Beginning to Spell

BEGINNING TO SPELL

A Study of First-Grade Children

REBECCA TREIMAN

New York   Oxford
OXFORD UNIVERSITY PRESS
1993

Oxford University Press

Oxford   New York   Toronto
Delhi   Bombay   Calcutta   Madras   Karachi
Kuala Lumpur   Singapore   Hong Kong   Tokyo
Nairobi   Dar es Salaam   Cape Town
Melbourne   Auckland   Madrid

and associated companies in
Berlin   Ibadan

Library of Congress Cataloging-in-Publication Data
Treiman, Rebecca.
Beginning to spell :
a study of first-grade children /
Rebecca Treiman.
p.   cm.   Includes bibliographical references (p. 337) and index.
ISBN 0-19-506219-1
1. English language—Orthography and spelling—
Study and teaching (Primary)
2. First grade (Education)   I. Title.
LB1526.T74   1993   372.6'32—dc20   92-27415

2 4 6 8 9 7 5 3 1

Printed in the United States of America
on acid-free paper

For Chuck, Joe, and Bobby

Preface

As schools place more emphasis on writing during the early grades, we are forced to confront the issue of spelling. Why do beginning spellers make so many errors? How should teachers respond to children's mistakes? Should children be encouraged to invent their own spellings for words or will this only teach them bad habits? Is the English writing system harder to master than other writing systems and, if so, why? To address these and other questions, we need to know more about how children learn to spell. Educational decisions can then be based on empirical facts rather than on preconceived ideas.

The study of children's spelling is important for psycholinguists as well as for educators. As I argue throughout this book, children attempt to represent the *phonological* or sound forms of words when they spell. Thus, the study of children's spelling can shed light on the nature of children's phonological systems. It can tell us how they organize sounds into larger units such as syllables and words, which sounds they consider to be similar to one another, and which sounds they consider to be different. The study of children's spelling forces us to ask how children acquire phonological knowledge and whether their phonological systems change as they learn to read and write.

Spelling also provides a good testing ground for theories about the nature of children's learning. The English writing system is regular and predictable in some ways (words never begin with *ck,* the sound /æ/ is almost always spelled with the letter *a*) and irregular and unpredictable in other ways (the sound /k/ may be spelled with *c, ck,* or *k,* among other possibilities). How do children learn such a quasi-regular system? How does the knowledge that they bring with them to the task interact with the knowledge that they pick up on their own and the knowledge that they gain from formal instruction to result—for most children—in eventual mastery of the system?

The last few decades have seen a great deal of research on beginning reading. There has been less research on children's spelling. The study described in this book is an attempt to redress this imbalance through a detailed examination of the spellings produced by a group of American first graders. The children in this study were encouraged to write from the beginning of the school year. They were expected to spell words themselves as best they could; their teacher did not tell them the correct spellings of words even if they asked. The writings produced by these children provide a rich source of evidence on how children learn to spell and the kinds of mistakes they make. In this book, I discuss the children's spellings in detail. I consider their implications for education, for psycholinguistics, and for the study of children's learning.

Chapter 1 introduces the present study and relates it to previous research on children's spelling. Important background material on the nature of the English writing system and the sound system of the English language is presented in this chapter. The section on the English sound system is particularly important for those readers with little background in linguistics.

The results of the study itself are presented in Chapters 2 to 10. Chapter 2 examines the children's spellings at the level of whole words. In this chapter, I ask why some words are harder to spell than others. What is the role of word frequency, regularity, and other characteristics of words in spelling difficulty? Chapter 2 also reports a study of adults' ability to decipher first graders' spellings. In Chapter 3, I move from the level of whole words to the level of individual sounds or *phonemes*. I ask why some phonemes are harder to spell than others. For example, why do children make more errors on vowel phonemes than consonant phonemes? I also ask why children sometimes spell a phoneme with a letter that is appropriate for a different phoneme. Chapters 4 and 5 present detailed information about how children spell specific phonemes of English. Chapter 4 focuses on vowels, while Chapter 5 examines consonants. In Chapter 6, I adopt an orthographic perspective to the study of children's spelling. I ask how the conventional spelling of a word or sound affects children's ability to spell it. One question addressed by this chapter concerns the degree to which children pick up the orthographic regularities of English, such as the restriction against *ck* at the beginnings of words, from their experience with print. Chapters 7 and 8 turn to omissions—cases in which children fail to represent a phoneme in their spelling. Vowel omissions are discussed in Chapter 7, while consonant omissions are discussed in Chapter 8. The question here is which phonemes tend to be omitted from children's spellings and why. In Chapter 9, I discuss reversals—cases in which children reverse the order of two phonemes when they spell. Again, I ask when children reverse phonemes in their spelling and why they do so. Chapter 10 examines the children's spellings of inflected words such as *jumped* and *cleaned* and derived words such as *eater* and *collection*. Finally, Chapter 11 discusses the implications of the results for education, psycholinguistics, and psychology.

The book includes two appendices, which present some of the basic data of the study. There is also a glossary in which definitions of linguistic terms and other technical terms may be found.

Throughout this book, I adopt the convention of indicating children's spellings in upper-case letters. The sound forms of spoken words are indicated using the phonemic symbols listed on the inside covers of this book. Phonemic forms are enclosed in slash marks. Thus, the word *blow* has the phonemic form /bl'o/. First graders sometimes misspell this word as BOW.

I would like to express my deep gratitude to two people without whom this research would not have been possible. One is the first-grade teacher Margaret Powers, who so generously shared her children's writings with me. The other is the linguist/computer scientist extraordinaire Brett Kessler, who designed and wrote many of the computer programs that were used to analyze the children's spellings.

For their help with the research, I would also like to acknowledge the contributions of Catalina Danis, Patrick Lavery, Gary McLaskey, Kathleen Straub, Michele Trappe, and Andrea Zukowski. A particular debt is owed to Jennifer Gross, for all her editorial help, and Jon Brewster, for his aid in taming the Wayne State University computer system. Ranka Bijeljac-Babic, Denise Berch, and Ellen Richmond-Welty also helped with editorial matters.

Many friends, relatives, colleagues, and students read all or part of the manuscript and offered helpful comments. They include Judith Bowey, Catalina Danis, Usha Goswami, Brett Kessler, Steve LaPointe, Joe Stemberger, Joan Treiman, Sam Treiman, Richard Wagner, and Andrea Zukowski. Special thanks go to the members of the Cognitive Reading Group at Wayne State University, who tackled the entire first draft. They are Patricia Siple, John Mullennix, Ranka Bijeljac-Babic, Annemarie Cwikiel-Glavin, Jennifer Gross, George Moutsiakis, Michael Neal, Meral Topcu, and Sara Weatherston. I am also grateful to Marilyn Adams and Charles Read, my reviewers for Oxford University Press, and Joan Bossert, my editor, for their many valuable suggestions.

Research takes money and time. The former was provided by grants from the Spencer Foundation through Indiana University and by grants from the National Institutes of Child Health and Human Development (Grants HD 18387 and 20276) and the National Science Foundation (Grant BNS 9020956). The latter was provided by a Research Career Development Award from the National Institutes of Child Health and Human Development (Grant HD 00769).

Detroit, Mich.   R. T.
March 1992

Contents

Beginning to Spell

1

Introduction

To be literate, people must be able to read and to write. There has been a large amount of research on the first aspect of literacy, reading. We now know a good deal about how adults read and about how children learn to read. We know much less about the second aspect of literacy, writing. One aspect of learning how to write is learning how to spell. How do children manage this, especially in a language like English that has so many irregular spellings? That is the topic of this book. In this book, I present a detailed study of the spellings produced by a group of American first-grade children. I ask what the children's spellings reveal about their knowledge of language and about the development of spelling ability.

In these days of computerized spelling checkers, is learning to spell correctly still necessary for being a good writer? I believe that it is. In her review of research on beginning reading, Marilyn Adams (1990, p. 3) states that "the ability to read words, quickly, accurately, and effortlessly, is critical to skillful reading comprehension—in the obvious ways and in a number of more subtle ones." Similarly, the ability to spell words easily and accurately is an important part of being a good writer. A person who must stop and puzzle over the spelling of each word, even if that person is aided by a computerized spelling checker, has little attention left to devote to other aspects of writing. Just as learning to read words is an important part of reading comprehension, so learning to spell words is an important part of writing.

In the study reported in this book, I focus on a group of American first-grade children who were learning to read and write in English. These children, like an increasing number of children in America today, were encouraged to write on their own from the very beginning of the first-grade year. Their teacher did not stress correct spelling. Indeed, she did not tell the children how to spell a word even if they asked. She told them to spell the word themselves as best they could. These first graders' spellings provide a rich source of evidence on how English-speaking children learn to spell and on what kinds of mistakes they make.

The study of children's spelling is important for both theoretical and practical reasons. Psychologists and linguists are interested in children's spelling because of what it reveals about children's knowledge of language and the nature of children's learning. For example, the study of children's spellings can shed light on how children organize sounds into syllables and which sounds they consider to be similar to one another. Educators are interested in children's spelling because spelling is something that children are expected to learn in school. If teachers understand the logic behind children's spelling errors, they can respond to the errors in the most helpful manner. They can design instruction to help children overcome their difficulties. An understanding of normal children's spelling errors is vital, too, in the diagnosis and remediation of children who are encountering problems in learning to spell and read. In this book, I consider both the theoretical and the educational implications of my findings.

A central idea of this book is that, for young children, spelling is largely an attempt to represent the sounds of words. In most cases, it is not a rote attempt to reproduce a memorized string of letters. To understand children's spellings, then, one needs to know a good deal about the *phonology* or sound system of the English language. The use of linguistic terms and concepts cannot be avoided in this or any other serious discussion of children's spelling. The glossary to this book defines the linguistic terms and other technical terms and should be helpful for readers with little knowledge of linguistics.

This chapter provides an introduction to the present study of spelling in first-grade children. I review earlier research on the topic of spelling and relate my study to the previous work. In addition, I present important background information on the sound system of the English language and the nature of the English writing system.

The Study

The study reported in this book is based on spellings collected from 43 first-grade children. These children were members of a single teacher's class during two different school years. Their school, a public or government-supported school, was located in a predominantly white, middle-class section of Indianapolis, Indiana. I studied the spellings of 26 children who attended the class during one school year and 17 children who attended the class during the following year. The children were between six and seven years old; their exact ages were not available.

Classroom Methods

The children's teacher was a strong believer in the *whole-language* philosophy of teaching reading and writing. Advocates of this view (e.g., Goodman, 1986) believe that children should read and write about topics of interest to them. Children should work with meaningful materials, including children's literature and stories generated by the children themselves. They should not be asked to read isolated words. Children's texts should have natural language patterns. They should not be distorted to include large numbers of words with particular types of spellings. Proponents of the whole-language approach do not advocate formal teaching about the relations between sounds and letters. Indeed, they believe that traditional phonics instruction may be harmful because it presents children with isolated words, meaningless sounds, and distorted texts. Whole-language advocates believe that children will figure out the relations between spellings and sounds on their own, from their experience with printed and spoken words. Although the first-grade teacher was a strong believer in the whole-language philosophy, she could not fully implement it in her classroom because of certain requirements that were set down by the school system. Thus, as I describe in detail shortly, she provided some traditional phonics and spelling instruction.

The teacher was influenced, too, by the *language-experience* approach to teaching reading and writing. This approach, a precursor to the whole-language movement, advocates a close relation between experiencing life and reading and writing about it. Often, children write stories and journals about their experiences. The goal is to convey that print is talk written down.

Beginning early in the school year, the first-grade students in the present study wrote for about a half hour almost every morning. To get the children started, the teacher sometimes read a story aloud. The children discussed the story and then wrote about it. Other times, the teacher told just the beginning of a story and the children wrote a potential ending. The children used crayons and pencils and large sheets of unlined paper. When the children had finished writing, they dictated what they had written to the teacher or teacher's aide. The adult wrote the children's words on their papers, using conventional spelling, and also wrote the date. Children thus saw the correct spelling of each word not long after they themselves had attempted the word. However, the adult did not say whether children had spelled the word correctly. According to the teacher, though, the children sometimes commented that their spelling agreed or did not agree with the adult's.

From the beginning of the school year, the teacher made clear that she wanted each child's *own* writing. She stated that the students did not copy spellings from one another. The teacher told her pupils that she would not tell them the correct spellings of words even if they asked. She followed this policy strictly. Consequently, the children rarely asked how to spell words.

During the first few months of the school year, and in a few cases for even longer periods of time, some children drew pictures and wrote their names but did not write anything else. Other children produced what seemed to be random strings of letters. For instance, Calvin drew a picture of some playground equipment and a large sun, as Figure 1.1 shows. At the top left corner of his page, he wrote ACR. To the teacher Calvin dictated, "I like swings and I like slides. And I like the sun." It is not clear which word(s) the letters A, C, and R were meant to represent, or whether Calvin even meant to represent words at all. By November, Calvin's writing had changed dramatically. He now drew a picture of two boys near a castle and wrote JAC JUPT, as Figure 1.2 shows. He dictated to the teacher, "Jack jumped." Clearly, JAC is an attempt to spell *Jack* and JUPT is an attempt to spell *jumped*. As the school year progressed, the children began to write more and more stories with recognizable words. Print began to take up more of the children's papers and pictures less. Figure 1.3 shows one of the more complex stories produced by a child in this study.

For the teaching of reading, the school system mandated the Ginn series of basal readers. Although these were not the books that the teacher preferred, she used them in a way that was consistent with her educational philosophy. When introducing a new story, for example, she asked the pupils to look at the pictures and

Figure 1.1. Calvin's writing, August.

predict what the words would say. She wrote sentences from the story on the blackboard and had the students read them aloud. As a matter of principle, she never wrote single words on the blackboard. The teacher supplemented the basal readers with books that were tailored to the whole-language approach. These books had predictable sentence structures and pictures that were chosen to help children guess the words.

The school system further required that phonics instruction be given using a particular phonics workbook (*Phonics Workbook Level A,* 1966). The exercises in this book were designed to help children identify the letters of the alphabet and their sounds. The children worked on their phonics book at a different time of day than they worked on writing and reading. Deliberately, the teacher only talked about individual letters and sounds during this time. The school system also required that the children memorize a list of six spelling words each week, beginning in January. The students were to be tested on these words each Friday. The teacher complied with this requirement.

The teacher's lack of enthusiasm for the phonics workbook and the weekly spelling lists was probably obvious to her students. The children must have sensed that writing was what mattered most in this classroom. The teacher proudly displayed her pupils' writings in the hall, even though some of her colleagues were surprised that work with so many misspelled words would be so honored.

The writings that I have described are a rich source of information about begin-

Figure 1.2. Calvin's writing, November.

ning spelling. The teacher had saved many of the children's writings from the two school years in question and made them available to me for this study. I used writings that were produced between the very beginning of each school year (late August) and near the end of the school year (the middle of April). In the next section, I describe the way in which I prepared these writings for analysis.

Preparing the Writings for Analysis

The first step in analyzing this large collection of writings was to pair the printed words in each story with the spoken words in the child's dictation. When Calvin wrote JAC JUPT and dictated "Jack jumped," for example, it is clear that JAC corresponds to *Jack* and JUPT corresponds to *jumped*. Sometimes, particularly near the beginning of the school year, it was not possible to pair the printed and spoken words in this way. In the story of Figure 1.1, for instance, there seems to be no relation between what Calvin wrote and what he dictated. I did not include such cases in my analyses. Thus, the spellings analyzed in this study are those produced by children who are writing reasonably productively. A further complication is that the children did not always leave spaces between their words when writing. When they did not, I tried to infer the location of the breaks from the spellings themselves and from the spoken words. In Figure 1.3, for example, WRTA must be a combination of WR for *were* and TA for *there*.

Annie Golldlocks in the three bas   3-19-80

Annie Golldlocks
Golldlocks Wint
to the fouist
and She let hre
purig kul win She
got Back the
three
bars wrta

thea ate hre
purig She was
anger thea
ran aowt av the haws.

Goldilocks and the three bears.

Goldilocks went to the Frest and she let her porridge cool. When she got back, the three bears were there.

They ate her porridge She was angry.

They ran out over the house.

Figure 1.3. Annie's writing, March.

Once the printed words and spoken words had been paired up, the next step was to symbolize the sound of each spoken word. I used a transcription system that was intended to represent the regional pronunciations of the words in the children's dialect. A linguist who was a native speaker of this dialect transcribed all of the words using the 24 consonant phonemes and 14 vowel phonemes listed on the inside covers of this book. Later in this chapter, I discuss the concept of a phoneme, the characteristics of English phonemes, and the specific properties of these children's speech.

Some English words tend to be pronounced differently in connected speech than they are in isolation. In the sentence *"We waited an hour,"* for example, *an* may be said with the unstressed vowel /ə/ rather than with the stressed vowel /æ/. Words like *the* and *of* undergo similar changes. I chose to transcribe words as they are pronounced in isolation. The assumption is that children spell words as they sound when said alone rather than as they may sound in connected speech. This view is supported by results presented later in this book.

I assumed that each printed word that a child produced was the child's attempt to symbolize the phonemes of the spoken word. The next step, therefore, was to determine which letters were intended to represent which phonemes. In many cases, this was easily done. For instance, the child who spelled *robe* as ROB probably intended *r* to stand for /r/, *o* to stand for /o/, and *b* to stand for /b/. Other cases are problematic. In REAMBER for *remember,* is *ea* a two-letter attempt to represent the vowel of the first syllable or does *e* stand for the vowel of the first syllable and *a* for the vowel of the second syllable?

To deal with such questions, a set of guidelines was developed for use in matching the letters of a child's spelling with the phonemes of the corresponding spoken word. According to these guidelines, it is possible that one or more phonemes in the spoken form of the word are not represented in the child's spelling. However, extraneous phonemes are never represented. All letters in the child's spelling must be accounted for. A phoneme may be symbolized by one letter or more than one letter. If more than one letter represents a single phoneme, the letters may be adjacent to one another. For example, the *a* and *e* of STAE (for *stay*) together stand for /e/. The letters may also be separated, as with the *a* and final *e* of RATE, which together represent /e/. Except in a few cases, such as *x* for /k/ followed by /s/, as in FOX, a single letter does not represent more than one phoneme. Using these guidelines, the linguist who prepared the phonemic transcriptions for this study matched the letters in each spelling with the phonemes in the spoken word. I independently coded 103 randomly chosen pairs. We agreed on 97% of the words and on 98% of the phonemes, a high degree of reliability.

To facilitate analysis of the spellings, a computer program called "Spell" was designed especially for this project. For each observation, a number of pieces of information were entered into the program. They included (1) the child's spelling of the word, (2) the pronunciation of the word, (3) the match between the child's spelling and the pronunciation, (4) the conventional spelling of the word, (5) the name of the child who produced the spelling, and (6) the date it was produced. The "Spell" computer program works interactively, allowing one to ask questions about the spellings, receive answers, and then ask further questions. For example, when asked how the children spelled the phoneme /b/, the program prints a table showing. the letters that the children used to represent /b/ and how often they used each one. The user may then ask more specific questions, such as how the children spelled /b/ when it was followed by a vowel or how Mary spelled /b/ during the month of September. Other information made available by the "Spell" program includes the number of times that the children attempted a particular word and the number of times that they spelled it correctly. I used the "Spell" program for many of the analyses reported in this book. In other cases, preliminary information garnered from the "Spell" program was transferred to other computer programs for statistical analyses.

As a first step in the analysis, the "Spell" program was used to tabulate how the children spelled each phoneme. The results are shown in Appendix I. As a guide to the interpretation of the results, consider the phoneme /i/. This phoneme occurred 1,138 times among the words that the children chose to spell. In 592 of these cases, the conventional spelling of the phoneme was *e*. For example, /i/ is spelled with *e* in *he* and *rodeo*. The children correctly spelled the phoneme as *e* in 526 of these 592 cases. They omitted the phoneme 16 times and produced various other spellings in their remaining attempts. As the Appendix shows, the conventional spelling of /i/ was not always *e*. This vowel was spelled in a number of other ways, including *i* as in *pizza* and *y* as in *city*. The children's spellings are shown separately for each conventional spelling.

The results in Appendix I are broken down by the conventional spellings of the phoneme because the children's spellings of most phonemes were affected by the conventional spellings. For example, the children were more likely to use *e* for /i/ when the conventional spelling of the phoneme was *e* (as in *he*) than when the conventional spelling of the phoneme was *i* (as in *pizza*). Conversely, the children more frequently used *i* for /i/ when the phoneme was spelled as *i* than when it was spelled as *e*.

To produce the tabulations of Appendix I, it was necessary to decide which letter or group of letters in the conventional spelling of each word represented each phoneme in the spoken form of the word. In most cases, these decisions were easy to make. With *help,* for instance, the /h/ of the spoken word /hɛlp/ is symbolized with *h,* the /ɛ/ with *e,* the /l/ with *l,* and the /p/ with *p*. Sometimes, however, difficult decisions had to be made. Generally, each letter in the conventional spelling of the word was assigned to a phoneme. For example, the final *e* of *cave* was considered to be part of the spelling of /e/. Thus, the /e/ of this word is symbolized with a two-part grapheme—*a* followed by final *e*. Exceptions to the principle that each letter is, or is part of, the spelling of some phoneme were made for words such as *family*. Here, the letter *i* does not correspond to any phoneme in the pronunciation /fæmli/.

As the preceding discussion shows, I had to make a number of assumptions in preparing the spelling data for analysis. Sometimes, the results themselves can help to show whether an assumption is true or false. For instance, the assumption that children try to spell words as they sound in isolated form rather than as they sound in connected speech is supported by results presented later in this book. Other assumptions are simplifications that, although true most of the time, are not always correct. For example, the words that the children dictated when reading their stories to the teacher were usually the words that they intended to write. However, this is not always true. First graders sometimes forget what they meant to write, even if only a few minutes elapse between writing a story and reading it back. Since I could not read the children's minds, I had to use the words they dictated.

The Sound System of English

To a large extent, children's spellings are attempts to represent the sounds of words. To understand the children's spellings, then, it is necessary to know a good deal about the sound system of the language. In this section, I present an overview of the phonological or sound structure of the English language.

Phonemes and Phones

Phonology is the part of linguistics that concerns the sounds and sound patterns of language. In describing the sound system of English and of other languages, linguists have found it useful to distinguish among various levels of abstraction, ranging from more abstract underlying representations to more concrete surface representations. For present purposes, I focus on two levels at which sounds may be described—the *phonemic* level and the *phonetic* level. The phonemic level is more abstract, more closely related to meaning. The phonetic level is more superficial, more closely related to the details of pronunciation. The units at the phonemic level are called *phonemes.* By convention, the symbols for phonemes are enclosed in slash marks. Thus, /t/, /s/, and /æ/ are phonemes. A phoneme may be defined as the minimal unit of sound that makes a difference in meaning. Thus, *tip* and *sip,* which differ by a single phoneme—/t/ versus /s/—have different meanings. The units at the phonetic level are called *phones* or *allophones.* By convention, the symbols for phones are enclosed in square brackets ([ ]).

The distinction between phonemes and phones is best explained by example. Consider the phoneme /t/. Its pronunciation differs depending on where in a word it occurs. When /t/ is at the beginning of a word, as in *tip,* its pronunciation is accompanied by a puff of air. This puff of air may be detected by putting one's hand close to one's mouth. Such /t/s are called *aspirated.* When /t/ occurs in a word like *city,* it is pronounced differently, by making a quick tap with the tip of the tongue on the ridge behind the upper teeth. This /t/ is called a *flap.* Thus, there are several phonetic variants or allophones of the phoneme /t/. Aspirated /t/ is indicated as [tʰ]; other phonetic variants are indicated with other symbols. Allophonic variation can be predicted from the phoneme's context and does not affect the word's meaning. If one were to say *city* with an aspirated /t/ rather than a flapped /t/, the pronunciation would sound unusual but the word would be perceived by native speakers of American English as an instance of *city.*

Thus, a phonemic symbol such as /t/ can be considered a cover term for a range of different sounds or phones. The phonemic representation does not symbolize such surface features as aspiration or flapping. Instead, it stands for the ideal or pro-

totypical "t." We may think of the phoneme as the speaker's internal representation
of a speech sound—an abstract representation that ignores predictable variations
in how the phoneme is actually pronounced. The phonetic representation, in contrast, is more detailed. It explicitly represents such low-level information as aspiration and flapping.

I will say more about the English writing system and its relation to the spoken
language later in this chapter. For now, I simply point out that the English writing
system represents the spoken language at the level of phonemes and at deeper levels.
It does *not* represent allophonic variation. Thus, /t/ is spelled with *t* whether it
occurs in *tap* or *city*. We do not use different letters for aspirated /t/ and flapped
/t/. One question addressed by the present study is whether first graders understand
which linguistic level the English writing system represents. Do children spell all of
the allophones of a phoneme alike or do they attempt to represent allophonic variation in their spelling?

The Vowel Phonemes of English

The transcription system adopted for this study included 14 vowel phonemes. In
this section, I discuss the properties of the vowel phonemes in some detail. For further information on this topic, see Chapter 4 of Ladefoged (1982).

Vowels are pronounced with a relatively open vocal tract. To form different
vowels, the shape of the vocal tract is varied by changing the position of the tongue,

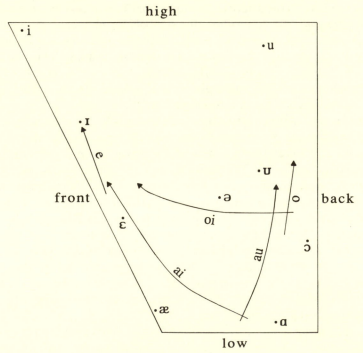

Figure 1.4. Characteristics of vowels in adult speakers of midwestern American English,
adapted from Ladefoged (1982).

the degree of rounding of the lips, and other factors. *High* vowels are those in which the body of the tongue is raised toward the roof of the mouth during the pronunciation of the vowel. *Low* vowels are those in which the body of the tongue is lowered. *Back* and *front* vowels differ from one another in whether the tongue is retracted toward the back of the mouth, as it is for back vowels, or whether the tongue remains toward the front of the mouth, as it is for front vowels. These dimensions are depicted in Figure 1.4, which plots the characteristics of vowels in midwestern American English. This figure is adopted from Ladefoged (1982), and is based on acoustic measurements of adult speakers.

The solid points in Figure 1.4 represent *monophthongs,* or vowels in which there is no appreciable change in quality during the course of the vowel. The lines in Figure 1.4 indicate the movements that are involved in *diphthongs,* or vowels that do show a change in quality. The diphthongized vowels of Figure 1.4 have two parts. The first part, which is relatively loud and steady, is called the *steady-state* portion of the diphthong. The second part is an *offglide,* or a rapid movement toward another vowel. One question addressed by the present study is whether children indicate the two-part nature of vowel diphthongs in their spelling.

Vowels may also be classified on the dimension of *rounded* versus *unrounded.* Rounded vowels are produced with a rounding of the lips; unrounded vowels are not. The front vowels of English are unrounded, while most of the back vowels are rounded. The vowels /ə/ and /ɑ/ differ from the other nonfront vowels in that they are not rounded.

Another dimension on which English vowels are often classified is that of *tense* versus *lax.* The vowels /i/, /e/, /ai/, /o/, and /u/, among others, are considered tense, while the vowels /ɪ/, /ɛ/, /æ/, /ʊ/, and /ə/ are called lax. Tense and lax vowels are primarily distinguished by the positions in which they occur in words. Tense vowels may occur in the final positions of stressed syllables, as in /h'i/ and /h'e/. Lax vowels may not; there are no English words like */h'ɪ/ and */h'ɛ/. (A * preceding a form means that it is illegal in the language.) Certain tense and lax vowels are grouped into pairs, where a pair consists of a tense vowel and a similar lax vowel. Three such pairs are /i/ and /ɪ/, /e/ and /ɛ/, and /u/ and /ʊ/.

I transcribed each vowel as having one of three levels of stress—primary stress, secondary stress, or no stress. For example, the first vowel in the spoken form of *baby* has primary stress. The second vowel of this word is unstressed. In *peanut,* the first vowel has primary stress and the second vowel has secondary stress. The symbol ' immediately preceding a vowel means that the vowel has primary stress; the symbol ˌ indicates secondary stress. Stress marks are placed before the affected vowel rather than before the syllable because the syllable boundaries within words are sometimes unclear, as discussed later in this chapter.

The Consonant Phonemes of English

Having discussed the vowels of English, I turn now to the consonants. Whereas vowels are produced with a relatively open vocal tract, consonants are produced with a more constricted vowel tract. Consonants may be classified in terms of the location and characteristics of this constriction. *Place of articulation* is the point at

Manner of articulation	Voicing	Place of articulation						
		bilabial	labio–dental	dental	alveolar	palato–alveolar	palatal	velar
Stop	Voiceless	p			t			k
	Voiced	b			d			g
Fricative	Voiceless		f	θ	s	ʃ		
	Voiced		v	ð	z	ʒ		
Affricate	Voiceless					ʧ		
	Voiced					ʤ		
Nasal	Voiced	m			n			ŋ
Liquid	Voiced				l/r			
Glide	Voiced	w					j	w

Note. h is not shown in this chart
l is lateral and r is nonlateral

Figure 1.5. The consonants of English.

which the airflow has the greatest degree of obstruction. *Manner of articulation* is the way in which the constriction is produced. Consonants also differ from one another in *voicing,* or whether the vocal cords vibrate during the articulation of the consonant. Figure 1.5 classifies the consonants of English along these dimensions. For a more detailed discussion of English consonants than I am able to provide here, see Chapter 3 of Ladefoged (1982).

The consonants of English may be divided into six categories according to their manner of articulation. The *stop* consonants are /p/, /t/, /k/, /b/, /d/, and /g/. To produce these sounds, the speaker completely obstructs the flow of air. When the air is released, a small burst of sound occurs. Stop consonants differ from one another in the point at which the obstruction of the airflow occurs, or place of articulation. Stop consonants also differ in voicing. Sounds that are produced when the vocal cords are vibrating are called *voiced;* sounds that are produced when the vocal cords are apart are *voiceless.* The phonemes /p/ and /b/ have a *bilabial* place of articulation, or an articulation that involves both lips. The phoneme /p/ is voiceless and the phoneme /b/ is voiced. The *alveolar* place of articulation involves the front part of the tongue and the *alveolar ridge,* or the part of the upper surface of the mouth that is immediately behind the front teeth. The two English stops with this place of articulation are /t/ (voiceless) and /d/ (voiced). Finally, /k/ (voiceless) and /g/ (voiced) have a *velar* place of articulation. For these sounds, the back of the tongue is raised so that it touches the back of the mouth, or *velum.*

The English *fricatives,* /f/, /θ/, /s/, /ʃ/, /h/, /v/, /ð/, /z/, and /ʒ/, form the second manner category in Figure 1.5. In the production of these sounds, the airstream is only partly obstructed so that a slight hissing sound results. Fricatives, like stops, differ from one another in place of articulation and in voicing. The voiceless /f/ and the voiced /v/ have a *labio-dental* place of articulation. The lower lip and the upper front teeth come together in the production of these sounds. The *dental* place of articulation, which is used for /θ/ (voiceless) and /ð/ (voiced), involves the front part of the tongue and the upper front teeth. The alveolar fricatives are the voiceless /s/ and the voiced /z/. The *palato-alveolar* fricatives are /ʃ/ (voiceless) and /ʒ/ (voiced). Here, the front of the tongue is close to the back of the alveolar ridge. The remaining fricative, /h/, is often said to have a *glottal* place of articulation. According to Ladefoged (1982), though, /h/ is just the voiceless counterpart of the following vowel.

English has two *affricates*, the voiceless /tʃ/ and the voiced /dʒ/. In this study, /tʃ/ and /dʒ/ were coded as single phonemes. However, an affricate may be considered as a sequence of a stop consonant followed by a fricative. Specifically, /tʃ/ may be thought of as /t/ followed by /ʃ/ and /dʒ/ may be thought of as /d/ followed by /ʒ/. The symbols for the affricates indicate their two-part nature.

English has three *nasals*, /m/, /n/, and /ŋ/. In the production of these sounds, the air is obstructed in the oral cavity but escapes through the nose. All the nasal consonants of English are voiced. The nasals differ from one another in place of articulation, /m/ being bilabial, /n/ alveolar, and /ŋ/ velar.

The remaining consonants of English are the *liquids* /r/ and /l/ and the *glides* /w/ and /j/. The phoneme /l/ is said to be a *lateral*, in that the air flows outward at the sides of the tongue. The phoneme /r/ is a nonlateral alveolar liquid. The phoneme /w/ is shown in two places in the chart of Figure 1.5. It is pronounced with a rounding of the lips, which makes it bilabial, and a raising of the tongue toward the velum, which makes it velar.

One controversial aspect of English transcription concerns the *syllabic liquids* that appear in the second syllables of words such as *reader* and *little*. Some linguists, including Trager and Smith (1951) and Prator and Robinett (1972), consider syllabic liquids to be sequences of /ə/ followed by /r/ or /l/. Many dictionaries adopt the same solution. However, other linguists (e.g., Kenyon & Knott, 1953) consider syllabic /r/, at least, to be a single phoneme. Here, syllabic liquids were coded as sequences of /ə/ plus a liquid. Thus, *reader* was transcribed as /rídər/ and *little* as /lítəl/. One question addressed by this study is whether children consider syllabic liquids as single units or as vowel-liquid sequences.

The Characteristics of Hoosier Speech

The transcriptions of this study were intended to represent the speech of these first-grade children at the phonemic level. After interviewing several of the children, I determined that they predominantly spoke in a certain southern Indiana accent. Henceforth, for the sake of convenience, I call this *Hoosier dialect*. When most speakers of this dialect use a particular form, that form was adopted for the present study. Because of limits on time and resources, I could not determine how each child in the study pronounced each word.

Several characteristics of Hoosier dialect distinguish it from other forms of American speech. In Hoosier dialect, vowels are *raised*, or pronounced with a higher position of the tongue, before nasal consonants. Thus, *pen* was coded as /pín/, *hem* as /hím/, and *sing* as /síŋ/. Raising may also occur before /g/; hence *egg* was coded as /ˈeg/ rather than /ˈɛg/. Certain sounds that belong to different pho-

Beginning to Spell

nemes in other dialects of English are collapsed in Hoosier speech. The vowel of *car* and the first vowel of *father* merge with the vowel of *odd,* all three vowels being transcribed with /ɑ/. The vowel of *up* merges with the final unstressed vowel of *sofa,* the symbol /ə/ being used for both vowels. The pronunciations of *witch* and *which* are the same for speakers from Indiana. *Mary, merry,* and *marry* all sound alike, the first vowel of each word being /ɛ/. One question addressed by the study is whether the children's Hoosier dialect affects their spelling.

Because interpretation of the children's spellings depends on assumptions about their pronunciations, I did not include in the analyses the spellings of children whose pronunciations differed from those of the group as a whole. Thus, the spellings of seven black students who were bused to the school from a different area of the city during the second year of the study were not analyzed. These children's dialect differed from that of the white students. Also excluded were the spellings of one white student who had a severe articulation problem. His spellings were not analyzed because they might have been affected by his mispronunciations. None of the other chidren were considered by school personnel to have articulation problems.

Sonority

So far, a number of different classes of phonemes have been discussed. These include stops, fricatives, affricates, nasals, liquids, glides, and vowels. Some of these phoneme classes share important similarities with one another, allowing them to be grouped into larger categories that behave alike with respect to certain linguistic processes. One important distinction is that between *sonorants* and *obstruents.* Sonorants include vowels and those consonants that are similar to vowels in having a relatively high amount of acoustic energy. Thus, the category of sonorants includes vowels, glides, liquids, and nasals. The other major category of phonemes—obstruents—includes stops, fricatives, and affricates. Obstruent consonants are less vowel-like than sonorant consonants. The mouth is less open and the flow of air is obstructed to some degree. As a result, obstruents have a relatively low amount of acoustic energy.

The distinction between sonorants and obstruents is fairly gross. The phonemes of English may be more finely classified in terms of their degree of sonority by means of what linguists call a *sonority scale.* According to Clements (1990) and other linguists, vowels are the most sonorous type of phoneme, ranking highest on the sonority scale. They are followed in turn by glides, liquids, and nasals. Obstruents rank lowest on the sonority scale. Thus, although vowels, glides, liquids, and nasals are all classified as sonorants, vowels have a higher degree of sonority than do glides. Glides are more sonorous than liquids, which are in turn more sonorous than nasals.

Some linguists have made finer distinctions of sonority than those just suggested. For example, Jespersen (1904), who was one of the first to rank speech sounds in terms of their sonority, put the liquid /r/ higher on the sonority scale than the liquid /l/. Although linguists disagree about such points of detail, the general concept of a sonority scale is widely accepted.

In English, as in other languages, some sequences of phonemes may occur in the language, while others may not. For instance, English syllables may begin with clusters of two consonants. If the first consonant of the cluster is /b/, the second consonant may be only /r/ or /l/. Thus */bnɪk/ could not be a word in English, although it could be a word in some other languages. To take another example, English syllables may end with some vowels but not with others. The syllable */h'ɪ/ is illegal in English while /h'ai/ is legal. We may say that */bnɪk/ and */h'ɪ/ violate the *phonological constraints* of English.

A phoneme's position on the sonority scale helps to predict where in a syllable the phoneme may occur. Phonemes that are high on the sonority scale, such as vowels, tend to occur in the middles of syllables. Phonemes that are low on the sonority scale, such as obstruents, tend to occur at the beginnings and ends of syllables. Thus, a syllable may start with /b/ (a low sonority obstruent) followed by /l/ (a higher sonority liquid) and then by /o/ (which, as a vowel, is even higher in sonority). The cluster /bl/, which shows an increase in sonority, may begin a syllable. However, /lb/, which shows a decrease in sonority, may not begin a syllable. Conversely, /lb/ may occur at the ends of syllables, as in *bulb,* but /bl/ may not occur at the end of syllables.

The Grouping of Phonemes into Larger Units

We do not speak in single phonemes. Almost all of the words of English or any other language are composed of more than one phoneme. How are the phonemes put together to form larger units such as words and syllables?

One important group of phonemes is the *morpheme.* A morpheme may be roughly defined as the smallest unit of meaning in a language. In *dishes,* for example, /dɪʃ/ is one morpheme and /əz/ is another. As another example, the morphemes of *helped* are the stem /h'ɛlp/ and the past tense marker /t/.

The *syllable* is another important linguistic unit. Linguists and native speakers generally agree among themselves on the number of syllables in a word. For example, *bay* contains one syllable and *baby* contains two syllables. However, as lay people may be surprised to learn, linguists do not always agree about the locations of syllable boundaries in words of more than one syllable.

Consider the word *baby.* Is the middle /b/ of this word part of the first syllable, part of the second syllable, or part of both syllables at once? According to many dictionaries and some linguists (e.g., Pulgram, 1970), the middle /b/ of *baby* belongs to the word's second syllable. According to other linguists, the situation is more complex. Selkirk (1982) believes that there is more than one level or type of phonemic representation. The middle /b/ of *baby* is the first phoneme of the second syllable at a deep level of representation but the final phoneme of the first syllable at a more superficial level. Kahn (1976) has a different view. He claims that the /b/ is the first phoneme of the second syllable in very slow speech. In normal rate and rapid speech, according to Kahn, the /b/ is simultaneously part of both the first and second syllables. The consonant is *ambisyllabic*—part of two syllables at the same time.

Although linguists disagree about the syllabification of words like *baby,* they agree about the syllabifications of certain other multisyllabic words. Three assumptions are widely shared. The first may be called the *vowel principle*. This assumption, which is common to all linguistic theories of which I am aware, is that each syllable of a spoken word contains a vowel (or a syllabic consonant, as in the second syllable of *little*). The vowel principle implies that, if two vowels are adjacent to one another, they must belong to different syllables. Thus, the syllable boundary in *Joey* must fall between /o/ and /i/.

The second common assumption about syllabification is the *maximum onset principle*. This principle, which is followed by many theorists (e.g., Hoard, 1971; Hooper, 1972; Kahn, 1976; Pulgram, 1970; Selkirk, 1982), states that as many consonants as possible, given the phonological constraints of the language, are placed at the beginning of a stressed syllable within a morpheme. In other words, the *onsets* or initial consonant portions of stressed syllables are maximized. Thus, both the /t/ and /r/ of *patrol* must belong to the stressed second syllable of this word since /tr/ is a possible initial cluster in English. In *Charlene,* both /r/ and /l/ may not belong to the stressed second syllable because /rl/ may not begin a syllable in English. Thus, /r/ must be the last phoneme of the first syllable and /l/ must be the first phoneme of the second syllable.

The third assumption about syllabification may be called the *legality principle*. This principle is a part of many theories (e.g., Hooper, 1972; Pulgram, 1970; Selkirk, 1982). It states that consonants are assigned to syllables in such a way that any consonants that occur at the beginning of a syllable within a word are legal at the beginning of a word. Likewise, any consonants that occur at the end of a syllable within a word are legal at the end of a word. The legality principle sometimes rules out all but one potential syllabification of a word. For example, *only* must be syllabified between /n/ and /l/ rather than after /l/ or before /n/. This is because /n/ is legal at the ends of words and /l/ is legal at the beginnings of words but /nl/ is illegal both as a final cluster and as an initial cluster. In other cases, as with *baby,* the legality principle permits more than one syllabification. This is because /b/ may occur both at the beginnings and at the ends of English words.[1]

The three principles just discussed—the vowel principle, the maximum onset principle, and the legality principle—have been tested in experimental work with children (Fallows, 1981) and adults (Treiman & Danis, 1988; Treiman & Zukowski, 1990). In these studies, people are asked to do such things as reverse the order of syllables within a word or pause between syllables when pronouncing a word. For the most part, the syllable boundaries revealed by people's performances in these tasks agree with the syllable boundaries predicted by the linguistic principles.

I have discussed the issue of syllabification in some detail because this issue has important implications for the study of children's spelling. For example, as I show in Chapter 8, children sometimes fail to spell the /l/ of *blow* and the /r/ of *troll*. Why do they do this? One possibility is that children tend to omit the second consonants of clusters that occur at the beginnings of words. Another possibility is that children tend to omit the second consonants of clusters that occur at the beginnings of syllables, whether or not the syllables are word-initial. To distinguish between these possibilities, one must determine how children spell syllable-initial clusters in the *middles* of words. If the domain of omissions is the word, second-consonant omissions should not occur with syllable-initial clusters in the middles of words. If the domain of omissions is the syllable, second-consonant omissions should occur with syllable-initial clusters in the middles of words just as with syllable-initial clusters at the beginnings of words. But which sequences of consonants within a word form the initial cluster of a syllable? To answer this question one must make decisions about syllabification. In the analyses reported in this book, I use the three principles just discussed—the vowel principle, the maximum onset principle, and the legality principle—to help break words into syllables.

Now that I have discussed the division of words into syllables, I turn to the structure of syllables themselves. Are syllables linear strings of phonemes, each phoneme following the previous phonemes like beads on a string? Alternatively, are the phonemes in syllables organized into groups or units? Many linguists (e.g., Fudge, 1969, 1987, 1989; Selkirk, 1982) maintain that English syllables are not simple strings of phonemes. Rather, they have a hierarchical internal structure. According to these linguists, English syllables contain two main units. The first unit of the syllable, as Figure 1.6 shows, is the *onset*. The onset is the initial consonant or consonant cluster. For instance, the onset of *tea* is /t/ and the onset of *brick* is /br/. English syllables do not necessarily have an onset. *It,* for example, does not have a consonant onset. The second major unit of the syllable is the *rime*. The rime contains the vowel and any following consonants. The rime of *tea* is /i/ and the rime of *brick* is /ɪk/. All syllables must have a rime.

The rime of an English syllable contains two parts. The first part of the rime, and one that all rimes must possess, is the *peak*. (This unit is sometimes called the *nucleus*.) The vowel, the type of phoneme that is highest on the sonority scale, belongs to the peak. The second part of the rime, which is optional, is a consonantal *coda*. For example, *teeth* contains the onset /t/ and the rime /iθ/. The peak of the rime is /i/ and the coda is /θ/. *Tea* contains the onset /t/ and the rime /i/. This rime has the peak /i/ but does not have a coda.

There is some disagreement among linguists about the nature of the peak. Selkirk (1982) states that a sonorant consonant that immediately follows a vowel may be part of the peak. This can happen, Selkirk claims, when the vowel is one of the so-called short vowels, such as /ɪ/ or /ɛ/. In this view, the /n/ of /wɪnt/ *(went)* belongs to the peak. Together, /ɪ/ and /n/ form the peak; /t/ is the coda. An obstruent that follows the vowel cannot be part of the peak. It must belong to the coda. Thus, the peak of /wɪsp/ *(wisp)* is /ɪ/, with /s/ and /p/ forming the coda. Other linguists (e.g., Fudge, 1969) restrict the peak to vowels.

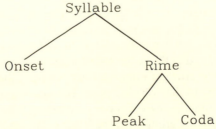

Figure 1.6. Hierarchical view of the structure of the English syllable.

Although many linguists claim that English syllables have two main units, the onset and the rime, other linguists disagree (Clements & Keyser, 1983; Davis, 1989). For instance, Clements and Keyser argue that English syllables have three parts—an onset, a vowel-containing peak, and a coda. In their view, the peak is no more closely tied to the coda than it is to the onset. There is no rime unit.

Experimental evidence supports the view that English syllables are composed of onset and rime units (see Treiman, 1989 for a review). In a number of situations—when they err in producing spoken words, when they misremember syllables, and when they learn new word games—adults tend to divide syllables at the boundary between the onset and the rime. For example, college students readily learn a new word game in which /krɪnt/ and /glʹəpθ/ combine to produce /krʹəpθ/. This response joins the onset of the first syllable with the rime of the second syllable. Blends that break the syllables at other points (i.e., /krʹɪnt/ + /glʹəpθ/ = /klʹəpθ/, /krʹɪpθ/ or /krʹɪnθ/) are harder to learn (Treiman, 1983, Exp. 7).

What does research have to say about the internal structure of the rime? In one experiment (Treiman, 1984b, Exp. 4), I compared college students' ability to learn two types of word games. In the first game, vowel-consonant-consonant rimes were divided between the vowel and the first consonant—a V/CC division. In the second game, the rimes were broken between the two consonants—a VC/C division. When the first consonant was a liquid (/r/ or /l/), the students learned the VC/C game more easily than the V/CC game. That is, they found it easier to treat the vowel and the liquid as a unit than to break them up. When a nasal such as /m/ or /n/ followed the vowel, the two games were comparable in difficulty. And when an obstruent (e.g., /s/, /p/) followed the vowel, the V/CC division was easier to master than the VC/C division. Interpreting these results within hierarchical theories of syllable structure, it appears that liquids may occupy the peak with the vowel. Obstruents belong to the coda rather than to the peak. Nasals, it seems, have an intermediate status, tied to both the peak and the coda.

Other experiments with adults suggest that the two English liquids, /r/ and /l/, differ in their cohesiveness with a preceding vowel (Derwing, Nearey, & Dow, 1987). A vowel and a following /r/ are even more tightly linked than a vowel and a following /l/. In Chapter 11, I discuss another linguistic framework—an alternative to the hierarchical theory—which may provide a better account of graded effects such as these.

Do children consider syllables to be linear strings of phonemes or do they organize the phonemes within syllables into larger units, as adults do? The study of children's spelling may help to answer this question. For example, first graders sometimes spell the sequence /ɑr/ with the single letter *r,* the name of which is /ɑr/. Children's use of letter-name knowledge to spell causes them to make errors like CR for *car* and PRK for *park.* First graders are less likely to spell /ti/ with just *t,* as in TTH for *teeth.* Why are letter-name spellings more frequent for *r* than for *t*? The work on syllable structure that I have discussed suggests an answer to this question. The phonemes /ɑ/ and /r/ are tightly bound. Both belong to the syllable's rime; both may, in addition, belong to the syllable's peak. Because the phonemes form a linguistic unit, children sometimes treat the phonemes as a group for spelling purposes, symbolizing the entire group with the letter *r.* The phonemes /t/ and /i/ are less closely joined. The consonant belongs to the syllable's onset while the vowel belongs to the syllable's rime. That is, the word *teeth* is parsed into /t/ and /iθ/ rather than into /ti/ and /θ/. Because /t/ and /i/ are not strongly linked, first graders do not usually treat them as a unit for spelling purposes. Thus, children organize the phonemes within syllables into groups and this organization affects their spelling.

The Writing System of English

Having completed my survey of the sound system of English, I now turn to the English writing system. It is widely believed that the English writing system is complex, illogical, and irregular. As a result, the system is extremely difficult for children to learn. These sentiments are expressed in such statements as:

> Our present spelling system is inconsistent, illogical, needlessly difficult and highly ineffective. . . . It is a major cause of reading difficulty and of high illiteracy rates. ("Why simplified spelling?", 1987, p. 1)

> It [our system] wastes a large part of the time and effort given to the instruction of our children, keeping them, for example, from one to two years behind the school children of Germany. . . . Moreover, the printing, typewriting, and handwriting of the useless letters which our spelling prescribes, and upon which its difficulty chiefly rests, wastes every year millions of dollars, and time and effort worth millions more. ("Simplified Spelling," 1906, p. 7, cited in Venezky, 1980)

The belief that the English writing system is complex and illogical has some important consequences. One consequence is the idea that English-speaking children's difficulties in learning to spell occur for one reason and one reason alone—the irregularity of our writing system. If only our system were regular, the argument goes, children would learn to spell with ease. Children who are learning a language with a regular writing system, such as Italian or Finnish, should learn to read and write much more rapidly than English-speaking children. Severe difficulty in learning to spell and read should be much less common in Italy or Finland than it is in the United States or England.

The view that English spelling is inconsistent and irregular has consequences, too, for our ideas about the processes that children use to spell. Because the system is so irregular, the argument goes, children's only hope of success is to memorize the spelling of each word. The rules of English are so complex and so riddled with exceptions that children cannot figure out how to spell words on their own. Thus, learning to spell is a matter of rote memorization. It requires diligence and effort but little intelligence or thought. In line with this belief, some well-educated people are almost proud to admit that they are poor spellers. They seem to imply that they are so creative and so busy that they never took time to laboriously memorize the spellings of words.

To evaluate these widely held beliefs, it is necessary to discuss the properties of the English writing system. Why is our writing system so maligned? In what ways is it "inconsistent" and "illogical"? Without a detailed understanding of the writing system itself, we cannot begin to understand how children learn the system and what kinds of difficulties they face.

The English writing system is, basically, an *alphabet*. An alphabetic writing system represents the spoken language at the level of phonemes. Each phoneme in the spoken form of a word is symbolized with a *grapheme*—a letter or group of letters—in the printed form of a word. For example, the spoken form of *back* has three phonemes—/b/, /æ/, and /k/. The phoneme /b/ is symbolized with the one-letter grapheme *b*, the phoneme /æ/ is symbolized with the one-letter grapheme *a*, and the phoneme /k/ is symbolized with the two-letter grapheme *ck*.

The ideal alphabet, it is often thought, has *one-to-one* relations between phonemes and graphemes. Each phoneme is always represented with the same grapheme every time it occurs. Each grapheme symbolizes only one phoneme. This state of affairs is depicted in the top panel of Figure 1.7, where numbers represent phonemes and letters represent graphemes. In the figure, the phoneme /1/ is always spelled with the grapheme *a*. The grapheme *a* does not represent any other phoneme. The phoneme /2/ is always spelled with the grapheme *b*. This grapheme represents only the phoneme /2/; it never stands for any other phoneme. It was necessary to use abstract numbers and letters rather than real English graphemes and phonemes in the figure because English has no cases that match this ideal! In such a system, the spelling of each word is totally predictable for a given dialect. Because there is only one way to spell each phoneme, the speller does not have to choose from among several possibilities.

An alphabetic system may also have *one-to-many* relations from phonemes to graphemes. The middle panel of Figure 1.7 shows a fragment of a system of this

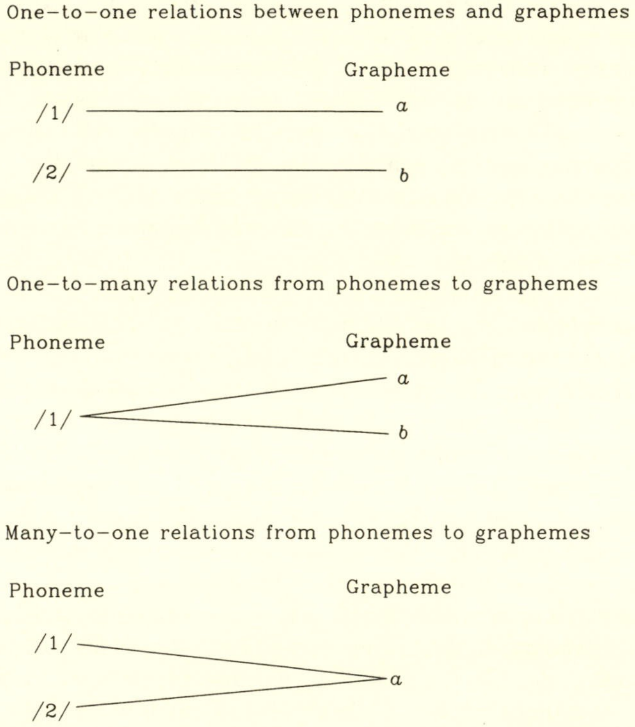

One–to–one relations between phonemes and graphemes

Phoneme — Grapheme
/1/ ———————— a
/2/ ———————— b

One–to–many relations from phonemes to graphemes

Phoneme — Grapheme
/1/ a, b

Many–to–one relations from phonemes to graphemes

Phoneme — Grapheme
/1/, /2/ a

Figure 1.7. Possible relations between phonemes and graphemes.

type. In the example, the phoneme /1/ has two possible spellings, *a* and *b*. This phoneme is spelled as *a* in some words and *b* in others. This is the situation that holds in English, except that many phonemes have more than two spellings. For example, /k/ may be spelled with *c*, as in *cat*, *k*, as in *kite*, or *ck*, as in *back*, among other possibilities. The spellings of /i/ include *e*, as in *he*, *i*, as in *pizza*, *y*, as in *happy*, *ie* as in *chief*, and others.

For phonemes that map onto more than one grapheme, the mappings may vary in their predictability. At one extreme, the mappings are wholly unpredictable. There is nothing that allows one to choose among the possible spellings of a phoneme. For instance, suppose that the phoneme /1/ is spelled as *a* half the time it occurs. It is spelled as *b* the other half of the time. The words in which /1/ is spelled as *a* do not differ in any systematic way from the words in which /1/ is spelled as *b*. It is impossible to predict which of the two spellings occurs in any given word.

At the other extreme, suppose that one can always choose the correct spelling of a phoneme by considering the phoneme's context or other factors. For example, suppose that the phoneme /1/ is spelled as *a* when it is at the end of a word. When at the beginning of a word or in the middle of a word, the phoneme is always spelled as *b*. In this case, there is a rule that allows one to correctly spell the phoneme /1/. The rule has no exceptions. Thus, even though the phoneme may be spelled in more than one way, people who know the rule can always spell the phoneme correctly. They can do this even if they have never seen the word in print and so cannot spell it correctly from memory.

An intermediate possibility is that a rule or pattern exists but that it has exceptions. Suppose that /1/ is usually spelled as *a* when it occurs at the ends of words. However, there are a few words that end with /1/ in which /1/ is spelled with *b*. The many words in which word-final /1/ is spelled with *a* may be called *regular* words. The few words in which word-final /1/ is spelled with *b* may be called *irregular* or *exception* words. In this case, people who know the rule can usually spell the phoneme /1/ correctly. They will be correct on the regular words. However, they will be incorrect on the irregular words unless they happen to have memorized the conventional spellings of these words. Spellers will *regularize* the irregular words, writing /1/ at the ends of these words with *a* rather than with *b*.

This intermediate possibility—rules plus exceptions—is often found in English. One of the most clear-cut rules concerns the phoneme /oi/. Generally, /oi/ is spelled as *oy* at the ends of morphemes (e.g., *toy, boyfriend*) and before vowels (e.g., *royal*). It is spelled as *oi* elsewhere (e.g., *oil, coin*). There are a handful of exceptions to this pattern, including *oyster*. A person who knew the rule governing the alternation of *oy* and *oi* could generally spell /oi/ correctly. However, this person would misspell the irregular word *oyster* as *oister*. Most English rules have a larger number of exceptions. For example, one possible rule of English is that /i/ is spelled as *ie* when it is followed by /f/, as in *belief* and *chief* (Hanna, Hanna, Hodges, & Rudorf, 1966). However, /i/ is sometimes spelled as *ee* or *ea* in this context, as in *beef* and *sheaf*. A person who used the rule that /i/ is *ie* before /f/ would have difficulty with words like *beef*.

The bottom panel of Figure 1.7 shows yet another possible state of affairs—a *many-to-one* mapping from phonemes to graphemes. In the example, the phoneme

/1/ has a single spelling. It is always symbolized with *a*. As a result, the spelling of /1/ is completely predictable. The phoneme /2/ also has a single spelling. It, too, is always spelled with *a*. Thus, the grapheme *a* represents two different phonemes, /1/ and /2/. There is a two-to-one mapping from the phonemes /1/ and /2/ to the grapheme *a*. The English phonemes /θ/ and /ð/ exemplify this type of mapping. The phoneme /θ/ is virtually always spelled with *th*. The phoneme /ð/ is virtually always spelled the same way. The few exceptions are mostly technical terms like *phthalic*, a type of acid. For all practical purposes, especially where children are concerned, /θ/ and /ð/ are both consistently spelled with *th*. The grapheme *th* therefore represents two different phonemes, /θ/ and /ð/.

To summarize the discussion to this point, English has one-to-many relations from phonemes to graphemes, as in the middle panel of Figure 1.7. It also has many-to-one relations from phonemes to graphemes, as in the bottom panel of Figure 1.7. English does not have the simple one-to-one mappings from phonemes to graphemes that are thought to characterize the ideal alphabetic writing system.

Turning to words that contain more than one morpheme, another characteristic of the English writing system becomes apparent. With such words, English sometimes deviates systematically from the alphabetic principle. Consider the past tense verbs *helped* and *cleaned*. The spoken form of *helped* actually ends with /t/, so the phoneme-grapheme correspondences of English predict the spelling *helpt*. The spoken form of *cleaned* ends with /nd/ rather than with a vowel plus /d/, so the phoneme-grapheme correspondences predict final *nd*. Yet the words are spelled as *helped* and *cleaned* rather than as *helpt* and *cleand*. To see why, consider that past tense verbs contain two morphemes. The first morpheme is the verb stem, *help* or *clean* in the examples. The second morpheme is the past tense marker, here called *-D*. The pronunciation of *-D* differs according to the final phoneme of the verb stem to which it is attached. When the verb ends with /p/, the past tense marker is realized as /t/, as in *helped*. When the verb ends with /n/, the past tense marker is /d/, as in *cleaned*. Although the past tense morpheme is pronounced differently in the two cases, it is spelled as *ed* in both. The English past tense morpheme is spelled in a consistent manner, ignoring predictable variations in its phonemic form.

Words like *helped* and *cleaned* are called *inflected* words. In English, inflections are added to the ends of words to mark such things as tense and number. The past tense suffix *-D* is one inflectional ending. The plural marker, here called *-Z*, is another. Both *-D* and *-Z* are spelled in a consistent way despite changes in their phonemic forms.

The same principle holds for many *derived* words, in which *affixes* (prefixes or suffixes) have been added to change the meaning of the word. One derivational prefix is *re-*, which may be added to *read* to form *reread*. Derivational suffixes include *-ion* and *-ic*, as in *relation* and *conic*. *Relation* retains the *t* of *relate* even though the consonant changes from /t/ to /ʃ/. Similarly, *conic* retains the *o* of *cone* even though the vowel changes from /o/ to /ɑ/. In these and many other cases, the morphemes of derived words are spelled consistently. Meaning relations among derived words are not *always* preserved in spelling, however. For instance, the second *o* of *pronounce* is dropped in *pronunciation*.

As these examples of inflected and derived words show, the English writing system represents morphological as well as phonemic information. One question addressed by this study is whether first graders appreciate that meaning relations among words are often marked in spelling.

To conclude, the English writing system is complex in at least four ways. First, the system has one-to-many relations from phonemes to graphemes. Most phonemes are not symbolized with the same grapheme every time they occur. For example, /k/ is sometimes symbolized with *k,* sometimes with *c,* and sometimes with other graphemes. Second, for those phonemes that have more than one spelling, it is not always possible to predict when each spelling occurs. The rules that do exist often have exceptions. Yet a third source of complexity is that English has many-to-one relations from phonemes to graphemes. Two or more phonemes are sometimes spelled with the same grapheme, as when /θ/ and /ð/ are both spelled with *th.* A final source of complexity is that links between phonemes and graphemes are sometimes overridden by morphological considerations. In English, morphemes are often spelled in a consistent manner, making the relations between phonemes and graphemes less consistent. Thus, there are several things that one could mean when one says that the English writing system is inconsistent and illogical. Which of these characteristics, if any, causes problems for children learning to spell? The present study addresses this question.

Previous Research on Children's Spelling

Spelling as Memorization

Traditionally, it was thought that children learn to spell by memorizing the letters in printed words. Children learn one word at a time until they have mastered the spellings of all of the words that they need to know. This view of spelling is based on the idea that the English writing system is inconsistent and illogical. Children's only hope of mastering the system is rote visual memorization.

The view of spelling as rote, word-by-word memorization has had a lasting effect on spelling instruction. Even today, many elementary schools teach spelling as a separate subject from reading. All children, regardless of their reading skills, receive the same list of words to memorize for a weekly spelling test. The idea of spelling as rote memorization has also affected society's attitudes about spelling. Learning to spell is thought to be arduous and time-consuming. It is thought to require attentiveness and a good visual memory but little intelligence or linguistic ability.

If children spell by memorizing the letters in printed words and then reproducing the memorized sequences, their errors should be viewed by reference to the correct spellings of the words. Indeed, traditional methods of classifying children's spelling errors do exactly this (see Spache, 1940). These systems recognize several major types of error. In an *omission* error, the child leaves out one or more letters of the word's spelling. For instance, a child may spell *fine* as FIN or *butter* as BUTTR. In these cases, it is thought, the child has forgotten one of the letters in the memorized sequence. A second kind of error involves the *addition* of a letter. A child may spell *bike* as BICKE, adding a *c. Reversals* of the letters from a word's conventional spelling may also occur. Here, the child recalls the sequence of letters in the wrong order, as in CRIDE for *cried*. Finally, in a *substitution* error, one or more letters of the correct spelling is replaced with an incorrect letter or letters, as in BAD for *bed*.

The idea that learning to spell involves the memorization of letter strings meshed well with the experimental psychology of the middle part of this century. The psychologists of this time focused on the learning of meaningless strings of items. The stimuli in psychological experiments were lists of digits or lists of letters; the participants in the experiments attempted to memorize these sequences. Psychologists found a *serial position curve* when plotting people's recall of the memorized sequences. People did relatively well on items at the beginning of a list—the *primacy effect*. They did relatively well, too, on items at the end of a list—the *recency effect*. However, people did poorly on items in the middle of a list. Several experimental psychologists became interested in spelling because it seemed a real-world analogue of the laboratory learning task. In the words of Jensen (1962, pp. 105–106):

> Since a word consists of a series of letters, and since spelling a word consists of putting each letter in its proper order, we might ask whether the serial position effect, which is generally manifested in every form of serial learning investigated in the laboratory, is also manifested in spelling.

In experimental work with students at the junior high school level and above, Jensen *did* find serial position effects in spelling. This result suggested to him that spelling is similar to serial learning.

Charles Read's Research

In the 1960s, psychologists became less concerned with serial learning and rote memorization. They became more interested in learning of a creative kind—learning in which people implicitly figure out the rules of a particular domain. To the psycholinguists of the 1960s, children's learning of spoken language was the epitome of creativity. Two- and three-year-olds who produce sentences like "He goed" or "Sally throwed the ball" are not learning to speak by memorizing the words and sentences that they hear. Instead, the children are apparently trying to induce the rules of spoken English—in this case, the rules for the past tense. In so doing, the children make *regularization errors* on irregular verbs. Learning to produce *spoken* language, which was thought to be the height of creativity, was studied intensively in the 1960s. It was not until the work of Charles Read, in the 1970s, that learning to produce *written* language began also to be seen as an example of creative learning.

Working on his doctoral dissertation in linguistics and education at Harvard University, Read made an important observation. This observation clashed with the traditional view that children learn to spell by laboriously memorizing the letters in each word. Some preschoolers, Read found, begin to write on their own, without formal teaching. For these children, spelling is largely an attempt to symbolize the sounds of words. It is not just an attempt to reproduce memorized strings of letters. These children learn to spell by inducing principles of sound-spelling correspondence that apply to a number of words. They do not learn just one word at a time.

Read's conclusions came from his study of 32 children who began to write as preschoolers, before they were able to read. These children started to write when they were between about two and a half and four years old. Typically, the children learned to recognize and name the letters of the alphabet at an early age. They then learned that a letter often stands for a phoneme that occurs in the letter's name. This realization typically occurred when a child learned the first letter in his or her name or the letters of some common word. For example, a girl named Becky might learn that the first letter of her name is *b*. From this, she might infer that *b* symbolizes the phoneme /b/.

The children began to spell words using the principle that letters represent phonemes in the letters' names. Thus, the children generally spelled *bay* as BA since the name of the letter *b* contains /b/ and the name of the letter *a* is /e/. What makes spelling challenging for children, and interesting for researchers, is that some English phonemes do not occur in the name of any letter. For example, no English letter contains /θ/ or /oi/. According to Read, the children sometimes asked an adult how to spell these sounds. In other cases, they invented their own spellings for the sounds. For comprehensive discussions of this work, see Read (1971, 1975, 1986).

Read's work signaled a shift from viewing spelling in visual terms, as an attempt to memorize strings of letters, to viewing spelling in linguistic terms, as an attempt to represent the sounds of words. In addition, Read's findings signaled a shift from viewing spelling as a rote process to viewing spelling as a creative process. When Read reviewed the research on children's spelling in 1986, he titled his book *Children's Creative Spelling*. This title would have been unthinkable in earlier years, when spelling was seen as a learned habit.

If children spell creatively, attempting to represent the linguistic structure of speech, their spellings should provide important information for linguists and psycholinguists. Indeed, Read showed that children's spellings can shed light on their linguistic knowledge. Consider the vowel /ε/, as in *bed*. No vowel letter in English has /ε/ as its name. Thus, children cannot use a simple letter-name strategy to spell this vowel, as they can with vowels like /o/ and /i/. The name of the letter *a*, however, is similar to /ε/. As pointed out earlier, /e/ and /ε/ are both front unrounded vowels. Children often spell /ε/ with *a*, suggesting that they unconsciously recognize the similarity between /ε/ and /e/ and use it to guide their spelling. Children's spellings suggest that they consider some pairs of phonemes (e.g., /ε/ and /e/) to be similar to one another and other pairs of phonemes to be dissimilar.

One of the strengths of Read's work is its combination of naturalistic and experimental methods. I have already described Read's naturalistic research. Read also carried out experiments to replicate and extend his naturalistic findings. One goal of the experiments was to determine whether older children produce some of the same spelling errors discovered among preschoolers. Another goal of the experiments was to pinpoint the reasons for particular misspellings.

A weakness of Read's research is that he sometimes overreacted against the earlier view of spelling as a purely visual process. Read sometimes failed to consider how children's experience with printed words could have contributed to their errors. As one example, the preschoolers in Read's study sometimes misspelled /ð/ with *t*. One reason for this error, which Read did not discuss, is that /ð/ is normally spelled with *t* followed by *h*. The children had probably seen *th* in words like *the* and *they*. They may have spelled /ð/ as *t* in a partly successful attempt to recall the two-letter spelling. Thus, children's spelling is affected by their knowledge of conventional orthography. In this book, I discuss the orthographic influences on children's spelling as well as the phonological influences.

Read's research set the stage for other research on children's spelling in the 1970s and 1980s. Indeed, much of the subsequent research was largely based on Read's findings in that it looked for the same errors that he found and interpreted them in the same way that he did. This study extends Read's pioneering work. It examines a new collection of beginning spellings, looking at a broad range of phenomena with a fresh eye. In this way, the results of this study should add to our knowledge of how children learn to spell and the kinds of errors they make.

In some ways, this study is similar to Read's. Both studies involve detailed linguistic analyses of large collections of beginning spellings. In both cases, the spellings were produced in a natural situation rather than in an experiment.

One difference between the studies is the type of children involved. The children in Read's study began to write on their own before they entered school and even before they learned to read. Writing and spelling were activities that they chose themselves, not activities that their parents or teachers expected them to perform. The children in my study were first graders. They wrote, at least at first, because they were asked to do so. These children were learning to read at the same time that they were learning to write. Almost all of the children in Read's study came from educated, professional families. Some attended private schools. The children in my study were from middle-class backgrounds and attended a public school. Finally, Read's subjects showed an interest in and aptitude for writing that is unusual among children their age. The children in my study were not precocious or advanced. They simply happened to be assigned to a first-grade teacher who encouraged independent writing. Given the many differences between the two groups of children, it is important to ask whether a similar picture of beginning spelling emerges from the two studies. Do the spellings of gifted preschoolers who begin to write on their own differ qualitatively or quantitatively from the spellings produced by more typical first-grade children?

Another important difference between the two studies is that Read examined only misspelled words. Because he was primarily concerned with children's invented spellings, he did not include correctly spelled words in his collection of data. I analyzed correctly spelled words as well as errors. Thus, I can ask certain questions that Read was not able to address, such as whether some types of words are easier for children to spell correctly than others.

The tabulations in Appendix II of this book are useful in comparing my results with Read's. Appendix II lists how the children in this study spelled each phoneme in misspelled words only. These results may be compared with the results in Appendix A of Read (1975), which are also based on misspelled words. Because Read did not break down children's spellings of each phoneme according to the conventional spellings of the phoneme, Appendix II is arranged in the same fashion.

University of Virginia Research

Read's research broke new ground in the study of children's spelling. However, because the work was limited to a special group of children, some scholars (e.g., Gibson & Levin, 1975) questioned the generalizability of the results. Edmund Henderson and his doctoral students at the University of Virginia's McGuffey Reading Center wondered whether the spellings of children who learn to write at school resemble the spellings of Read's preschoolers. They therefore examined the spellings of elementary school children. I refer to this body of work as the University of Virginia research, because that is where it began. It has since spread beyond these geographical boundaries. Descriptions of this work may be found in Beers, Beers, and Grant (1977), Beers and Henderson (1977), Gentry (1982), Henderson and Beers (1980), and Henderson (1985). The work of Linnea Ehri (e.g., Ehri, 1986) has also been influenced by the University of Virginia tradition.

The Virginia researchers combined analyses of children's naturally produced spellings with experimental work, the same combination that proved so successful for Read. Based on their findings, they proposed a theory of spelling development. According to this theory, children pass through a series of stages in learning to spell. Descriptions of these stages vary slightly from one study to the next; I adopt here the description of Gentry (1982).

The first level of spelling development is the *precommunicative stage.* At this stage, children string together letters of the alphabet in an apparently random fashion. Numbers as well as letters may appear in spellings. Children show no knowledge of the correspondences between phonemes and graphemes at this stage. When Calvin says that ACR stands for "I like swings and I like slides. And I like the sun" (see Fig. 1.1), he is at the precommunicative stage of spelling development. The term "apparently random" is used for a reason; research by Ferreiro and Teberosky (1982) and Tolchinsky Landsmann and Levin (1985, 1987) suggests that the spellings are less random than they first seem. The important point for present purposes, however, is that the letters do not represent speech sounds at the phonemic or phonetic level.

The second stage of spelling development is the *semiphonetic stage.* Children now realize that letters stand for the segments in spoken words. At this stage, Gentry (1982) and others imply, children take spelling to represent the *phonetic* level of speech rather than the *phonemic* level. "Letters used to represent words provide a partial (but not total) mapping of phonetic representation for the word being spelled" (Gentry, 1982, p. 194). As this description states, semiphonetic spellers do not code all of the phonetic segments of a word in their spelling. They represent some phones and omit others. For example, children may spell *old* as OD, omitting the *l*. Although Gentry (1982) does not specify which segments tend to be omitted in semiphonetic spelling, other investigators (e.g., Ehri, 1986; Morris & Perney, 1984) imply that vowels in the middles of words and word-final consonants are particularly susceptible to omission. For example, children may spell *mail* as M or ML. A further characteristic of the semiphonetic stage is that spellers use a letter-name strategy whenever possible. When they encounter a phone or series of phones that matches the name of a letter, they spell it with the corresponding letter. For instance, semiphonetic spellers may write *are* as R, *you* as U, and *carpet* as CRPT.

During the *phonetic stage,* children continue to represent the phonetic level of speech in their spelling. This stage differs from the preceding one in that omissions no longer occur. "All of the surface sound features of the words being spelled are represented in the spelling" (Gentry, 1982, p. 195). Phonetic spellers continue to use a letter-name strategy. They do not yet know which sequences of letters are acceptable in English and which sequences are not acceptable. For instance, a phonetic speller might spell *cut* as CKUT, not knowing that *ck* is barred at the beginnings of English words.

Transitional spellers move away from the reliance on sound that marked the earlier stages. They now adhere to the basic conventions of English orthography. Errors like CKUT for *cut* no longer occur. The letter-name strategy also disappears. Children no longer spell *car* as CR, as they did earlier. They use a vowel letter followed by *r* to represent the letter-name sequence. As another example of the move away from a letter-name strategy, children symbolize the vowel of *dive* with *i* followed by final *e* rather than with just *i*. Transitional spellers begin to use meaning relations among words to guide their spelling. If they know how to spell *eight,* they may spell *eighty* as EIGHTEE. They do not spell it as ATE, as they did earlier.

The final stage of spelling development, according to Gentry (1982), is the *correct stage.* Knowledge of the English writing system is now firmly established. Expanding on Gentry's scheme, Henderson (1985) divided the correct stage into two stages that deal with the spelling of multisyllabic words. During a *syllable juncture stage,* Henderson (1985) proposed, children learn that double consonants mark "short" vowels. Thus, they learn to double the middle consonants of words like *rabbit* and *getting.* During the final stage of development, spellers learn about the derivational principles that guide the spelling of multisyllabic words.

The University of Virginia researchers, like Read, consider children's early spellings (those produced during the semiphonetic and phonetic stages) as attempts to represent the sounds of words rather than as attempts to reproduce memorized sequences of letters. According to the Virginia researchers, it is only later (during the transitional stage and beyond) that children's spellings begin to be influenced by the printed forms of words they have seen.

One of the main goals of the University of Virginia researchers is to apply the results of spelling research in the classroom. In this, they differ somewhat from Read, whose study of children's spelling was largely motivated by his interest in linguistics. The Virginia researchers have helped to make teachers aware of the reasons for children's spelling errors. They have suggested instruction that is appropriate at each level of spelling development. The Virginia work has been influential, in part, because of the growing interest in whole-language and language-experience approaches to reading and spelling at the elementary level. The idea that children progress naturally through a sequence of stages in learning to spell fits well with these approaches, as does the idea (Gentry, 1982, p. 198) that "purposeful writing is the key to cognitive growth in spelling."

From the perspective of the University of Virginia researchers, the spellings in this study are all at the semiphonetic stage or higher. As mentioned earlier, some of the children produced apparently random strings of letters at the beginning of the school year. Because I did not include these spellings in my analyses, I can draw no conclusions about the earliest beginnings of writing development. The findings of this study apply to children who can spell words in an independent manner. They do not tell us what enables children to reach this point but rather shed light on the nature of the spellings produced by children who have begun to write.

I have chosen not to divide the spellings in this study into semiphonetic, phonetic, and transitional categories. Most of the analyses that I report are carried out on the pooled results for the school year as a whole, although I sometimes compare the spellings from the first semester of the school year with the spellings from the second semester. Although the children's spellings certainly improved across the course of the school year, I believe that the developmental stages proposed by the Virginia researchers are too simple. Semiphonetic, phonetic, and transitional spellings are less distinct and less well defined than they first appear to be.

Linguistic Awareness

Learning to speak and understand a language is something that almost all children accomplish, beginning at an early age. By the time they are four years old or so, children can speak grammatically and can understand a wide variety of sentence forms. Learning to read and write is more difficult. Written language differs from spoken language in that it is learned later, usually requires formal instruction, and causes great difficulty for some children who are developing normally in all other respects. Why is learning to speak and understand a language relatively easy, while learning to read and write a language is relatively hard? In 1971, a conference was held to discuss this question. Researchers in the fields of linguistics, psychology, and education were invited. The proceedings of the conference were published in an influential book edited by Kavanagh and Mattingly (1972).

Several of the conferees suggested an answer to the question that had motivated the conference. Reading and writing are difficult, they argued, because these processes require a degree of *linguistic awareness* that speaking and understanding do not. In order to read and write, it is not enough for a person to know how to use language. The person must also have some awareness of the parts of which language is made up, including words, morphemes, syllables, and phonemes. With an alphabetic writing system, awareness of phonemes is especially important. As Donald Shankweiler and Isabelle Liberman observed (Shankweiler & I. Y. Liberman, 1972, p. 309):

> In reading an alphabetic language like English, the child must be able to segment the words he knows into the phonemic elements that the alphabetic shapes represent. In order to do this, he needs to be consciously aware of the segmentation of the languages into units of phonemic size. . . . He has to be consciously aware that the word "cat" that he knows—an apparently unitary syllable—has three separate segments. His competence in speech production and speech perception is of no direct use to him here, because this competence enables him to achieve the segmentation without ever being consciously aware of it.

Adults who are literate in an alphabetic writing system do possess phonemic awareness. They know that /k'æt/ *(cat)* contains three sounds and that /pl'æn/ *(plan)* contains four. They know that /bl'æk/ *(black)* and /br'en/ *(brain)* share a sound at the beginning. Most preschool and kindergarten children lack this awareness. Although they use phonemes *implicitly* when they speak and understand, they have difficulty counting phonemes, comparing phonemes, and performing other *explicit* phonemic awareness tasks (e.g., I. Y. Liberman, Shankweiler, Fischer, & Carter, 1974; Treiman & Zukowski, 1991).

In the years since the 1971 conference, children's phonemic awareness has become a major topic of research. One strand of research has focused on the relations among phonemic awareness, reading, and spelling. We now know that phonemic awareness plays an important role in learning to read and write. Indeed, children's performance on short tests of phonemic awareness predicts their reading achievement better than does their performance on long, comprehensive intelligence tests (Stanovich, 1992). Although there has been a good deal of research on the relation between phonemic awareness and reading, there has been little research on the relation between phonemic awareness and spelling. However, the research that does exist shows that phonemic awareness plays a role in learning to spell (Burns & Richgels, 1989; I. Y. Liberman, Rubin, Duques, & Carlisle, 1985; Lundberg, Olofsson, & Wall, 1980). In fact, phonemic awareness may be even more critical for spelling than it is for reading (Goswami & Bryant, 1990). This is because, in order to spell a word (at least a word whose conventional spelling is unfamiliar to the child), the child must be able to analyze the spoken form of the word into phonemes so as to represent each phoneme with a grapheme.

Given the role of phonemic awareness in learning to spell and read, it becomes important to learn more about the nature and development of phonemic awareness itself. A second strand of research has addressed this issue. We now know that not all tasks that require children to analyze spoken syllables into smaller units are equally difficult. Tasks that can be solved via an onset/rime division of the syllable are relatively easy (Bowey & Francis, 1991; Kirtley, Bryant, Maclean & Bradley, 1989; Treiman, 1985a; Treiman, 1992; Treiman & Zukowski, 1991). For example, some preschoolers and kindergarteners can tell that *plank* and *plea* sound the same at the beginning (i.e., share an onset, /pl/). Some preschoolers and kindergarteners can tell that *spit* and *wit* rhyme (i.e., share a rime, /ɪt/). Children have more difficulty judging that *plank* and *prove* sound the same at the beginning. This task is hard because it requires children to analyze the onsets /pl/ and /pr/ into their component phonemes. Children also have difficulty telling that *spit* and *flat* sound the same at the end. This task is hard because it requires children to analyze the rimes /ɪt/ and /æt/. Although researchers have not directly investigated children's ability to analyze peaks (e.g., the /ɪl/ of *milk*) or codas (e.g., the /ft/ of *sift*) into phonemes, I suspect that this level of phonemic segmentation is especially difficult.

Thus, children's phonemic awareness skills are not fully developed when they enter the first grade. Most middle-class first graders *can* analyze spoken syllables into onsets and rimes at this time. However, many have trouble analyzing the subunits of the syllable—including onsets, rimes, peaks, and codas—into their component phonemes. As I show in the following chapters of this book, these difficulties affect the children's spellings.

Although most middle-class children have some degree of phonemic awareness when they enter first grade, a few do not. These will be the children who cannot invent spellings at all or who produce things like ACR for "I like swings and I like slides. And I like the sun." We know that such children exist. They are the children who, if things do not improve, may eventually be labeled "reading disabled" or "dyslexic." Because of the nature of this study, I can say very little about the characteristics of these children or of their spellings. The modal child in this study, readers should keep in mind, is a child who has enough phonemic awareness to spell words independently.

Cognitive Psychologists Look at Spelling: The Dual-Route Model

Within the field of psychology, the cognitive revolution of the 1960s led researchers away from studies of serial learning and rote memorization. Instead, psychologists began to study the mental processes that people use to perform real-life tasks. Not surprisingly, many cognitive psychologists became interested in reading. A good deal of research was done on how adults read and on how children learn to read. In the late 1970s, Uta Frith observed that spelling had received little attention. She convinced a number of researchers to turn their efforts to spelling. Their findings were published in 1980 under the title *Cognitive Processes in Spelling* (Frith, 1980).

The consensus in this book, as in most of the cognitive psychological research on spelling of this period, is that children (and adults) may use one of two different processes to spell a word. The first process in these *dual-route* models is similar to the traditional one of rote, word-by-word memorization. Children memorize the sequence of letters in each word and read off this sequence from memory when trying to spell the word. The second process is more creative. Spellers try to construct or generate a spelling for the word based on the word's phonological form. To do this, children analyze the spoken word into phonemes, using the phonemic analysis skills discussed earlier. Children then symbolize each phoneme with a letter or group of letters. To do this, children use their knowledge of the relations between phonemes and graphemes in the English language. For example, a child may analyze the spoken form of *cat* into /k/, /æ/, and /t/. The child may choose the grapheme *k* for the phoneme /k/, the grapheme *a* for the phoneme /æ/, and the grapheme *t* for the phoneme /t/, producing the incorrect but plausible spelling KAT. Spellers may use one route or the other for a particular word. Alternatively, they may use both routes in combination.

Similar dual-route models have been put forward for reading (see Coltheart, 1978). In the case of reading, one process involves a direct association between the word's spelling and its pronunciation or meaning. The second process involves a rule-governed mapping from the spelling of a word to its sound.

Dual-route models of spelling are compatible with the finding that phonemic awareness plays a role in learning to spell. Although phonemic awareness is not needed to use the memorization route, it *is* needed for the phonological route. A child who cannot segment spoken words into phonemes cannot learn the relations between phonemes and graphemes and cannot construct the spelling of a word from its sound.

In keeping with their tendency to dichotomize, dual-route modelers typically divided spelling errors into two main categories. The first type of error is the *legal* or *phonetic* error. The spelling, although incorrect, is a reasonable representation of the spoken word. KAT for *cat* and CRIDE for *cried* are examples of legal errors. The second type of error is *illegal* or *nonphonetic*. The error is not a possible representation of the spoken word. Examples are BRAOD for *broad* and PELCH for *peach*.

Legal errors are thought to indicate the use of the phonological spelling route. The child who spelled *cat* as KAT successfully analyzed the spoken word into phonemes and assigned a plausible letter to each phoneme. However, the child did not produce the correct spelling. Illegal errors point to use of rote memorization or unsuccessful use of the phonological route. For instance, the child who spelled *broad* as BRAOD remembered that the printed word contained the letters *b, r, o, a,* and *d* but did not reproduce the letters in the right order.

Another dichotomy that was widely accepted by the cognitive psychologists of the 1970s and early 1980s was the dichotomy between *regular* words and *irregular* (or *exception*) words. Regular words can be correctly spelled (or read) via the phonological route. Examples are *thin* and *bad*. Irregular words cannot be correctly spelled (or read) via the phonological route. Their spellings, or at least certain portions of their spellings, must be memorized. *Come* and *said* are considered to be irregular words.

Where Read and the University of Virginia researchers employed both naturalistic and experimental methods in the study of spelling, most dual-route modelers used an experimental approach. In a typical study (e.g., Barron, 1980), children are given lists of regular and irregular words to spell. The researcher attempts to equate the two types of words in advance for other variables that may influence children's performance. For example, the regular and irregular words contain the same numbers of letters and are equally common in children's reading materials. Any difference between the two types of words in level of performance or in type of errors is taken to reflect the difference in regularity.

Connectionist Models

In recent years, dual-route models have come under attack (see Humphreys & Evett, 1985; Van Orden, Pennington, & Stone, 1990). For example, adults do not always pronounce the nonword *mave* as /m'ev/, as they should if following spelling-to-sound translation rules of the kind envisaged by dual-route theorists. Because *mave* is similar to the irregular but frequent word *have,* people sometimes pronounce it as /m'æv/ (Glushko, 1979; Jared, McRae, & Seidenberg, 1990; Treiman & Zukowski, 1988). Although most criticisms of the dual-route models have been raised in the context of adult reading, Campbell (1985) provided some evidence from children's spelling that appears to speak against the dual-route view.

In place of dual-route models, a new class of models has been put forward— *connectionist* models (Seidenberg & McClelland, 1989; Van Orden et al., 1990). Within connectionist models of reading, there are links or connections from orthographic units to phonological units. The weights on these connections are adjusted to reflect the relations between spellings and sounds in the words to which readers are exposed. Thus, when people pronounce a nonword like *mave,* their performance is affected by all of the similar-looking words that they know. This includes both "regular" words like *save* and *gave* and "irregular" words like *have*. In place of frozen spelling-to-sound rules such as *a* followed by final *e* goes to /e/, the body of words to which readers have been exposed takes on primary importance.

The rise of connectionist models is closely linked to the increasing use of computers in the study of cognitive processes. This endeavor, which brings together traditional cognitive psychology and computer science, is known as cognitive science. Cognitive scientists have found it necessary to implement connectionist models on computers in order to determine the properties of these models and to study how they work.

To date, connectionist modeling has focused on reading rather than spelling. However, connectionist models of spelling may also be envisaged. In such models, there are connections from phonological units to orthographic units. Learning to spell involves modifying the weights on the connections to reflect the relations between sounds and spellings in the words to which the person has been exposed.

Dialect and Spelling

If spelling is the rote recall of memorized sequences of letters, then people's dialects should not affect their spelling. Children who speak different dialects of English should make the same kinds of spelling errors, provided that the children have the same exposure to printed words. However, if children construct spellings from words' sounds, then children who pronounce words in different ways may spell them differently. To take an example, people in many parts of the United States pronounce *pen* with /ε/. However, people from the area of this study, like many people from the southern United States, pronounce *pen* with /ɪ/. For these speakers, *pen* and *pin* sound alike. If spelling reflects phonemic form, children who speak such dialects may spell *pen* and *pin* alike, writing PIN for both.

We know relatively little about the effects of dialect on children's spelling. The research that has been done is chiefly experimental work with children in the late elementary grades or even older. By this time, children's knowledge of conventional spelling might be expected to outweigh any effects of dialect. Although the evidence is scanty, it appears that children's dialect *does* affect their spelling (see Read, 1986). For example, black third graders sometimes misspell *south* as SOWF, a mistake that fits the pronunciation of this word in their dialect as /s'auf/. White children are less likely to make this error (O'Neal & Trabasso, 1976).

As I have discussed, dialect was considered in the present study. The phonemic transcriptions used here represent the typical pronunciations of words in Hoosier speech. When discussing the results of the study, I point out certain spelling errors that appear to reflect the children's dialect. However, because the study does not include a second group of children who speak a different dialect of English, I cannot draw strong conclusions about the effects of dialect. To do this, it would be necessary to compare children who speak different dialects.

The Relation Between Spelling and Reading

How are spelling and reading related to one another? According to some investigators, the relationship is very close. For example, children who are good readers are usually good spellers. This is true even at the first-grade level (Gough, Juel, & Griffith, in press). Findings reported by Ehri (1986) further support the idea that spelling and reading are closely linked. Ehri found that, when first graders are taught to read a set of words, their spelling of these words improves even if they do not practice writing the words.

According to other investigators, reading and spelling are not all that closely related. Supporting this view, the association between spelling and reading is not perfect. Some children and adults read well but spell appallingly. Bryant and Bradley (1980) suggested that spelling and reading are particularly disconnected for young children. They found that normal children of six and seven sometimes spell words like *bun* and *mat* but cannot read them. This happens, according to Bryant and Bradley, because the children adopt a phonological strategy when they spell but a visual strategy when they read. (But see Gough et al., 1992, for some questions about this finding.)

The present study focuses on spelling rather than reading. Because no information was collected about the children's reading, no conclusions can be drawn about the relation between an individual child's spelling ability and that child's reading ability. However, I do attempt to determine whether children's spellings are influenced by the knowledge that they have gained from reading. Such an influence would suggest that reading and spelling are not totally disconnected. Children learn about printed words from their reading, and this knowledge, in turn, affects the spellings that they produce.

Naturalistic Versus Experimental Approaches to the Study of Spelling

Two approaches have been used in the study of children's spelling—a naturalistic approach and an experimental approach. In a naturalistic study, one examines the spellings that children produce in writings done at home or in school. In an experiment, one presents children with a list of selected words or nonwords to spell. Each type of study has its advantages and disadvantages. The present study is a naturalistic one and has all the strengths and weaknesses that this entails.

One strength of a naturalistic study is that the spellings are produced by real children doing real writing. Children spell words of their own choosing, not words chosen by an experimenter who is testing a particular theory about spelling. Thus, the results may potentially shed light on a broad range of issues. An experiment, in contrast, is typically designed to study a single phenomenon. Moreover, the children in naturalistic studies usually do not know that their writings will be collected and studied. They spell the way they normally do in the context of meaningful writing. The children do not adopt unusual strategies to deal with an artificial single-word spelling task or to please an experimenter.

Although naturalistic studies have notable strengths, they also have some weaknesses. One problem is that the researcher is at the mercy of what the children choose to spell. In this study, as in other naturalistic studies, the children did not spell large numbers of words of certain types. For example, the children attempted relatively few words containing /dʒ/ or /oi/, which are among the less common phonemes of English. In such cases, one cannot draw strong conclusions from the naturalistic evidence alone. Sometimes, as in the case of /ʤ/, other research exists to bolster the conclusions from the naturalistic study. In these cases, I discuss the relevant research in this book. In other cases, the necessary work has not yet been done.

Another problem with naturalistic research is that some children spell more than others. In my study, some of the children were prolific writers. Others were not. It turned out that the children who contributed many spellings to the collection did not spell more accurately than the children who contributed few. There was no significant correlation between the total number of spellings that a child produced and the percentage of those spellings that were correct ($r = .03$). Nor was there a correlation between the number of *different* words that a child attempted to spell and the child's percentage of correct spellings ($r = .05$). These near-zero correlations suggest that the teacher succeeded in her goal of having the children write without worrying about the correctness of their spellings. If the poorer spellers knew that they were making many errors, and if they felt that errors were to be avoided, they would have written little.

Even though the children who wrote a great deal were not necessarily more accurate spellers than the children who wrote less, the unequal numbers of spellings contributed by different children could still cause problems. The prolific writers may have attempted more difficult words or made more advanced types of errors. Moreover, a phenomenon that occurred among only a few children could have a large influence on the group results if those children wrote a great deal. These limitations should be kept in mind when interpreting the results of the study.

The spellings collected in this or any other naturalistic study are an example of what has been called the fragmentary data problem (Brown & McNeill, 1966). The spellings produced by a given child do not involve the same words, the same number of words, or even the same time periods during the school year as the spellings produced by another child. The spellings of one word are not produced by the same children as the spellings of another word, different words yield different numbers of spellings, and the dates at which one word is attempted are not the same as the dates at which another word is attempted. Fragmentary data should be reported fully and analyzed in several different ways. I attempt to do so in this study.

Two main statistical approaches are used to analyze the results. One is multiple regression. This approach is necessary because words that differ in one way often differ in other ways as well. For instance, past tense verbs such as *jumped* and *hemmed* are longer than present tense verbs such as *jump* and *hem*. When one finds that children make more errors on *jumped* and *hemmed* than on *jump* and *hem,* as I did, the reason for the difference is not immediately apparent. Does it reflect the past tense ending or does it reflect the additional length? Multiple regression allows one to ask whether words like *jumped* and *hemmed* are harder to spell than words like *jump* and *hem* once the difference in length is statistically taken into account.

In other cases, the question is whether a particular spelling is more common in one situation than another. For example, is the use of *c* and *ch* for /t/ more common for /t/ before /r/, as in *truck,* than for /t/ in other contexts, as in *tie*? In such cases, I typically use chi-square tests to determine whether there is an association between type of spelling (*c* and *ch* spellings versus other spellings in the example) and context

(/t/ before /r/ versus /t/ in other contexts). Statistically, there are some problems with the use of chi-square tests with the present data. The observations are not totally independent, as they should be for the use of chi-square. For instance, a child who spelled the /t/ of *truck* with *c* might also spell the /t/ of *tie* with *c* for the sake of consistency. However, because the spellings of a given child were often separated by weeks or months, and because children often spelled the same phoneme or the same word in different ways even on the same day, the problem of nonindependence is not as serious as it otherwise would be. In many cases, because of the relatively small number of spellings of a particular phoneme or a particular type of word, there is no good alternative to the chi-square test.

Ultimately, the best way to learn about children's spelling is through a combination of naturalistic and experimental methods. Considering the complementary strengths and weaknesses of the two types of studies, results that are found in both types of research are most secure. I hope that the naturalistic findings reported in this book will stimulate additional research of both naturalistic and experimental kinds on children's spelling.

Notes

1. A possible extension of the legality principle (e.g., Pulgram, 1970) states that syllables with lax vowels must be closed with a consonant. Thus, the /m/ of *lemon* must be in the first syllable because English syllables may not end with lax vowels such as /ɛ/. However, not all linguists agree with this extension of the legality principle.

2

Spelling of Words

In studying the first graders' spellings, it is reasonable to begin at the simplest possible level of analysis. The most basic way to look at the children's spellings is at the level of whole words. At this level, the simplest possible question is whether a word is spelled correctly or incorrectly. Once children's spellings are classified as correct or incorrect, a number of questions arise. Are some words easier for children to spell correctly than others? If so, what kinds of words are easy to spell and what kinds of words are hard to spell? The answers to these questions should shed light on the difficulties that children face in learning the English writing system. For example, if children have more trouble on irregular words than on regular words, one could suggest that the irregularity of the English system is one source of difficulty in learning to spell. If children often misspell inflected and derived words, one could suggest that the morphological basis of the English writing system is a problem for first graders. Such issues are addressed in the first section of this chapter.

Although it is easy to classify children's spellings of whole words as correct or incorrect, this simple classification may obscure potentially important information. For example, although KARE is the wrong spelling of *care,* this error is a plausible rendition of the word's spoken form. The letter *k* is a reasonable rendering of the phoneme /k/; /k/ is spelled as *k* in words like *kite* and *king.* In the terms introduced in Chapter 1, KARE is a legal misspelling of *care.* On the other hand, CA is an illegal spelling of *care.* It contains no representation of the /r/. In this chapter, I take a first step beyond the correct/incorrect distinction by classifying errors on whole words as legal or illegal. I ask whether some kinds of words give rise to more legal errors than other words and why.

Legal errors are not all alike. They differ from one another in a number of ways, one of which is how easy they are to decipher. Given KARE, a teacher or parent readily appreciates that it is an attempt to spell *care.* Other legal errors are harder to interpret. For teachers to respond to children's errors most effectively, they must be able to figure out what children meant to write. Thus, a final section of this chapter reports a study of the factors that affect adults' ability to interpret children's legal spelling errors.

Correct Spellings

In this section, I classify children's spellings of whole words in the simplest way possible, as correct or incorrect. Table 2.1 shows the results of this classification. Of the 5,617 spellings in the collection, 2,877 or 51.2% were correct, pooling over both semesters of the school year. The other spellings were incorrect. Accuracy increased over the course of the school year, from 43.9% correct in the first semester (August through December) to 55.3% correct in the second semester (January through April). I discuss these changes in more detail later in this chapter. For now, I consider the results for the entire school year as a whole.

Of course, the 5,617 spellings in the collection were not spellings of 5,617 different words. The students attempted many words more than once. The total number of *different* words in the collection was 889. Examining the percentage of correct spellings for each of the 889 words, I observed a great deal of variability. Some words, such as *can, the,* and *up,* were almost always spelled in the conventional fashion. Other words, such as *come, jumped,* and *Christmas,* were usually misspelled. What explains these differences in spelling accuracy?

From the examples just given, one might hypothesize that short, common words that contain a single morpheme and that are spelled in a regular fashion are most likely to be correct. For example, *the* may have an advantage due to its high frequency. *Up,* although less common than *the,* may be easy to spell because it is short and regular. Thus, several factors may contribute to the likelihood that a word will be spelled correctly.

How can one determine whether a particular factor is related to spelling difficulty? Suppose that one wishes to find out whether inflected words are harder to spell than noninflected words. If one simply compared the percentages of correct spellings for inflected words and noninflected words, one would find that the percentage was lower for inflected words. However, this difference could arise, wholly or in part, from the fact that inflected words tend to be longer than noninflected words. Long words are harder to spell than short words, as shown later in this chapter. To determine whether inflection makes a difference, above and beyond the effect of word length, both variables must be considered simultaneously. Standard (or simultaneous) multiple regression is well suited for this purpose. This statistical technique permits one to consider a number of different variables together. One asks whether each variable adds to the prediction of spelling accuracy, over and above the predictability afforded by all the other variables.

In the following sections, I will present the main results of the analyses of correct

Table 2.1. Numbers of Whole-Word Spellings of Various Types

	First Semester	Second Semester	Both Semesters
Correct spellings	888	1,989	2,877
Errors	1,135	1,605	2,740
Legal	313	643	956
Illegal	822	962	1,784

spellings in a nontechnical manner. The statistical details will be discussed in a separate section, which readers may skip if they wish.

Factors Associated with Correct Spellings of Words

One factor that proved to be associated with correct spelling was the frequency or commonness of a word. The children spelled frequent words more accurately than infrequent words. One measure of word frequency was the number of times that the printed word occurred in a large collection of reading materials designed for children in the third to ninth grades (Carroll, Davies, & Richman, 1971). This frequency measure is based on a large and carefully chosen sample of children's reading materials. However, the materials were written over twenty years ago and were targeted for children above the first grade. Therefore, other measures of word frequency were used as well. These measures were based on the number of times that the first graders in the study themselves attempted the words. These measures yielded somewhat stronger frequency effects than the measures based on Carroll et al. (1971).

The relation between word frequency and spelling correctness suggests that children's experience with reading affects their spelling. If children see a word in print many times, as they do with words like *the* and *can,* they have a chance to memorize the word's conventional spelling. For uncommon words, children must work out the spellings themselves. In so doing, they may produce errors.

A second factor associated with the correctness of children's spellings was proper names. Proper names were easier to spell than expected on the basis of other factors. For example, even though *Jimmy* does not rank high in the word frequency norms of Carroll et al. (1971), and even though it was not attempted all that often by the children in this study, the children usually spelled it correctly.

The benefit for proper names, like the benefit for frequent words, may reflect children's reading experience. Although most proper names have relatively low frequencies in Carroll et al. (1971), and although specific proper names were used relatively infrequently by the children *as a group,* a child who spelled a particular name probably did so because it was the name of the child's friend or sibling. The child had therefore seen the name many times. Thus, the proper names that children spell tend to be high-frequency words for them. They are easy to spell for the same reason that high-frequency words like *the* are easy to spell.

Another factor associated with spelling difficulty was word length. Long words were more often misspelled than short words, even controlling for other factors. This held true whether length was defined by number of letters or number of phonemes. The students' difficulty with long words is not surprising. If children spell a word by constructing a spelling from the word's phonemic form, long words should be harder than short words. The more phonemes in the word, the greater the chance for error. If children spell a word by trying to remember the letters in its printed form, errors should also increase with the number of letters to be recalled.

In addition, inflected words were hard to spell. The students misspelled inflected words more often than noninflected words, even controlling for such things as the greater length of inflected words. Two things may help to explain the children's difficulties with inflected words. First, as pointed out in Chapter 1, the spellings of inflectional morphemes do not always match their phonemic forms. *Helped* ends not with the *t* that would be expected from the spoken form /hʼɛlpt/ but with *ed.* *Cleaned* ends not with the *nd* that would be expected from the spoken form /klʼind/ but with *ed.* Apparently, many first graders do not yet know that the past tense marker is spelled in a consistent manner despite variations in its phonemic form. They tend to spell alphabetically, using one letter or group of letters for each phoneme, rather than morphemically, using one letter or group of letters for each morpheme. Thus, children often misspell *helped* as HELPT or *cleaned* as CLEND (see Chapter 10). These spellings, even though they are incorrect, accurately symbolize the morphemes' phonemic forms.

There is, in addition, a second reason for children's difficulty with inflected words. First graders sometimes omit inflectional endings altogether, as when they write HELP for *helped* (see Chapter 8). These omissions may arise when children forget that they are using the past tense. The children use the present tense verb instead of the past tense verb.

The children also had difficulty on words with *multiple-letter graphemes.* To understand the nature of this difficulty, consider the words *din* and *thin.* Each phoneme in the spoken form of *din* is transcribed with a single letter. The phoneme /d/ is spelled with *d,* the phoneme /ɪ/ is spelled with *i,* and the phoneme /n/ is spelled with *n. Din* has no multiple-letter graphemes. *Thin,* in contrast has one multiple-letter grapheme. The phoneme /θ/ is symbolized with the consonant *digraph th.* The first graders misspelled words with digraphs and other multiple-letter graphemes more often than anticipated from other factors.

Why are words like *thin* hard for children to spell? To make sense of the *thin* spelling, children must divide the printed word into graphemes and must link each grapheme to a phoneme. But there is no logical basis for the division of *thin* into graphemes. There is no extra space after the *h*—no way to know that the *t* and the *h* of this word form a unit, as opposed to, let us say, the *h* and the *i.* The division of printed words into graphemes is especially difficult since the same two letters may behave differently in different words. For example, *t* and *h* form one grapheme in *thin,* where the two letters represent the single phoneme /θ/. The letters *t* and *h* form two graphemes in *anthill,* where they represent /t/ followed by /h/. In contrast, a word like *din* is easily divided into graphemes: Each letter is a grapheme.

Even if children succeed in analyzing *thin* into the graphemes *th, i,* and *n,* the link between *th* and /θ/ is difficult to learn and remember. This is because there are two letters to remember, as compared with only one for the link between *d* and /d/. Thus, the link between a two-letter grapheme and a phoneme is more difficult to learn than the link between a one-letter grapheme and a phoneme, even when both links are equally regular and predictable.

Another factor associated with spelling correctness was regularity. To examine the effects of regularity, I divided the words in the collection into the two categories familiar to cognitive psychologists—regular words and irregular (or exception) words. The children performed better on the regular words than on the irregular words. This held true using two definitions of regularity. The first measure of regularity, the *context-free* measure, did not consider the context in which a phoneme occurred. A word was coded as regular if each phoneme was symbolized with the grapheme that most often represented that phoneme in the words of the collection. For instance, *s* is the most common spelling of /s/, *e* is the most common spelling of /ɛ/, and *t* is the most common spelling of /t/. Thus, *set* is a regular word by the context-free measure. *Seth* is also regular, since *th* is the most common—indeed the only—spelling of /θ/. *Said* and *death* are irregular by the context-free measure since neither *ai* nor *ea* is the most common spelling of /ɛ/. The second measure of regularity was the *context-sensitive* measure. This measure took account of the fact that the spelling of a phoneme sometimes depends on the phoneme's position in a word and on the surrounding phonemes. For example, /ŋ/ is spelled as *ng* at the ends of words, as in *tang,* but as *n* before /k/, as in *tank.* In this way, the phoneme's environment helps to determine its spelling. Even though *ng* is, overall, a more common spelling of /ŋ/ than *n* is, *tank* (which uses *n*) is regular by the context-sensitive measure. *Tang* is also regular.

A context-sensitive measure of regularity cannot be developed in a vacuum. It must rest on a theory that specifies the context in which each phoneme-grapheme correspondence occurs. The present context-sensitive measure of regularity was based on the rules developed by Hanna and his colleagues in their study of approximately 17,000 English words (Hanna et al., 1966). To get a flavor of these rules, consider the rule for /ɛ/. This rule states that /ɛ/ in the middle of a word is spelled as *ea* when it is followed by /θ/ but as *e* otherwise. Thus, *set* and *death* are regular while *said* and *Seth* are irregular. The work of Hanna et al. (1966) does not provide an ideal description of children's knowledge of the relations between phonemes and graphemes. One reason for this is that many of the words in the Hanna et al. (1966) study are not familiar to young children. However, no other description of English phoneme-grapheme correspondences was available when I carried out this study.

The context-free and the context-dependent definitions of regularity do not always agree with one another. The two systems give the same result for *set* and *said.* Both classify *set* as regular and *said* as irregular. However, the measures disagree for *Seth* and *death.* According to the context-free definition, *Seth* is regular and *death* is irregular. According to the context-sensitive definition, the assignments are reversed: *Seth* is irregular and *death* is regular. As this example shows, the two systems give different results when the rules of Hanna et al. (1966) state that a less common grapheme—*ea* for /ɛ/, in this case—is preferred in a particular context.

Although each measure of regularity contributed significantly to the prediction of correct spellings, the context-free measure predicted children's performance slightly better than did the context-sensitive measure. This result may mean that the pupils did not yet know all of the factors that cause certain spellings of a phoneme to be preferred in some environments and other spellings to be preferred in other environments. In addition, even when children *do* use context-sensitive rules, their rules may not perfectly match those of Hanna et al. (1966).

The most important point, though, is that the children spelled regular words more accurately than irregular words. This difference suggests that spelling involves more than rote visual memorization. Rather, children actively search for links between the phonemes in spoken words and the graphemes in printed words. They use these links when spelling words. As a result, children sometimes misspell words like *said*—words that have unusual or atypical relations between sound and spelling.

I also examined the first graders' performance on *destressable words,* or words that often occur in unstressed form in connected speech. Examples include *an, the,* and *of* (see Kenyon, 1969). Destressable words are short and frequent and should therefore be easy to spell. In fact, the children performed *even better* on destressable words than expected on the basis of these factors. The children's good performance on destressable words supports the assumption that children try to spell words as they sound when pronounced separately rather than as they sound in connected speech (see Chapter 1). If children's spellings reflected the forms of words in rapid speech, then words like *an* should have been hard to spell. This is because *an* is often pronounced with unstressed /ə/ rather than with stressed /æ/ in rapid speech. As shown later in this book, children often fail to spell phonemes in unstressed syllables. N for *an,* in which the vowel is left out, is not correct.

It is not clear why words that may be unstressed in rapid speech were significantly easier to spell than anticipated from other factors. Perhaps, as in the case of proper names, frequency counts like those of Carroll et al. (1971) underestimate first graders' exposure to words like *an, the,* and *of.* Reading materials for first graders may have shorter sentences and higher concentrations of grammatical words than reading materials for third through ninth graders, on which the Carroll et al. (1971) norms are based. Yet the first graders did better than expected on destressable words even when their *own* attempts at these words were used to measure word frequency.

Whatever the explanation for the children's unexpectedly good performance on destressable words, an important conclusion follows. These first graders spelled the grammatical words of English—the words like *an, the,* and *of*—at least as well as they spelled the nouns, verbs, adjectives, and so on. The students did not have particular problems with grammatical words. Thus, concrete and imageable words are not necessarily easier to spell than other words.

Factors Not Significantly Associated with Correct Spellings of Words

So far, I have discussed the factors that had significant effects—either positive or negative—on the children's correct spellings of words. In this section, I consider some factors that did *not* reliably affect the percentage of correct spellings. Before beginning the discussion, a caveat is in order. If a factor does not significantly aid in the prediction of correct spellings, I cannot necessarily conclude that the factor has no effect. My collection of spellings may be too small to show a significant association. Even given the problems in interpreting null results, it is worth mentioning those factors that were not associated with correct spellings.

Derived words like *eater* and *collection* were not harder to spell than expected given other factors. As discussed in Chapter 1, the morphemes of derived words, like the morphemes of inflected words, often retain their spellings. For example, the *t* of *collect* appears in *collection.* This word does not contain *sh,* which would be more appropriate given the word's phonemic form but which would obscure the relation to *collect*. Earlier, I suggested that most of the first graders in this study did not yet understand the morphological basis of English spelling. This lack of understanding, I proposed, caused children to misspell inflected words. If this explanation is correct, why did the children not have difficulty with derived words? One reason may be that the children attempted relatively few derived words. Of the derived words that they did attempt, there were only a handful for which phoneme-grapheme rules would yield wrong spellings, such as COLLEKSHUN for *collection*. Words of this kind do not occur in significant numbers in children's compositions until later than first grade. Thus, difficulties with derived words may not surface in children's spontaneous writings until later.

Another factor that failed to reach significance in the analyses of correct spellings was the number of consonant clusters in the spoken word. If spelling is an attempt to represent the phonological forms of words, phonologically complex words should be difficult to spell. The number of consonant clusters in a word may be one measure of the word's phonological complexity. If so, words with several consonant clusters should be harder to spell than words with few or no consonant clusters. This result was not observed. However, as I show later in this chapter, the number of consonant clusters in a spoken word *was* significantly associated with the likelihood of producing a legal spelling. Children were more likely to produce illegal spellings for words with many consonant clusters than for words with few or no consonant clusters.

Finally, the children had no special difficulty with *homophones*. Homophones are words like *there* and *their* that have the same pronunciation but different spellings and different meanings. The children did not perform worse on words like *there* and *their* than expected on the basis of other factors.

Statistical Analyses

I used simultaneous multiple regression analyses in an attempt to predict percentage correct, or the percentage of spellings of each word that were correct. Several measures of word frequency were used. The first, Carroll et al. frequency, was the frequency of the word in the third- through ninth-grade reading materials in Carroll et al. (1971). The children attempted some words that did not appear in the Carroll et al. norms; these words were assigned a frequency of zero. A second measure of word frequency, attempts, was the number of times that the children themselves tried to spell the word. I also used log transforms of Carroll et al. frequency and number of attempts, since the untransformed variables were positively skewed. That is, there were many words that had relatively low frequencies but a few that had very high frequencies.

Length was measured by the number of phonemes in the spoken form of the word or by the number of letters in the word's conventional spelling. Clusters was the number of groups of two or more adjacent consonants in the spoken word. For example, *garden* contains one cluster (/rd/) and *plants* contains two clusters (/pl/ and /nts/). A word was coded as a homophone if there was one or more other words in the collection with the same pronunciation but a different spelling. The variables of inflected words, derived words, and proper names are self-explanatory. All of these were two-valued or binary variables. Another binary variable was included for destressable words, or words that are often unstressed in connected speech. The list of destressable words was from Kenyon (1969, pp. 105–112). Multiple-letter graphemes refers to the number of cases in the word's conventional spelling in which a phoneme is symbolized with more than one letter, whether the letters are adjacent to one another or not. *She* and *cake* both contain one multiple-letter spelling—*sh* in *she* and *a* plus final *e* in *cake*.

Regularity was measured in two ways. For the context-free measure, a word was coded as regular if each phoneme was spelled with the grapheme that most often represented that phoneme in the standard spellings of words in my collection. For the context-sensitive regularity measure, a word was coded as regular if its spelling could be constructed from its phonemic form in Hoosier dialect using the rules of Hanna et al. (1966, pp. 115–118). For both measures, the definition of regularity was based on the forms of words in Hoosier speech (the dialect of the children in this study) rather than the forms of words in general American speech. As discussed in Chapter 1, these forms sometimes differ. For instance, people from southern Indiana and throughout the southern United States pronounce *ten* as /t'ın/. Many other Americans pronounce it /t'ɛn/. Thus, *ten* was classified as irregular by both measures for the children in this study, although it would be regular by both measures for many other children. Although the context-free and the context-sensitive measure of regularity correlated significantly with one another ($p < .001$), the correlation was not particularly high ($r = .32$).

The predictors of log attempts, length in number of phonemes, inflected words, proper names, destressable words, multiple-letter spellings, and context-free regularity explained 26.2% (25.7% adjusted) of the variance among words in percentage correct ($p < .001$) when all 889 words in the collection were included in the analysis. Each of the variables contributed significantly to the prediction of percentage correct—$p < .001$ for the variables of log attempts, length, context-free regularity, proper names, and destressable words, and $p < .005$ for the variables of multiple-letter spellings and inflected words. The largest effects were for length and regularity. No significant additional variance was explained when the variables of derived words, clusters, or homophones were included in the regression. The percentage of explained variance changed little when length in letters was used in place of length in phonemes. It fell by about 1% when attempts, Carroll et al. frequency, or log of Carroll et al. frequency were used in place of log attempts, and by about 2% when context-sensitive regularity was substituted for context-free regularity.

For the regression analyses just described, as well as for the other regressions reported in this book, I checked that the predictor variables were not highly intercorrelated before running the analyses. High correlations among the predictor variables are statistically undesirable.

Thus, when all of the words in the collection were included in the analysis, slightly more than one-quarter of the variance in percentage correct was explained using the predictors I have described. However, the true percentage of variance explained by the predictors may be much greater. This is because the children attempted many words just a few times. As an extreme example, consider those words that were attempted only once, as many were. For these words, the value of percentage correct can only be 0 or 100. Intermediate values are not possible.

Regression analyses were carried out on subsets of the data produced by successively eliminating words that occurred once, twice, and so on, up to five times. The percentage of variance explained by the regression reached a maximum of 55.1% (54.7% adjusted; $p < .001$) when words that occurred five or fewer times were eliminated from the analysis. (This analysis used log attempts as a measure of word frequency, length in phonemes as a measure of length, and context-free regularity as a measure of regularity; it included 189 words.) Apparently, then, over half of the variance in percentage correct can be explained if fairly stable estimates of percentage correct are available. This figure is reasonably high, implying that many of the factors associated with correct spellings have been uncovered.

Comparison with Results of Other Studies

To my knowledge, no previous study has examined the effects of a large number of variables on children's correct spellings, as done here. However, some of the factors considered in this study have been investigated in earlier research.

Many investigators (Beers et al., 1977; Bloomer, 1961, 1964; Goyen & Martin, 1977; Groff, 1982, 1984; Mangieri & Baldwin, 1979) have reported that children spell frequent words more accurately than infrequent words. Bloomer (1961, 1964) also found an effect of word length. The grade level at which half of the children tested correctly spelled a word was lower for short words than for long words. Effects of word length were also reported by Mangieri and Baldwin (1979). The present results confirm that word frequency and word length are associated with spelling accuracy. Moreover, these effects emerge as early as first grade. Although word length and word frequency are related, with frequent words tending to be shorter than infrequent words, the two variables have independent effects on spelling accuracy.

Other researchers have asked whether regular words are easier to spell than irregular words. The previous studies focused on children well beyond the first grade; none of them compared different measures of regularity, as done here. Most of the earlier studies found regularity effects. Treiman (1984a) found such effects with third and fourth graders; Waters, Bruck and Seidenberg (1985) found them with third graders; Mangieri and Baldwin (1979) found them with students in the fourth, sixth, and eight grades. Dodd (1980) reported that 14-year-old students with normal hearing were more accurate at spelling regular words than irregular words, although profoundly deaf students showed no difference between the two types of words. The only negative note was sounded by Goyen and Martin (1977), who found no significant regularity effect in a study of eighth graders. The present results add to the evidence for a regularity effect. Importantly, they show that this effect emerges early in the development of spelling ability. Even first graders seek out relations between sounds and spellings, and even first graders have difficulty with words that do not conform to the regularities that they have extracted.

In reading, regularity effects are stronger for frequent words than for infrequent words (e.g., Seidenberg, 1985; Taraban & McClelland, 1987). Irregularity has little or no effect for very common words but is detrimental for less common words. These results have been interpreted to mean that readers process familiar words as visual patterns. Only for less familiar words do they use spelling-sound relations. Unfortunately, I was unable to determine whether the effects of regularity on spelling varied with word frequency. Because the children attempted infrequent words less often than frequent words, my estimates of spelling difficulty are less reliable for infrequent words.

The present results show that, even accounting for other factors, words with multiple-letter graphemes are difficult for children to spell correctly. To my knowledge, no previous study has focused specifically on children's spelling of multiple-letter graphemes. Groff (1986) did report that pupils in the second, third, and fourth grades made more errors on words with consonant digraphs and consonant clusters than on words without these features. Unfortunately, Groff did not distinguish between digraphs and clusters. A sequence of letters that represents a single phoneme, such as *th* for /θ/, is a digraph. A sequence of letters that represents a group of phonemes, such as *fl* for /f/ followed by /l/, is a cluster. Linguistically, these two cases are quite different. My results suggest that digraphs and other multiple-letter graphemes are particularly difficult for children to spell.

In previous work, researchers have often tried to isolate the effect of a particular factor on spelling accuracy by selecting words that differ on that factor but that are alike in other ways. For example, to determine whether regular words are easier to spell than irregular words, researchers attempt to match regular and irregular words on other factors that are known to affect spelling accuracy. Unless the stimuli are carefully equated, one cannot be sure that any differences between the regular words and the irregular words are actually due to regularity. Most researchers have considered word frequency when designing their stimuli. However, they have overlooked other factors that, judging from the results of my study, also influence spelling accuracy. For example, researchers who have compared regular words and irregular words have not reported whether the two types of words contain comparable numbers of multiple-letter graphemes. The present results suggest that it is important to equate regular and irregular words in this way. The findings of previous research must be interpreted with caution in view of such limitations.

Legal Spellings

So far, I have classified the children's spellings of whole words as correct or incorrect. This is the simplest possible way of classifying children's spellings. However, the correct/incorrect distinction may obscure important information. For instance, PLA, PA, BLAY, and PAYL are all incorrect spellings of *play.* However, the four errors are actually rather different. PLA may be considered a legal misspelling of *play* since /e/ is spelled as *a* in words like *baby.* PA, BLAY, and PAYL are all illegal. PA is illegal because /l/ is not represented at all; BLAY is illegal because /p/ is spelled with *b,* a letter that is never used for /p/ in English; PAYL is illegal because /e/ and /l/ are represented in the wrong order. In this section, I distinguish between legal errors like PLA for *play* and illegal errors like PA, BLAY, and PAYL for *play*. I ask whether the legal/illegal distinction affords insights beyond those afforded by the correct/incorrect distinction. Because the legal/illegal distinction has been widely employed in previous research, it is useful to make this distinction in this study.

According to the cognitive psychologists who popularized the legal/illegal distinction, legal and illegal errors arise for different reasons. The child who makes a legal error like PLA for *play* has attempted to use the phonological spelling route and has done so fairly well. The child has analyzed the spoken word into phonemes and has symbolized each phoneme with a grapheme that represents that phoneme in English. The only thing that the child does not know is that /e/ is spelled with *ay* in *play*. The child who makes an illegal error has not used the phonological route or has not done so successfully. The child who writes PAYL for *play* may have used the visual route, trying to recall the letters in the printed word *play* but producing them in the wrong order. The child who spells *play* as PA may have tried to use the phonological route but may have overlooked /l/ when analyzing the spoken word into phonemes.

I classified an error as legal if the child spelled each phoneme with a grapheme that represented that phoneme in the standard spelling of at least one word in my collection, without regard to the context in which that spelling occurred. By this criterion, PLA is a legal misspelling of *play*. This is because /e/ is symbolized as *a* in many words in the collection, including *a* and *baby*. BULOON is a legal spelling of *balloon* because *u* is a possible spelling of /ə/ (e.g., *us*) and *l* is a possible spelling of /l/ (e.g., *look*). BOLON is also a legal spelling of *balloon,* since /ə/ is sometimes spelled with *o* (e.g., *brother*) and /u/ is sometimes spelled with *o* (e.g., *do*). Because words such as *didn't* contain no separate letter for /ə/, I scored errors like BLON for *balloon* as legal.

I classified an error as illegal if: (1) the child represented at least one phoneme in the word with a grapheme that was not correct for that phoneme in any word in the collection; (2) the child failed to represent one or more phonemes in the word (except when the phoneme was one of the few that may be omitted in English); or (3) the child represented the phonemes in the wrong order. For example, BLUME is an illegal spelling of *balloon* by criterion (1). The phoneme /n/ is not spelled with *m* in any word in my collection. BK for *back* is illegal by criterion (2). The phoneme /æ/ is not represented but the spellings of all words in the collection that contain /æ/ use one or more letters to represent this phoneme. Finally, WNET for *went* is illegal by criterion (3). The phonemes are represented in the wrong order.

Two features of the present definition of legal and illegal spellings require special comment. First, an error such as PNOT for *not* is scored as illegal. This is because there are no words in my collection in which /n/ is spelled with *pn*. Some uncommon English words, such as *pneumonia, do* use *pn* for /n/. However, the first graders never attempted words like *pneumonia*. Most likely, they had never seen such words.

A second important feature of the present distinction between legal and illegal spellings is that *any* possible representation of a phoneme counts as a legal spelling.

Context is disregarded. For example, FOD for *food* was scored as legal because *o* may symbolize /u/ in English. Normally, single *o* is used for /u/ at the ends of words, as in *do* and *who*. In the middles of words, /u/ is not typically spelled as *o*. If context were used to distinguish between legal and illegal spellings, FOD for *food* would be illegal. The present classification system, however, did not consider context.

In some cases, the classification of errors as legal or illegal without respect to context gives the same result as the classification of errors as legal or illegal with respect to context. For instance, THAY for *they* is legal by both context-free and context-dependent criteria. THY for *they* is illegal by both criteria. However, many errors, including FOD for *food,* are legal when context is disregarded but illegal when context is considered. For the first graders in this study, errors of this latter kind actually formed the majority of legal errors.

I defined legality without regard to context because this procedure seemed most reasonable at the first-grade level. A child who knows that /u/ is spelled as *o* in words like *do* and *who* might well apply this knowledge to other words containing /u/, spelling *food* as FOD. Of course, students must *eventually* learn to take context into account. They must learn that /u/ in the middle of a word is not usually spelled with single *o*, while /u/ at the end of a word may be spelled this way. For first graders, however, errors that reflect a knowledge of possible grapheme-phoneme pairings are a sign of genuine progress. This is true even if the children have not yet sorted out the contexts in which the various pairings occur.

One might object to calling FOD for *food* a legal error because it does not sound like the intended word when read aloud. *If* children know that *o* before a consonant is generally pronounced as /ɑ/ when translating from spelling to sound, provided that no final *e* is present, and *if* children use this knowledge to check their spellings, they could eliminate FOD as a spelling of *food*. However, first graders may not yet know the relevant grapheme-phoneme correspondences. Moreover, even if first graders use certain correspondences when they read, they may not always use reading to check their spelling. To do so, children must temporarily disengage from the spelling task. They must put themselves in the place of the reader for whom the message is intended, asking whether their spelling makes sense for that reader. Given the effort that is required for many young children to produce a spelling, and given young children's difficulties in putting themselves in the place of other people, it is likely that first graders do not always use their knowledge of reading to check their spelling.

Supporting the argument just made, first graders sometimes fail to read back their spellings even when their reading skills would permit them to do so. For example, a first grader who participated in one of my experiments confidently spelled the nonword /tʼez/ as TAS, a legal spelling by the criteria used here. When the spelling test was over, I asked the child to read TAS. She unhesitatingly pronounced it /tʼæs/. Had the child read her spelling to herself when she first produced it, she would presumably have been unsatisfied with her attempt and tried to change it. However, she did not do this. Observations like this, together with findings reported elsewhere in this book, suggest that first graders often do not use reading to check their spelling. I therefore decided that spellings like FOD for *food* should be classified as legal even though they do not match the intended word when read aloud.

Factors Associated with Legal Spellings of Words

Using the criteria just described, I classified each error on each word as legal or illegal. For some words, such as *face,* a high percentage of the errors were legal. For other words, such as *helped,* the percentage of legal errors was low. Why are some words easier to spell in a legal manner than others? To address this question, regression analyses were carried out. The results of the analyses are presented first, followed by the statistical details.

Three factors helped to predict the percentage of errors that were legal. The first was the number of consonant clusters, or groups of adjacent consonant phonemes, in the spoken word. For words with many consonant clusters, the percentage of errors that were legal tended to be low. For words with few consonant clusters, the percentage of legal errors tended to be high. For example, the children made fewer legal errors on *helped,* which contains the cluster /lpt/, than on five-phoneme words without consonant clusters.

Why were errors on words with consonant clusters less likely to be legal than errors on words without consonant clusters? To spell most consonant clusters in a legal fashion, children must represent each phoneme of the cluster with a separate grapheme. If children fail to represent one of the phonemes in the cluster, the error is illegal. With *helped,* for instance, children must include letters for /l/, /p/, and /t/. With *plants,* children must represent the /p/ and /l/ of the /pl/ cluster and the /n/, /t/, and /s/ of the /nts/ cluster. As I show in Chapter 8, children sometimes fail to spell consonants in clusters. They make errors like HEPT for *helped* and PAS for *plants.* These errors seem to reflect a difficulty in analyzing consonant clusters in spoken words into phonemes. Students' difficulty in apprehending the internal structure of consonant clusters contributes to the relatively high rate of illegal errors on words with consonant clusters.

Word length, as measured either by the number of phonemes in the spoken word or the number of letters in the printed word, was also associated with the percentage of errors that were legal. Misspellings of long words were less likely to be legal than misspellings of short words. The longer a word, the more chances there are to spell a phoneme in an illegal manner, omit a phoneme, or reverse phonemes.

One of the two measures of regularity, the context-free measure, was significantly associated with the percentage of errors that were legal. Recall that a word was classified as regular by this criterion if each phoneme was spelled with the grapheme that most often represented that phoneme in the words of the collection. Words that were irregular by the context-free measure yielded higher percentages of legal errors than words that were regular. Why is this? Children sometimes substitute a more common grapheme for a less common grapheme, producing an incorrect but legal spelling—a regularization error. For example, if children make an error on the irregular word *said,* their error is relatively likely to be the legal spelling SED. In contrast, if children spell the regular word *bed* in an analogous fashion, they are of course correct.

The second measure of regularity, that based on the context-sensitive rules of Hanna et al. (1966), did not yield significant results. Even though *Seth* is classified as irregular by Hanna et al. (1966), in that /ɛ/ before /θ/ is spelled with *e* rather than the *ea* that is expected under this system, children do not often regularize it as SEATH. This result supports my earlier suggestion that first graders do not yet know many of the context-sensitive rules of English spelling.

None of the other variables investigated, including word frequency, proper names, destressable words, inflected words, derived words, multiple-letter graphemes, or homophones, was significantly associated with the percentage of errors that were legal.

Statistical Analyses

In this section, I describe the statistical analyses of legal errors. The dependent variable in these analyses was the percentage of errors on each word that were legal by the present criteria, or percentage legal. Although there were 889 words in the collection, the children made no errors on 92 of the words. Thus, the maximum number of cases in the analyses of percentage legal was 797. The predictor variables in the analyses of percent legal were the same as those in the analyses of percent correct.

A regression using the predictors of clusters, length in phonemes, and context-free regularity accounted for 6.9% of the variance in percentage legal (6.5% adjusted, $p < .001$) when all 797 words were included in the analysis. Clusters contributed at the .001 level, context-free regularity at the .005 level, and length at the .05 level. The results were similar when length in letters was used in place of length in phonemes. None of the measures of word frequency added significantly to the prediction. The variables of proper names, destressable words, inflected words, derived words, multiple-letter graphemes, or homophones did not have significant effects either.

Although the regression was significant, the percentage of variance explained by the regression was quite low—much lower than the figure of over 25% in the case of percentage correct. One reason for the low value is that the value of percentage legal was based, for many words, on just a few errors. I therefore repeated the analyses deleting cases in which the number of errors was one, two, and so on, up to five errors. The maximum percentage of variance explained by a regression using clusters, length in phonemes, and context-free regularity was 13.6% (12.9% adjusted, $p < .001$). This value was reached when words with just one error were omitted from the analysis, leaving 389 cases. Although this value is higher than that observed in the analysis including all cases, it is still rather low.

The low percentage of variance explained by the regression forces us to question the classification of errors as legal or illegal. Do legal errors and illegal errors actually arise for different reasons? Do legal errors reflect successful use of the phonological route? Do illegal errors reflect use of the visual route or unsuccessful use of the phonological route? If the distinction between legal and illegal errors is not wholly valid, attempts to predict whether an error is legal or illegal will meet with little success. I return to these important issues later in this chapter.

Comparison with Results of Other Studies

To my knowledge, no previous study has examined the effects of a large number of variables on the legality of children's spelling errors, as done here. However, research by Bruck and Treiman (1990) and Treiman (1991) supports one conclusion of the present study—that children are less likely to produce legal spellings for words with consonant clusters than for words without consonant clusters. In these experiments, children spelled words such as *blow* and *bowl,* which differed in the presence or absence of an initial cluster. The two types of words were similar in frequency, number of phonemes, and identity of phonemes. Bruck and Treiman (1990) studied first and second graders who performed at a second-grade level on standardized spelling and reading tests. They also studied older children who were identified as dyslexic and who performed at the same second-grade level on the spelling and reading tests. Treiman (1991) studied first graders. In both experiments, children produced fewer legal spellings for words like *blow* than for words like *bowl.* Similarly, children produced fewer legal spellings for nonwords that began with consonant clusters than for nonwords that did not. Thus, at least for consonant clusters at the beginnings of words, there is converging evidence that children sometimes fail to spell words with clusters in a legal manner.

Barron (1980) examined the effects of regularity on the legality of children's spelling errors. He found that the percentage of errors that were legal was higher for irregular words than for regular words for pupils in the fourth, fifth, and sixth grades. Almost all of the irregular words in Barron's study would be classified as irregular by both my context-free and context-sensitive measures. With my first graders, too, the percentage of errors that were legal was higher for irregular words like *said* than for regular words like *set.* However, this result only held when regularity was defined using the context-free measure.

Changes in Correct and Legal Spellings Over the School Year

So far, I have considered the students' spellings for the school year as a whole. To find out how the spellings changed over the course of the year, I now compare spellings produced during the first semester of the school year to those produced during the second semester.

The numbers in Table 2.1 show that 43.9% of all the spellings were correct during the first semester of the school year. The figure was 55.3% for the second semester ($p < .001$ for the difference by a chi-square test). Moreover, the percentage of errors that were legal increased from the first semester to the second semester. During the first semester, 27.6% of all errors were legal by my criteria. During the second semester, the figure was 40.1% ($p < .001$ for the difference by a chi-square test).

Thus, the children's spellings improved over the course of the school year. Importantly, improvement was evident not only in conventional standards of correctness but also in the types of errors that the children made. The increase in the percentage of errors that were legal suggests that the present distinction between legal and illegal errors has some degree of validity. On the whole, legal errors *do* seem to be more advanced than illegal errors.

Types of Words Attempted

Having discussed some of the factors that are associated with correct spellings and with legal spellings, I now ask whether these same factors are associated with the types of words that the students tried to spell. For example, children make more errors on long words than short words. Moreover, their errors on long words are less likely to be legal than their errors on short words. In view of these differences, do children avoid long words? *If* children are aware of their difficulties with long words, and *if* they strive to produce correct spellings, the answer to this question should be yes. If these conditions do not hold, the answer may well be no.

To study what kinds of words the first graders chose to spell, regression analyses were performed to predict attempts, or the number of times that the children tried to spell each word. Not surprisingly, the frequency of the word in Carroll et al. (1971) was the best predictor of how often the children attempted it. The children spelled frequent words more often than they spelled infrequent words. Even though the Carroll et al. (1971) word frequency norms are based on reading materials designed for third- through ninth-grade children, and even though they are somewhat dated, they have some validity for the first graders in this study.

Do variables that affect the correctness of children's spellings or the legality of their errors add significantly to the prediction of number of attempts once word frequency is taken into account? To address this question, I asked whether length, clusters, inflected words, proper names, destressable words, multiple-letter graphemes, and regularity (either the context-free measure or the context-sensitive measure) added significantly to the regression. Destressable words made a small additional contribution. The children attempted destressable words even more often than expected given the high frequencies of these words. Because first graders' sentences tend to be short, their writings contain many destressable grammatical words like *the* and *an*. The context-free measure of regularity also made a small additional contribution. The children attempted regular words more often than otherwise expected. However, the context-sensitive measure of regularity did not have a significant effect.

Statistical support for the conclusions just presented comes from the results of hierarchical multiple regressions to predict attempts. Carroll et al. (1971) word frequency was entered first. The seven other variables just listed were then entered as a group. The frequency of the word in Carroll et al. (1971) explained 49.8% of the variance in attempts. Of the other variables, only destressable words and the context-free measure of regularity made significant additional contributions ($p < .005$ and $p < .05$, respectively). However, the amount of extra variance explained by these two variables was small, only 1.3%.

Analyses were also carried out using log transforms of attempts and Carroll et al. frequency. The pattern of significant and nonsignificant results was similar to that just described, except that a small but significant tendency to avoid inflected words appeared in some of the analyses. However, the percentage of variance explained in the regression analyses using transformed variables was not as high as in the regression analyses using untransformed variables.

Thus, there is little evidence that these first graders avoided difficult words when they wrote. Although long words and words with multiple-letter graphemes were hard to spell, the children did not attempt these words any less often than expected based on the words' frequencies. Nor did the children avoid words with consonant clusters. Easy-to-spell proper names were not overrepresented in the children's compositions. Although there was some sign of overrepresentation of regular words, the effect was quite small.

One possible interpretation of these results is that the children did not know whether their spellings were correct or incorrect or did not know what kinds of words were hard for them to spell. However, the teacher stated that the children *did* compare their spellings with those that she or the teacher's aide wrote. The children sometimes commented that they had spelled a particular word correctly. Thus, the children had at least some awareness of the accuracy of their spellings. A more plausible interpretation of the results is that the pupils were not particularly motivated by a desire to produce correct spellings or by a fear of producing wrong ones. If the story that they were writing demanded a particular word, they included it. The teacher seemed to have succeeded in her goal of encouraging students to write without worrying about the correctness of their spellings.

Adults' Ability to Interpret Legal Misspellings

So far, I have classified children's spelling errors as legal or illegal. But not all legal errors are alike. One way in which legal errors differ is in their degree of transparency. Some legal errors are relatively easy for adults to interpret. Others are more difficult. To respond to children's spelling errors in the most effective manner, teachers should be able to figure out what children meant to write. Asking children is not always effective: If an hour or a day has gone by, a first grader cannot always tell what word he or she had in mind.

Legal misspellings such as BOI for *boy* and KAT for *cat* are relatively easy to interpret. Even when these errors are taken out of context, adults easily guess the intended words. Adults know that these spellings, although incorrect, reveal a good deal of knowledge on the children's part about the phonemes in spoken words and how these phonemes are symbolized in print. Other legal errors are less transparent. For example, HY for *he* is legal by the criteria used here because *y* stands for /i/ in words like *happy*. However, adults may not realize that HY is a reasonable rendition of *he*.

The context of an error may help adults to interpret it. For instance, HY is fairly easy to decipher in a context that leads one to expect "he." Here, however, I wish to determine which features of the error *itself* make it more or less easy to interpret. To study these features, adults were presented with errors in isolation, removed from the stories in which they had appeared.

The participants in the error-interpretation experiment were 23 adults who were experienced observers of young children's spellings. They included teachers of kindergarten, first grade, and second grade and researchers who study spelling among children of these levels. Each participant was given a list of almost all the unique legal errors that were produced by the first graders in the present study—a total of 579 errors.[1] The adults were told that each error was a child's attempt to spell a real English word, including common first names. The participants were further told that each item was an error, even though it might coincidentally look like another real word. The adults were asked to write down the word that they thought the child had intended in each case.

Overall, the adults did well on the error-interpretation test. Of their responses, 79.3% were the words that the child had, in fact, intended. (The adults were counted as correct if they guessed a homophone of the intended word, such as *there* for *their*.) The many correct responses for spellings presented out of context show that experienced teachers and researchers are good at interpreting children's legal misspellings.

Not all of the errors were easy to interpret, however. In some cases, as with BOI (for *boy*), HAPE (for *happy*), and CRASMUS (for *Christmas*), almost all of the adults answered correctly. Errors such as HY (for *he*), YDR (for *eater*), and TEKN (for *chicken*) were more difficult. Analyses were carried out to study the linguistic factors that make some legal errors easier to decipher than others. The results of the analyses are discussed next, followed by the statistical details.

If an error was pronounced as the intended word using conventional English spelling-to-sound correspondences, the adults guessed the intended word more easily than if the error was pronounced in some other manner. For example, both HEE and HY are legal misspellings of *he*, since /i/ is spelled as *ee* in some words (e.g., *asleep*) and *y* in others (e.g., *happy*). However, HEE is read as *he* according to the spelling-sound rules of English. HY is pronounced like *high*. Correspondingly, the adults were more often correct on HEE than HY. This result suggests that adults try to interpret children's errors by reading them to themselves. If the error sounds like a real word, adults often assume that this word must be the one the child had in mind. Understandably, adults do not always realize that an error that does not sound like a certain word when read aloud may be a plausible spelling of that word.

The more misspelled consonants in an error, the harder it was to interpret. For example, the adults performed less well on BICK for *bike*, which has one consonant error (*ck* rather than *k* for /k/), than on BIK for *bike*, which has no consonant errors. The effect of number of consonant errors is not surprising. The more deviant an error, the harder it is to interpret.

Errors on vowels may be divided into two categories—letter-name errors and non-letter-name errors. Letter-name errors use the letter *a* to represent the phoneme /e/, the letter *e* to represent the phoneme /i/, *i* for /ai/, *o* for /o/, and *u* for /u/. In the first four cases, the name of the letter matches the phoneme that it symbolizes. In the case of *u* for /u/, the name of the letter, /ju/, contains the phoneme /u/. Thus, the vowel error in BIK—*i* in place of *i* followed by final *e* for /ai/—is a letter-name error. Another example of a letter-name error is *e* for *ea* in EDR for *eater*. Non-letter-name errors include *ie* for *i* followed by final *e* in BIEK for *bike* and *y* for *ea* in YDR for *eater*.

The impact of vowel errors depended on the type of error. Letter-name vowel errors did not significantly impede adults' ability to guess the intended word, while non-letter-name vowel errors did. Seeing an error such as BIK, adults readily interpret *i* as an attempt to represent the phoneme /ai/, its name. Errors of this kind caused no measurable difficulty. However, BIEK, which includes a non-letter-name vowel error, was harder to interpret.

BIK for *bike,* which contains a letter-name vowel error, is not pronounced as /b'aik/ according to English spelling-to-sound rules. This is because vowels have their so-called short pronunciation (/ɪ/ in this case) rather than their long pronunciation (/ai/) before a final consonant. Most errors that included vowel letter names, like BIK for *bike,* did not match the intended word when read aloud. However, the associations between vowel letters and their names seem to be strong in adults—strong enough that they easily guess that BIK represents *bike.* Later in this book, I will show that children also have strong associations between letters and their names.

Another factor associated with adults' ability to interpret children's legal misspellings was word length. The longer the intended word, either in number of phonemes or number of letters, the easier it was to guess. For example, even though CRASMUS is not read as *Christmas* according to English spelling-to-sound rules, and even though it contains several consonant errors and non-letter-name vowel errors, all of the adults inferred that it was an attempt to spell *Christmas.* When the intended word is long, a legal misspelling contains many clues to the word's identity.

Errors that were themselves common real words seemed to be harder to interpret than errors that were not. For example, the fact that AT is a real word may make it difficult for people to realize that it could spell *ate.* Errors on common words seemed to be easier to guess than errors on uncommon words.

Statistical support for the results just presented comes from regression analyses that attempted to predict the percentage of correct responses to each legal error. One of the predictors was pronunciation regularity, defined as whether the error was pronounced as the intended word using the spelling-to-sound rules of Venezky (1970). In a few cases in which these rules were not decisive, missing values were coded for this variable. The second predictor was the number of consonant errors in the legal misspelling. Other predictors were the numbers of letter-name and non-letter-name vowel errors and the length of the intended word in number of phonemes or number of letters. I also included measures of the frequency of the error itself and the frequency of the intended word, either their raw frequencies in Carroll et al. (1971) or log transforms of the Carroll et al. frequencies.

With log transforms of the frequency variables and length in phonemes as a measure of length, the variables just described explained 25.1% of the variance in percentage correct (24.1% adjusted, $p < .001$) in an analysis including 563 cases. Pronunciation regularity, consonant errors, non-letter-name vowel errors, word length, and log frequency of the intended word each made significant contributions to the prediction of percentage correct ($p < .001$ for each). The largest effect was that of word length. The log frequency of the error itself also contributed significantly to the regression ($p = .01$). Performance did not decline significantly as the number of letter-name vowel errors increased. The results were virtually identical when length in letters was used in place of length in phonemes. Substituting raw frequencies for transformed frequencies, the percentage of variance explained by the regression dropped to 19.9% (19.2% adjusted, $p < .001$). The frequency of the error and the frequency of the intended word no longer contributed significantly to the regression.

To summarize, teachers and other adults who are familiar with children's spelling are fairly good at interpreting children's legal spelling errors, even when the errors are taken out of context. However, adults do better on some legal misspellings than others. Errors that are easy to decipher include those that match the intended word when read aloud, those that include only letter-name vowel errors, those in which the consonant spellings deviate less from the intended word, and those that represent long words. In addition, errors on common words and errors that are not themselves words may be easier to decipher than other errors.

Summary of Findings

Before discussing the implications of the results presented in this chapter, it is useful to summarize the main findings. Such a summary follows.

1. The first graders were more likely to spell a word correctly if they had seen the word frequently than if they had not.
2. Long words were less likely to be correct than short words. In addition, errors on long words were less likely to be legal than errors on short words.
3. The children made more errors on inflected words (e.g., *helped, cleaned*) than on noninflected words.
4. The children had difficulty spelling words that contained phonemes that are represented with more than one letter, as in *thin*.
5. The first graders often misspelled irregular words such as *said*. There was some evidence that errors on irregular words were more likely to be legal than errors on regular words.
6. Errors on words that contained clusters of adjacent consonants (e.g., *plant*) were less likely to be legal than errors on words without such clusters.
7. For the children in this study, the most important determinant of how often they attempted a word was the word's frequency. The children did not avoid grammatical words or words that are difficult to spell.
8. Adults who are experienced with young children's spelling are good at interpreting students' legal misspellings. However, their knowledge of context-sensitive spelling-sound correspondences can make it hard for them to realize that a spelling that does not sound like a certain word when read aloud may nevertheless represent that word.

Implications

The results in this chapter have implications for several issues, including the impact of the writing system on children's spelling, the processes by which children spell, the teaching of spelling, and the classification of spelling errors.

Writing Systems and Spelling

As discussed in Chapter 1, the English writing system is notoriously difficult to learn. This difficulty is usually attributed to one thing and one thing alone—the irregularity of English spelling. In English, most phonemes may be spelled in more than one way. It is not always possible to predict when each spelling will occur. For example, /f/ is usually spelled with *f,* as in *fox.* However, /f/ is sometimes symbolized with *ph,* as in *elephant* and *telephone.* These one-to-many relations from phonemes to graphemes are thought to explain children's difficulties in learning to spell.

The present results confirm that the one-to-many relations between phonemes and graphemes are a problem for children learning to spell. The children in this study made more errors on words in which /f/ is spelled as *ph* (i.e., irregular words) than on words in which /f/ is spelled as *f* (i.e., regular words). If /f/ were always spelled as *f,* the results suggest, children would make fewer errors. The findings imply that a writing system with one-to-one relations from phonemes to graphemes would be easier for children to learn than a writing system with one-to-many relations from phonemes to graphemes.

Although the irregularity of the English system is one source of difficulty in learning to spell, it is by no means the only one. Another problematic aspect of the English writing system is that graphemes sometimes contain two or more letters. For instance, the grapheme that symbolizes /θ/, *th,* has two letters. Although *thin* is regularly spelled by any reasonable criterion, first graders have difficulty with this word because of the two-letter grapheme. The present results imply that a system with few or no multiple-letter graphemes would be easier to learn than a system with many multiple-letter graphemes. This would be true even if both systems were completely regular.

Yet a third characteristic of the English writing system also causes difficulty for beginning spellers. This is the fact that morphemes are often symbolized in the same way from one word to another, even when their phonemic forms change. This characteristic of the writing system causes problems for first graders, who tend to spell phonemically—one symbol for each phoneme—rather than morphemically—one symbol for each morpheme. Thus, children often misspell inflected words such as *helped.* They write this word with *t* rather than *ed* at the end. If *helped* were spelled as *helpt,* the results imply, first graders would make fewer errors.

Thus, it is not just the irregularity of the English spelling system that makes the system difficult to master. Although the irregular mappings from phonemes to graphemes do cause trouble, so do the regular mappings from phonemes like /θ/ to graphemes like *th.* In addition, first graders have difficulty appreciating the higher-level regularities that exist in English, such as the fact that the past tense marker is spelled with *ed.*

Not all of children's difficulties in learning to spell stem from the nature of our writing system. In addition to the problematic aspects of the English writing system—its one-to-many relations from phonemes to graphemes, its use of multiple-letter graphemes, and its tendency to spell morphemes consistently despite changes in their phonemic forms—the nature of *spoken* English also contributes to children's difficulties. Spoken English words contain many consonant clusters—initial clusters as in *blue,* final clusters as in *jump,* and medial clusters as in *garden.* Children's spellings of words with consonant clusters are less likely to be legal than their spellings of words without consonant clusters. This is because, as shown in Chapter 8, first graders sometimes produce illegal spellings like BOO for *blue* and JUP for *jump.* My results imply that beginning spellers would have less difficulty, at least in the sense of producing fewer illegal errors, in languages whose spoken forms contain few or no consonant clusters than in languages whose spoken forms contain many consonant clusters. Holding the nature of the writing system constant, the characteristics of the *spoken* language may affect children's spelling.

Another feature of spoken English that contributes to children's spelling difficulties is that our language contains many long, multisyllabic words. Children produce more errors and higher percentages of illegal errors on long words than on short words. Other things being equal, a language with short words would be easier for children to spell than a language with long words.

Thus, the English writing system deserves *some* of the blame, but not *all* of the blame, for children's difficulties in learning to spell. Even if English had one-to-one relations between phonemes and graphemes—the ideal writing system, according to many—learning to spell would not be effortless. Children would still have problems on words with consonant clusters and on long words.

Just as spelling difficulties *within* a language have multiple causes, differences *among* languages are also multiply determined. These differences reflect not only differences among the writing systems but also differences among the spoken languages. Thus, conclusions from previous cross-linguistic studies may need to be reevaluated. For example, Lindgren, De Renzi, and Richman (1985) argued that, at least for reading, Italian is easier to learn than English. These researchers attributed the difference between Italian and English to the greater regularity of spelling-sound correspondences in Italian. However, differences between the spoken languages may also play a role. For instance, the most frequent type of syllable in Italian is the simple consonant-vowel syllable. Except for a few borrowed words, Italian syllables do not end with consonant clusters (Agard & DiPietro, 1965). English, of course, has a wide variety of syllable types. Consonant clusters occur at both the beginnings and ends of syllables. These differences between the *spoken* languages may contribute to the apparent difference in the ease of learning the *written* languages.

Models of the Spelling Process

The present finding that common words are easier to spell than uncommon words is consistent with dual-route models of spelling. According to these models, two different processes are available for spelling. The first process involves memorization: The speller attempts to reproduce a previously memorized spelling for the whole word. The second process is more creative: The speller constructs a spelling from the word's phonological form. According to dual-route models, the spellings of common words are more likely to be stored in memory than are the spellings of uncommon words. With common words, children can sometimes spell the word by recalling its conventional spelling. With uncommon words, this is not possible. Children must construct a spelling and, in so doing, may err.

That common words are easier to spell than uncommon words would also be consistent with connectionist models of spelling. These theories postulate links between phonological units and orthographic units that vary in strength. The weights on the connections are adjusted to reflect the words to which the model is exposed. Connectionist models of reading, like dual-route models, perform better on frequent words than on infrequent words (Seidenberg & McClelland, 1989). Thus, the frequency effects in children's spelling do not allow us to distinguish between dual-route models and connectionist models.

My results *do* suggest that children require a fair amount of exposure to master the correct spelling of a word. Supporting this claim, the children sometimes misspelled even extremely common words like *a, the,* and *and.* In a few cases, like ARD for *and,* the child may have known the correct spelling but produced it incorrectly because of a temporary lapse of attention or because of sloppy penmanship. However, other errors on frequent words seem to reflect phonological processes. An example is AAD for *and.* This error is consistent with children's tendency to delete the first consonants of final clusters (see Chapter 8). Another error that points to the use of phonology in spelling is VU for *the.* This error shares no letters with *the* but does reflect the similarity in sound between /v/ and /ð/. Within the dual-route framework, errors like AAD for *and* and VU for *the* suggest that, even with common words, children sometimes try to generate a spelling from the word's spoken form rather than produce a spelling from memory. Within the connectionist framework, these errors suggest that many exposures to a word are required for flawless performance.

Given that phonology plays an important role in spelling, how do children generate spellings of words from the words' phonological forms? At least two things seem to be required. First, children must be able to divide spoken words into smaller units. They must possess some degree of phonemic awareness. Second, children must know something about the relations between phonemes and graphemes in the English language. The two processes of analyzing a spoken word into phonemes and choosing a grapheme to symbolize each phoneme are not necessarily performed in sequence. Particularly with long words, children may analyze and spell one part of the word, then analyze and spell another part of the word, and so on.

Errors may occur in the analysis of spoken words into phonemes, the assignment of graphemes to phonemes, or both. For words with consonant clusters, many errors seem to occur during the process of phonemic analysis. The child who spelled *plants* as PAS, omitting the /l/ of the initial cluster and the /n/ and /t/ of the final cluster, apparently treated the clusters of the spoken word as units. For irregular words, errors often occur in choosing the appropriate grapheme to represent each phoneme. The child who spelled *said* as SED correctly analyzed the spoken word into phonemes and represented each phoneme with a reasonable grapheme. However, the child spelled /ɛ/ with the grapheme that usually represents this phoneme, *e,* rather than the grapheme that is correct for this word, *ai.*

To summarize, phonology plays a role in children's spelling of even frequent words. To spell a word, children use their knowledge of the sounds in the spoken word and their knowledge of the relations between phonemes and graphemes.

The Teaching of Spelling

Because correct spelling is the ultimate goal of instruction, teachers naturally focus on whether their pupils' spellings are correct or incorrect. Although this is useful, it is not enough. In many cases, one can get a more complete picture of children's spelling performance by examining their errors. Misspellings shed light on children's developing phonemic awareness skills and on their increasing knowledge of the relations between phonemes and graphemes. A careful examination of children's errors can illuminate the reasons for the errors and can suggest what feedback will be most effective.

As an example of the knowledge that lies behind many spelling errors, consider KAT for *cat*. The child who makes this error can hear the spoken word, analyze it into phonemes, remember the identity and order of the phonemes, and assign a plausible spelling to each phoneme. The only thing that the child does not know—and it is a small thing in comparison with the many skills that the error reveals—is that the /k/ of this word is spelled with *c*. If one only scored the spelling as incorrect, one might overlook the knowledge that lies behind it. By going beyond a simple correct/incorrect distinction, teachers can better appreciate the progress that children are making.

KAT for *cat* is a "good" error—a spelling that, although wrong, reveals a mastery of several important processes. Experienced teachers appreciate the knowledge that lies behind such errors. With KAT, for instance, the adults in the error-interpretation experiment readily guessed the intended word, even when the error was out of context. Knowing that the child's only mistake was choosing *k* rather than *c* for /k/, teachers may decide to ignore the error altogether. They may even praise it as a good attempt to spell the word. If teachers *do* correct the error, they may say that /k/ is sometimes spelled with *k* but that it happens to be spelled with *c* here. Such a response, which acknowledges the reasonableness of the child's spelling, is most beneficial to the child.

Other errors that deserve the kind of response just described are less likely to get it. Consider HY for *he*. Although this error is legal, in that *y* may represent /i/, teachers or parents will probably read HY as *high* (/h'ai/). In this case, adults' well-developed knowledge of the relations between spellings and sounds in English hinders their interpretation of children's errors. Given their years of experience in reading words like *by, my,* and *fly*, adults may overlook the fact that *y* may also represent /i/. Because teachers may not realize that HY is a "good" error for *he*, their response to the error may be inappropriate. Teachers may repeat the spoken word *he*, stressing that it ends with /i/ rather than /ai/. However, the children who produce HY probably hear the difference between *he* and *high* perfectly well. They probably know that *he* ends with /i/. The children may be puzzled by the adult's assumption that they do not know these things. If such episodes continue, children may even start to doubt their ability to hear spoken words and to analyze them into phonemes. A more appropriate response would be to say that HY is a good attempt to spell *he,* that /i/ is indeed spelled with *y* in words like *city,* but that the sound happens to be spelled with *e* here. (See Read, 1986, p. 18 for a related discussion.)

Although experienced teachers are good at interpreting students' legal spelling errors, the powerful biases that are engendered by their own mature reading skills mean that there is room for improvement. The most natural way to decipher an error, the results of the error-interpretation experiment suggest, is to read it back using one's knowledge of how letters are pronounced together with one's knowledge of letter names. Reliance on this approach means that one may fail to notice that HY is a plausible misspelling of *he* or that BOS is a plausible misspelling of *bus.* To better interpret students' errors, teachers should know that spellings that do not match the intended word when read aloud may still be reasonable. Teachers should also know that a spelling that looks like one word, such as *at,* may actually be an attempt to spell another word, such as *ate.*

The need to appreciate the knowledge that lies behind incorrect spellings is there regardless of the particular teaching method used. Whether or not teachers provide formal instruction in spelling and whether or not they explicitly point out and correct spelling errors, they must know that misspellings often reflect a great deal of knowledge on the child's part. A careful study of children's misspellings can show where children are in the process of learning to spell and what they should be taught next. Corrections, if and when they are made, should acknowledge what children have done right as well as what children have done wrong.

With respect to the teaching methods used in the classroom studied here, my results suggest that children taught by these methods do not worry about spelling words correctly. The first graders in this study did not feel constrained to produce simple stories that contained only words whose spellings they already knew. They attempted long or unfamiliar words when their stories called for them. Clarke (1988) likewise found that first graders who were encouraged to invent their own spellings wrote longer stories and used a greater variety of words than children who were encouraged to spell conventionally.

Although this study focuses on spelling rather than composition, a few words about composition are appropriate at this point. The students' willingness to try unfamiliar words may have allowed them to write longer, more complex, and more imaginative stories than would have otherwise been the case. This freedom may have helped the children to develop as writers. Similar benefits might accrue if teachers using other approaches overlooked misspellings in young children's imaginative writings or used suggestions that were carefully tuned to the children's level of knowledge.

Classification of Spelling Errors

In this chapter, I studied children's spelling at the level of whole words. I began with the simplest possible way of classifying spellings, as correct or incorrect. Such a classification, simple though it is, produced useful results. It was found that certain types of words—uncommon words, long words, inflected words, and irregular words, among others—are difficult to spell correctly. Other types of words are easier to spell. Because one indication of spelling ability, and the one that is most critical to parents, teachers, and society in general, is the ability to spell correctly, information about the types of words that children tend to misspell is important.

If the correct versus incorrect classification captured all of the information in a child's spelling, I could stop there. However, it does not. The correct/incorrect distinction carries with it the implication that all incorrect spellings are alike. It further implies that all misspellings reflect a lack of knowledge about how words sound and about how the writing system works. These implications are clearly false. Some spelling errors reveal a sophisticated knowledge about the linguistic properties of words and about how these properties are represented in print. Other errors suggest less knowledge of these fundamentals.

How should we capture the partial knowledge that lies behind many of children's spelling errors? Many investigators have suggested that misspellings be divided into two categories. The first category is the legal or phonetically accurate error. The second category is the illegal or phonetically inaccurate error. A child who makes a legal error, it is thought, has successfully used the phonological route. The child has correctly analyzed the spoken word into phonemes and has represented each phoneme with a grapheme that may spell that phoneme in English. A child who makes an illegal error, it is thought, has used the phonological route unsuccessfully or not at all.

Although the legal/illegal classification has been widely employed in spelling research, there has been relatively little discussion of the criteria that should be used to make the distinction or of the assumptions behind it. With respect to criteria, should legal spellings be defined with regard to context or without regard to context? If context is disregarded, FOD for *food* is a legal error because *o* may spell /u/. If context is considered, FOD for *food* is illegal because /u/ is not usually represented with *o* in the middle of a word. My results show that the two criteria yield quite different answers about the prevalence of legal errors in first graders. The same is true in older students (Bruck & Waters, 1988). Thus, researchers who use one definition of legality could well reach different conclusions than researchers who use the other. (See Bruck & Waters, 1988 for an example of such a case.)

A more fundamental issue in the classification of errors as legal or illegal is what these two types of errors mean. Do legal spellings always imply that children have successfully analyzed the spoken word into phonemes and have used a spelling for each phoneme that they know to occur in English? Do illegal spellings alway imply that children have used the phonological route unsuccessfully or not at all?

Many of children's legal errors probably *do* reflect an ability to analyze spoken words into phonemes, together with a knowledge of mappings from phonemes to graphemes in the conventional English system. Consider the error COAK for *Coke*. The girl who produced this error probably analyzed the spoken word into the phonemes /k/, /o/, and /k/. The child chose the correct spellings for the two consonant phonemes; her only error was in assigning a spelling to the vowel. The child probably symbolized the vowel with *oa* because she knew that /o/ is spelled as *oa* in other English words. In this case, there is no way to predict that /o/ is spelled with *o* plus final *e* rather than with *oa*. Either spelling may occur before final /k/, as shown by *poke* and *soak*. Children must learn, through experience with printed and spoken words, that the /o/s in *Coke* and *poke* are spelled with *o* plus final *e* while the /o/s in *soak* and *oak* are spelled with *oa*.

BOI for *boy* is another case in which the assumptions underlying the concept of legal errors are probably correct. The child who made this error probably analyzed the spoken word into the phonemes /b/ and /oi/. The child probably knew that *oi* may spell /oi/. In English, /oi/ is typically spelled with *oy* at the end of a morpheme (e.g., *boy, boyfriend*) or before a vowel (e.g., *foyer*). It is spelled with *oi* elsewhere (e.g., *coin*). Children who know this pattern can spell /oi/ correctly even in words they have never seen in print. The child who misspelled *boy* as BOI apparently knew neither the rule governing the alternation between *oi* and *oy* nor the correct spelling of the word. However, this child *could* analyze the spoken word into phonemes and *did* know that *oi* may spell /oi/.

Although legal errors often reflect an ability to analyze spoken words into phonemes, together with a knowledge of conventional phoneme-grapheme mappings, this is not always true. Consider the error BAD for *bed*. This error was scored as legal because words such as *Mary* are pronounced with /ɛ/ by the children in this study. However, the children who spelled /ɛ/ as *a* may not have been using words like *Mary* as a guide. As discussed in detail in Chapter 4, there is an another possible explanation for this error. This explanation is based on the similarity in sound between /ɛ/ and other vowels that are commonly spelled with *a,* namely /æ/ and /e/. Students may spell /ɛ/ as *a* not because they know about this correspondence from words like *Mary* but because they know that vowels that sound similar to /ɛ/ are often spelled with *a.* Another case in which the assumptions about legal spellings may be incorrect is that of BLOON for *balloon*. I scored this error as legal because /ə/ is not spelled with a separate letter in words such as *didn't.* However, the students who wrote *balloon* as BLOON may not have known this convention. They may have failed to spell /ə/ because this unstressed vowel is not salient in the spoken form of the word (see Chapter 7). Thus, legal errors do not necessarily mean that children can successfully analyze a spoken word into phonemes.

Moreover, illegal errors do not necessarily mean that children are unsuccessful at using the phonological route. As an example, CHRUCK for *truck* must be considered illegal since /t/ is never symbolized with *ch* in English. But, as discussed in more detail in Chapter 5, /t/ before /r/ sounds similar to /tʃ/. Almost surely, the child who spelled *truck* as CHRUCK tried to represent the phonological form of the spoken word. The child used phonological information to spell and, what is more, did so in a reasonable manner.

These problems with the legal/illegal distinction may help to explain why the statistical analyses reported in this chapter were less successful at predicting the percentage of errors that were legal than the percentage of spellings that were correct. Although the distinction between legal and illegal errors has some degree of validity, it also has some serious problems.

All of the analyses reported in this chapter were carried out at the level of whole words. The spellings of each word were scored as correct or incorrect and as legal or illegal. However, analyses that are restricted to the level of whole words are not sufficiently detailed for an alphabetic writing system such as English. In an alphabetic system, there are links between the *parts* of spoken words, or phonemes, and the *parts* of printed words, or graphemes. Any study of children's spelling that is confined to the level of whole words is incomplete. In the following chapters, therefore, I move from the level of whole words to the level of phonemes. I ask what children know about the relations between individual phonemes and individual graphemes.

Notes

1. Excluded were attempts at unusual proper names and forms such as /kˈipt/, which children occasionally used as the past tense of *keep* in place of the irregular form *kept*.

3

Spelling of Phonemes: Correct Spellings, Legal Substitutions, and Illegal Substitutions

So far, I have examined children's spellings at the level of whole words. The results show that children have more difficulty with some kinds of words than others. For example, children often misspell words that contain multiple-letter graphemes, words such as *that* and *sang.* Children often misspell irregular words, words such as *said* and *come.* One would guess that *th* is the trouble spot in *that* and *ai* is the trouble spot in *said.* However, because the analyses presented so far are confined to whole words, I cannot say for sure. To determine which parts of words are difficult to spell, I must move from the level of whole words to the level of individual phonemes and individual graphemes.

The need to examine children's spellings at the level of phonemes and graphemes stems from the nature of the English writing system itself. As discussed in Chapter 1, the English writing system is basically alphabetic. Although most phonemes may be spelled in more than one way, there *are* relations between phonemes and graphemes. For instance, /k/ may be spelled with *k,* as in *key, c,* as in *care,* or *ck,* as in *back,* among other possibilities. Adults cannot always choose the correct spelling from among these possibilities, but we know that /k/ could never be written with *m* or *b.* Our knowledge of phoneme-grapheme correspondences tells us that *Carl* or *Karl* are reasonable renditions of the spoken form /k'ɑrl/ but that *Marl* is not.

Traditionally, it was thought that children learn to spell on a visual basis, by memorizing the sequence of letters in each word. In this view, children treat printed words as wholes. They do not learn relations between the parts of printed words (graphemes) and the parts of spoken words (phonemes). The traditional view further implies that children memorize one word at a time. They do not learn relations between sounds and spellings that apply to many different words. Findings reported in Chapter 2 suggest that this traditional view of learning to spell is incorrect. For example, children's difficulty on irregular words like *said* and *come* suggests that children learn about the correspondences between phonemes and graphemes. Words with irregular or unusual correspondences are harder to spell than words with more typical correspondences.

In this chapter, I study children's knowledge of the links between phonemes and graphemes in more detail. To do so, I divide the children's spellings of phonemes into three broad categories—*correct spellings, substitution errors,* and *omission errors.*

In a correct spelling, the student spells the phoneme in the standard manner. For instance, the child who spells *birthday* as BRDDAY represents the phoneme /e/ in the conventional way, even while misspelling other parts of the word. As another example, /p/ is correct in SPRAD for *sprayed.*

In a substitution error, the child symbolizes the phoneme with a grapheme that is not correct for the word in question. For example, the child who spells *brain* as BRAN transcribes /e/ with *a* rather than the conventional *ai.* The child who spells *hope* as HOM represents /p/ with *m.* These are both substitution errors.

Substitutions may be divided into two categories, legal and illegal. In a legal substitution, the child's spelling is a correct representation of that phoneme in some *other* word in the collection. The use of *a* for the /e/ of *brain* is a legal substitution since /e/ is symbolized as *a* in words such as *a* and *baby.* In an illegal substitution, the child's spelling does not represent the phoneme in any word in the collection. The use of *m* for /p/, as in HOM for *hope,* is illegal since /p/ is never spelled as *m.*

The distinction between legal and illegal substitutions for phonemes is closely tied to the distinction between legal and illegal spellings for words, as discussed in Chapter 2. If each phoneme in a word is spelled correctly or using a legal substitution, and if the phonemes are represented in the right order, the spelling of the whole word is legal in the sense presented in Chapter 2.

The final type of spelling is an omission error. Here, the student fails to represent the phoneme altogether, causing an error. For example, /p/ is omitted when *spines* is rendered as SINSE; /e/ is omitted when *cave* is rendered as CV. Note that certain phonemes are occasionally omitted in standard English. For instance, *K-mart* does not include a separate letter for the first vowel. Thus, if a child fails to represent this vowel when spelling *K-mart,* the omission counts as a correct spelling of the phoneme rather than an omission error.

I used the tabulations of Appendix I to place each spelling of each phoneme into one of the categories of correct spellings, legal substitutions, illegal substitutions, or omissions. The results for consonants and vowels are shown in Table 3.1.

Table 3.1. Numbers of Correct Spellings, Substitution Errors, and Omission Errors on Consonant and Vowel Phonemes

Type of Spelling	Consonants		Vowels	
	Number	Percent	Number	Percent
Correct spelling	8,592	79.3	3,900	58.3
Substitution error	1,439	13.3	2,174	32.5
Legal	823	7.6	1,452	21.7
Illegal	616	5.7	722	10.8
Omission error	800	7.4	619	9.2
Total	10,831	100.0	6,693	100.0

A glance at Table 3.1 suggests that the students performed quite differently on consonants and vowels. Statistical tests confirmed this impression ($p < .001$ by a chi-square test for the relation between type of phoneme [consonant, vowel] and type of spelling [correct, substitution, omission]). Consonants were more likely to be spelled correctly than vowels. The percentage of correct spellings was 79.3% for consonants as compared with 58.3% for vowels ($p < .001$ by a chi-square test). Vowels were more susceptible than consonants to both substitution errors and omission errors (both differences significant by chi-square tests, $p < .001$). Moreover, consonants and vowels differed in the *types* of substitution errors that they engendered. For consonants, 823 of the 1,439 substitution errors, or 57.2%, were legal. For vowels, 1,452 of the 2,174 substitution errors were legal, or 66.8% ($p < .001$ for the difference by a chi-square test). Thus, given that a substitution error was made, it was more likely to be legal when the phoneme was a vowel than when it was a consonant.

Why did the students perform so differently on consonant phonemes and vowel phonemes? There are two general types of explanations for the observed differences. First, the results could reflect intrinsic differences between consonants and vowels. Explanations in this category may be labeled *phonological,* since they attribute the results to the phonological characteristics of the two classes of sounds. Second, the different patterns for consonants and vowels could reflect the different ways in which consonants and vowels are spelled in English. This second type of explanation may be called *orthographic,* since it attributes the results to properties of the English writing system itself.

To make the distinction between phonological and orthographic hypotheses more concrete, consider the finding that children were more often correct on consonants than on vowels. One possible phonological explanation for this finding would invoke the different properties of consonant and vowel phonemes. The boundaries between vowel phonemes are less distinct than the boundaries between consonant phonemes (Ladefoged, 1982). For instance, a consonant can be a nasal or a fricative but cannot be halfway between the two. A vowel, however, can be intermediate between two other vowels. Correspondingly, the perception of vowels is typically more continuous than the perception of consonants (A. M. Liberman, Cooper, Shankweiler, & Studdert-Kennedy, 1967). If vowel phonemes are less distinct or less well defined than consonant phonemes, children may have more difficulty spelling vowels. According to this version of a phonological hypothesis, children's problems with vowels do not reflect the specific characteristics of the English writing system. Rather, difficulties with vowels reflect the phonological properties of languages and should occur across a wide range of alphabetic writing systems.

An orthographic hypothesis for children's better performance on consonants than on vowels appeals to particular properties of the English writing system. In English, the system of vowel spellings is more complex than the system of consonant spellings. Vowels have more different possible spellings than consonants (Hanna et al., 1966). English-speaking children may misspell vowels because they do not know which of the several graphemes to use. According to this orthographic hypothesis, students' performance on vowels relative to consonants depends on the characteristics of the writing system they are learning. Children learning to spell in English should have more difficulty with vowels than consonants but children learning to spell in other languages should not. Difficulty with vowels should not be universal.

One goal of this chapter is to explore the reasons for the observed differences between consonants and vowels. In particular, I attempt to distinguish between phonological and orthographic hypotheses of the kinds just described. In the following discussion, I report quantitative analyses of correct spellings, legal substitutions, and illegal substitutions on phonemes. Omission errors are not discussed in this chapter but are considered in Chapters 7 and 8.

Correct Spellings

The first type of spelling to be discussed is correct spellings. When one examines the children's performance on phoneme-grapheme correspondences—correspondences such as that between /e/ and *a* and /f/ and *f*—one finds that the children did better on some phoneme-grapheme correspondences than others. For example, the children were usually correct on the correspondence between /f/ and *f*, as in *fox*. They did poorly on the correspondence between /f/ and *ph*, as in *elephant*.

Why are correspondences like that between /f/ and *f* easier for children to master than correspondences like that between /f/ and *ph*? A number of factors could play a role. For one thing, /f/ is usually spelled as *f*. The *ph* spelling occurs in relatively few words; none of these words is especially common. Moreover, *f* is a single letter while *ph* is two letters. The names of the letters could also be important. The name of *f*, /ɛf/, contains the phoneme that the letter represents. Neither the name of *p* nor the name of *h* contains the phoneme /f/. Teaching may also help to explain why the children did better on *f* than *ph*. The *f* spelling of /f/ appeared in the children's phonics book and in the spelling words that they were asked to memorize each week, beginning in January. The *ph* spelling was not included in these activities. Thus, several factors could help to explain why the children did better on some phoneme-grapheme correspondences than others. To disentangle the effects of these factors, I used multiple regression techniques, as done in Chapter 2. As in Chapter 2, I first discuss the results of the analyses and then present the statistical details.

Factors Associated with Correct Spellings of Phoneme-Grapheme Correspondences

Several factors proved to be associated with children's performance on phoneme-grapheme correspondences. The first and most important factor concerned the frequency or dominance of the correspondence. The children did better on dominant correspondences than on less dominant correspondences.

To measure the dominance of a phoneme-grapheme correspondence, I calculated the probability of the grapheme given the phoneme in the words of the collection. If a phoneme has only one possible spelling, the probability of the grapheme given the phoneme is 1.0. In this case, there is a one-to-one relation from the phoneme to the grapheme. For example, *th* is the only spelling of /θ/. If a phoneme has more than one spelling, the probability of each grapheme given the phoneme is less than 1.0. In this case, there is a one-to-many relation from the phoneme to the graphemes. For example, among the conventional spellings in the collection, /f/ was spelled as *f* 89% of the time. Thus, the probability of *f* given /f/ was .89. The phoneme /f/ was spelled as *ph* 8% of the time, making the probability of *ph* given /f/ .08.

Other things being equal, the children performed better on correspondences for which the probability of the grapheme given the phoneme was high than on correspondences for which the probability of the grapheme given the phoneme was low. Thus, the children performed better on the correspondence between /f/ and *f* than on the correspondence between /f/ and *ph*. This relation between the relative probability of a grapheme given a phoneme and children's use of the grapheme to spell the phoneme suggests that one-to-one relations from phonemes to graphemes are easier to learn than one-to-many relations. The one-to-many relations from phonemes to graphemes that exist in English *are* one source of difficulty in learning to spell. If /f/ had only one spelling, as /θ/ does, the system would be easier for children to master.

In Chapter 2, I showed that irregular words such as *said* cause trouble for beginning spellers. Children perform better on words in which each phoneme is represented with the most common grapheme (i.e., words that are regular by the context-free definition) than on words in which this is not the case. The present results confirm that *ai* is the trouble spot in *said*. If /ɛ/ were symbolized with *e*, the most common spelling of this vowel, the word would be easier for children to learn.

The results further imply that children's experience with reading affects their spelling. Children observe that some links between sounds and letters, like the link between /f/ and *f*, occur frequently in the words that they know how to read. Other phoneme-grapheme links, like that between /f/ and *ph*, are less common. As a result, children are more likely to choose *f* than *ph* when attempting to spell /f/.[1]

Thus, children are active learners. They analyze the printed words that they see into graphemes. They analyze the spoken versions of these words into phonemes. They search for relations between the graphemes in the printed words and the phonemes in the spoken words. They use these relations when it comes time to spell new words. This is a far cry from the rote, word-by-word memorization envisioned by traditional views of spelling.

Another factor associated with correct spelling of phoneme-grapheme correspondences was the number of letters in the grapheme. Some graphemes, like *f*, contain a single letter. Other graphemes, like *ph*, have two or more letters. Other things being equal, the students performed worse on phoneme-grapheme correspondences for which the grapheme contained more than one letter than phoneme-grapheme correspondences for which the grapheme contained one letter. Recall from Chapter 2 that the first graders often misspelled words like *that* and *sang*—words that contain multiple-letter graphemes. The present results confirm that *th* and *ng* are the trouble spots in *that* and *sang*. Digraphs are one difficult aspect of the English writing system.

The first graders' difficulty with multiple-letter graphemes is not surprising. To link graphemes and phonemes, children must divide printed words into graphemes and spoken words into phonemes. Children must relate the graphemes in printed words to the phonemes in spoken words. For words like *bath,* which contain four letters and only three phonemes, it is not clear how the printed word should be segmented. Do *t* and *h* go together, symbolizing a single phoneme, or do *a* and *t* perhaps go together? Even if children correctly parse the printed word into *b, a,* and *th,* they must learn the link between *th* and /θ/. From children's point of view, there is no good reason why /θ/ should be spelled with *th* rather than with some other letter or group of letters. The two letters in *th* make it especially difficult to learn and remember.

When a phoneme is spelled with a multiple-letter grapheme, the letters may or may not be adjacent to one another in the printed word. In *cake,* the letters that symbolize the vowel—*a* and final *e*—are separated by other letters. In *they,* the letters *e* and *y* are adjacent to one another. There was no significant difference between performance on multiple-letter graphemes with separated letters and performance on multiple-letter graphemes with adjacent letters.

Another factor associated with performance on grapheme-phoneme correspondences concerns the *names* of letters. Letter names are one of the earliest reading-related skills that children acquire. Indeed, most middle-class children learn to recite the alphabet and to associate the names of letters with the letters' forms in kindergarten or even earlier (e.g., Mason, 1980). The children's knowledge of letter names affected their spelling. The children did best on those phoneme-grapheme correspondences for which the name(s) of the letter(s) matched or contained the phoneme being spelled.

To understand these letter-name effects, consider the case of vowels. Sometimes, the name of a letter *exactly* matches the vowel that it spells—*a* for /e/, *e* for /i/, *i* for /ai/, and *o* for /o/. In these cases the children performed very well. The link between /e/ and *a* is not arbitrary for children who know their letter names. Children assume that /e/ must be spelled with *a* because /e/ is the name of the letter *a.* The link between /e/ and *a*—a link that usually develops long before children start to read and write—affects children's spelling.

For consonants, the name of a letter never *exactly* matches the phoneme that it spells. The names of consonant letters are syllables like /bi/ and /ɛl/ rather than single phonemes like /b/ and /l/. Indeed, stop consonants like /b/ cannot even be pronounced in isolation. They must be followed or preceded by a vowel. However, the names of many consonant letters *contain* the phonemes that the letters typically spell. For example, the name of *b,* /bi/, contains /b/.

The children in this study performed relatively well on correspondences like that between /b/ and *b.* This is because they associated the letter name /bi/ with the letter *b* and because their linguistic awareness was well enough developed that they knew that the syllable /bi/ contains the phoneme /b/ (the onset of the syllable). The children did relatively poorly when the name of the letter did not contain the phoneme being spelled. For instance, knowledge of letter names does not help on the correspondence between /g/ and *g.* The name of the letter *g,* /dʒi/, does not contain /g/.

Thus, some correspondences between phonemes and graphemes are arbitrary for children while others are not. For children, there is no good reason why /g/ should be spelled with *g* as opposed to some other letter. There is no good reason why /θ/ should be spelled with *th*. These correspondences are difficult for children to learn because they do not fit with the knowledge that children bring with them to the task. Other correspondences between phonemes and graphemes make more sense to children. The links between /e/ and *a* and /b/ and *b* are not arbitrary for pupils who know the names of letters and who (in the case of *b* for /b/) have a certain amount of phonological awareness. Because the correspondences are motivated rather than arbitrary, they are relatively easy to learn.

The formal instruction that the children received also affected their learning of phoneme-grapheme correspondences. Other things being equal, the students did better on phoneme-grapheme correspondences for which some direct instruction was provided in the classroom than on phoneme-grapheme correspondences for which there was no direct instruction. As an indication of whether a correspondence was deliberately taught, I determined whether it appeared in the children's phonics book or in the spelling words that they memorized each week, beginning in January. Some correspondences, like those between /b/ and *b* and /oi/ and *oy,* were included in one or both of these activities. Other correspondences, like those between /ŋ/ and *n* and /oi/ and *oi,* were not. (See Table 3.2 for a list of the taught spellings for each phoneme.) The students performed better on the taught corre-

Table 3.2. Spellings in Phonics Workbook and Spelling Lists, Listed in Alphabetical Order

Phoneme	Spelling(s)	Phoneme	Spelling(s)
/b/	*b*	/v/	*f, v*
/d/	*d*	/w/	*w, wh*
/ʤ/	*j*	/z/	*s, z*
/ð/	*th*	/ʒ/	none
/f/	*f*	/θ/	*th*
/g/	*g*	/ai/	*i, i & e, ie, y*
/h/	*h*	/au/	*ou, ou & e, ow*
/j/	*y*	/æ/	*a*
/k/	*c, k, q, (x)*	/a/	*o*
/l/	*l*	/e/	*a & e, ai, ay, e*
/m/	*m*	/ɛ/	*e*
/n/	*n*	/ə/	*a, o, u*
/ŋ/	*ng*	/i/	*e, e & e, ea, ee, ey, i, y*
/p/	*p*	/ı/	*i, e*
/r/	*r*	/o/	*o, o & e, oa, oe, oo, ou, ow*
/s/	*s, (x)*	/oi/	*oy*
/ʃ/	*sh*	/ɔ/	*o*
/t/	*t*	/u/	*o, oo, u & e, ue, ui*
/ʧ/	*ch*	/ʊ/	*oo*

Note. The symbol & indicates that the letters or groups of letters in a spelling are not adjacent. For example, *a & e* represents /e/ in *came.* When a letter is enclosed in parentheses, this indicates that the letter represents a phoneme in addition to the one under consideration. For example, *x* represents both /k/ and /s/ in *fox.*

spondences than expected on the basis of other factors. Thus, even though the children in this study had relatively little formal teaching about spelling, the instruction that they did receive had a detectable effect on their use of phoneme-grapheme correspondences.

Factors Not Associated with Correct Spellings of Phoneme-Grapheme Correspondences

So far, I have discussed those factors that were significantly associated with children's performance on phoneme-grapheme correspondences. Other factors did not yield significant results. Although null results must always be interpreted with caution, it is worth discussing those factors that were not related to children's performance.

Earlier, I presented two classes of hypotheses about why English-speaking children spell consonants more accurately than vowels. Hypotheses in the first class, or phonological hypotheses, attribute the difference in accuracy to the different phonological properties of consonants and vowels. Hypotheses in the second class, or orthographic hypotheses, attribute the difference to properties of the English writing system. If phonology is important, the phonological category of the phoneme— vowel versus consonant—should contribute significantly to the regression after other factors are taken into account. If orthography is critical, phonological category should not make an independent contribution. Phonological category did not add to the regression, supporting an orthographic hypothesis. The children performed better on consonants than vowels because the two types of phonemes are spelled differently in English, not because of intrinsic phonological differences between the two types of sounds.

What specific orthographic differences between consonants and vowels could make vowels harder to spell? One important difference is that, in English, vowels have many more spellings than consonants do. As a result, the probability of each grapheme given the phoneme tends to be lower for vowels. A second orthographic difference is that the spellings of vowels tend to contain more letters than the spellings of consonants. Together, these orthographic factors are sufficient to explain the children's poorer performance on vowels. Although consonants and vowels certainly differ in their phonological properties, there is no evidence that these differences directly affect spelling accuracy in first-grade children.

Earlier, I showed that the single best predictor of children's performance on a phoneme-grapheme correspondence was the probability of the grapheme given the phoneme. The first graders performed better on high-probability correspondences, like that from /f/ to *f,* than on low-probability correspondences, like that from /f/ to *ph.* In contrast, the probability of the phoneme given the grapheme was *not* influential. Consider the graphemes *ph* and *th.* The grapheme *ph* symbolizes only one phoneme, /f/. There is a one-to-one relation from the grapheme to the phoneme. The probability of /f/ given *ph* is 1.0. The grapheme *th* may represent either /θ/ or /ð/. The probability of /θ/ given *th* is less than 1.0, as is the probability of /ð/ given *th.* Although *ph* and *th* differ in the probability of the phoneme given the grapheme, this difference did not affect the children's performance. After other factors were taken into account, the students did not do especially well on *ph* or especially poorly on *th*.

These results are important because they suggest that first graders do not normally use their knowledge of reading to check their spelling. Suppose that a girl spells *cat* correctly. She then checks whether she comes up with /k'æt/ when she pronounces *cat*. The grapheme *c* is ambiguous: It may represent either /k/ or /s/. The girl might therefore read *cat* as /s'æt/. Because this is not what she meant to write, she might change her spelling from the correct CAT to an incorrect spelling, say CKAT. My results did not support this idea. The students did *not* have special difficulty when a grapheme mapped onto two or more phonemes. Apparently, first graders do not usually use their knowledge of how words are pronounced to check their spelling. For first graders, the processes involved in producing a spelling for a word are not closely connected to the processes involved in pronouncing a printed word.

Once other factors were taken into account, common phonemes were not easier to spell than uncommon phonemes. Specifically, the number of times that a phoneme occurred in my collection was not related to the students' accuracy on correspondences involving that phoneme. Nor was the number of occurrences of a grapheme in the standard spellings of words of my collection (pooling across the phonemes that the grapheme represents) related to children's performance on correspondences involving that grapheme. Apparently, the frequency of the *relation* between a phoneme and a grapheme is more important than the frequency of the phoneme by itself or the frequency of the grapheme by itself.

Earlier, I reported that correspondences in which the name of the letter matched or contained the phoneme being spelled were easier than other correspondences. One might expect to find some differences *within* the letter-name category. Children might do best when the name of the letter exactly matches the phoneme; they might do better when the consonant being spelled is at the beginning of the letter's name than when it is at the end of the letter's name. No such differences were found, possibly because the amount of unique variance explained by letter names was in any case rather small.

Finally, spelling difficulty did not seem to be related to pronunciation difficulty. For example, normal first graders may mispronounce /θ/, saying *thumb* as /f'əm/, *thin* as /f'ɪn/, and so on. They rarely mispronounce stop consonants such as /b/ and /k/. However, the children did no better on phoneme-grapheme correspondences involving easy-to-pronounce consonants than on phoneme-grapheme correspondences involving difficult-to-pronounce consonants.

Statistical Analyses

I carried out regression analyses to predict percentage correct, or the percentage of correct spellings for each of the phoneme-grapheme correspondences in the words of the collection. The total number of phoneme-grapheme correspondences was 185. One predictor was the probability of the grapheme given the phoneme in the conventional spellings of words in the collection. Each occurrence of each word was counted separately, giving frequent words a greater weight than infrequent words.

A second predictor was the length of the grapheme in number of letters. A grapheme such as *a* followed by final *e,* in which the two letters are not adjacent, was coded as a two-letter spelling, as was a grapheme such as *ay.* The third predictor was that of letter names. A correspondence was coded as a letter-name spelling if the name of the letter matched or contained the phoneme being spelled. For a multiple-letter grapheme, the names of all of the letters had to contain the phoneme for the correspondence to count as a letter-name spelling. The fourth predictor was whether the correspondence was included in the words in the children's phonics book or spelling lists.

Together, the four predictors explained 61.0% (60.1% adjusted) of the variance in percentage correct ($p < .001$). There were significant effects for the probability of the grapheme given the phoneme ($p < .001$), grapheme length ($p < .001$), letter names ($p < .001$), and taught correspondences ($p = .001$). The largest effect by far was for the probability of the grapheme given the phoneme. A regression using only this variable explained 45.4% of the variance in percentage correct.

Consideration of the phonological category of the phoneme—consonant or vowel—did not reliably increase the percentage of variance explained by the regression. This was true even though there was a significant simple correlation ($p < .001$, one tailed) between phonological category and percentage correct. Nonsignificant results were also obtained for the probability of the phoneme given the grapheme, the number of occurrences of the phoneme in the collection, and the number of occurrences of the grapheme in the conventional spellings of words of the collection.

As a measure of articulation difficulty for consonants, I used the results of Snow (1963). Snow asked 438 first graders, none of whom had received speech therapy, to pronounce words containing each English consonant. She reported the percentage of correct pronunciations for each consonant. I included these percentages in a regression analysis that was restricted to consonants.[2] Ease of articulation did not contribute significantly to the regression once the other variables were taken into account. Because I could find no published study giving articulation data for vowels for a large group of first-grade children, I did not study the relation between ease of articulation and spelling accuracy for vowels.

The figure reported here for the percentage of variance explained by the regression, although it is over 60%, may underestimate the true value. If a correspondence occurs only a few times in the collection of spellings, as some did, the estimate of percentage correct is poor. Regression analyses using the predictors of probability of the grapheme given the phoneme, grapheme length, letter names, and taught correspondences were therefore carried out on subsets of the data produced by successively eliminating correspondences that occurred once, twice, and so on, up to five times. The percentage of variance explained by the regression reached a maximum of 69.7% (68.9% adjusted) when only those correspondences that occurred more than twice ($n = 150$) were included in the analysis. This is an impressive figure. It suggests that the variables uncovered here explain much of the variance among correspondences in ease of learning.

An additional analysis explored the effect of grapheme length. This analysis focused on phoneme-grapheme correspondences for which the grapheme was two or more letters long (*n* = 116). Graphemes were coded as having separated letters, as in, *a* followed by final *e,* or adjacent letters, as in *ay.* There was no significant difference between the two types of multiple-letter spellings.

Factors Associated with Correct Spellings of Phonemes

So far, I have studied the children's performance on various phoneme-grapheme correspondences. Another way to look at the results is to examine children's performance on individual phonemes. For example, instead of considering each spelling of /p/ separately, one can examine *all* spellings of this phoneme. One can ask how often the students spelled /p/ correctly and why /p/ was easier to spell than /θ/ or /i/.

Children's performance on individual phonemes was well predicted from only two variables. The first variable will be called *spelling uncertainty.* It reflects the difficulty or uncertainty involved in selecting a spelling for the phoneme from among the graphemes that may represent it. If a phoneme has only one possible spelling—if the mapping from the phoneme to the grapheme is one-to-one—then there is no uncertainty in selecting a spelling for the phoneme. If a phoneme has more than one possible spelling—if the mapping is one-to-many—then there is some uncertainty. The speller has some chance of selecting the wrong alternative. The more alternatives there are, and the more similar the probabilities of the alternatives are, the more uncertainty there is.

The children did better on phonemes for which there was little spelling uncertainty than on phonemes for which there was more uncertainty. For example, there is little uncertainty for /p/. This phoneme has one dominant spelling *(p)* and one relatively uncommon variant *(pp).* There is much more uncertainty for /i/. This phoneme may be spelled in a number of different ways. Correspondingly, the children found /p/ easier to spell than /i/.

The second important variable was the number of letters in the spellings. For instance, /p/ is usually spelled with single *p.* Its other spelling, *pp,* contains two letters, but this spelling is not very common. In contrast, /θ/ is always spelled with two letters, *th.* Other things being equal, the students performed better on phonemes whose conventional spellings contained few letters than on phonemes whose conventional spellings contained many letters.

Once uncertainty and the length of the spellings were taken into account, the phonological category of the phoneme—consonant or vowel—had no effect. This result suggests that the children were less accurate at spelling vowels than consonants because there is more uncertainty involved in selecting spellings for vowels. Vowels have more possible spellings than consonants do. Moreover, these spellings are likely to have similar frequencies. The spellings of vowel phonemes also tend to contain more letters than the spellings of consonant phonemes. Thus, properties of the English writing system may explain why English-speaking first graders have particular trouble with vowels. It does not appear that the phonological characteristics of vowels make them intrinsically difficult to spell.

The frequency of the phoneme itself did not affect the students' ability to spell it once other factors were taken into account. Consistent with findings reported earlier in this chapter, whether a phoneme is spelled in a consistent manner is more important than how often the phoneme occurs.

Finally, there was little or no relation between ease of articulation and spelling accuracy. When uncertainty and grapheme length were taken into account, consonants that were easy to pronounce were not generally easier to spell than consonants that were hard to pronounce.

Statistical Analyses

To measure the uncertainty involved in selecting a spelling for a phoneme, I used a measure, H, that was suggested by Fitts and Posner (1967). H is calculated as:

$$ H = \sum_{i=1}^{N} p_i \log_2 1/p_i $$

where p_1 is the probability of the first grapheme that may spell the phoneme, p_2 is the probability of the second grapheme, and so on. H is zero when a phoneme has only one spelling. H increases as the number of alternatives increases and as their probabilities become more similar to one another. As a measure of grapheme length I used the average length of the conventional spellings of the phoneme, weighted according to the number of times each grapheme occurred. Together, the two predictors explained 61.8% of the variance (59.6% adjusted) in the percentage of correct spellings for phonemes ($p < .001$). Each predictor was significant at the .001 level, with grapheme length having the larger effect. The percentage of variance explained by the regression did not increase significantly when the phonological category of the phoneme (consonant or vowel) was included. This was true even though the simple correlation between percent correct and phonological category was reliable ($p < .01$, one tailed). The number of occurrences of the phoneme did not contribute significantly to the regression.

The analyses described so far included all 38 phonemes. However, the children attempted /ʒ/ only four times, making estimates of the percentage of correct spellings for this phoneme somewhat suspect. When /ʒ/ was removed from the analysis, the percentage of variance explained by uncertainty and grapheme length increased to 75.7% (74.3% adjusted; $p < .001$). Thus, these two factors explain a large percentage of the variance in correct spellings of phonemes.

To study the possible influence of articulation difficulty on spelling accuracy, I again used the results of Snow (1963), who reported the percentage of correct pronunciations for each consonant in a large group of first-grade children. In an analysis including all 24 consonants, the articulation measure accounted for a significant amount of variance above and beyond the contribution of uncertainty and length. However, this finding was entirely due to /ʒ/. This phoneme was difficult to pronounce and seemed difficult to spell as well. However, the children attempted /ʒ/ so rarely that it is difficult to estimate the percentage of correct spellings for this phoneme. When /ʒ/ was removed from the analysis, the contribution of pronunciation difficulty to the regression disappeared. For most consonants, then, there is no relation between pronunciation difficulty and spelling difficulty in this group of first graders.

Substitution Errors

Having discussed some of the factors associated with correct spellings, I now turn to the second broad category of spellings—substitution errors. Children make a substitution error when they spell a phoneme with the wrong grapheme. In this section, I distinguish between legal substitution errors, in which the grapheme used in error symbolizes the phoneme in some *other* word in the collection, and illegal substitution errors, in which it does not.

Legal Substitutions

When children use a legal but incorrect spelling for a phoneme, which of the possible spellings of the phoneme do they choose? Consider children's legal substitutions on /p/. This phoneme is symbolized in two different ways in my collection of words—*p* and *pp*. When the correct spelling of /p/ was *not p*, children often used *p* in error. Examples are CHOPED for *chopped* and APOS for *apples*. In contrast, the children rarely substituted *pp* for *p*. Thus, *p* was a common legal substitution for /p/ while *pp* was uncommon.

Why were legal substitutions like *p* for /p/ more common than legal substitutions like *pp* for /p/? To address this question, I carried out regression analyses to predict the percentage of errors on a phoneme that involved each phoneme-grapheme correspondence. This variable will be called percentage substitutions. For example, percentage substitutions for the correspondence between /p/ and *p* was 76.7%, since 76.7% of children's errors in spelling /p/s that were conventionally spelled with something *other* than *p* were *p*. For the correspondence between /p/ and *pp*, percentage substitutions was 2.7%, meaning that only 2.7% of children's errors on all /p/s that were conventionally spelled with a grapheme other than *pp* used *pp*.

Before discussing the results of the analyses, note that there was a close relation between percentage substitutions and percentage correct ($r = .71, p < .001$). Just as the children were more often correct on the correspondence between /p/ and *pp* than the correspondence between /p/ and *pp*, so they more often substituted *p* for *pp* than the reverse. One would expect some of the same variables associated with percentage correct to be associated with percentage substitutions, and indeed this was so.

The single best predictor of percentage substitutions, just as it was the single best predictor of percentage correct, was the probability of the grapheme given the phoneme in the words of the collection. For example, the probability of *p* given /p/ is high. The probability of *pp* given /p/ is low. Correspondingly, *p* was a more common substitution than *pp*. These results show that the children were more likely to substitute a frequent spelling for an infrequent one than vice versa.

The children's knowledge of letter names influenced their substitution errors, just as it influenced their correct spellings. Substitutions like *a* for /e/ were common, in part, because the name of *a* is /e/. Other things being equal, students were more likely to substitute a letter-name spelling for a non-letter-name spelling than the reverse.

So far, the results for percentage substitutions are similar to the results for percentage correct. However, there were several differences. The frequency of the grapheme itself was significantly associated with percentage substitutions but not with percentage correct. For example, pooling across all of the phonemes that it represents, *a* is quite common. Correspondingly, children often used *a* in substitution errors. In the analysis of percentage substitutions, the length of the grapheme did not have a significant effect once the probability of the grapheme given the phoneme, letter names, and grapheme frequency were taken into account. Grapheme length did have a significant effect on percentage correct. Another factor that was associated with percentage correct but not with percentage substitutions was whether the phoneme-grapheme correspondence appeared in the children's phonics book and spelling lists.

The results just described come from regression analyses to predict the percentage of errors on each phoneme that used each of the conventional phoneme-grapheme correspondences for that phoneme. The maximum number of cases in the analyses was 179. This figure is less than the total number of phoneme-grapheme correspondences in the words of the collection (185) because cases in which a phoneme was not spelled with a letter (as with the /e/ of *K-mart*) were omitted. The correspondences between /θ/ and *th* and /ð/ and *th* also had to be excluded. Because /θ/ and /ð/ are always spelled with *th* in the words of my collection, legal substitutions are not possible on these phonemes.

A regression using the predictors of the probability of the grapheme given the phoneme in the words of the collection, letter names, and number of occurrences of the grapheme in the conventional spellings of words of the collection explained 76.1% (75.7% adjusted) of the variance in percentage substitutions ($p < .001$). The figure rose by about 2% ($p < .001$) when the four cases for which the denominator for percentage substitutions was two or less were eliminated from the analysis. Although all three predictors made significant contributions ($p < .001$ for each), the largest effect by far was for the probability of the grapheme given the phoneme. A regression using this variable alone explained over 70% of the variance in percentage substitutions.

Illegal Substitutions

So far, I have focused on substitutions that are legal from the perspective of the conventional writing system. Although legal substitutions outnumbered illegal substitutions, illegal substitutions were by no means rare. Indeed, 43.3% of all consonant substitutions and 33.2% of all vowel substitutions were illegal. For example, the first graders used *g* for /k/, as in GARY for *care,* *t* for /θ/, as in TREE for *three,* and *i* for /ɛ/, as in LIT for *let.* In English, these letters are never used to symbolize these phonemes. Why did the students make these errors? Are they random errors or are they somehow systematic?

The examples just given suggest that knowledge of phonology and partial knowledge of conventional orthography play a role in illegal substitutions. Children's use of *g* for /k/ may reflect the similarity in sound between /g/ and /k/, two stop consonants that differ only in voicing and that are rated as similar by adults (Singh, Woods, & Becker, 1972). Children may substitute *i* for /ε/ because of similarity between the two front unrounded vowel phonemes /ε/ and /ɪ/. These vowels are rated as similar by adults (Fox, 1983; Singh & Woods, 1971) and children (Read, 1973). Partial knowledge of conventional spelling may help explain errors like *t* for /θ/. Children may use *t* because it is the first letter of *th*.

To study the effects of phonemic similarity and other factors on illegal substitutions, I first attempted to infer which phoneme the students had in mind when they made a particular illegal substitution. Once errors were classified in this way, I could ask whether the substitutions reflect the similarity of the phonemes involved. For consonants, I could classify a majority of illegal substitutions in the manner just described. For example, consider the use of *t* for /p/. Since *t* is the most common spelling of /t/, I took *t* as an attempt to represent /t/. Although *t* may also spell /ʧ/, as in *fortune*, I assumed that *t* represented /t/ rather than /ʧ/ because *t* is the most common spelling of /t/ and a less common spelling of /ʧ/.

Some errors could not be unambiguously assigned to a phoneme according to the criteria just described. For instance, *s* is ambiguous because it is the most common spelling of both /s/ and /z/. The letter *c*, which represents either /k/, /s/, or /ʃ/, also cannot be assigned to a single phoneme. Ambiguous substitutions such as these were excluded from the analyses. Also excluded were letters or letter groups that stand for more than one phoneme, such as *kl* and *x*.

For consonants, 61.5% of the illegal substitutions could be classified as attempts to represent a specific phoneme. Although this figure is high enough to justify further analyses, the need to exclude over one-third of the data means that the results must be interpreted cautiously. The number of classifiable errors was much lower for vowels. Here, a majority of illegal substitutions were ambiguous. For example, *i* is the most common spelling of both /ɪ/ and /ai/ while *o* is the most common spelling of four different vowels. When the children used *i* or *o*, it was not clear which phoneme they had in mind. Because most illegal vowel substitutions could not be assigned to a single phoneme, I could not correlate the number of substitutions with the similarity of the phonemes involved.

I carried out regression analyses to study the factors associated with illegal substitution errors on consonants. One important factor was phonemic similarity. Illegal substitutions were more likely to involve similar phonemes than dissimilar phonemes. Two global measures of phonemic similarity were about equally successful as predictors of illegal substitutions. The first of these measures was the number of *distinctive features* that distinguish the two phonemes. Distinctive features are properties that differentiate phonemes from one another. For example, /k/ and /g/ share all features but one, the feature of voicing. /k/ is voiceless, while /g/ is voiced. The spellings of phonemes that differed in few features were more often substituted for one another than were the spellings of phonemes that differed in many features. The second global measure of phonological similarity was *rated similarity*. This measure was taken from a study (Singh et al., 1972) in which adults rated the similarity of pairs of syllables such as /k'a/–/g'a/ and /k'a/–/m'a/, using a scale from 1 (most similar-sounding pair) to 7 (most dissimilar-sounding pair).[3] The closer two phonemes were rated, the more often a spelling of one phoneme was substituted for a spelling of the other phoneme.

To study the effects of phonemic similarity in more detail, I next considered three separate dimensions of similarity. These dimensions are manner of articulation, place of articulation, and voicing. As discussed in Chapter 1, the air through the vocal tract must be obstructed in some way to form a consonant. Consonants may be classified according to the manner and place of this obstruction. As a glance back at Figure 1.5 shows, English consonants are grouped into six categories for manner of articulation—stops, fricatives, affricates, nasals, liquids, and glides. The figure shows seven categories for place of articulation—bilabial, labio-dental, dental, alveolar, palato-alveolar, palatal, and velar. Finally, consonants may be classified as voiced or voiceless according to whether the vocal cords vibrate during the obstruction.[4]

Consonants that were alike in manner of articulation and place of articulation were often substituted for one another. However, the substituted phoneme did not necessarily agree with the intended phoneme in voicing. In other words, substitutions often involved consonants from the same manner category, especially consonants that are produced in the same or nearby locations in the mouth. There were many confusions between pairs of consonants that differed only in voicing, such as /k/ and /g/.

Why do first graders sometimes confuse the spellings of similar-sounding consonants, especially consonants that are alike in all respects but voicing? One possibility is that children cannot distinguish between the phonemes. For instance, if children do not hear the difference between /k/ and /g/ or do not produce the distinction in their own speech, they may spell /k/ as *g*. However, this hypothesis cannot explain most of the illegal substitutions observed in this study. Normal first graders easily distinguish words such as *cot* and *got* in their own speech and the speech of others. A first grader who did not differentiate these words would be considered to have a severe articulation problem; none of the first graders in this study had such problems. Moreover, results reported earlier in this chapter showed little or no relation between the ease of articulation of a consonant and children's ability to spell it.

If errors like *g* for /k/ do not reflect a failure to distinguish between /g/ and /k/, perhaps they reflect children's experience with the English writing system. In English, pairs of phonemes that differ only in voicing are sometimes spelled alike. For example, /ð/ and /θ/, which differ only in voicing, are both spelled as *th*. /s/ and /z/ are both often spelled as *s*. Knowledge of these aspects of the English writing system may play some role in errors like *g* for /k/, but I doubt that it is the *only* cause of these errors.

I suspect that the intrinsic similarity between phonemes that differ only in voicing explains *both* children's voicing confusions in spelling and the occasional neglect of voicing by the English writing system. The similarity between phonemes such as /ð/ and /θ/ and /g/ and /k/ causes children (and adults) to sometimes ignore voicing in spelling and in other situations.

To summarize the results on phonological similarity, illegal substitutions often involve similar phonemes, especially consonants that are alike in all respects but voicing. These substitutions do not usually reflect an inability to hear the difference between similar-sounding phonemes or an inability to distinguish them in pronunciation.

Phonological similarity was not the only factor associated with children's illegal substitution errors on consonants. Another factor was partial knowledge of common digraphs. A digraph is a grapheme like *th* for /θ/ in which two different letters symbolize a single phoneme. When a digraph was the most common spelling of a consonant phoneme, the children sometimes used the first letter of the digraph rather than the entire digraph. Illegal substitutions involving the second letter of the digraph seemed also to occur, but were less common. For example, the first graders sometimes used *t* for /θ/. Other times they used *h*. These errors reflect orthographic knowledge (partial familiarity with *th*) rather than phonological knowledge (similarity in sound between /θ/ and /t/ and /θ/ and /h/).

Earlier in this chapter, I reported that first graders perform poorly on multiple-letter graphemes. The present results show what kinds of errors they make on one common multiple-letter grapheme—the digraph. When attempting to spell a digraph, students sometimes produce just one of the letters. Often, as with *t* or *h* for /θ/, the resulting error is illegal. With digraphs like *th,* errors that use the first letter are especially common.

These digraph effects were limited to cases in which the digraph was the most common spelling of the phoneme. With /θ/, whose only spelling is *th,* the children produced *t* errors and apparently also *h* errors above the rate predicted by phonemic similarity between /θ/ and /t/ and /θ/ and /h/. With /f/, on the other hand, *ph* is not the most common spelling. The children did not produce *p* errors or *h* errors at elevated rates. Thus, the children knew something about common digraphs like *th* for /θ/ but not uncommon digraphs like *ph* for /f/.

Multiple-letter spellings had another effect on illegal substitutions, in addition to those just described. Errors in which the students used multiple-letter graphemes were less common than expected on the basis of other factors. For example, illegal substitutions involving /tʃ/ for /dʒ/ were relatively uncommon. By the present criteria, the only spellings that count as unambiguous attempts to represent /tʃ/ are multiple-letter spellings like *ch*. The children produced few such spellings, consistent with their tendency to avoid multiple-letter spellings.

Finally, visual similarity among letters played some role in illegal substitutions, at least with *b* and *d*. The children confused *b* and *d* more often than expected given the similarity between the phonemes. These confusions presumably reflect the similarity between the letters. However, the effects of visual similarity seemed smaller than the effects of phonological similarity.

Statistical support for the conclusions just described comes from regression analyses in which I attempted to predict the number of substitutions of each possible consonant for every other one. Two global measures of phonemic similarity served as predictors. The first, feature similarity, was the number of features that distinguish the two phonemes in the system of Chomsky and Halle (1968). The second, rated similarity, was the rated similarity of the phonemes in word-initial position in the study by Singh et al. (1972). The two measures of phonemic similarity correlated significantly with one another ($r = .51$, $p < .001$). Two additional predictors concerned the effects of digraphs. A substitution like /s/ for /ʃ/ was coded as a first-letter-of-digraph substitution because the most common spelling of /ʃ/ is *sh* and this substitution uses just the first letter of the digraph.[5] The substitution of /h/ for /ʃ/ was a second-letter-of-digraph substitution. Finally, a substitution was coded as involving a multiple-letter spelling if the only substitution that unambiguously represented the phoneme contained two or more letters.

The first regression used the variables of feature similarity, first letter of digraph, second letter of digraph, and multiple-letter spelling. There were 483 cases in the analysis. Together, the four predictors explained 70.7% of the variance (70.5% adjusted) in number of substitutions ($p < .001$). As the number of features on which the phonemes differed increased, the number of substitutions decreased ($p < .001$). Substitutions that involved multiple-letter spellings occurred less often than otherwise expected ($p < .05$); substitutions that used the first or second letter of a digraph occurred more often than otherwise expected ($p < .001$). The variable of first-letter-of-digraph substitutions had a larger effect than the variable of second-letter-of-digraph substitutions.

In a second regression, rated similarity was used in place of feature similarity. The number of cases in this analysis was 420. This is less than the number of cases in the preceding analysis because phonemes that may not occur at the beginnings of words were not included in the Singh et al. rating study. The percentage of variance explained by the regression was almost identical to that in the analysis using feature similarity. The pattern of significant and nonsignificant results was also similar. Now, though, the variable of second-letter-of-digraph substitutions did not contribute significantly once the other variables were taken into account ($p = .11$).

To study the effects of phonemic similarity in more detail, I performed another analysis using the predictors of manner of articulation, place of articulation, voicing, first letter of digraph, second letter of digraph, and multiple-letter spelling. This regression explained 73.0% of the variance in illegal substitutions (72.6% adjusted, $p < .001$). Significant effects appeared for both manner of articulation ($p < .001$) and place of articulation ($p < .005$). However, there was *no* significant effect of voicing. Both first letter of digraph and second letter of digraph made significant contributions ($p < .001$), with the weighting for first letter greater than that for second letter. Multiple-letter spellings were less often involved in substitutions than otherwise expected ($p < .01$).

In the analyses reported so far, I coded an error as a first-letter-of-digraph error or a second-letter-of-digraph error if the digraph was the most common spelling of the phoneme. A broader definition of digraph errors includes *all* digraph spellings, common or uncommon. However, once digraph errors narrowly defined were included in the analyses, there were no additional effects due to digraph errors broadly defined.

In English, only the categories of stops and fricatives contain pairs of phonemes that are alike in manner of articulation and place of articulation and that differ just in voicing. Such pairs include the stops /g/ and /k/ and the fricatives /v/ and /f/. My results imply that many errors involve such pairs of phonemes. To verify this suggestion, I examined errors on stops and fricatives separately. Confusions involving the /b/–/d/ pair were not analyzed because visual similarity contributed greatly to these errors, as described below. Substitutions that differed in voicing only (e.g., /g/ for /k/) were most frequent, occurring 47 times. Errors that differed in place of articulation only (e.g., /p/ or /t/ for /k/) occurred 24 times, while errors that differed in both voicing and place (e.g., /b/ or /d/ for /k/) occurred 11 times. The distribution of errors differs significantly from that expected by chance. Voicing errors were more common than expected and errors that differed in both voicing and place were less common than expected ($p < .001$ by chi-square tests).

To summarize the results so far, the analyses of illegal substitutions have been quite successful. Regardless of how one measures the similarity among phonemes, phonemic similarity, digraph spellings, and multiple-letter spellings together explain over 70% of the variance in illegal substitutions on consonants. This figure suggests the major factors associated with illegal substitutions have been uncovered.

Some of the variance in illegal substitutions that is not explained by the variables just described may reflect visual similarity among pairs of letters. According to the regressions, /b/ substitutions for /d/ should have occurred about twice. In fact, they occurred 25 times. The discrepancy between the predicted value and the actual value was larger for /b/–/d/ than for any other case in the analyses. Substitutions of /d/ for /b/ were also much more common than predicted. These errors must reflect the visual similarity between the letters *b* and *d*.

Unfortunately, a measure of visual similarity could not be included in the analyses. This is because the visual similarity of letters differs according to whether they are written in upper or lower case and according to the style of print that is used. I did not code such information in this study. Thus, although similarity between letters does contribute to illegal substitutions, at least with /b/ and /d/, the influence of this factor is hard to quantify. Note, however, that the percentage of variance explained by the regressions increased by about 10% when /b/–/d/ confusions were omitted from the analyses. Other than the case of /b/ and /d/, scrutiny of the data revealed no other cases in which confusions clearly reflected visual similarity between letters. In general, visual similarity seems to play a smaller role than phonemic similarity in children's illegal substitution errors.

Legal Substitutions Relative to Illegal Substitutions

On the whole, the students made more legal substitutions than illegal substitutions. However, consonants and vowels differed in the types of substitution errors that they engendered. The percentage of substitution errors that were legal was higher for vowels, 66.8%, than for consonants, 57.2%.

Why do consonants and vowels differ in the percentage of substitution errors that are legal? As in the case of correct spellings, there are two general types of explanation for the difference. First—a phonological hypothesis—the difference could reflect intrinsic linguistic differences between consonant and vowel phonemes. Second—an orthographic hypothesis—the difference could reflect properties of the English writing system itself.

One property of the English writing system that could cause the percentage of legal substitution errors to be higher for vowels than for consonants is that vowels have more possible spellings than consonants do. Consider, as an extreme example, the vowel /ə/. If a child spelled this phoneme with any single vowel letter or with *y,* the error would be legal. This is because each of these spellings occurs for /ə/ in some English word. Thus, even children who have no idea how to spell /ə/ may produce a legal spelling by guessing. With /θ/, on the opposite extreme, a random guess would be very unlikely to produce the legal spelling *th.*

This orthographic hypothesis, then, is that the percentage of legal substitution errors is higher for vowels than for consonants because vowels have more spellings than consonants do. The results of a regression analysis supported this hypothesis. This analysis was carried out across all 38 phonemes. The dependent variable was the percentage of all substitution errors on each phoneme that were legal. The predictors were the uncertainty involved in selecting a grapheme for the phoneme from among the various possibilities (measured by the H statistic described previously) and the length of the graphemes (measured by the weighted average length of the graphemes that represent the phoneme). The percentage of variance explained by the regression was 51.4% (48.6% adjusted, $p < .001$). The figure increased by over 10% when the two phonemes for which the total number of substitutions was three or less were omitted from the analysis. As uncertainty increased, the percentage of substitution errors that were legal increased ($p < .001$). As the length of the spellings increased, the percentage of substitution errors that were legal decreased ($p < .001$). Once uncertainty and length were taken into account, consideration of a phoneme's category—consonant or vowel—did not help predict the percentage of substitution errors that were legal. This result supports the orthographic hypothesis that the percentage of legal substitutions is higher for vowels than for consonants because vowel phonemes have more possible spellings. Substitution errors on vowels are more likely to be scored as legal than substitution errors on consonants because random or educated guessing is more likely to produce legal substitutions in the case of vowels.

These findings raise an important concern. If some legal substitutions stem from guessing, especially with vowels like /ə/, legal substitutions do *not* necessarily mean that the child knows the conventional spellings of a phoneme. The first grader who spells *but* as BIT does not necessarily know that *i* is sometimes used to spell /ə/. The child may have simply guessed *i* from among the vowel letters. These results point to a problem in the classification of substitutions as legal or illegal. Later in this chapter, I further discuss the limitations of the legal/illegal distinction.

Summary of Findings

Before discussing the implications of the findings in this chapter and comparing them with the findings of previous research, a brief review is in order. The major findings of this chapter may be summarized as follows:

1. The most important determinant of how often the first graders used a particular grapheme to represent a phoneme was how often that phoneme-

grapheme pair occurred in the printed words to which the children were exposed. For the children in this study, the role of formal teaching was also evident, although not as strong.

2. Single-letter graphemes (e.g., *t, a*) were easier to learn than multiple-letter graphemes (e.g., *th, ai*).

3. The first graders' knowledge of letter names affected their spelling. It caused them to use correspondences like those between /e/ and *a* and /p/ and *p* more often than expected given the frequency of these correspondences.

4. The children made more errors on vowels than consonants. This difference reflects the nature of the English writing system, primarily the fact that vowels have more possible spellings than consonants do.

5. In general, there was no relation between how easy the consonant was to pronounce and how easy it was to spell.

6. The first graders sometimes confused the spellings of similar-sounding consonants. These confusions often involved pairs of consonants that were alike in all respects but voicing, such as /g/ and /k/.

7. The children confused *b* and *d* more often than expected based on the similarity of the phonemes /b/ and /d/. These confusions reflect the visual similarity of the letters *b* and *d*.

8. When trying to spell a consonant that is usually spelled with a digraph, the first graders sometimes used the first letter or, less commonly, the second letter of the digraph.

Comparison with Results of Other Studies

Read's Research

The most comprehensive and linguistically sophisticated study of children's spelling to date is that of Charles Read. Read identified 32 preschoolers who started to spell on their own before they entered school. He examined their spelling errors from a linguistic perspective. Fortunately for present purposes, Read presented tables showing how the children in his study spelled each phoneme. These tables allow me to compare my results with Read's.

In making the comparisons, it is important to recall that Read's collection of spellings includes incorrectly spelled words only. Read did not collect or analyze correct spellings. My collection includes both correct spellings and errors. The total number of words in Read's collection, 2,517, is slightly less than the total number of misspelled words in my collection, 2,740. However, the average number of phonemes per incorrectly spelled word is somewhat higher in Read's study than in the present study, so the total number of phonemes in misspelled words is higher in Read's study.

One complication that arises in comparing my results with Read's is that the two studies assume slightly different phonemic analyses of English. The major difference is that Read separated the /ə/ category of the present study into two phonemes—a stressed vowel, /ʌ/, and an unstressed vowel, /ə/. For comparability, these cases are eliminated from the analyses to be reported.

To compare my results on correct spellings, legal and illegal substitutions, and omissions with those of Read, I used the tabulations in my Appendix II and in Read's Appendix A. These data show how children in each study spelled each phoneme in incorrectly spelled words. I classified each spelling of a phoneme in a misspelled word into one of the three categories shown in Table 3.3.

The first category in Table 3.3 contains correct spellings and legal substitution errors. These are grouped together because Read's results are not presented in a way that allows them to be distinguished. For instance, Read gives the total number of times that children spelled /ɪ/ as *e*. One does not know how often *e* was the correct spelling of the phoneme and how often some other spelling, such as *i*, was correct. The criteria of the present study were employed to classify the spellings in Read's study as correct/legal or illegal.[6] The second category of spellings in Table 3.3 is illegal substitutions and the third is omissions.[7]

Examining Table 3.3, one observes a surprising result. The children in Read's study, although younger than the children in my study, were actually *better* spellers. The distribution of spellings among the three categories of Table 3.3 differs significantly for the two studies ($p < .001$ by a chi-square test, pooling over consonants and vowels). The percentage of spellings in the correct plus legal category is lower in my study than in Read's study. The percentage of spellings in the illegal category is higher in my study than in Read's study, as is the percentage of omissions ($p < .001$ for both by chi-square tests). Although the total number of phonemes in incorrectly spelled words is smaller in my study than in Read's study, my study includes more illegal substitutions and almost twice as many omissions.

Why did the children in my study make more illegal substitutions and more omissions than the children in Read's study? The children in my study were first graders, whereas the children in Read's study were preschoolers. One would think that first graders would be better spellers than preschoolers, not worse spellers. Moreover, Read stressed the nonstandard nature of his preschoolers' spellings; he spoke of the spellings as invented. However, the preschool spellings that Read collected seem to be *more* influenced by conventional orthography than my first-grade spellings.

There are at least two explanations for the surprising finding that my collection of first-grade spellings contains fewer correct and legal spellings than Read's collec-

Table 3.3. Spellings of Phonemes in Incorrectly Spelled Words Only in Present Study and Read's (1975) Study (numbers in parentheses are percentages)

Type of Spelling	Present Study			Read's Study		
	Consonants	Vowels	Both	Consonants	Vowels	Both
Correct/legal	5,580	1,771	7,351	7,514	2,692	10,206
	(79.7)	(65.2)	(75.6)	(87.6)	(83.8)	(86.6)
Illegal	619	682	1,301	664	363	1,027
	(8.8)	(25.1)	(13.4)	(7.7)	(11.3)	(8.7)
Omission	806	262	1,068	397	159	556
	(11.5)	(9.7)	(11.0)	(4.6)	(4.9)	(4.7)

tion of preschool spellings. First, Read's preschoolers may actually have been better spellers than my first graders. Although Read's subjects were younger, they may have known more about conventional spelling. Their parents may have put more emphasis on reading and writing and may have read to the children more often. This explanation is plausible since the parents of the children in Read's study were well educated and, judging from their acceptance of their children's attempts to write, placed a high value on literacy. In contrast, my study involved more typical middle-class families whose children happened to be assigned to a first-grade teacher who stressed writing.

In addition, the way in which the spellings were collected could be important. The children in my study indicated which words they meant to write by dictating their stories to the teacher soon after they wrote them. The children in Read's study did not do this. In some cases the children's parents or teachers reported what the children said they wrote, but in other cases Read had to use context to infer the children's intentions. Context is not always sufficient, however. For example, looking at Johnny's I LIT MY FURND HAVE TEKN, which is accompanied by a drawing of five people, it is hard to guess what TEKN means. However, Johnny dictated the story as, "I let my friend have chicken." I therefore coded TEKN as an attempt to spell *chicken*. As another example, it is hard to tell that PAS represents *plants* without the student's dictation. If Read could not interpret a spelling, he did not include it in his collection. In contrast, many errors that I found hard to interpret *were* included based on the children's dictations. Consequently, my collection contains many errors that deviate greatly from standard spelling; that is, many errors with illegal substitutions and omissions.[8]

There is, therefore, a *quantitative* difference between the spellings in my collection and the spellings in Read's collection. Contrary to expectations, the spellings in my collection are more primitive. In this chapter and later in this book, I ask whether the spellings observed here are *qualitatively* similar or dissimilar to the spellings observed by Read.

One important similarity is that children's knowledge of letter names affected their spelling in both cases. The preschoolers studied by Read used their knowledge of letter names to gain entrance into the writing system. Having inferred that a letter often spells a phoneme in the letter's name, they tended to spell /e/ as *a*, /b/ as *b*, and so on. Read's children had no choice but to use letter names. They received little or no direct instruction in spelling and, at the time they began to write, could read only a few words. The first graders in my study were in a rather different situation. Although their teacher favored whole-language and language-experience approaches to the teaching of reading and writing, she did provide some formal instruction in phonics and in spelling. The children were learning to read at the same time that they were learning to spell. Even so, the first graders used their knowledge of letter names as a guide to spelling. Like Read's preschoolers, they often spelled /e/ as *a* and /b/ as *b*. The first graders used these and other letter-name correspondences more often than expected given the frequency of the correspondences in the words that they read. Thus, letter names play a role in spelling for children who learn at school as well as for children who learn on their own at home.

Other Studies

Previous research suggests that phonemes that may be spelled in many different ways are harder to spell correctly than phonemes that have just a few spellings. This is true for both children and adults (e.g., Cahen, Craun, & Johnson, 1971; Jorm, 1977; Kreiner & Gough, 1990). My findings support the claim that ambiguous phonemes are difficult to spell, even for first graders. However, my results go beyond the previous findings by showing that ambiguity is not the *only* determinant of how accurately first graders spell a phoneme. The number of letters in the spellings is also important. For first graders, phonemes whose conventional spellings contain a single letter are easier to spell than phonemes whose conventional spellings contain more than one letter.

Implications

Writing Systems and Spelling

The English writing system is notoriously difficult to master. According to many of its critics, its difficulty lies in its irregularity. If only there were one-to-one mappings between phonemes and graphemes, the critics claim, English would be simple for children to learn and simple for adults to use. The results in this chapter and Chapter 2 confirm that irregularity is a problem in learning to spell. If each phoneme were spelled in a single way, the results imply, children would do better.

However, irregularity is not the *only* source of difficulty for children learning to spell in English. Another problem is that the spellings of English phonemes often contain more than one letter. For first graders, graphemes like *sh* cause difficulty even when they are consistently linked to phonemes. Given two writing systems that had one-to-one mappings from phonemes to graphemes, a system with single-letter graphemes would be easier to learn than a system with multiple-letter graphemes.

Another important factor, and one that has often been overlooked in comparisons among writing systems and proposals for spelling reform, concerns the names of letters. My results suggest that children would learn to spell most easily if letters' names always matched or included the sounds that the letters made in words. For example, if /e/ were always spelled with a letter named /e/, children would have little difficulty learning to spell this phoneme. If /e/ were spelled with a letter *not* named /e/, children would do more poorly, even if the mapping from the phoneme to the grapheme were totally regular. Given two writing systems that had one-to-one mappings between phonemes and graphemes, a system in which the letters' names matched or contained the phonemes that the letters symbolized would be easier to learn than a system in which this was not the case.

Just as writing systems differ from one another in whether they have one-to-one mappings between phonemes and graphemes and in whether they have multiple-letter graphemes, so they differ from one another in their system of letter names. In English, letter names are not highly predictable. For many consonants, the letter's name contains the sound that it typically represents followed by /i/. Examples are

b, which is named /bi/, and *t,* which is named /ti/. However, the names of consonant letters do not always follow this principle. The names of a few consonants,
such as *j,* end with /e/. The names of other consonants, such as *s,* begin with vowels.
In a few cases, a letter's name has little or no relation to its sound. For example, the
name of *y* is /wai/ but *y* is never pronounced as /w/.

In Korean, on the other hand, letter names are highly systematic. The letter that
represents /b/ is named "biub" and the letter that represents /d/ is named "diud."
("Iu" refers to a vowel that does not have an exact English equivalent.) This principle holds for almost all consonant letter names. For vowels, the names of the letters match the sounds that the letters make in words. Because letter names in
Korean are so systematic, letter names may be more beneficial for Korean children
than for English-speaking children.

Thus, irregularity is not the only source of difficulty in learning to spell in
English. Other problems are that some spellings contain more than one letter and
that letter names do not always provide a good guide to spelling.

It has often been noted that English-speaking children have more trouble spelling vowels than consonants (e.g., Jorm, 1977; Stage & Wagner, 1992). The present
results confirm this observation and, more importantly, suggest a reason for it. First
graders' difficulties with vowels reflect, in large part, the properties of the English
writing system. Because vowel phonemes have more different spellings than consonant phonemes and because the likelihoods of the alternatives are more similar,
children more often misspell vowels. Although vowels and consonants certainly differ phonologically, there is no evidence that these phonological differences directly
cause children's problems in spelling vowels at the first-grade level.[9]

My conclusion—that properties of the English writing system can explain first
graders' high error rate on vowels as compared with consonants—fits well with conclusions reached from studies of reading. In reading, as in spelling, English-speaking
children have difficulty with vowels (Fowler, I. Y. Liberman, & Shankweiler, 1977;
Seidenberg, Bruck, Fornarolo, & Backman, 1986; Shankweiler & I. Y. Liberman,
1972; Treiman & Baron, 1981). Several investigators have sought the reasons for
this difficulty (Fowler, Shankweiler, & I. Y. Liberman, 1979; Shankweiler & I. Y.
Liberman, 1972). Children's problems, the findings suggest, reflect the complexity
of English spelling-sound correspondences for vowels. In alphabetic systems with
simpler relations between spellings and sounds, such as Serbo-Croatian, vowels are
not necessarily harder to read than consonants (Lukatela & Turvey, 1980). My findings point to similar conclusions in the case of spelling. The difficulties that English-
speaking children experience with vowels, both in reading and in spelling, largely
reflect the nature of the English writing system. Difficulties with vowels may not be
a necessary or universal feature of alphabetic writing systems.

Models of the Spelling Process

To understand the mental processes that children use to spell, two general questions
must be addressed. First, what do children know about the relations between
sounds and spellings? Second, how do children put this knowledge to use when they
spell? The results presented in this chapter shed light on these important questions.

First, consider children's knowledge of the relations between phonemes and graphemes. The dual-route model, at least in its simplest form, implies that children have a list of the graphemes that may represent each phoneme. These graphemes are divided into two groups. One group contains the "regular" spelling—the grapheme that usually symbolizes the phoneme. The second group contains one or more "irregular" spellings. For example, the regular spelling of /ɛ/ is *e*. The irregular spellings include *ai*, as in *said*, and *ea*, as in *dead*. My results do not support this simple view. A grapheme that is not the most common spelling of a phoneme but that occurs fairly often is more likely to be involved in a substitution than is a very uncommon grapheme. In other words, phoneme-grapheme correspondences seem to vary in strength.

Connectionist models could capture the idea that links between phonemes and graphemes vary continuously in strength. According to such models, each phoneme-grapheme correspondence has a weight. The weights vary from strong to weak; they are not limited to just two values, as the simple dual-route model implies. My results show that several factors affect the weights that children assign to phoneme-grapheme correspondences. For the children in this study, the most important factor is the relations between phonemes and graphemes that are embodied in the printed language, or more accurately that portion of the language to which the children are exposed. Another factor is children's knowledge of letter names. Links like that from /e/ to *a* are stronger than expected given the frequency with which *a* represents /e/ in English words. The number of letters in graphemes and the teaching that children receive are also influential. Weighted phoneme-grapheme correspondences fit well into connectionist models.

One can gain some insight into how children put their knowledge of phoneme-grapheme correspondences to use by considering why they sometimes make errors like *g* for /k/. As discussed earlier, children distinguish between /k/ and /g/ when they speak and listen. However, children sometimes substitute the spelling of one phoneme for the spelling of the other. At what point in the spelling process does the similarity between /k/ and /g/ cause children to make errors?

One point at which errors like *g* for /k/ may happen is in the process of analyzing a spoken word into phonemes. In order to construct a spelling for a word, children must attend to the sound of the word, specifically to the individual phonemes within it. As discussed in Chapter 1, this is difficult for some young children. Although children implicitly use phonemes when they talk and understand, they have little explicit awareness of phonemes. In one of my previous studies, I found that children sometimes make voicing confusions when they analyze spoken words into phonemes (Treiman, 1985b, Exp. 2). In that study, five-and-a-half-year-old children were asked whether spoken nonsense syllables such as /sɑp/, /vᵘul/, and /zⁱir/ began with a target phoneme such as /s/. I made sure that the children correctly repeated each syllable before making their judgments. Thus, if children say that /zⁱir/ begins with /s/, the error does *not* reflect mispronunciation of the syllable. I asked whether children made more errors on syllables whose initial phonemes were similar to the target phoneme than on syllables whose initial phonemes were less similar to the target. The correlation between number of errors and measures of phonemic similarity was not significant, perhaps because of the relatively small number of syllables in the experiment. However, the error rate was highest when the first phoneme of the syllable differed from the target phoneme only in voicing. For instance, the children mistakenly said that /z̆ir/ began with /s/ one third of the time. Similar voicing confusions were also found in another experiment (Treiman, 1985b, Exp. 3). These results suggest one reason why children sometimes misspell /k/ as *g*. When attempting to analyze a spoken word like *care* into phonemes, children may abstract out the phoneme /g/ instead of the phoneme /k/. Consequently, they may use *g* as the first letter of the word.

Another phase of the spelling process during which confusions among similar-sounding phonemes may occur is in memory. As children analyze a spoken word into phonemes, they must place the phonemes into short-term memory while deciding how to spell each one. Research by Eimas (1975) on six-year-olds' short-term memory for stop consonant-vowel syllables shows that memory confusions tend to involve phonemes that sound similar to one another. Children are especially likely to confuse phonemes that differ only in voicing. Thus, even if children correctly analyze *care* into phonemes, they may misremember /k/ as /g/ and consequently spell it as *g*.

Finally, confusions among similar-sounding phonemes may occur as children apply phoneme-grapheme correspondences. Correspondences like those between /k/ and *k* and /g/ and *g* may be next to each other, in some sense, in children's long-term memory stores. As a result, confusions may be more likely between *g* and *k* than between, say, *g* and *m*.

Thus, the process of generating a spelling from a word's phonological form has at least three steps. First, children must analyze the spoken word into smaller units. For children to benefit most from an alphabetic writing system, these units will usually be phonemes. Second, children must place the units into short-term memory. Third, children must assign a spelling to each unit. These processes may be carried out in sequence for the word as a whole. Alternatively, students may analyze and spell one part of a word before tackling the next part of the word. Errors may arise at each step—analyzing the spoken word into smaller units, remembering the identity and order of the units, or choosing a spelling for each unit. In each case, errors that involve similar-sounding phonemes—especially phonemes that differ only in voicing—are particularly common.

Children's Phonological Systems

When spelling, children attempt to represent the phonological forms of words. By studying children's spellings, then, psycholinguists may learn about their phonological systems.

The present findings on children's illegal substitutions suggest that children tacitly categorize the consonants of their language according to their similarities and differences. Although normal first graders readily distinguish among consonant phonemes, they consider some consonants to be similar to one another and other consonants to be less similar. Consonants that share manner of articulation and consonants that share place of articulation are particularly similar. With stops and fricatives, the closest pairs are those that are alike in *both* manner and place and that differ only in voicing.

Thus, part of language development lies in coming to recognize the similarities among phonemes that one has previously learned to treat as different. Such a system of similarities is in place by at least first grade, and probably sooner (see Read, 1975). Moreover, first graders' judgments of the relations among consonants largely resemble those of adults. Although there are some differences (Read, 1975, pp. 139–143), I would not have found a relation between *children's* illegal consonant substitutions and *adults'* ratings of phoneme similarity if children's systems differed greatly from adults'.

Evidence about which phonemes children consider to be similar and different is difficult to obtain in other ways. One cannot ask children to rate hundreds of pairs of syllables for similarity, as one can ask adults to do. Experimental procedures *have* been devised to tap children's phonological judgments, but these procedures are limited by children's short attention span, difficulty in following instructions, and other factors (see Read, 1973, 1975). Children's spellings, therefore, can be very useful in the study of children's phonological systems.

The Teaching of Spelling

In this book, I found it necessary to move from the level of whole words to the level of phonemes when analyzing the first graders' spellings. Similarly, teachers must move below the whole-word level when examining their students' spellings. If teachers view their pupils' spelling errors at the level of phonemes, they will realize that many errors reveal a deeper knowledge than appears on the surface. For example, even if a student has misspelled a word, the student may have correctly spelled some of the phonemes. Even if a student has spelled a phoneme incorrectly, the error may be a possible spelling of the phoneme in another word, one letter of the phoneme's conventional spelling, or a spelling of a similar-sounding phoneme. All misspellings are not alike. By analyzing the errors that their students make, teachers can get a good idea of where the children are in the process of learning to spell. They can get a good idea of what instruction the students need in order to develop further.

The Classification of Spelling Errors

Spelling errors have traditionally been classified orthographically, by reference to the conventional spelling of the word. For instance, a child who misspells *pizza* as PEZZA is said to have substituted *e* for *i*. A child who misspells *pizza* as PIZZ is said to have omitted *a*. The results in this chapter suggest that any classification system that is based solely on words' conventional spellings will fail to capture important features of children's errors. Thus, it is wrong to say that children have a tendency to replace *i* with *e*. When the intended phoneme is /i/, *e* substitutions for *i are* frequent, as in PEZZA. When the intended phoneme is /ai/, however, *e* substitutions for *i* are rare. To understand children's errors, one must consider the phonemes that the letters represent, not just the letters themselves. One must view the errors phonologically, not just orthographically.

If errors are to be viewed from a phonological perspective, how should they be classified? It is often suggested that errors be divided into two categories–legal and illegal. In this chapter and in Chapter 2, I followed this suggestion. Although the distinction between legal errors and illegal errors is useful, it also has some serious problems.

One problem is that the legal/illegal division is based on the relations between phonemes and graphemes in the conventional writing system. However, children who use a conventional phoneme-grapheme correspondence do not necessarily know any of the words in which this correspondence occurs. Consider the error NAK for *neck.* Although *a* does spell /ɛ/ in words such as *Mary,* the first graders substituted *a* for /ɛ/ at a high rate, much higher than expected given the rate at which *a* is used to spell /ɛ/ in English and other factors. According to the regression presented earlier in this chapter, *a* substitutions for /ɛ/ should have occurred at a rate of 11.3%. In fact, they occurred at a rate of 54.5%, meaning that over half of the students' errors on /ɛ/s that were not spelled with *e* were *a.* As I discuss in more detail in Chapter 4, children spell /ɛ/ as *a* because /ɛ/ is similar to other phonemes that are spelled as *a,* namely /e/ and /æ/. Thus, children's phonological knowledge suggests the use of *a* for /ɛ/. This spelling does *not* usually occur because children know that /ɛ/ may be spelled with *a* in English.

Another substitution that is classified as legal but that may not reflect children's knowledge of conventional phoneme-grapheme correspondences is *d* for /t/, as in WODER for *water.* Children make such errors not because they know that /t/ may be spelled with *d* (as in *used* [*to*]) but because the /t/ of *water* sounds similar to /d/ (see Chapter 5). Thus, children who substitute *a* for /ɛ/ and *d* for /t/ do not necessarily know that /ɛ/ may be spelled with *a* and that /t/ may be spelled with *d.* These substitutions reflect not orthographic knowledge but knowledge of the phonological properties of /ɛ/ and /t/.

In other cases, guessing may yield a substitution that is scored as legal. This is particularly true for /ə/. Any spelling of /ə/ with a single vowel letter or with *y* counts as a legal substitution since all these spellings occur in some English word. A student who guesses randomly from among the vowel letters is guaranteed to produce a legal substitution for /ə/. Thus, although BIT for *but* is scored as legal, children who make this error do not necessarily know that /ə/ is sometimes spelled with *i.*

The concept of illegal substitutions is also problematic. The term "illegal" implies that the substitution is haphazard or unmotivated. However, this is far from true. Illegal substitutions *are* systematic in many ways. They often involve similar-sounding phonemes, such as /g/ and /k/. They sometimes reflect partial knowledge of common digraphs such as *th.* That over 70% of the variance in illegal consonant substitutions could be explained by linguistic factors shows that illegal substitutions are by no means haphazard.

Thus, the classification of spellings as legal or illegal does not always reflect what is going on in children's minds. The terminology may prevent us from appreciating the knowledge that lies behind even "illegal" errors. These problems apply to the present study as well as to other studies that have classified errors as legal or illegal. To understand why children spell the way they do, one must go beyond a simple, mechanical distinction between legal and illegal spellings. Toward this end, Chapters 4 and 5 take a more qualitative approach to the study of children's spelling. Chapter 4 focuses on vowels and Chapter 5 discusses consonants.

Notes

1. I assume here that the probability of a grapheme given the phoneme in the conventional spellings of the words in the collection reflects the relations between sounds and spellings in the words to which children have been exposed. This assumption is reasonable in light of Chapter 2's finding that the words that the first graders attempted to spell tend to be words that occur frequently in reading materials designed for children.

2. For /ʒ/, Snow's results on the word *garage* were excluded from the calculation of percentage correct. As Snow states, it is probably unreasonable to consider the pronunciation of this word with final /dʒ/ as an error.

3. The adult study was used because I know of no comparable rating studies with young children.

4. A distinction between lateral and nonlateral is needed to distinguish between /r/ and /l/; this distinction was not considered in the present analysis.

5. The use of phonemes in coding means that *tt* for /θ/ was coded as a substitution of /t/ for /θ/ even though it does not use just the first letter of the digraph spelling. However, such errors were rare.

6. An exception is that *e* for /e/ was not counted as legal for Read since none of his subjects apparently spoke a dialect in which words like *leg* are pronounced with /e/.

7. All omissions were placed in this category even if, as with the omission of the first vowel of *K-mart,* they might have been correct spellings. This was done because Read did not indicate the conventional spellings of the words that the children attempted.

8. This explains why the misspelled words in Read's collection were longer than the misspelled words in my collection. As shown in Chapter 2, legal spelling errors that are difficult for adults to interpret tend to represent short words. Many of the errors that Read eliminated because of uncertainty about which word the child meant to write may, therefore, have been spellings of short words.

9. The phonological differences between vowels and consonants may be an *indirect* cause of children's difficulties with vowels. In the history of English, vowel pronunciations have changed more than consonant pronunciations, leading to a greater diversity of spellings for vowels.

4

Vowels

In this chapter, I focus on vowel phonemes. Because a study that is strictly based on a distinction between legal and illegal spellings has some serious problems, this chapter employs a more descriptive and qualitative approach. I discuss how the first graders in the study spelled each vowel phoneme of English. What do the children's spellings reveal about their knowledge of the English writing system and about their knowledge of spoken English?

The analyses reported in Chapter 3 uncovered some factors that affect how children spell phonemes. For the children in this study, the most important of these factors was exposure to phoneme-grapheme correspondences in printed words: Children used frequent correspondences more often than infrequent correspondences. Another factor was letter names: Children used correspondences in which the name of the grapheme contained the phoneme more often than correspondences in which the name of the grapheme did not contain the phoneme. A third factor was formal teaching: Children were more often correct on correspondences that were taught in the classroom than on correspondences that were not directly taught. In this chapter, I ask how these and other factors influenced the children's spelling of specific vowel phonemes.

Sometimes, the children's choices of spellings for vowel phonemes mirrored the choices embodied in the English writing system. The children used the spellings that occur most frequently in English, whether or not these spellings were explicitly taught. In other cases, the children's choices did not mirror the conventional ones. There are two different ways in which this occurred. First, the children sometimes used a spelling that is illegal in the conventional system; that is, a grapheme that never represents the phoneme. In these cases, something other than knowledge of conventional spelling must explain the "invented" spelling. I ask what the reasons are. In discussing these illegal substitutions, I have chosen, somewhat arbitrarily, a cut-off of 2.5%. Illegal substitutions that occurred at rates of 2.5% or more out of all spellings are singled out for discussion. A second way in which children's choices sometimes failed to mirror those of conventional English was in overuse of particular spellings. When children used a legal spelling more often than expected given its frequency in English, something other than knowledge of conventional spelling must be responsible. I ask what this "something" is. In this chapter and the following one, I employ binomial tests to diagnose overuse of legal spellings. It was necessary to perform several binomial tests for each vowel phoneme, since all vowel phonemes had more than one possible spelling. Therefore, the .05 significance level was divided by the number of tests performed for each phoneme. Only results that met this more stringent level are reported as significant.

Children's Spellings of Vowel Phonemes

In this section, I discuss how the children spelled each vowel phoneme. The reader may find it helpful to refer to the vowel diagram of Figure 1.4 when reading this section.

/i/

As Appendix I shows, the most common spelling of /i/ in my collection was *e*. For example, /i/ is spelled as *e* in *he* and *rodeo*. Likewise, the children's most frequent spelling of /i/ was *e*. The children used *e* in 62.2% of all their attempts to spell /i/; the figure was 52.0% for the conventional spellings of the same words. The difference was statistically significant ($p < .001$ by a binomial test). In other words, the children used *e* more often than expected given its frequency as a standard spelling. Table 4.1 shows some cases in which children used *e* in place of other spellings of /i/.

Why do children so often spell /i/ as *e*? The most likely reason is their knowledge of letter names. First graders know that the name of *e* is /i/. In searching for a way to symbolize /i/, children often choose *e* because they associate /i/ with *e*.

Table 4.1. Errors Based on Children's Knowledge of the Names of Vowel Letters

Phoneme	Error	Examples
/i/	*e*	HAPE for *happy* PESUE for *pizza* SEPS for *sheeps* [sic] CEG for *king*
/e/	*a*	BRTA for *birthday* THA for *they* RAN for *rain* WAZ for *weighs*
/ai/	*i*	BIK for *bike* MI for *my* NIT for *night* CIS for *cries*
/o/	*o*	BLO for *blow* BOT for *boat* PLO for *pillow* TOR for *tore*
/u/	*u*	FLU for *flew* FUD for *food* SUP for *soup* LUS for *loose*

Overuse of *e* for /i/ was widespread among the first graders. Almost 90% of the children who attempted /i/ produced at least one wrong *e* spelling. Among those children who attempted at least four words in which /i/ was symbolized with a letter other than *e*, *e* errors occurred at rates of up to 70%.

After *e*, the children's second most common spelling of /i/ was *i*. Surprisingly, *i* was also the second most common standard spelling of /i/ in my collection of words. In Hoosier speech, as in general American speech, /i/ is written with *i* in words such as *encyclopedia* and *pizza*. In addition, people from Indiana pronounce words such as *king* and *think* with /i/. These /i/s result from a process called *raising*, by which /ɪ/ changes to /i/ before /ŋ/. The vowel is written with *i*, making *i* a common spelling of /i/ in Hoosier speech. The students' use of *i* for /i/ reflects their knowledge of printed words such as *king* and *think*, together with their dialect.

To grasp the effect of dialect on the children's spelling of /i/, compare children's performance on words like *king*, in which *i* corresponds to /i/, with their performance on words like *him*, in which *i* corresponds to /ɪ/. These two types of words are spelled with the same vowel letter. Many Americans pronounce them with the same vowel phoneme. The children in this study, however, pronounced the words differently. Their spellings showed corresponding differences. The children relatively often (22.5% of the time) replaced the *i* of words like *king* with *e*. They produced errors like CENG for *king* and MORNEG for *morning*. These errors make sense given that the children pronounced the words with /i/ and given that /i/ is more often spelled with *e* than with *i*. The substitution of *e* for *i* was significantly less common on words like *him* than on words like *king* (11.0% versus 22.5%; $p <$ .001 by a chi-square test). In addition, the children more often produced the correct *i* for words like *him* than for words like *king* (74.2% versus 38.5%; $p < .001$ by a chi-square test). Together, these results suggest that the children's dialect affected their spellings of vowels.

Although the students often misspelled the vowels of words like *king*, they were more likely to use the correct *i* than the incorrect *e* (38.5% versus 22.5%; $p < .005$ by a chi-square test). Thus, although the children's dialect caused them some difficulty on the vowels of words like *king*, they were beginning to overcome this difficulty and to spell the vowels correctly.

The dialect errors just described were widespread among the pupils in this study. Of the children who attempted one or more words containing an /i/ that was spelled as *i*, 65% replaced *i* with *e* at least once. Among children who attempted at least four words of this kind, the rate of *e* errors ranged from 0% to 80%. Several of the children produced no correct *i* spellings at all. For example, Tony produced errors such as THEC for *think* and KENG for *king*. The only time he spelled /i/ with something other than *e* was in LOWRUN for *luring*.

Because *i* is used for /i/ in words like *pizza*, the use of *i* in place of other spellings of /i/ is a legal substitution. Thus, KIP is a legal spelling of *keep* and FIT is a legal spelling of *feet*. These errors provide a good example of how adults may fail to recognize the logic behind a child's error. Understandably, adults read KIP as /kɪp/. They may not realize that KIP is a reasonable attempt to spell *keep*. From the child's point of view, however, /i/ is spelled with *i* in words like *king* and *pizza* and so might also be spelled with *i* in *keep*.

After *e* and *i*, the next most common standard spelling of /i/ was *y*. In English, there is a rule that allows one to choose between *y* and *i*. Usually, *y* occurs at the end of morphemes (e.g., *happy, babysit*), while *i* occurs elsewhere. In Chapter 6, I ask whether the children appreciated this pattern.

/e/

In my collection, the most common conventional spelling of /e/ was *a*, as in *a* and *baby*. This was also the children's most common choice. However, the students used *a* significantly more often than expected given its frequency in the standard spellings of the words. Of the children's spellings of /e/, 60.5% were *a*, as compared with 47.5% for the conventional spellings ($p < .001$ by a binomial test). Table 4.1 shows some errors in which children substituted *a* for other spellings of /e/. The use of *a* for /e/, like the use of *e* for /i/ discussed earlier, reflects the children's knowledge of letter names. In searching for a way to spell /e/, children often chose *a* because they associate /e/ with *a*.

Letter-name spellings of /e/ were common among the first graders. Almost 90% of the children who attempted at least one /e/ that was symbolized with a letter other than *a* produced one or more incorrect *a*. The error rate varied greatly: Among children with four or more attempts, the rate of *a* errors ranged from 0% to 75%.

The *a* spelling of /e/ was not taught in the pupils' phonics book, nor was it included in the words on their spelling lists. The phonics textbook stressed, instead, that /e/ is often spelled with *a* followed by final *e*, as in *tape*. Single *a* was taught as a spelling of /æ/, as in *tap*. Despite the instruction that the children received, they often misspelled words like *tape* as TAP.

The children's second and third choices for /e/—*a* followed by final *e* and *ay*, respectively—were also the second and third most common spellings of /e/ in the words of my collection. The children's fourth choice, however, was a spelling that never occurred for /e/ in the words of the collection—*ae*.[1] The children used *ae* in 2.9% of their attempts to represent /e/. Examples include AET for *ate*, SAEC for *steak*, and BAEBSTET for *babysitted*.

The *ae* spelling of /e/ was not widespread. Of the students who attempted /e/, a little over a quarter produced *ae;* the rate of these errors among children who spelled /e/ four or more times never exceeded 12%. However, the fact that different children independently chose the same spelling suggests that it is more than a random error. Charles Read also observed some *ae* spellings for /e/ among preschoolers.

Why did some children spell /e/ as *ae*? An answer to this question is suggested by the diphthongal nature of /e/. This vowel begins with a sound that is similar to /ɛ/ and moves toward a high front vowel. Children may add an *e* to the *a* that is suggested by the letter name in an attempt to represent the diphthongal nature of the vowel. Actually, the final part of /e/ is closer to /ɪ/ than to /i/. The *e* of *ae* seems to be an attempt to represent /i/. It may be that the *target* of the glide—the phoneme toward which it moves, but does not reach—is /i/. Children may use *e* to indicate this. Further support for this analysis of the *ae* error is provided later in this chapter, where I show that the children produced illegal spellings ending in *e* for the other diphthongs with similar offglides, /ai/ and /oi/.[2]

Other legal spellings of /e/ that occurred at low rates were *e, ey, ea,* and *ai.* The inclusion of *e* as a legal spelling of /e/ deserves comment. Words such as *egg* and *legs* are often pronounced with /e/ rather than /ɛ/ in Hoosier speech due to the process of vowel raising mentioned earlier. In this dialect, therefore, /e/ may be spelled as *e.*

Although /e/ has several possible spellings, it is sometimes possible to predict the correct one. The digraph ending in *y, ay,* typically occurs before vowels and at the ends of morphemes (e.g., *mayor, birthday*). The digraph ending in *i, ai,* generally appears elsewhere (e.g., *rain*). Children's appreciation of this pattern in the case of /e/ and other vowels is discussed in Chapter 6.

/ai/

The most common spelling of /ai/ in my collection was *i.* Correspondingly, *i* was also children's most common spelling. However, the students used *i* significantly more often than expected based on its frequency in the standard system (62.4% versus 53.7%; $p < .001$ by a binomial test). Table 4.1 shows some examples in which children used *i* in place of other spellings of /ai/. Children pick *i* to spell /ai/ because the name of the letter *i* is /ai/. Children's knowledge of letter names makes them likely to choose *i* when deciding how to spell /ai/.

Incorrect letter-name spellings of /ai/ were widespread among the first graders. Over 80% of the students who attempted /ai/s that were spelled with letters other than *i* produced at least one wrong *i* spelling. The error rate, among children with four or more attempts, ranged from 0% to 75%.

The children's second and third most common spellings of /ai/—*y* and *i* followed by final *e,* respectively—were also the second and third most common standard spellings. The children's fourth choice for /ai/ was *ie.* Although this spelling did not appear in the children's phonics book or spelling lists, it does occur in words like *fries.* However, the children used *ie* significantly more often than expected based on its frequency as a standard spelling (1.6% versus 0.4%; $p < .001$ by a binomial test). Examples include BIEK for *bike,* SGIE for *sky,* and LIEKT for *liked.*

Although children's percentage of *ie* spellings of /ai/ was below my cut-off of 2.5%, I will briefly consider the reasons for this error. Some children may use *ie* in an attempt to represent the diphthongal nature of /ai/. The diphthong /ai/ begins with a low central vowel and ends with a glide toward a high front vowel. Children may add an *e* to the *i* suggested by the letter name in an attempt to indicate the diphthongal nature of /ai/, just as they sometimes added an *e* to the *a* spelling of /e/ in an attempt to indicate the diphthongal nature of that vowel.[3]

/o/

In the standard spellings of my collection, /o/ was most often spelled as *o.* Likewise, *o* was children's most common spelling of /o/. The students used *o* 59.5% of the time, significantly exceeding the 42.2% rate of *o* spellings in the conventional forms of the words ($p < .001$ by a binomial test). Table 4.1 shows examples of the children's incorrect *o* spellings. Children overuse *o* for /o/ because *o* is the name of the phoneme /o/. As in the other cases that I have examined, the knowledge of letter names that children bring with them to school affects their spelling.

Overuse of *o* for /o/ was common among the first graders. Almost 80% of the children who attempted /o/s that were not spelled with *o* produced *o* errors. The rate of these errors, among children with four or more attempts, ranged from 0% to 56%.

Besides *o,* children's other common spellings of /o/ were the legal *ow* and *o* followed by final *e.* No other legal spelling of /o/ was significantly overused with respect to its frequency in standard spelling and no illegal substitution occurred at a rate of 2.5% or more.

/u/

The most common standard spelling of /u/ was *o,* as in *do.* In second place was *oo,* as in *food.* The students' first and second choices for /u/ mirrored the choices of the conventional system: Their most frequent spelling was *o* and their second most frequent spelling was *oo.*

At this point, the children's choices diverged from the choices embodied in standard English. The first graders used *u* significantly more often than expected (5.5% versus 1.7%; $p < .001$ by a binomial test). About a quarter of the children produced at least one *u* spelling for /u/s that were spelled with graphemes other than *u.* However, *u* errors were quite frequent in some children, occurring 60% of the time in one child. Table 4.1 shows some instances in which children used *u* in place of other spellings of /u/. The correspondence between /u/ and *u* was not included in the children's phonics book or spelling lists, so the *u* error does not reflect formal teaching. Rather, it reflects children's knowledge of letter names. First graders know that the name of *u,* /ju/, contains /u/. As a result, they sometimes spell /u/ with *u.*

In addition to overusing one legal spelling of /u/, the students produced one illegal spelling at a rate of over 2.5%. This illegal spelling, *ow,* occurred 3.4% of the time. Examples are DOW for *do,* BLOW for *blue,* and NOW for *new.* The use of *ow* for /u/ was not widespread: Less than 20% of the children who attempted /u/ produced *ow* and no child with four or more attempts produced these errors more than 25% of the time. However, *ow* seems to be more than a random error.

Children may use *ow* for /u/ because *ow* represents both /o/ and /au/ in conventional English. Both /o/ and /au/ are back vowels with offglides in the direction of /u/. As such, both are similar to /u/. The results of Fox (1983) suggest that adults are sensitive to the similarity among /u/, /o/, and /au/. In Fox's study, /o/ and /au/ were in the top third of vowels in their similarity to /u/, with /u/ and /o/ being rated as more similar than /u/ and /au/.[4] Students may use *ow* for /u/ because of the similarity between /u/ and /o/ and, to a lesser extent, the similarity between /u/ and /au/.

/ɑ/

The phoneme /ɑ/ is pronounced fairly far back in the mouth, like /o/ and /u/. Unlike /o/ and /u/, /ɑ/ is not rounded. In the conventional spellings of my collection, /ɑ/ was most often symbolized with *o,* as in *got* and *fox.* Its second most common spelling was *a*. Examples are *garden* and *water,* the first syllables of which were considered to contain /ɑ/ for these children. The children's preferred spellings for /ɑ/, *o* and *a,* mirrored those of the standard system. Because the *a* spelling of /ɑ/ did not appear in the children's phonics book or spelling lists, the children's reading experience—specifically, their exposure to words like *garden* and *water*—must have affected their spelling.

The children produced two nonstandard spellings for /ɑ/ at rates of 2.5% or more. These were *i* and *u*. Table 4.2 shows examples of these errors.

The students used *i* for /ɑ/ 5.1% of the time. To understand why they made this error, recall that *i* was the children's most common spelling of /ai/, in part because the name of *i* is /ai/. The vowels /ɑ/ and /ai/ are similar to one another. The diphthong /ai/ begins with a vowel that is low like /ɑ/ but more central. It ends with an offglide in the direction of /i/. The similarity between /ɑ/ and the first or steady-state part of the /ai/ diphthong may lead children to group /ɑ/ with /ai/. As a result, children sometimes symbolize /ɑ/ with a letter that is appropriate for /ai/, namely *i*.[5]

About a third of the pupils who attempted /ɑ/ produced *i* errors. One child used *i* for half his spellings of /ɑ/, writing *Mom* correctly several times but otherwise representing /ɑ/ as *i*. The other children who spelled *o* four or more times used *i* less than 20% of the time.

The other nonstandard spelling of /ɑ/ to be discussed was *u*. The children spelled /ɑ/ as *u* 3.0% of the time. Conventional English never uses this spelling. Why did the children sometimes do so? The children may have picked *u* for /ɑ/ because *u* often represents a sound that is similar to /ɑ/. As I will discuss presently, *u* was the most common spelling of stressed /ə/ when it was not part of a syllabic liquid. The vowels /ə/ and /ɑ/ are similar to one another. Both are low, nonfront vowels (/ə/ being relatively central and /ɑ/ somewhat farther back); both differ from the other nonfront vowels of English in that they are not rounded. Indeed, adults rate /ə/ and /ɑ/ as quite similar to one another (Fox, 1983; Singh & Woods, 1971). The similarity between /ɑ/ and /ə/ may explain why children sometimes spell /ɑ/ with *u*. However, these spellings were not widespread. They occurred among less than 20% of the children and never at a rate of more than 20%.

/ɔ/

In the words that the students chose to spell, *o* was the most common spelling of /ɔ/, as in *dog*. Second was *a,* as in *all*. Children's first and second choices for /ɔ/

Table 4.2. Examples Containing Misspellings of /a/

Error	Examples
i	DIL for *doll* SIPN for *shopping* WITR for *water*
u	FURMUR for *farmer* FUMR for *farmer* SUP for *shopping*

Table 4.3. Examples Containing Misspellings of /ɔ/

Error	Examples
oo	FOOR for *for*
	BOOL for *ball*
	OOLWIAS for *always*
	BEIKOOS for *because*
ol	SOL for *saw*
	SIDEWOLK for *sidewalk*
	GRAPOL for *grandpa*

mirrored those of standard English. Their most frequent spelling was *o* and their second most frequent spelling was *a*. Children used *a* for /ɔ/ even though this spelling was not taught in their phonics book or spelling lists.

The children's third choice was a grapheme that never occurs for /ɔ/ in English—*oo*. This spelling constituted 4.6% of all the children's spellings of /ɔ/. Examples appear in Table 4.3. Although the use of *oo* for /ɔ/ was not widespread, occurring among only 15% of children who attempted /ɔ/, one child produced this error over one-third of the time. *Oo* for /ɔ/, then, is more than a random error. Why do some children adopt *oo* for /ɔ/? An answer is suggested by the fact that *oo* is the most common spelling of /ʊ/. The vowels /ɔ/ and /ʊ/ are similar in that both are rounded back vowels. The adults studied by Fox (1983) rated /ʊ/ as among the most similar vowels to /ɔ/, although those studied by Singh and Woods (1971) did not. Children may be sensitive to the similarity between /ʊ/ and /ɔ/ and may use *oo* for /ɔ/ for this reason.

One other nonstandard spelling for /ɔ/ occurred more than 2.5% of the time— *ol*. The first graders used *ol* to represent /ɔ/ 3.0% of the time. Examples are shown in Table 4.3. This error may reflect the *velarization* of /l/ that takes place after vowels. Velarization refers to the fact that, after a vowel, /l/ is pronounced with the back of the tongue raised. In this way, it is similar to /u/. The spelling of /ɔ/ as *ol* may reflect the similarity between /ɔ/ and /o/ or /ɑ/ plus /u/.

/au/

Among the words of the collection, /au/ was most often spelled as *ou,* as in *mountain* and *about*. The children's most common spelling of /au/ was *a*, as Table 4.4 shows. The use of *a* for /au/ may be considered an illegal substitution, since /au/ is never symbolized as *a* in English. No spelling of /au/ among the words of the collection even contains *a*. However, *a* for /au/ was the most frequent illegal spelling for any vowel in this study, occurring at a rate of 18.0%.

Why did the students use the unconventional *a* more often than they used any of the conventional spellings of /au/? An answer is suggested by the fact that *a* is the most common spelling of /æ/ in English. The vowel /au/ is a diphthong whose initial or steady-state portion is a low vowel intermediate between /æ/ and /ɑ/. Children may use *a* for /au/ in an attempt to represent the initial portion of /au/. Children apparently categorize the first part of the diphthong as being similar to /æ/ and therefore use *a* to spell it.[6]

Table 4.4. Examples Containing Misspellings of /au/

Error	Examples
a	KA for *cow*
	DAN for *down*
	ABAT for *about*
	HAS for *house*
o	FOD for *found*
	ABOT for *about*
	HOS for *house*
al	MALS for *mouse*
	ALT for *out*
	CAL for *cow*
ao	AOT for *out*
	PAOCH for *pouch*
	FIRHAOS for *firehouse*

The use of *a* for /au/ was widespread among the first graders. Over half of the children who attempted /au/ produced one or more *a* errors. The rate of these errors among children with four or more attempts to spell /au/ ranged from 0% to 40%.

Although *a* was the students' most common illegal substitution for /au/, four other illegal spellings occurred at rates exceeding 2.5%. The first of these was *o*. The *o* spelling of /au/ was used 9.9% of the time and by about one-third of the children. Table 4.4 shows some examples. There are two possible reasons for this error. The first stems from the diphthongal nature of /au/. Because the steady-state portion of /au/ is intermediate between /æ/ and /ɑ/, children may sometimes use *a* and sometimes use *o* to spell it. A second reason why children may pick *o* for /au/ is that all spellings of /au/ begin with *o*. Children may have seen graphemes such as *ou* and *ow* for /au/ and, in line with their tendency to omit the second letters of digraphs, reproduced these spellings as *o*.

Other illegal substitutions for /au/ were *aw* and *al*. The children used *aw* on 6.8% of their attempts to spell /au/ and *al* on 5.6% of their attempts. Examples appear in Table 4.4. Less than 20% of the children who attempted /au/ produced *aw*, but one child did so on five of his seven attempts to spell this vowel. Similarly, *al* errors were produced by a small percentage of the children but were used more than once by these children.

Why did some children use *aw* and *al* to represent /au/? One possibility is that *aw* and *al* may stand for /ɔ/, as in *saw* and *walk.* The phonemes /ɔ/ and /au/ are similar to one another in that both are back vowels with some degree of rounding. (Rounding occurs during the offglide of /au/.) The adults studied by Fox (1983) considered /ɔ/ to be the most similar vowel to /au/. If children do too, they may extend spellings that are appropriate for /ɔ/ to /au/.

In the case of *al* for /au/, there is another possible reason for the error. The sequence of phonemes /æl/ is similar to the single phoneme /au/. This is because, as mentioned earlier, /l/ is velarized after a vowel. Because the raised position of the back of the tongue for syllable-final /l/ resembles the tongue position for /u/, /æl/ is similar to /æ/ followed by /u/, or /au/. Children may therefore symbolize /au/ with a sequence of letters that is appropriate for /æl/.

Finally, the children spelled /au/ as *ao* 3.1% of the time (see Table 4.4). In the conventional spellings in my collection, *ao* is never used for /au/ or any other vowel. Why did the children produce this spelling? Children may use *ao* in an attempt to represent the diphthongal nature of /au/. They may employ *a* to represent the first part of diphthong, as in the *a* spellings discussed previously. They may add *o,* which is their most common spelling of /u/, to indicate that the diphthong has an offglide in the direction of /u/.

/oi/

In the standard spellings of my collection, /oi/ was most often spelled with *oy,* as in *boy.* This was also the children's most common spelling. However, the students produced two illegal spellings at rates of 6.8% each—*o* and *oe.* In the case of /oi/, which the children attempted less than any other vowel, a 6.8% rate corresponds to only three spellings. Nonetheless, I may ask why some children use *o* and *oe* to spell /oi/.

The use of *o,* as in TOS for *toys* and CON for *coin, may* be an attempt to represent the first part of the /oi/ diphthong. This diphthong begins with a steady-state portion that is similar to /o/. Alternatively, children may use *o* because they have seen words like *boy* and *coin* which contain digraph spellings of /oi/. Children sometimes omit the second letters of these digraphs when trying to reproduce them.

The *oe* error, as in BOE for *boy,* provides stronger evidence that some children analyze /oi/ into two parts. These children may use *o* to symbolize the first part of the diphthong. They may add *e* to show that the diphthong ends with a glide in the direction of /i/. The *oe* spelling of /oi/ is similar to the *ao* spelling of /au/ in that both are attempts to represent the two parts of a dipthong.

/ɪ/

The vowel /ɪ/ is generally spelled with *i,* as in *him* and *it.* Likewise, the first graders most often spelled /ɪ/ with *i.* The second most frequent spelling of /ɪ/ in my collection was *e.* In Hoosier speech, words such as *men* and *end* contain /ɪ/ rather than /ɛ/ due to the process of vowel raising mentioned earlier. Thus, there are a number of words in which /ɪ/ is spelled with *e.* Other dialects contain only a few words of this kind, such as *pretty.* Not surprisingly, the children's second most common spelling of /ɪ/ was *e.*

Because *e* symbolizes /ɪ/ in words such as *men* and *pretty,* the use of *e* for /ɪ/ is a legal error. Table 4.5 shows examples of these errors. Although such errors may be hard for adults to decipher, they probably reflect children's knowledge that /ɪ/ is sometimes spelled as *e.* Children reason that, because the /ɪ/ of *men* is spelled with *e,* the /ɪ/ of *if* may also be so spelled. As a result, they sometimes write *if* as EF.

To study the effect of dialect on the children's spelling of /ɪ/, we may compare their performance on words like *men* and words like *met.* Many speakers of American English pronounce these two words with the same vowel, /ɛ/. These speakers expect the two words to be spelled with the same vowel, as they are. Hoosiers, however, pronounce the first word with /ɪ/ and the second word with /ɛ/. Because /ɪ/ is

Table 4.5. Examples Containing Misspellings of /ɪ/

Error	Examples
e	EF for *if*
	HES for *his*
	GEV for *give*
	DENNRE for *dinner*
i	WIN for *when*
	WIT for *went*
	INDE for *ending*
	SINTR for *center*
a	KALR for *killer*
	FRAND for *friend*
	AF for *if*

more often spelled with *i* than *e,* Hoosier children should often misspell *men* as MIN. They should be less likely to misspell *met* as MIT, since /ɛ/ is never spelled with *i.* Confirming these predictions, incorrect *i* spellings occurred 36.9% of the time on words like *men,* resulting in errors like those shown in Table 4.5. Incorrect *i* spellings occurred only 5.1% of the time on words like *met* ($p < .001$ for the difference by a chi-square test). Moreover, correct *e* spellings were more frequent on words like *met* than words like *men* (52.5% versus 33.5%; $p < .001$ by a chi-square test). These results suggest that children's dialect affects their spelling of vowels.

For words like *men,* incorrect *i* spellings, which are consistent with the students' dialect, were not significantly more common than correct *e* spellings (36.9% versus 33.5%; difference not significant by a chi-square test). If the children knew nothing about the correct *e* spelling, *i* spellings should have predominated. Apparently, the conventional spelling, *men,* was beginning to replace *min,* the spelling that fits with the children's dialect.

Dialect errors like MIN for *men* occurred among a majority of the children in this study. Sixty percent of the students who attempted /ɪ/s that were spelled with *e* produced at least one *i* error. The rate of these errors, among children with four or more attempts, ranged up to 80%. Indeed, some of the children produced no correct *e* spellings at all, even on common words. For example, Tisha spelled *when* as W during October, omitting the vowel altogether. Later in the school year, she spelled this word as WIN. She also spelled *went* as WIT.

After *i* and *e,* the children's third most frequent spelling of /ɪ/ (not counting omissions) was *a.* Occasionally *a* is used to spell /ɪ/, as in *any.* However, the children used *a* significantly more often than expected given its frequency in conventional English (5.1% versus 0.5%, $p < .001$ by a binomial test). Examples appear in Table 4.5. The overuse of *a* for /ɪ/ was fairly widespread. Almost half of the children who attempted /ɪ/ produced at least one *a* error, although none of the children who attempted /ɪ/ four or more times produced *a* spellings at rates greater than 30%.

Why might children overuse *a* for /ɪ/? The answer does not lie in formal teaching. The *a* spelling of /ɪ/ did not appear in the pupils' phonics book or the words on their spelling lists. Rather, the overuse of *a* for /ɪ/ may reflect the link between the letter *a* and the phonemes /æ/ and /e/. The letter *a* is the most common spelling of both /æ/ and /e/. The link between *a* and /e/ is further strengthened by the fact that the *a* is named /e/. The unrounded front vowels /æ/ and /e/ are rated as similar to the unrounded front vowel /ɪ/ (Fox, 1983; Singh & Woods, 1971). Children may use *a* for /ɪ/ because of the similarity between /e/ and /ɪ/ and the similarity between /æ/ and /ɪ/.

/ɛ/

In my collection, the most common standard spelling of /ɛ/ was *e,* as in *best* and *help.* This was also the children's most frequent spelling. Although the children spelled /ɛ/ as *e* 39.6% of the time, they spelled it as *a* almost as often—34.5% of the time. The letter *a* represents /ɛ/ in words like *Mary* and *carrots,* but children used *a* for /ɛ/ at a rate far exceeding the 3.1% expected based on the use of *a* to spell /ɛ/ in standard English ($p < .001$ by a binomial test). This discrepancy—34.5% usage in children's spelling as compared with 3.1% usage in conventional spelling—is the largest such discrepancy in the present study. Table 4.6 shows some of the errors in which *a* was used for /ɛ/. Although standard English primarily employs *a* to represent /ɛ/ before /r/, the children used *a* for /ɛ/ in a variety of environments.

Why did the children so often use *a* to spell /ɛ/? Phonological factors are largely responsible. The letter *a* is the most common spelling of both /æ/ and /e/ and the name of the letter *a* is /e/. Both /æ/ and /e/ are similar to /ɛ/. All three vowels are front and unrounded. Studies with adults (Fox, 1983; Singh & Woods, 1971) and kindergarteners (Read, 1975, pp. 120–122) reveal that people consider /ɛ/ and /æ/ and /ɛ/ and /e/ to be similar. The studies disagree on which of the two pairs is more similar. Read (1975, pp. 124–126) and Fox (1983) found that people rate /ɛ/ and /æ/ as closer than /ɛ/ and /e/. Singh and Woods (1971) found the opposite. Despite this discrepancy, it is clear that /æ/ and /e/ are both similar to /ɛ/. Probably, both relations combine to produce the many *a* spellings for /ɛ/.

The erroneous use of *a* for /ɛ/ was widespread among the first graders. Almost three-quarters of the students who attempted /ɛ/ produced at least one *a* error. Among students who attempted /ɛ/ four times or more, one-third made *a* errors more than half the time. The rate of *a* errors was nearly 80% in some children. For example, Jason spelled /ɛ/ as *a* five times and as *i* once (see below). He produced only one correct *e* spelling.

Table 4.6. Examples Containing Misspellings of /ɛ/

Error	Examples
a	AVR for *ever*
	HAP for *help*
	ALFFNE for *elephant*
	NAK for *neck*
	LAG for *collection*
	TAR for *there*
	SAD for *said*
i	LITCH for *lets*
	GIST for *guessed*
	TID for *teddy*

Importantly, the children used *a* for /ɛ/ even though they were taught otherwise. Their phonics workbook and their spelling words included only one spelling of /ɛ/ —*e*. The workbook and spelling lists also taught only one correspondence for /æ/ —*a*. These "short vowel" spellings were among the first vowel spellings taught in the classroom. However, the consistent instruction that the children received was not enough to counteract their tendency to spell /ɛ/ as *a*.

After *e* and *a*, the first graders' third most common spelling of /ɛ/ (not counting omissions) was *i*. The children used *i* to represent /ɛ/ 4.7% of the time (see Table 4.6). These spellings are classified as illegal since *i* may not represent /ɛ/ in English. Why, then, did the children sometimes use *i* for /ɛ/? The letter *i* is the most common spelling of /ɪ/. The phoneme /ɪ/, like /ɛ/, is a front, unrounded vowel. The two vowels differ in height, the difference in height between /ɪ/ and /ɛ/ being comparable to the difference in height between /ɛ/ and /æ/. Adults rate /ɪ/ and /ɛ/ as highly similar (Fox, 1983; Singh & Woods, 1971), as do children (Read, 1973).[7]

The use of *i* for /ɛ/ was not as widespread as the use of *a* for /ɛ/. About a quarter of the children who attempted /ɛ/ produced *i*. Of those children who spelled /ɛ/ at least four times, none used *i* at a rate above 20%. Only one relation—the relation between /ɪ/ and /ɛ/—supports *i* for /ɛ/. Two relations—the relation between /æ/ and /ɛ/ and the relation between /e/ and /ɛ/—support *a* for /ɛ/. Therefore, children are more likely to spell /ɛ/ as *a* than as *i*.

/æ/

The children spelled /æ/ more consistently than any other vowel. They used *a* to represent /æ/ a full 85% of the time. The children did not use any illegal spelling more than 2.5% of the time; they did not use any legal spelling more often than expected based on its frequency in English.

Why did the students spell /æ/ in such a consistent manner? First, and probably most important, this vowel is consistently represented in English. More than any other vowel, /æ/ approaches the ideal of a one-to-one mapping from phoneme to grapheme. Second, /æ/ is located at a "corner" of the vowel space (see Fig. 1.4). It is not similar to a large number of other vowels. The relative lack of neighbors may contribute to children's correct spellings of /æ/.

The children's consistent spelling of /æ/ does *not* appear to reflect their teaching. True, the children were taught only one spelling of /æ/, *a*. However, they were taught only a single spelling for several other vowels as well, including /ɛ/. With /ɛ/, the children often used a spelling other than the one they were taught. With /æ/, they did not. The teaching that the children received cannot explain why their spelling was so much more consistent in one case than the other.

/ʊ/

The most frequent spelling of /ʊ/, and the only one that was explicitly taught, was *oo,* as in *book.* This was also the children's most common spelling. The children's second choice for /ʊ/ was *o.* The letter *o* may represent /ʊ/, in *woman,* but children used *o* much more often than expected on this basis (17.6% versus 3.9%; $p < .001$ by a binomial test). Table 4.7 shows some examples. The overuse of *o* for /ʊ/ was

Table 4.7. Examples Containing Misspellings of /ʊ/

Error	Examples
o	POT for *put*
	TOCK for *took*
	POD for *pulled*
i	GID for *good*
	CRIS for *crooks*
	WIMN for *woman*
a	LAS for *looks*
	PLAD for *pulled*
	WAT for *wouldn't*
ua	LUA for *looks*
	KUAD for *could*
	TUAC for *took*

fairly widespread: Over 40% of the children who attempted /ʊ/ made one or more *o* errors.

Why did the children overuse *o* for /ʊ/? Teaching does not seem to be responsible, as the children's phonics book and spelling lists did not contain any words in which /ʊ/ is spelled with *o*. Beyond this, it is difficult to pinpoint the cause of the error. It may reflect partial knowledge of conventional spelling: The common *oo* spelling of /ʊ/, as in *book,* contains *o*. Similarity relations among vowels may also play a role. Because *o* is the most frequent spelling of four different nonfront vowels—the rounded /u/, /o/, and /ɔ/, and the unrounded /ɑ/—one cannot be sure which sound children had in mind when they used *o*. Evidence from adults suggests that /ʊ/ and /u/ are particularly close (Fox, 1983; Singh & Woods, 1971). The relation between /ʊ/ and /u/ may help to explain why children sometimes spell /ʊ/ as *o*.

Three additional illegal substitutions on /ʊ/ occurred at rates above 2.5%. These were *i* (3.9%), *a* (2.9%), and *ua* (2.9%). Examples appear in Table 4.7. Because of the small number of attempts at /ʊ/, these error rates correspond to only three or four cases each. Thus, it is not clear that the errors are systematic.[8] Similarity between /ʊ/ and /ɪ/, which is generally spelled with *i,* might cause children to use *i* for /ʊ/. Although /ɪ/ is an unrounded front vowel and /ʊ/ is rounded and further back, the two vowels are comparable in height. Both are classified as lax. Adults, however, do not consider /ɪ/ and /ʊ/ to be particularly similar (Fox, 1983; Singh & Woods, 1971). The letter *a* may represent /æ/ or /e/, but neither one of these is especially close to /ʊ/.

/ə/

In this study, words such as *us* and *asleep* were coded as containing /ə/. Also, words with unstressed and stressed syllabic liquids, such as *bigger, little,* and *girl,* were transcribed with /ə/. The phoneme /ə/ had more different spellings than any other phoneme—a total of 16. When all cases of /ə/ were considered together, the most frequent standard spelling was *e,* followed by *a* and *u.* However, the distribution of spellings differed according to the stress and context of the vowel. When /ə/ was stressed and not followed by a liquid, it was most often spelled with *u*, as in *us* and *peanut*. In the case of stressed syllabic /r/, *i* was the most common spelling, as in *girl*, with *e* a close second, as in *her*. Finally, *e* was the typical spelling of unstressed /ə/, as in *bigger* and *landed*.

The first graders failed to spell /ə/ approximately one-third of the time. This was the highest omission rate of any vowel. As I show in Chapter 7, these omissions were often in the context of syllabic liquids. For example, children spelled *bird* as BRD and *bigger* as BIGR. As I discuss in more detail in Chapter 7, children may omit the vowel in words like *bird* and *bigger* because they do not consider these words to contain a separate /ə/ before the /r/.

When the children *did* spell /ə/, *u* was their most common choice. The children employed *u* for /ə/ 19.6% of the time, significantly more often than the 14.1% expected based on the frequency of *u* as a standard spelling ($p < .001$ by a binomial test). Examples include MUNEY for *money*, WUS for *was*, UV for *of*, SEVUN for *seven*, and UWY for *away*. These errors may arise, in part, because *u* was the most common spelling of /ə/ in the children's phonics workbook and spelling lists. Outside of school, too, a child who asked how to spell /ə/ would probably be told to use *u*.

Importantly, the students only overused *u* for /ə/ when /ə/ was not followed by /r/ or /l/ ($p < .001$ by binomial tests for both the stressed and unstressed cases). That is, the children did *not* extend *u* to words such as *bird, bigger*, and *cereal*. This finding supports the view that many children do not consider these words to contain a separate /ə/. Rather, children consider these words to contain the syllabic liquids /r/ and /l/.

Changes in Vowel Spellings Between the First and Second Semesters

How did the students' spellings of vowels change from the first semester to the second semester of the school year? To address this question, I calculated the rate of each of the vowel spellings that has been discussed for the two semesters of the school year. For the most part, differences between semesters were small and not significant. However, two clear patterns did emerge.

One finding concerns the spellings of the so-called long vowels /e/, /i/, /ai/, /o/, and /u/. During the first semester, 61.9% of all spellings of these vowels were the letter-name spellings *a, e, i, o,* and *u*. During the second semester, the percentage of letter-name spellings fell to 52.9% ($p < .001$ by a chi-square test). As letter-name spellings decreased, spellings with final *e* increased. Spellings of /e/, /i/, /ai/, /o/, and /u/ with *a & e, e & e, i & e, o & e,* and *u & e*, respectively went from 2.2% in the first semester to 8.8% in the second semester ($p < .001$ by a chi-square test). Importantly, this increase appeared to be specific to final *e* spellings. No significant increase was seen for other multiple-letter spellings of long vowels, such as *ai* for /e/. These spellings occurred at a 16.1% rate during the first semester and a 17.8% rate during the semester, not a significant difference.

A second finding was an *increase* in the use of *a* to represent /ε/, from 25.5% in the first semester to 40.5% in the second semester ($p < .025$ by a chi-square test).

This increase seems to reflect a decrease in omissions. Children who at first failed to represent /ε/ altogether often used *a* when they began to spell it. This result underlines the strength of children's tendency to spell /ε/ as *a*. That children so often spelled /ε/ as *a*, despite the rarity of this correspondence in the words that they read and despite the fact that they were taught to spell /ε/ as *e*, suggests that strong *internal* factors push them toward this spelling.

Comparison with Results of Other Studies

Read's Research

How do my findings on vowels compare with those of Charles Read? Recall that Read analyzed a large collection of spellings produced by preschoolers. Although the children studied by Read were younger than the children studied here, the percentage of correct and legal spellings was higher in Read's collection than in my collection (see Chapter 3). That is, the spellings that Read analyzed were *more* influenced by conventional spelling than the spellings that I analyzed. In this section, I ask whether the two collections of spellings, despite the quantitative difference, are qualitatively similar. To address this question, I compared the tables in Appendix II of this book, which show how the children in my study spelled each vowel phoneme in incorrectly spelled words only, to the tables presented by Read (1975), which are also based on incorrectly spelled words. This comparison reveals a fair degree of similarity between the results of the two studies.

Consider, first, the role of letter names in children's spelling of vowels. Both studies found children's most common spellings of /e/, /i/, /ai/, and /o/ to be *a, e, i,* and *o,* respectively. In both studies, too, *u* was a fairly common spelling of /u/. These results by themselves do not prove that children use letter names to spell vowels, for the spellings in question are common in English. Generally, Read did not compare the frequencies of correspondences in children's spelling with the frequencies of the same correspondences in standard English. However, the children in my study employed each of the letter-name spellings significantly more often than expected based on its frequency in standard English.[9]

The children in Read's study began to write as preschoolers, before they had received systematic instruction in spelling or reading. It is not surprising that these children used letter names to guide their spelling. Essentially, the children had no other choice. Not having been taught how to spell /e/, they could only use the letter whose name is /e/. The children in my study began to write in school. Although their teacher favored a whole-language approach, she did provide some instruction in phonics. This instruction strongly discouraged a letter-name strategy. For example, the children's phonics book taught that *a* followed by final *e* stands for /e/, as in *tape,* while single *a* stands for /æ/, as in *tap.* The children did exercises in which words like *tape* and *tap* were printed next to one another and they were to circle the word that contained the "long *a*" sound. Despite the instruction that they received, the children often made errors like TAP for *tape.*

Apparently, a letter-name strategy comes naturally to beginning spellers. Whether children start to write at home or at school, they often misspell *tape* as

TAP and *bike* as BIK. Judging from the results of Beers et al. (1977), these errors persist beyond first grade for infrequent words. Phonics instruction—at least the kind and amount given to the children in this study and the study of Beers et al. (1977)—does not eliminate children's use of letter names to guide their spelling.

My results agree with Read's in suggesting that some children are sensitive to the change in vowel quality that occurs within a diphthong. Children sometimes attempt to indicate the two-part nature of vowel diphthongs in their spelling. Errors that point to such a conclusion and that occurred in both my study and Read's are *ae* for /e/, *ie* for /ai/, *oe* for /oi/, and *ao* for /au/. In addition, both studies found that children sometimes spelled /ɑ/ as *i*, an apparent attempt to represent the first and linguistically more prominent part of a diphthong.[10]

The main difference between the two studies with regard to children's spellings of diphthongs concerns the diphthong /au/. The children in my study often spelled it as *a*, which represents the first part of the diphthong. The children in Read's study more often used *aoo*, which represents both parts of the diphthong. Spellings that symbolize both parts of a diphthong are more complete and more sophisticated than spellings that symbolize only one part of a diphthong. Thus, the different findings of the two studies fit with the idea that the spellings in Read's study were more advanced than the spellings in my study. Despite this difference, the major point remains: Children may spell a diphthong by representing both of its parts or by representing one part only. When children symbolize just one part of a diphthong, this part is the steady-state portion rather than the brief offglide.

In both studies, children sometimes misspelled vowel phonemes with letters that were appropriate for similar vowels. The two studies point to many of the same vowel similarities as bases for beginning spellings. In both studies, *a* and to a lesser extent *i* were common errors for /ɛ/. In both studies, too, children sometimes used *a* for /ɪ/. Whether children start to write at home or at school, they implicitly recognize the similarity among /ɪ/, /ɛ/, /e/, and /æ/. All of these vowels are front and unrounded. Also, the children in both studies seemed to group together the non-front unrounded vowels /ə/ and /ɑ/, sometimes using *u* for /ɑ/. The errors *ow* for /u/, *aw* for /au/, and *o* for /ʊ/ also occurred in both studies. These errors apparently reflect the similarity among the back rounded vowels of English.

Errors that were found in my study but that were not prevalent in Read's study were *oo* and *ol* for /ɔ/, *al* for /au/, and *i*, *ua*, and *a* for /ʊ/. Although the *i* and *a* errors for /ʊ/ in my study seemed to point to similarity between front unrounded vowels and a back rounded vowel, the fact that these errors did not appear in Read's study suggests that vowel substitutions do not generally involve groupings of front and back vowels.

There were several errors that occurred in both studies but for which different explanations were offered. The different explanations reflect the different dialects of the children in the two studies. One such error was *e* for /ɪ/. For the children in my study, /ɪ/ is spelled as *e* not only in words such as *pretty*, as in general American English, but also in words such as *when* and *them*. Errors like HEM for *him*, WELL for *will*, and BEG for *big* were classified as legal substitutions. The children in my study did not use *e* for /ɪ/ any more often than expected given the frequency of this spelling in the words to which they were exposed. Such a difference would have been expected if there were a special phonological similarity between /i/ and /ɪ/. Read also found errors like HEM for *him* and WELL for *will*. However, because *e* was not a common spelling of /ɪ/ for the dialects of his children, he attributed these errors to the similarity between /i/ and /ɪ/. These vowels are unrounded front vowels. They differ in tenseness, with /i/ tense and /ɪ/ lax.

Another error that was explained differently in the two studies was *i* for /i/. In Hoosier speech, *i* is a fairly common spelling of /i/. It occurs in words such as *king* and *think,* which are pronounced with /i/ in Hoosier speech, as well as in words such as *pizza,* which are pronounced with /i/ by everyone. The use of *i* for /i/, as in FIT for *feet,* SI for *see,* or RILEE for *really,* was considered a legal substitution. The children in my study did not use *i* for /i/ more often than expected based on its frequency in the standard system. Read also found errors like FIT for *feet.* However, he attributed these errors to the similarity between the tense vowel /i/ and the corresponding lax vowel /ɪ/ rather than to children's knowledge that /i/ may be spelled with *i.*

Finally, errors such as NELS for *nails,* although not numerous in the present study, were considered legal substitutions. This is because, in Hoosier speech, /e/ is symbolized as *e* in words such as *legs.* Read observed these errors too but interpreted them differently. Read proposed that these errors stem from the similarity between /e/ and /ɛ/. The vowels /e/ and /ɛ/ are both front and unrounded. They differ in tenseness, with /e/ tense and /ɛ/ lax.

The observations just described led Read to suggest that children make specific groupings of vowels within the broader categories of front unrounded vowels and back rounded vowels. In particular, Read claimed, children consider vowels that are alike in all but tenseness to be especially similar. In the front unrounded category, such pairs are /i/ (tense) and /ɪ/ (lax) and /e/ (tense) and /ɪ/ (lax). In the back rounded category, one pair is /u/ (tense) and /ʊ/ (lax). Although Read focused on children's pairing of tense and lax vowels as an explanation for certain vowel errors, such pairings were not common in my study. Moreover, experimental findings show that, although children do consider pairs of front vowels that differ only in tenseness to be similar to one another, this similarity is weaker than other similarity relations within the class of front unrounded vowels (Read, 1973; Read, 1975, Chapter 5). The strongest relations within the class of front unrounded vowels appear to be that between /ɪ/ and /ɛ/, which are alike in tenseness and different in height, and that between /ɛ/ and /æ/, which are also alike in tenseness and different in height. Thus, children do relate front unrounded vowels to one another and back rounded vowels to one another, but these groupings do not necessarily, or even predominantly, involve pairs of tense and lax vowels.

University of Virginia Research

As discussed in Chapter 1, the University of Virginia researchers have proposed that students pass through a series of stages in learning to spell. During the first, or precommunicative stage, children string letters together in an apparently random fashion. Although some of the first graders in my study produced such spellings at the beginning of the school year, I did not analyze them. The earliest spellings investigated here should belong to the second, or semiphonetic stage of spelling development.

During the semiphonetic stage, students are said to use a letter-name strategy whenever possible. They spell phonemes or groups of phonemes with the letters that have those names. For /e/, /i/, /ai/, and /o/, my results support this claim. The first graders used letter-name spellings about 60% of the time for these vowels, pooling over the results from throughout the school year. Letter-name spellings occurred at a much lower rate—about 6%—for /u/. Thus, letter-name spellings are not equally common for all long vowels, as has sometimes been implied (Beers & Henderson, 1977). Later in this book, I will show that letter-name spellings are not equally common for all consonants either. Thus, it does not appear that first graders use a letter-name strategy whenever possible.

Even though letter-name spellings were much more frequent for words like *feel* than for words like *pool,* I may ask whether children who made many errors like FEL for *feel* also made a greater than average number of errors like PUL for *pool.* Such a result should be found if some students rely on a letter-name strategy more than others. For each of /e/, /i/, /ai/, /o/, and /u/, I calculated the percentage of the time that each child used the letter-name spelling when this spelling was not correct. I examined the correlations among the percentages of letter-name spellings for the five vowels. Spellings from 33 of the 43 pupils were included in the analysis; ten pupils did not attempt any words in one or more of the categories. Thus, there were ten correlation coefficients, one for each vowel with every other vowel. Nine of the ten correlations were positive, but only three reached the .05 level of significance by a one-tailed test. The average value of the correlation coefficients was rather low ($r = .17$). Thus, there is modest support for the idea that children who use letter-name spellings for one vowel tend to do the same for other vowels.

According to the University of Virginia researchers, letter-name spellings of long vowels begin in the semiphonetic stage of spelling development and persist during the following stage, the phonetic stage. When learners reach the next stage, the transitional stage, things change. Spellings like TIPE for *type* now replace letter-name spellings like TIP. Consistent with this claim, letter-name spellings like *i* for /ai/ decreased from the first semester of the school year to the second semester. Vowel plus final *e* spellings increased. However, a similar increase was not apparent for other multiple-letter spellings of long vowels, such as *ai* for /e/. This result does not support the statement that "especially liberal use of vowel digraphs like *ai, ea, ay, ee,* and *ow* appears" during the transitional stage (Gentry, 1982, p. 197). If this were true, spellings like *ai* for /e/ should have been substantially more frequent during the second semester of the school year than during the first semester. In this respect, the present results do not appear to support the Virginia researchers' characterization of the transitional stage.

Factors That Affect Children's Spellings of Vowels

The findings in this chapter point to four factors that help to explain why children spell vowels the way they do. These factors are experience with printed English, knowledge of letter names, the phonological properties of vowels, and dialect. I will discuss each of these factors in turn, showing how they interact to account for children's spellings of English vowels.

Exposure to Print

Children are surrounded by print—in the classroom, at home, and elsewhere in their environment. This exposure affects them powerfully, as children learn about many aspects of spelling from the print around them.

When they learn that the printed word *big* stands for the spoken word /bɪg/, many children induce that *b* symbolizes /b/, that *i* symbolizes /ɪ/, and that *g* symbolizes /g/. When attempting to spell /ɪ/ in a word whose spelling they do not know, children generally use *i,* the most frequent spelling of /ɪ/ in the words that they do know. For the children in this study, the phoneme-grapheme correspondences in the words that they knew seemed to influence their spelling to a greater extent than the phoneme-grapheme correspondences that they were taught at school. For example, the children sometimes spelled *dog* as DAG. Although *a* was not taught as a spelling for /ɔ/, the children had learned this spelling from reading such words as *all* and *tall.*

Thus, children are not passive whole-word learners. When they learn to read a word like *big,* first graders do not, or at least not always, treat the printed word as a unitary whole. They segment it into the graphemes *b, i,* and *g.* At least some of the time, children also segment the spoken form of the word into the phonemes /b/, /ɪ/, and /g/. The children relate the graphemes in the printed word to the phonemes in the spoken word, concluding that *b* stands for /b/, *i* for /ɪ/, and *g* for /g/. In this way, children actively try to make sense of the print to which they are exposed.

The present findings on print exposure mesh with those of recent studies with older children (Cunningham & Stanovich, 1991) and adults (Stanovich & West, 1989). These studies have found that, other things being equal, people who read a lot are better spellers (and better readers) than people who read less. My results corroborate these findings by showing that exposure to printed words facilitates spelling even at the first-grade level.

Although exposure to print plays an important role in learning to spell, the results should not be taken to mean that children master *all* aspects of the English writing system from this exposure. For example, children's choices of spellings for vowel phonemes do not always mirror the choices embodied in conventional English. Children produce certain spellings that never occur in the standard system, sometimes at relatively high rates. Children also overuse certain conventional spellings by large margins. In these cases, one cannot look only to knowledge of the conventional writing system to explain children's errors. One must also consider other factors, some of which are discussed below.

Nor should the present results be construed to mean that *all* children grasp the relations between phonemes and graphemes as a result of learning to read. The analyses reported here are based, for the most part, on group data. Some children, even though they can read some common words, do not do so in an analytic manner. These children have been called *logographic* readers (Frith, 1985; Gough & Hillinger, 1980). Logographic readers focus on one attribute of each word that distinguishes it from all of the other words they know. For example, they may recognize *dog* by virtue of the "tail" at the end. Such children have difficulty analyzing printed words into graphemes, analyzing spoken words into phonemes, and relating the phonemes to the graphemes. Correspondingly, they are very poor spellers (Juel, Griffith, & Gough, 1984). Logographic readers, it appears, do not pick up links between phonemes and graphemes on their own.

Despite the caveats just mentioned, many first graders do learn aspects of the English spelling system without formal instruction. Previous studies (Bissex, 1980; Read, 1975) have shown this to be the case for certain gifted preschoolers. The present results suggest that the same holds true for many "average" first graders. What students learn, in spelling as in other domains, is not just what they are taught. With their power of observation and their ability to relate things to one another, children learn a great deal on their own.

Letter Names

One influence on children's spellings of vowels, above and beyond their knowledge of conventional spelling, is their knowledge of letter names. The children in this study often used *a, e, i,* and *o* for /e/, /i/, /ai/, and /o/, respectively. Going beyond the results of previous studies, I found that children employed these letter-name correspondences significantly more often than expected given the frequency of the correspondences in standard English. Children did this because they knew that the names of the letters *a, e, i,* and *o* are /e/, /i̵/, /ai/, and /o/, respectively.

The children's overuse of letter-name spellings was not limited to the four cases just discussed in which the name of the vowel letter *exactly* matches its sound. The children also used *u* for /u/ more often than expected. They did this because they knew that *u* is named /ju/ and because they possessed sufficient phonemic awareness to know that the syllable /ju/ contains the phoneme /u/.

Letter-name spellings were not equally common in all cases. For /e/, /i/, /ai/, and /o/, children used letter-name spellings about 60% of the time. For /u/, they used the letter-name spelling only about 6% of the time. One reason for this difference may be that /e/, /i/, /ai/, and /o/ exactly match the name of a letter, while /u/ does not. A second and more important reason is that *a, e, i,* and *o* are often used to spell /e/, /i/, /ai/, and /o/ in English. For these vowels, children are encouraged in their use of a letter-name strategy by the fact that letter-name spellings are often correct. In contrast, *u* is not a common spelling of /u/. Having observed that /u/ is not usually written as *u,* the first graders did not often use this spelling. For first graders, then, use of a letter-name strategy is modified by their experience with print.

In many cases, as with *baby* and *both,* children who use a letter-name strategy will spell the vowel correctly. However, this is not always true. The use of letter names to spell often leads to errors, as in BIK for *bike* and PUL for *pool.* Although the use of letter names is natural for beginners, it is not an unmixed blessing for children learning to spell in English.

Phonology

Children are not blank slates when they begin to spell. To understand why children make the mistakes they do and to understand why some aspects of conventional spelling are easier for them to master than others, one must consider the knowledge that children bring with them to the task of learning to spell. One body of knowledge that is crucial in this regard is phonological knowledge. Even before they start to write and read, children know a good deal about the sounds of their language. They know implicitly about the properties of phonemes and about the relations among phonemes. Many of children's spelling errors reflect this knowledge.

At least some children are sensitive to whether a vowel is a diphthong or a monophthong; that is, to whether there is an appreciable change in quality during the course of the vowel. Certain errors on diphthongs suggest that children (implicitly) recognize the change in quality, analyze the diphthong into two parts, and attempt to represent both parts. These errors are *ae* for /e/, *ie* for /ai/, *oe* for /oi/, and *ao* for /au/. Another and apparently less sophisticated type of error represents only one part of a diphthong. For the English diphthongs discussed here, the first part is linguistically more prominent. This portion (the steady-state portion) is longer and steadier than the second portion (the offglide). Correspondingly, certain spelling errors seem to be attempts to symbolize the first parts of diphthongs. These errors include *i* for /ɑ/ and *a* for /au/. The children who spelled /ɑ/ as *i* apparently analyzed the diphthongal name of the letter *i*, /ai/, as beginning with a sound similar to /ɑ/. In the case of *a* for /au/, the first part of the diphthong does not match a letter name and so was spelled with a letter representing /æ/. The use of *o* for /au/ and /oi/ may also be attempts to represent the first parts of diphthongs. However, these errors may also occur because the conventional spellings of /au/ and /oi/ begin with *o*. Although certain of children's errors represented only the first or steady-state part of a diphthong, no common errors represented only the offglide.

Do the children's two-part spellings of diphthongs mean that they consider diphthongs to be two phonemes rather than one? The question of whether a segment is one phoneme or two phonemes need not have a definite answer. Children (and adults) may consider a diphthong to be a unit that has two parts. The parts are so tightly linked that they usually function as a group. However, the two elements of the diphthong are sometimes treated separately, leading to spellings like *ao* for /au/.

Only some of the first graders produced the errors on diphthongs that have been discussed. This finding could be taken to mean that only some first graders divide vowels into the categories of diphthongs and monophthongs. Alternatively, many children may be sensitive to the distinction between diphthongs and monophthongs but few may choose to represent it in their spelling. Other students may know the conventional spellings of diphthongs or may feel that the change in vowel quality within a diphthong is too small to deserve representation in print. Thus, although a study of children's spellings tells us about the phonological categorizations that children are *capable* of making, it does not tell us how widespread such categorizations are. To determine whether most first graders distinguish between diphthongs and monophthongs, one would need to develop a more direct test of this distinction.

In addition to categorizing vowels along the dimension of monophthong versus diphthong, children also seem to categorize vowels along the dimensions of front versus nonfront and rounded versus unrounded. Evidence that children group front unrounded vowels comes from their use of *a* and *i* for /ɛ/. These spellings do not reflect knowledge of conventional English, knowledge of letter names, or direct instruction. Instead, they seem to reflect the similarity in sound between /ɛ/ and /æ/, /ɛ/ and /e/, and /ɛ/ and /ɪ/. Further evidence for the category of front unrounded vowels comes from *a* errors on /ɪ/. Together, these errors suggest that children implicitly appreciate the similarity among /ɪ/, /e/, /ɛ/, and /æ/. These vowels are alike in frontness and in lack of lip rounding; they differ from one another in other ways. I did not find evidence that children place /i/ in the category of front unrounded vowels, but Read reported such evidence. (English, unlike some other languages, does not have a class of front rounded vowels.)

Other substitutions reflect the similarity among the back rounded vowels of English. These errors include *ow* for /u/, *oo* for /ɔ/, *aw* (and possibly also *al*) for /au/, and *o* for /ʊ/. These spellings suggest that children group together /u/, /ʊ/, /o/, /au/, and /ɔ/.

The evidence for the class of nonfront unrounded vowels is weaker than the evidence for the preceding classes. It rests on the erroneous use of *u* for /ɑ/, which seems to reflect the similarity between /ə/ and /ɑ/. These are the only vowels of English to be both nonfront and nonrounded. Children may consider them as similar for this reason. Read also found that children grouped /ə/ and /ɑ/, strengthening the evidence for a category of central to back unrounded vowels.

Although /o/ and /au/ are diphthongs, children seemed to classify them with the back rounded monophthongs for spelling purposes. Likewise, they placed the diphthong /e/ with the unrounded front monophthongs. The similarity in front/back position and in lip rounding apparently outweighs the monophthong/diphthong difference. However, /oi/ and /ai/ did not seem to fall into the categories defined in terms of front versus back and rounded versus unrounded. This may be because /oi/ and /ai/ involve a large change along the front/back dimension, a larger change than for the other diphthongs.

To summarize the discussion to this point, children implicitly categorize vowels along several dimensions. These dimensions include diphthong versus monophthong, front versus nonfront, and rounded versus unrounded. Substitutions tend to involve vowels that are alike in the categories defined by these dimensions but that differ in height. Thus, height seems to be the least salient vowel dimension for children—the dimension that is easiest to ignore. Vowel height is similar in this way to consonant voicing, which children sometimes also ignore when they spell (Chapter 3).

Most of the substitutions that occurred at rates above my cut-off of 2.5% fit the pattern just described. The only exceptions were *i* and *a* for /ʊ/, which appear to reflect similarity between front unrounded vowels and a back rounded vowel. These errors were rare and, as I have discussed, were not found by Read. Thus, they do not change the general picture.

How do children's vowel categories affect their spelling? For example, given that children consider /ɛ/ to be similar to /æ/, why do they sometimes use a letter appropriate for /æ/ when trying to symbolize /ɛ/? The confusions may arise for several reasons. When segmenting a spoken word into phonemes, children may abstract out a vowel that is similar but not identical to the vowel in the spoken word (Ehri, Wilce, & Taylor, 1987). Once children have analyzed a spoken word or part of a spoken word into phonemes, they must remember the phonemes while trying to spell them. Errors may arise in short-term memory, as children replace one vowel with another vowel that is phonemically similar. Finally, when applying correspondences between phonemes and graphemes, children may confuse the graphemes that are linked to similar phonemes.

In most cases, spelling errors involving similar vowels do *not* arise because children fail to differentiate among the vowels in their own speech or the speech of others. Although some normal first graders spell *bet, bat,* and *bait* alike, using BAT for all three, they pronounce the words differently. Likewise, adults know that *wound* (an injury) and *wound* (the past tense of *wind*) sound different, even though they spell them alike. A first grader who did not distinguish among /ɛ/, /æ/, and /e/ would be considered to have a severe speech problem; none of the children in this study had such problems.

Recall that no conclusions about how children categorize vowels could be drawn from the study of illegal substitutions reported in Chapter 3. There, I mechanically determined which phoneme the child intended in each illegal substitution error and then asked how the substituted phoneme differed from the target phoneme. Although this approach was fairly successful for consonants, it did not work for vowels. Because many vowel graphemes symbolize more than one vowel phoneme, I could not tell which phoneme was intended in many cases. This problem has not been eliminated in the analyses reported in this chapter. However, I have tried to show that similarity among vowel phonemes is the most plausible explanation for certain errors and that other explanations are less likely.

Not all the first graders produced the spelling errors that implicated similarity relations among vowel phonemes. However, the fact that a student fails to make a particular spelling error does *not* mean that the student fails to recognize the similarity. For example, a good first-grade speller might never misspell /ɛ/ as *a*. However, this child might still consider /ɛ/ to be similar to /e/ and /æ/. To determine whether children recognize similarity relations among vowels, one must develop tests that do not depend on spelling. Read (1973, 1975), who has devised such tests, has found that even kindergarteners can judge the relations among vowel phonemes. Their judgments correspond fairly closely to the ones that children's spelling errors lead us to expect. Thus, it is not just a few children who implicitly appreciate similarity relations among vowels. Many kindergarteners and first graders do so.

In sum, children have a surprisingly fine appreciation of the properties of vowel phonemes. Even when they consider vowel phonemes to be different, children recognize certain similarity relations among the phonemes. The dimensions of similarity to which children are sensitive include frontness versus backness, presence versus absence of lip rounding, and monophthong versus diphthong. These are all qualities that linguists have identified as important. Thus, the results support the psychological reality of these dimensions. By at least six years of age, children implicitly appreciate the critical properties of vowel phonemes.

The learning that is most obvious to an observer of children's phonological development is the learning of distinctions among phonemes. Children come to distinguish phonemes in their own speech and the speech of others. The present results suggest that another type of learning occurs as well—learning about the similarities and differences among phonemes. We know little about how this learning takes place. Clearly, explicit teaching is not required. Parents and teachers do not tell children that /ɪ/ and /ɛ/ sound similar to one another, whereas /ɪ/ and /u/ sound quite different. Nor is reading experience responsible for young children's vowel groupings. Indeed, the way in which the English writing system groups vowels is sometimes at odds with children's implicit classifications. For example, /ɪ/ and /ai/ are linked in terms of spelling in that the first is often spelled with *i* while the second is often spelled with *i* followed by final *e*. First graders, however, do not consider /ɪ/ and /ai/ to be particularly similar. If anything, reading experience works *against* the phonological categories seen here. Again, we are forced to conclude that much of children's learning is driven from within. On their own, children organize the material that they are learning, recognizing relations and forming categories. They do this with the phonemes of their spoken language just as they do it with printed words.

Dialect

The children in this study spoke a dialect that differed from general American English in several ways. The children's dialect seemed to affect their spellings of vowels. Errors such as MIN for *men* and THIM for *them* exemplify the apparent influence of dialect. These errors are reasonable representations of the children's own pronunciations of these words. Spellings like KENG for *king* and THENK for *think* may also reflect the children's dialect. People from southern Indiana pronounce these words with /i/ rather than /ɪ/. Correspondingly, children who speak this dialect sometimes spell the words with *e*.

Although I suggest that misspellings like MIN for *men* and KENG for *king* reflect the children's dialect, I cannot say this for sure. Children who speak dialects of English in which vowels are not raised before nasals sometimes make the same errors. It would be important to show that errors like MIN for *men* are more common among a group of children who speak Hoosier dialect than a group of children who do not. The present study did not include such a control group.

If errors like MIN for *men* reflect the children's dialect, how does dialect exert its effect on spelling? I have assumed that the children in this study represented *men* as /mɪn/. If so, words like *men* are irregularly spelled for these children in the same way that words like *pretty* are irregularly spelled for all present-day speakers of American English. For people from southern Indiana and throughout the southern United States, *min* is more consistent with the word's phonemic form than is *men*. In the same way, *pritty* is more consistent with this word's phonemic form than is *pretty*. Thus, children's difficulty with words like *men* is one instance of their general difficulty with irregular words (see Chapter 2). Importantly, regularity and irregularity must be defined relative to a person's own dialect.

Although the children sometimes spelled men as MIN, they also produced many correct *men* spellings. These correct spellings confirm that exposure to print plays an important role in learning to spell. Although children have some trouble learning irregular words like *men* and *pretty,* tending to replace the *e*s with *i*s, they do eventually shift to *e*. This shift from *i* to *e* does *not* necessarily imply a shift in children's phonemic representations. Just as people can learn the spelling *pretty* while still pronouncing the word with /ɪ/, so people can learn *men* while maintaining the /ɪ/ vowel.

Implications

Classification of Spelling Errors

Traditional systems of classifying spelling errors are based on words' conventional spellings. In such orthographically based classification systems, BAD for *bed* involves a substitution of *a* for *e*. Children are said to have a strong tendency to replace the letter *e* with the letter *a*. However, this statement is not actually correct. When *e* stands for /ɛ/, *a* *is* often substituted for *e*. However, when *e* stands for /ə/, few such substitutions occur. Children often misspell the vowel of *bed* with *a* but they do not often misspell the second vowel of *dishes* with *a*. As this example shows, an understanding of children's errors requires one to consider the spoken forms that the spellings represent. If one considered only the words' spellings, certain regularities would be missed.

The claim that an orthographically based classification system does not suffice to capture all the regularities in children's spelling should not be taken to imply that orthography is unimportant. Indeed, as I show in Chapter 6, learning about the letter sequences that occur in English words is an important part of learning to spell. My claim is that the learning of orthographic patterns, on its own, cannot fully explain children's errors. One must also consider the spoken forms of words.

Given that phonology must be considered in the classification of children's spelling errors, how should this be done? Many researchers have suggested that errors be divided into two categories—phonologically legal errors and phonologically illegal errors. Legal errors accurately represent the phonological forms of words. Illegal errors do not. My results suggest that the distinction between legal and illegal errors is an overly simple approach to a complex phenomenon. In some cases, illegal errors are excellent representations of phonology. For example, *ao* for /au/, although illegal from the view of the conventional writing system, accurately captures the diphthongal nature of /au/.

The Teaching of Spelling

Informal Spelling Instruction. One of the best ways to teach children to spell is to respond to the errors that they produce while writing (see Henderson, 1985). Informal instruction is not planned in advance. It is improvised in response to the needs of the individual child or group of children. To respond to children's spelling errors in the most helpful manner, we must realize that many errors are more reasonable than they first appear. The errors reflect a good deal of knowledge about the English writing system and about the sounds of English words. To appreciate this knowledge, we must go beyond viewing children's spellings simply as correct or incorrect. We must understand that, even when a child's spelling is wrong, there may be a good reason for the error.

An error that does not match the intended word when read aloud may still be reasonable. Consider DAN for *down*. It is pronounced as the name *Dan* rather than as *down*. However, the student who produced this error apparently knows that the diphthong /au/ is similar to /æ/. The error is not unmotivated. As another example, NAK does not match *neck* when read aloud. Nonetheless, the child who made this error seems to know that /ɛ/ is similar to /æ/ and /e/.

Adults' well-developed literacy skills can make it hard for them to understand the reasons behind vowel errors such as these. Adults readily appreciate that DAN might be an attempt to spell *Dane:* They group /æ/ and /e/ together because /æ/ is the "short" pronunciation of *a* and /e/ is the "long" pronunciation. However, adults may not recognize DAN as a reasonable attempt to spell *down*. They are not used to considering /au/ as a two-part sound, the first part of which is similar to /æ/. Their knowledge of spelling suggests, if anything, that the vowel of *down* is similar to /o/. Training in phonetics can help adults overcome their spelling-centered view of sounds. With some such training, teachers can more easily put themselves in the place of children who understand the basic properties of sounds but who know little about conventional spelling.

An appreciation of the knowledge that lies behind children's errors can help teachers respond to the errors appropriately. Consider the child who spelled *neck* as NAK. This child probably did not mishear or mispronounce the word. It would do little good to have the child repeat the word or to tell the child that *neck* sounds different from *knack*. Rather, the child might be assured that /ɛ/ *does* sound similar to /æ/ and /e/ but that /ɛ/ is usually spelled with *e*. As another example, the pupil who spelled *down* as DAN does not need help in hearing the difference between *down* and *Dan*. The child probably distinguishes the spoken words perfectly well. Nor does the child need to be reminded that *a* spells /æ/. The child's knowledge that /æ/ is spelled as *a* probably contributed to the error in the first place. Rather, the teacher might acknowledge that the first part of /au/ does sound similar to /æ/ and that the child did a good job of trying to spell the word as it sounds. The teacher could point out, however, that /au/ is usually spelled with two letters, *o* and *w* in this case. In these and other cases, a careful examination of children's misspellings can shed light on the reasons for the errors. This, in turn, can indicate what type of feedback will be most constructive and effective.

In suggesting how teachers might informally respond to certain misspellings, I do *not* wish to imply that teachers should correct all of the spelling errors that first graders make. When first graders are writing stories, for example, it is often wise to focus on composition rather than on spelling. At times, however, it *is* appropriate to pay attention to spelling. At these times, teachers' responses will be kinder and more helpful if they are guided by an appreciation of the logic behind the students' errors.

Dialect. In interpreting children's vowel misspellings, we must be sensitive to the dialect that children speak. For children who speak a dialect in which *pen* and *them* are pronounced with /ɪ/, errors such as PIN and THIM are reasonable. They are "good" errors in the same way that PRITTY for *pretty* is a "good" error. These misspellings reveal that students can analyze a spoken word into phonemes and can represent the vowel with the most common grapheme. The only problem, in the case of PIN and THIM, is that the phonemic form being analyzed is the children's own pronunciation, not the pronunciation heard on national television.

Just as teachers might ignore the error PRITTY for *pretty* in a first or second grader, recognizing that the word is irregular and that the error conforms to the child's phonemic form, so teachers might ignore THIM for *them*. Misspellings like PRITTY and THIM will decline as children see the conventional spellings of the words. If teachers do respond to an error like THIM, it is unwise to try to "correct" the pupil's /ðɪm/ pronunciation. Such a correction could imply that the child's way of speaking is wrong or substandard. In any case, dialects are not easily changed. Better to accept the pupil's pronunciation but to say that *them* is usually spelled with *e*. A speaker of Hoosier English is perfectly capable of learning the spellings *them* and *pen* while retaining the pronunciations /ðɪm/ and /pˈɪn/. In the same way, a speaker of general American English is perfectly capable of learning the spelling *pretty* while retaining the pronunciation /prˈɪti/. Learning to spell does *not* require people to change their accents.

Textbooks, too, should take dialect differences into account. Unfortunately, they do not always do so. For example, the phonics book used in this first grade— a book that is distributed throughout the United States—included an exercise in which children were to color the pictures of objects whose names contained the "short *e*" sound. One of the "correct" pictures was that of a tent; another was that of a pen. Children who pronounce these words with /ɪ/, as many people from the southern United States do, might well give the "wrong" answers to these items. It cannot help children to be scored as wrong when they have correctly analyzed the spoken words according to their own dialect.

Formal Spelling Instruction. Advocates of a whole-language approach to reading and writing claim that children learn to write (and read) by doing it themselves and by seeing it done. Formal teaching about the correspondences between individual letters and individual sounds is not necessary. Such instruction may even be harmful, since it requires teachers to present single words, letters, and sounds out of context. This, whole-language advocates claim, draws children's attention away from the important part of language—its communicative function. What do my results have to say about these ideas?

There is some truth to the whole-language philosophy. Many children do pick up correspondences between letters and sounds on their own, even when the correspondences are not explicitly taught. However, the insight behind the whole-language approach—that children can learn many things on their own—should not be pushed too far. For one thing, not all children easily pick up relations between phonemes and graphemes on their own. For another thing, this learning is more rapid for some correspondences than for others. In my view, children should be given as many opportunities to learn as possible. These opportunities should include exposure to print, informal instruction, and formal instruction.

With respect to print experience, children should be read to and classrooms should be filled with books, labels, and signs. Students should be given the opportunity to learn words that are important to them. These suggestions, which are advocated by proponents of the whole-language and language-experience approaches, may be followed in all types of classrooms. As discussed earlier, teachers should also provide informal spelling instruction by analyzing the errors that children produce when writing and tailoring feedback to the nature of the errors.

Formal instruction about the relations between sounds and spellings should focus on those things that students find hardest to pick up on their own. Less time should be spent on those things that children learn easily and without direct instruction. To take an example, the students in the present study, like many other first graders, received about the same amount of instruction on the correspondence between /æ/ and *a* as on the correspondence between /ɛ/ and *e*. Their phonics book allotted approximately the same amount of space to the two correspondences. However, the children had little difficulty spelling /æ/ as *a* but great difficulty spelling /ɛ/ as *e*. The children often misspelled /ɛ/ as *a*, I argued, because /ɛ/ sounds similar to other vowels that are commonly spelled with *a*. They did well on /æ/ because this vowel is spelled so consistently in English and because it is not similar to many other vowels. My findings suggest that the allocation of time to the short *e* and short *a* vowels should be changed. More time should be spent on the link between /ɛ/ and *e* than on the link between /æ/ and *a*. Formal spelling instruction should be most effective when it concentrates on those things that are hardest for children to pick up on their own.

Letter-Name Knowledge.   There has been much debate about the importance of letter names in learning to write and read (see Adams, 1990; Ehri, 1983). Many studies have shown that children's knowledge of letter names is a good predictor of their ability to learn to read (e.g., Bond & Dykstra, 1967; Chall, 1967). Although the research findings are clear, the interpretation of the findings is less clear. One possible interpretation is that letter-name knowledge directly facilitates the learning of spelling and reading. Another possible interpretation is that children who know the names of letters before they enter school come from homes in which parents pay attention to the children, read books to them, and talk to them about words and letters. If so, knowledge of letter names is a sign that children are cognitively and emotionally ready to learn to read; that they recognize and discriminate the letters of the alphabet. In this view, however, knowledge of letter names does not *directly* facilitate the reading or spelling of specific words.

For spelling, the question is whether students use the names of the letters when they are spelling words and whether this strategy leads to correct spellings. My results show that first graders do use their knowledge of letter names to spell vowels. However, this does not always help them to spell correctly. Knowledge of the names of *a, e, i,* and *o* sometimes helps children to spell /e/, /i/, /ai/, and /o/. For these vowels, letter-name spellings are often correct, as in *baby* and *both.* Use of letter names causes errors on words like *bike,* where the letter-name spelling, BIK, is not correct. However, adults interpret these errors without much trouble (see Chapter 3). With /u/, a letter-name strategy usually leads to errors. This is because the vowel letter with the most similar name, *u,* is not a common spelling of /u/. For the nine English vowels *other* than /e/, /i/, /ai/, /o/, and /u/, letter names are of no direct use in spelling the vowels correctly. Thus, although knowledge of letter names has some benefits for the spelling of vowels, these benefits are restricted to a minority of vowel phonemes. For middle-class first graders, like the children in this study, teaching that focuses on the *sounds* of letters is likely to be of greater benefit for spelling than drill on the *names* of letters.

Notes

1. *Ae* spells /e/ in the name *Rae,* but the children in this study did not attempt this word, nor did the word appear in Carroll et al. (1971). Even if I were to classify *ae* for /e/ as a legal spelling, I would probably find that children used *ae* more often than expected based on its frequency in standard English.

2. An alternative explanation for the use of *ae* for /e/ is that *a* followed by *e* at the end of the morpheme often spells /e/. Children may err by putting *e* immediately after *a* rather than at the end of the morpheme. If this explanation is correct, *oe* errors for /o/ should be as common as *ae* errors for /e/, since *o* followed by *e* at the end of the morpheme often spells /o/. In both my study and Read's, *ae* errors for /e/ were more common than *oe* errors for /o/. However, the differences were not significant.

3. Another possible explanation for the use of *ie* for /ai/ is that /ai/ is often spelled with *i* plus final *e.* Children may sometimes err by placing *e* immediately after *i.* If this were the only basis for *ie* spellings of /ai/, *ie* errors for /ai/ should be no more common than *oe* errors for /o/. *Ie* errors were more frequent than *oe* errors in my study and Read's study, but the differences were not significant.

4. Fox (1983) presented the results for each subject separately; these were averaged for present purposes.

5. *I* is also the most common spelling of /ɪ/, but /ɪ/ and /ɑ/ are not very similar according to Figure 1.4 or according to the ratings of Fox (1983) and Singh and Woods (1971).

6. *A* is also the most common spelling of /e/, but /e/ and /au/ are not very similar according to Figure 1.4 or according to the ratings of Fox (1983).

7. *I* is also the most common spelling of /ai/, but /ɛ/ and /ai/ were not rated as particularly similar in the study of Fox (1983).

8. One of the errors that was coded as using *i* for /ʊ/ was WILL for *would.* The intended word was taken to be *would* since that was how the child dictated it, but the child probably meant to write *will.*

9. Read did report such a comparison in the case of *o.* He suggested that children were *less* likely to use *o* for /o/ than expected based on the frequency of this correspondence in standard spelling. However, the estimate for standard spelling came from Venezky's (1970) study of the 20,000 most common words of English. Since the printed words that first graders have seen probably number in the thousands rather than the tens of thousands (Just & Carpenter, 1987; Lorge & Chall, 1963), it seems preferable to base estimates about standard spelling on the words that the children attempted, as done here. Moreover, Venezky (1970)

counted each word once, regardless of its frequency of occurrence in the language. In any collection of children's spellings, frequent words are represented more often than infrequent ones.

10. In Read's study, most of the *i* spellings of /ɑ/ came from a single child. My results show that this error was not an isolated idiosyncrasy: One child in this study made the error more often than the other children but almost a third of the children spelled /ɑ/ as *i* at least once.

5

Consonants

Learning to spell involves learning about the relations between the phonemes of the spoken language and the graphemes of the printed language. In Chapter 4, I asked how children learn these relations for vowels. The results showed that a number of factors affect children's learning, including their exposure to printed words, their knowledge of letter names, and their phonological systems. In this chapter, I turn to consonants. I ask whether these same factors affect children's spelling of consonants. This chapter focuses on substitution errors and, to a lesser extent, correct spellings. Consonant omission errors will be considered in detail in Chapter 8.

Sometimes, the first graders' most common spellings of consonant phonemes were those spellings that are most frequent in the conventional English system. However, the children's spellings did not always mirror those of conventional English. The children sometimes used a grapheme that never represents the phoneme in the standard system; that is, an illegal spelling. As in Chapter 4, I focus on illegal spellings that occurred at rates of 2.5% or more. I ask why the children selected that particular grapheme to represent the phoneme. In other cases, the students used a legal spelling significantly more often than expected given its frequency in the conventional system. Again, factors other than exposure to the relations between phonemes and graphemes in English words must be responsible for the error. I ask what these factors are. As in Chapter 4, I use binomial tests to compare the frequencies of correspondences in children's spelling to the frequencies of the correspondences in the conventional spellings of the same words.

Children's Spellings of Consonant Phonemes

In this section, the children's spellings of various consonant phonemes are discussed. The reader may find it helpful to refer to the consonant chart of Figure 1.5 when reading this section.

Stop Consonants

The stop consonants of English are /p/, /t/, /k/, /b/, /d/, and /g/. In discussing how the children spelled these consonants, I will first consider the children's spellings without regard to the contexts in which the consonants occurred. Next, I will discuss some errors that occurred for stop consonants in particular contexts.

Overall, the most frequent illegal substitutions on stop consonants were *d* for /b/, as in DEG for *big* and DOOKS for *books,* and *b* for /d/, as in BAEY for *day* and SOB for *showed.* These substitutions occurred at rates of 4.3% and 3.0%, respectively. Half of the first graders used *d* for /b/ or *b* for /d/ at least once. The rate of these confusions among children who attempted the phonemes at least four times ranged from 0% to almost 25%.

Children may confuse *b* and *d* for at least two reasons—the phonemic similarity between the sounds /b/ and /d/ and the visual similarity between the printed letters *b* and *d.* In terms of their sounds, /b/ and /d/ are alike in that both are stop consonants and both are voiced. The phonemes /b/ and /d/ differ from one another only in their place of articulation—bilabial for /b/ and alveolar for /d/. In terms of how they are written, *b* and *d* look similar whether they are in upper-case or lower-case letters.

If phonemic similarity were the only cause of confusions between *b* and *d,* confusions involving /p/ and /t/ should be as common as confusions involving /b/ and /d/. This is because the relation in sound between the voiceless stops /p/ and /t/ is parallel to the relation in sound between the voiced stops /b/ and /d/. In fact, /b/–/d/ confusions outnumbered /p/–/t/ confusions (3.5% versus 0.1%; $p < .001$ by a chi-square test). The reason must be that *b* and *d* look very similar while *p* and *t* do not.

Other than *d* for /b/ and *b* for /d/, no other illegal substitutions on stop consonants occurred at rates of 2.5% or more. However, there was one case in which the children used a legal spelling significantly more often than expected based on its occurrence in standard English. This was *d* for /t/. The letter *d* is an uncommon but legal spelling of /t/ (as in *used* [*to*]). However, the children employed *d* significantly more often than expected on this basis (2.5% versus 0.1%; $p < .001$ by a binomial test).

Why did the students overuse *d* for /t/? A look at their errors suggests two reasons. Most of the erroneous *d* spellings of /t/ occurred in words such as *latter.* As I discuss, the /t/s in such words sound similar to /d/. Also, /t/ after initial /s/ was subject to *d* spellings.[1] These errors, too, are based on sound.

I now turn to a discussion of some particular contexts in which the children misspelled stops. The first context to be discussed is that of flaps.

Flaps. In the speech of most Americans, the /t/ in a word like *latter* is produced differently than the /t/ in a word like *pretend.* In *pretend,* the tip of the tongue is raised to the alveolar ridge (the small protuberance behind the upper teeth) and remains there for some time before it is released. The /t/ of *pretend* is voiceless, as is usual for /t/. In *latter,* the tongue gives a rapid tap against the alveolar ridge and then drops away. The /t/ of *latter* is voiced rather than voiceless. It is called a *flapped* /t/. The phoneme /d/ also undergoes flapping; it is typically flapped in words like *ladder.* The middle consonants of *latter* and *ladder,* which are both voiced flaps, sound alike for most speakers. For many people, though, the words differ in the duration of the /æ/. The vowel is longer in *ladder* than *latter,* consistent with a general tendency for vowels to be longer before voiced consonants than before voiceless ones.

Because the flaps of *latter* and *ladder* are pronounced alike, linguists consider them to be the same at the phonetic level. However, the flaps are often thought to differ at the phonemic level. The middle sound of *latter* is considered an instance of /t/; the middle sound of *ladder* is considered an instance of /d/. Consistent with this assumption, I transcribed *latter* as containing /t/ and *ladder* as containing /d/. I will call the middle sound of *latter* flapped /t/ and the middle sound of *ladder* flapped /d/.

Within a word, /t/ flaps when it follows a vowel (or a vowel plus /r/) and precedes an unstressed vowel (Kahn, 1976). The /t/ of *latter* and the /t/ of *hearty* are in this context and are therefore flapped. The /t/ of *pretend* is not flapped, since it comes before a stressed vowel. Similarly, /d/ is flapped in *ladder* and *hardy* but not in *predict* (where it precedes a stressed vowel) or *handy* (where it follows /n/).

How did the first graders spell flapped /t/ and flapped /d/? The top part of Table

Table 5.1. Spellings of Flapped /t/ and /d/ and Medial Nonflapped /t/ and /d/

Spelling	Example	Number	Percent
Flapped /t/			
t or *tt*	EATR for *eater*	61	66.3
d or *dd*	WODR for *water*	19	20.7
omitted	LIOL for *little*	8	8.7
other	FUFFERBY for *flutterby*	4	4.3
	Total	92	100.0
Medial /t/ in nonflapped contexts[a]			
t or *tt*	PRTINEG for *pretending*	56	83.6
d or *dd*	WOND for *wanted*	3	4.5
omitted	WUNED for *wanted*	4	6.0
other	MNRIA for *mountains*	4	6.0
	Total	67	100.1
Flapped /d/			
t or *tt*	NOBUTTY for *nobody*	11	22.9
d or *dd*	MEDO for *meadow*	29	60.4
omitted	DUN for *didn't*	8	16.7
	Total	48	100.0
Medial /d/ in nonflapped contexts[b]			
t or *tt*	BITING for *building*	1	2.9
d or *dd*	HRDLIE for *hardly*	27	79.4
omitted	CANY for *candy*	4	11.8
other	UPRE for *under*	2	5.9
	Total	34	100.0

[a]After vowel (or vowel plus /r/) and before a stressed vowel or consonant, as in *pretend* or *outside;* after a consonant other than /r/ and before an unstressed vowel, as in *wanted*. The /t/ of *pizza* is not included in these figures since it is not spelled with *t* or *tt*.

[b]After vowel (or vowel plus /r/) and before a stressed vowel or consonant, as in *crocodile* or *sidewalk;* after a vowel and a consonant other than /r/ and before an unstressed vowel, as in *candy*.

5.1 shows the results for flapped /t/. The children's most common error, occurring 20.7% of the time, was to use *d* or *dd* in place of *t* or *tt*. This figure may be compared with the percentage of cases in which *non*flapped /t/ in the middle of a word was spelled with *t* or *tt*. The phoneme /t/ is not flapped in words such as *pretend* and *outside.* Here, the children symbolized /t/ with *d* or *dd* only 4.5% of the time. The children were more likely to spell /t/ with *d* or *dd* when it was flapped than when it was not flapped ($p < .01$ by a chi-square test).

Just as the children sometimes misspelled flapped /t/ with *d* or *dd,* they sometimes misspelled flapped /d/ with *t* or *tt*. As Table 5.1 shows, the children spelled flapped /d/ with *t* or *tt* 22.9% of the time. This rate is statistically indistinguishable by a chi-square test from the 20.7% rate of *d* or *dd* spellings for flapped /t/. The children were much more likely to spell flapped /d/ with *t* or *tt* than to spell non-flapped /d/ in the middle of a word in this manner (22.9% versus 2.9%; $p < .05$ by a chi-square test).

Examination of individual students' spellings confirmed that the use of *t* (or *tt*) for flapped /d/ was as common as the use of *d* (or *dd*) for flapped /t/. Of the children who attempted flapped /d/, 37% made at least one *t* (or *tt*) error. Likewise, 37% of the children who attempted flapped /t/ made at least one *d* (or *dd*) error. Because most children did not attempt a large number of flaps, I could not further investigate individual patterns of performance.

Thus, the students confused the spellings of /t/ and /d/ when these phonemes were in a particular environment—the environment in which flapping occurs in English. Moreover, the confusions were specific to /t/ and /d/, which are the only English stops that flap. When /p/, /b/, /k/, and /g/ occurred in the same environment in which /t/ and /d/ flap, as in *happy* and *babies,* their spellings were confused only 2.6% of the time. This is much less than the 21.4% confusion rate for the spellings of flapped /t/ and /d/ ($p < .001$ by a chi-square test). The specificity of confusions between *t* and *d*—specificity as to environment and specificity as to phonemes—shows that the confusions reflect the flapping of /t/ and /d/.

So far, I have examined /t/ and /d/ flaps *within* a word. Within a word, flapping occurs in the appropriate environment unless the word is pronounced in a very slow and artificial manner. In connected speech, /t/ and /d/ may also flap at the ends of words. Flapping may occur when /t/ and /d/ are preceded by /r/ or a vowel and when the following word starts with an unstressed vowel. Thus, the /t/ in the phrase *set Ann* may sound like the /d/ in *said Ann.* Although final /t/ and /d/ may flap in connected speech, the children did not seem to indicate this in their spelling. Final /t/ preceded by /r/ or a vowel was rarely spelled as *d* or *dd* and final /d/ preceded by /r/ or a vowel was rarely spelled as *t* or *tt*. Such errors occurred only 0.8% of the time, not significantly greater than the 0.0% rate for /t/ and /d/ at the beginnings of words, which never flap. This outcome supports my assumption that children try to spell words as they sound in isolated form rather than as they sound in connected speech.

Stop Consonants After /s/. In English, stop consonants after initial /s/ are spelled as if they were voiceless. They are symbolized with letters that are appropriate for the voiceless stops /p/, /t/, and /k/ rather than with letters that are appropriate for the voiced stops /b/, /d/, and /g/. Thus, we use the spellings *spy, sty,* and *sky* rather than **sby*, **sdy*, and **sgy*. Correspondingly, most linguists consider stops after /s/ to be voiceless at the beginning of a word or syllable. Following this assumption, I transcribed *sky* with /k/ rather than /g/.

Although stops after /s/ are usually thought to be voiceless, there are important similarities between stops after /s/ and voiced stops. In English, stops after /s/ are *unaspirated*, meaning that they are not pronounced with a following puff of air. Stops after /s/ are similar in this way to voiced stops, which are also unaspirated. They differ from voiceless stops, which—at least at the beginnings of words and syllables—are *aspirated*. Thus, the first sound of *pie* is aspirated, while the first sound of *buy* and the second sound of *spy* are not aspirated. The similarity between stops after /s/ and voiced stops emerges in measurements of *voice onset time* (VOT), which is defined as the length of time between the release of the stop closure and the beginning of vocal cord voicing. In a study with adults (Klatt, 1975), the average VOT for stops after initial /s/ and before a vowel, as in *spy*, was 22 milliseconds. This value was almost as low as the value of 16 milliseconds for initial voiced stops before vowels, as in *buy*. The average VOT for single initial voiceless stops, as in *pie*, was 61 milliseconds, substantially longer.

Several investigators have found that English-speaking adults are sensitive to the similarity in sound between stops after /s/ and voiced stops (Lotz, Abramson, Gerstman, Ingemann, & Nemser, 1960; Reeds and Wang, 1961). In these studies, the /s/ portion was deleted from tape recordings of words like *spy*. Listeners, when asked to identify the remaining words, considered them to begin with voiced stops rather than voiceless stops. For instance, when /s/ was removed from *spy*, people almost always said they heard *buy* rather than *pie*.

Although stops after /s/ are similar in important ways to voiced stops, stops after /s/ also share properties with voiceless stops. Typically, a vowel after a voiced stop has lower pitch than a vowel after a voiceless stop. The pitch on vowels following /s/-stop clusters is similar to the pitch on vowels following voiceless stops (Caisse, 1981; Ohde, 1984). In this respect, stops after /s/ seem to be like voiceless stops. However, the results of Lotz et al. (1960) and Reeds and Wang (1961) suggest that, at least at the beginnings of words, the similarity in vowel pitch between stops after /s/ and voiceless stops is less important to listeners than is the similarity in VOT between stops after /s/ and voiced stops.

Given that stops after initial /s/ share the salient characteristic of lack of aspiration with initial voiced stops, it is important to ask how children spell stops after /s/. Do they transcribe these stops as voiced, do they transcribe them as voiceless, or do they mix voiced and voiceless spellings? Table 5.2 shows how the first graders spelled /p/, /t/, and /k/ when they followed /s/ at the beginning of a word. Also shown, for purposes of comparison, are the children's spellings of /p/, /t/, and /k/ at the beginnings of words. The children were more likely to omit /p/, /t/, and /k/ when they followed initial /s/ than when they began a word ($p < .001$ by a chi-square test). The omission of stops following /s/ is one sign of children's general tendency to delete the second phonemes of initial clusters and is discussed in Chapter 8. When the children *did* symbolize stops after /s/, they usually represented them as voiceless; that is, with spellings appropriate for /p/, /t/, and /k/. However, a few voiced spellings appeared. These voiced spellings occurred in 3.4% of all cases

Table 5.2. Spellings of /p/, /t/ and /k/ After Word-Initial /s/ and Word-Initial

Spelling	Example	Number	Percent
After word-initial /s/			
voiceless	SHCKARY for *scary*	53	59.6
voiced	SGIE for *sky*	3	3.4
omitted	SINSE for *spines*	30	33.7
other	SROY for *store*	3	3.4
	Total	89	100.1
Word-initial			
voiceless	TRN for *turn*	764	96.7
voiced	GARY for *care*	5	0.6
omitted	LAG for *collection*	1	0.1
other	WRIS for *cries*	20	2.5
	Total	790	99.9

or 5.1% of all cases in which the stop was represented. In contrast, the children spelled word-initial voiceless stops as voiced only 0.6% of the time. Voiced spellings were significantly more frequent after initial /s/ than at the beginnings of words ($p < .05$ by a chi-square test).[2]

Thus, the first graders occasionally spelled stop consonants after /s/ as voiced. Although the rate of such spellings in the children's spontaneous writings was low, the suggestion that some children misspell stops after /s/ as voiced is strengthened by the results of experiments discussed later in this chapter.

From the perspective of standard English, SGIE is an illegal spelling of *sky*. After all, /k/ is never symbolized with *g* in English. However, this error has a reasonable phonological explanation. In this case, as in many others, children's so-called illegal spellings reveal a surprisingly fine appreciation of the sounds of words.

/t/ and /d/ Before /r/. With flaps and stops after /s/, certain of children's misspellings accurately represent aspects of a word's sound. A similar phenomenon occurs with /t/ and /d/ before /r/. When /t/ precedes /r/, its articulation changes under the influence of the following /r/. The place of articulation moves back in the mouth, from alveolar (the tip of the tongue contacting the alveolar ridge) to palato-alveolar (the front of the tongue contacting the back of the alveolar ridge). Also, the closure is released slowly rather than quickly. Thus, /t/ before /r/ is somewhat affricated. Since it has some degree of affrication, it is similar to the voiceless palato-alveolar affricate /tʃ/. Just as the /t/ of *try* is similar to /tʃ/, so the /d/ of *dry* is similar to /dʒ/.

Given the properties of /t/ and /d/ before /r/, how did the students spell /t/ and /d/ in these contexts? The results are shown in Table 5.3. Although /t/ before /r/ was usually spelled with *t*, there were two cases in which *ch*, the most common spelling for /tʃ/, was used. These errors may reflect the similarity in sound between /tʃ/ and /t/ before /r/. In addition, there was one case in which /t/ before /r/ was spelled with *c* and one case in which it was spelled with *h*. Because *c* and *h* form the *ch* digraph, and because children sometimes omit one letter of a digraph, these errors

Table 5.3. Spellings of /t/ and /d/ before /r/

Spelling	Example	Number	Percent
/t/ before /r/			
t	TROK for *truck*	35	77.8
ch	CHRAP for *trap*	2	4.4
c	CID for *tried*	1	2.2
h	SHEG for *string*	1	2.2
omitted	SRAG for *string*	4	8.9
other	THRAP for *trap*	2	4.4
	Total	45	99.9
/d/ before /r/			
d	DRAST for *dressed*	6	75.0
j	JRAD for *drowned*	1	12.5
other	BRAINDED for *drowned*	1	12.5
	Total	8	100.0

may also reflect the affrication of /t/ before /r/. The children only attempted eight words with /d/ before /r/. The /d/ was usually spelled with *d,* but *j*—the most common spelling of /ʤ/—was used once. Counting *ch, c, h,* and *j* as attempts to represent affricates, /t/ and /d/ before /r/ were spelled as affricates 9.4% of the time.

Although the children sometimes spelled /t/ and /d/ before /r/ with letters that were appropriate for /ʧ/ and /ʤ/, they rarely (0.1% of the time) used such spellings for other /t/s and /d/s. Affricate spellings were significantly more frequent for /t/ and /d/ before /r/ than for /t/ and /d/ in other contexts ($p < .001$ by a chi-square test).

Affricate spellings of /t/ and /d/ before /r/ occurred among 15% of the students who attempted /tr/ and /dr/. Because most of the children did not spell a large number of words containing /tr/ and /dr/, it was not possible to determine whether children who spelled /t/ before /r/ as an affricate also tended to spell /d/ before /r/ as an affricate.

Errors such as CHRAP for *trap* and JRAD for *drowned* are illegal in standard English. However, like many of the illegal spellings discussed in this book, the errors are by no means random or haphazard. They accurately reflect the sounds of /t/ and /d/ before /r/. Although the similarity between /t/ before /r/ and /ʧ/ is not represented in the English writing system, it is no less real than those properties of sounds that are.

Changes in Stop Consonant Spellings Between the First and Second Semesters. For each of the stop consonant spellings that has been discussed, I compared the error rate during the first semester of the school year with the error rate during the second semester. Most of the differences were small and none was significant by a chi-square test.

Fricatives

The fricatives of English are /f/, /θ/, /s/, /ʃ/, /h/, /v/, /ð/, /z/, and /ʒ/. Only /θ/, /ð/, and /ʃ/ gave rise to illegal substitutions that exceeded my cut-off of 2.5%. In addition, one spelling of /z/ was significantly overused with respect to its frequency in standard spelling. In the following sections, I consider these phenomena in more detail.[3]

Fricatives with Digraph Spellings. The fricatives /θ/, /ð/, and /ʃ/ have digraphs as their most common spellings. These digraphs are *th* for both /θ/ and /ð/ and *sh* for /ʃ/. Many of the children's illegal substitution errors on /θ/, /ð/, and /ʃ/ reflected partial knowledge of these common digraphs. Errors that used the first letter of a digraph were especially frequent. The children spelled /ʃ/ as *s* 31.4% of the time, /θ/ as *t* 28.0% of the time, and /ð/ as *t* 9.0% of the time. Table 5.4 gives examples of these errors.

I have argued that children spell /θ/ as *t* because they are somewhat familiar with the *th* digraph. Another possible explanation for this error is that /θ/ is similar to *t* and that children spell it as *t* for this reason. However, this explanation does not fit with my results. On the grounds of phonemic similarity alone, *d* spellings of /ð/ should be as common as *t* spellings of /θ/. This is because the relation between /d/ and /ð/ is the same as the relation between /t/ and /θ/. However, *t* spellings of /θ/ were much more common than *d* spellings of /ð/ (28.0% versus 0.2%; $p < .001$ by a chi-square test).

Explanations based only on phonemic similarity also fail for the other errors under discussion. The relation between /ʃ/ and /s/ and /z/ is parallel to the relation between /θ/ and /f/ and /v/, but the children spelled /ʃ/ as *s* much more often than they spelled /θ/ as *f* or *v* (31.4% versus 5.0%; $p < .001$ by a chi-square test). In addition, the relation between /ð/ and /t/ mirrors the relation between /θ/ and /d/, but children spelled /ð/ as *t* more often than they spelled /θ/ as *d* (9.0% versus 0.6%; $p < .001$ by a chi-square test). Thus, the use of *t* for /θ/ and /ð/ and *s* for /ʃ/ must reflect partial knowledge of common digraphs.

Although errors that used only the first letter of a digraph were quite common,

Table 5.4. Examples Containing Misspellings of Fricatives

Phoneme	Error	Examples
/ʃ/	*s*	SE for *she*
		SALTR for *shelter*
		WOS for *wash*
	h	HEY for *she*
		HAPS for *sheeps* [sic]
/θ/	*t*	BIRT for *birth*
		TAYK for *think*
		TUT for *tooth*
	f	BUFE for *both*
		TF for *tooth*
/ð/	*t*	TA for *the*
		TAT for *that*
		ATRE for *other*
/z/	*z*	PAZ for *pounds*
		ROGZ for *rogues*
		CEZ for *cheese*
		HIZ for *his*

errors that used only the second letter were less frequent. The sole second-letter error to exceed my cut-off of 2.5% was *h* for /ʃ/. This error occurred 3.8% of the time (see Table 5.4).

Many of the first graders made errors that used only the first letter of a digraph. About half of the students who attempted /ʃ/ and /θ/ produced these errors, as did over a third of the students who attempted /ð/. The errors occurred at rates of 50% or more among some children. The use of *h* for /ʃ/ was less widespread. Only 12% of the children who attempted /ʃ/ ever misspelled it as *h*.

For the fricatives under discussion, only one other illegal substitution exceeded my cut-off of 2.5%. This was *f* for /θ/, which occurred 4.3% of the time. Examples appear in Table 5.4. This error probably reflects the similarity between /θ/ and /f/. These two phonemes are alike in manner of articulation and in voicing. They differ only in place of articulation—labio-dental for /f/ and the neighboring dental place of articulation for /θ/. Of the children who attempted /θ/, 13% produced *f* spellings.

I have argued that normal first graders' misspellings do not usually stem from mispronunciation. However, problems in pronouncing /θ/ could cause some of the *f* errors observed in this study. /θ/ is one of the hardest phonemes for English-speaking children to pronounce (Menyuk, 1971; Snow, 1963). Children sometimes substitute /f/ for /θ/. A first grader who occasionally mispronounced /θ/ as /f/ would not be considered to have a severe speech problem and so might have been included in the present study.

The errors discussed in this section tended to decrease from the first semester of the school year to the second. The decrease was significant in the cases of *t* for /θ/ (38.6% to 19.8%; $p < .025$ by a chi-square test) and *t* for /ð/ (12.5% to 6.6%; $p < .05$ by a chi-square test). The children seemed to learn the conventional *th* spelling as the school year progressed.

/z/. Children's spellings of /z/ are of special interest. Given the correspondences between phonemes and graphemes in the words that first graders know how to read, children should spell /z/ as *s*. This is because *s* is the most common spelling of /z/ in English.[4] However, two other things may cause children to spell /z/ as *z*—formal teaching and knowledge of letter names. The children's phonics book and spelling lists stressed the correspondence between /z/ and *z*. At home, too, children who asked how to spell /z/ would surely be told to use *z*. This is because teachers and parents think more in terms of how letters are pronounced than in terms of how sounds are spelled. Because *z* is almost always pronounced as /z/ when reading, people may overlook the fact that /z/ is often spelled with *s*. Children's knowledge of letter names may also cause them to spell /z/ as *z*. The phoneme /z/ appears in the name of *z* but not in the name of *s*. Thus, if experience with print is most important, children should generally spell /z/ as *s*. If teaching and letter names are more important, children should generally spell /z/ as *z*. The first graders in my study usually spelled /z/ as *s*. This held true whether I looked at all spellings of /z/ (78.3% *s* spellings) or just spellings of /z/ in incorrectly spelled words (68.9% *s* spellings). Corroborating findings reported in Chapter 3, the correspondences between phonemes and graphemes that are embodied in printed words had a greater effect on these first graders' spellings than did teaching and letter names.

Although the students frequently spelled /z/ as *s,* they *did* use *z* significantly more often than expected given its frequency in standard English (7.1% versus 0.2%; $p < .001$ by a binomial test). Table 5.4 gives some examples of the incorrect use of *z* for /z/. These occasional *z* spellings may reflect the teaching that the children received, together with the fact that /z/ occurs in the name of *z.* The *z* errors appeared in about a third of the children who attempted /z/. They were fairly numerous in some children, occurring at a rate of 44% in one child. The use of *z* for /z/ decreased from 13.7% in the first semester to 3.3% in the second semester ($p < .001$ by a chi-square test). Thus, the children became less likely to spell /z/ as *z* as they observed that /z/ is usually spelled with *s.*

Affricates

English contains two affricates, /ʧ/ and /ʤ/. Affricates are usually thought to be single phonemes; my transcriptions considered them as such. However, affricates actually contain two articulatory gestures. The affricate /ʧ/ starts with a stop portion similar to /t/ followed by a fricative portion similar to /ʃ/. Similarly, /ʤ/ may be analyzed as /d/ followed by /ʒ/. Do the children's spellings of affricates sometimes reflect the two-part nature of these consonants, just as children's spellings of vowel diphthongs sometimes reflect the two-part nature of these vowels?

The students' most frequent spelling of /ʧ/ was *ch.* However, *t* was tied with *c,* the first letter of the *ch* digraph, for second place. Although *t* may symbolize /ʧ/, as in *fortune,* this spelling was not taught in school. The children used *t* significantly more often than expected given its frequency in the conventional spellings of the words that they attempted (10.1% versus 1.3%; $p < .001$ by a binomial test). Table 5.5 provides some examples of the use of *t* for /ʧ/. For /ʤ/, children used the illegal *d* 4.3% of the time. Because the children did not attempt many words containing /ʤ/, this rate corresponds to only two spellings. These errors also appear in Table 5.5. Of the children who attempted /ʧ/ and /ʤ/, almost a quarter produced *t* or *d* spellings.

Children may spell /ʧ/ as *t* and /ʤ/ as *d* because the affricates begin with a stop consonant gesture. Supporting this view, consonant phonemes that were not stops and that did not begin with a stop consonant gesture were rarely symbolized with a grapheme appropriate for the stop consonant with the same voicing and the most similar place of articulation. For example, the children never spelled the fricative /z/ with a grapheme that was appropriate for /d/, the stop consonant that, like /z/, is voiced and has an alveolar place of articulation. Consonants that were not affricates or stops were spelled as the corresponding stop 0.1% of the time, significantly less than the 7.9% rate observed for affricates ($p < .001$ by a chi-square test).[5] In other words, the children sometimes used stop spellings for affricates, the articulation of which begins with a stop, but rarely used stop spellings for fricatives, nasals, liquids, and glides.

As I have shown, some spellings of affricates, like *t* for /ʧ/, represented only the initial stop part of the affricate. The children did not make any errors like *tsh* for /ʧ/—errors that represented *both* the stop and fricative portions of the affricate. For those children who think of affricates as two-part sounds, the first part of the "clus-

Table 5.5. Examples Containing Misspellings of Affricates

Phoneme	Error	Examples
/tʃ/	t	TEKN for *chicken*
		TESE for *cheese*
		TZ for *cheese*
		TETR for *teacher*
	c	CEZ for *cheese*
		COILE for *chili*
	s	TESUR for *teacher*
		WIS for *witch*
	ck	CKES for *cheese*
		KACK for *catch*
	th	THES for *cheese*
		PUTHT for *punched*
	g	CEG for *catch*
	j	JES for *cheese*
	k	KEC for *cheese*
/dʒ/	d	DAM for *jam*
		DOST for *just*
	s	ORESIS for *oranges*
		LOSUZ for *largest*

ter" must be more salient than the second. Thus, children sometimes symbolize only the first part of the affricate.

Other spellings of /tʃ/ included *c* (10.1%) and *s* (8.9%). Occurring at lower rates were *ck* (3.8%), *th* (3.8%), *g* (2.5%), *j* (2.5%) and *k* (2.5%). Because /tʃ/ was so uncommon, the last five errors occurred only two or three times each. Examples appear in Table 5.5.

Turning to /dʒ/, illegal *s* substitutions occurred at a rate of 4.3% (see Table 5.5). This rate corresponds to only two errors, given the few spellings of /dʒ/. The use of *s* for /dʒ/, like the occasional use of *s* and *th* for /tʃ/, suggests that children group affricates with fricatives having similar places of articulation.

The errors on affricates discussed in this section tended to decrease from the first semester to the second semester of the school year. However, none of the decreases were statistically reliable.

In sum, children implicitly group affricates with one another and also with fricatives that have similar places of articulation. In addition, children relate affricates to stop consonants that have similar places of articulation and the same value of voicing. Children's grouping of affricates with fricatives and stops as well as with other affricates reflects the hybrid nature of affricates—the fact that they begin with a stop consonant gesture and end with a fricative gesture.

Nasals

English contains three nasals, /m/, /n/, and /ŋ/. When spelling /m/ and /n/, the students did not make any illegal substitutions at rates of 2.5% or more. Nor did they use any legal spellings significantly more often than expected.

With /ŋ/, the children used the illegal *g* at a rate of 5.8%. Examples are KEGS for *kings,* ROG for *wrong,* and THGC for *think.* A quarter of the children who attempted /ŋ/ produced *g* errors, some at rates as high as 50%. The rate of these errors did not differ significantly between the first and second semesters of the school year.

Why did the students sometimes misspell /ŋ/ as *g?* The similarity between /g/ and /ŋ/ may contribute to these errors. If phonemic similarity were the only cause, however, *g* spellings of /ŋ/ should be no more common than *b* spellings of /m/ or *d* spellings of /n/. This is because the relation between /g/ and /ŋ/ (two voiced consonants that share place of articulation and that differ in manner of articulation, stop versus nasal) is parallel to the relation between /b/ and /m/ and the relation between /d/ and /n/. In fact, *g* errors for /ŋ/ outnumbered *b* errors for /m/ and *d* errors for /n/ (5.8% versus 0.1%; $p < .001$ by a chi-square test). Thus, children's *g* spellings of /ŋ/ must reflect partial knowledge of the *ng* digraph. Children sometimes use one letter of the digraph rather than both letters. In the case of *ng,* use of the first letter of the digraph is a legal error.

Liquids and Glides

English contains the liquids /r/ and /l/ and the glides /w/ and /j/. The children did not make any illegal substitutions at rates of 2.5% or more on these phonemes.

Comparison with Results of Other Studies

Read

How do the consonant spellings observed in this study compare with the consonant spellings observed by Charles Read? Despite the differences between the two studies in subjects, circumstances, and sampling procedures, the consonant substitutions in the two studies are similar in many respects.

The children in both studies sometimes spelled flapped /t/ as *d.* Read observed errors such as WOODR for *water* and BODOM for *bottom,* which are similar to errors found here. Read also reported some *t* spellings of flapped /d/, as in NOBUTE for *nobody.* Although Read did not present quantitative data on this point, he implied that errors like BODOM, in which flapped /t/ is spelled as *d,* outnumbered errors like NOBUTE, in which flapped /d/ is spelled as *t.* If so, Read's results on flaps differ from mine. In this study, *d* spellings of flapped /t/ and *t* spellings of flapped /d/ were equally common.

In the case of /t/ and /d/ before /r/, the preschoolers studied by Read produced spellings such as CHRIE for *try* and JRAGIN for *dragon.* These errors are similar to ones observed here. Although there were relatively few affricate spellings of /t/ and /d/ before /r/ in each study, their occurrence in two separate naturalistic studies, as well as in several experiments (Barton, Miller, & Macken, 1980; Read, 1975; Treiman, 1985b), confirms that they are not random errors.

Read focused on phonologically based errors; he paid little attention to orthographically based errors. However, the children in Read's study, like the children in my study, seemed to be influenced by exposure to print. Many of their errors appeared to reflect partial knowledge of common digraphs. In Read's study, like the present one, *c, s,* and *g* were the most frequent nonstandard spellings of /ʧ/, /ʃ/, and /ŋ/, respectively. The most frequent error on both /θ/ and /ð/ was *t*.

Confusions between *b* and *d* appeared among Read's preschoolers as among my first graders. However, *b–d* confusions were less frequent in Read's study than in mine and Read did not specifically discuss these errors. Thus, although beginning spellers do sometimes confuse *b* and *d,* these reversal errors are not as common as has sometimes been implied. In both Read's study and mine, many consonant errors occurred at rates substantially higher than the rate for *b–d* confusions.

To summarize, the preschoolers in Read's study and the first graders in my study made many of the same errors on consonants. This is an important result. It, together with the findings reviewed by Read (1986), shows that the phenomena discovered by Read are not restricted to precocious children of professional parents. Nor are they restricted to children who begin to write outside of school with little or no formal instruction in reading and writing. Rather, the errors in question occur among many children who are beginning to spell.

Treiman

Some of the phenomena observed here—*ch* spellings of /t/ before /r/, for example—were first discovered by Read. Other phenomena had not previously been investigated. For some of these latter observations, I have carried out experimental work to verify that the phenomena are real and to study them in more detail. This work will be reviewed in the following sections. I will also review experiments that were designed to address some remaining questions about certain of the phenomena discovered by Read.

Stops After Initial /s/. Although Read (1980) mentioned that children sometimes spell stop consonants after /s/ as voiced, he did not tabulate the spellings of stop consonants after /s/ separately from the spellings of stop consonants in other positions. In my study, there were significantly more voiced spellings for /p/, /t/, and /k/ after word-initial /s/ than at the beginnings of words. However, the evidence from the naturalistic study, on its own, is weak. The first graders did not spell many words beginning with /s/-stop clusters. When they *did* spell such words, they sometimes omitted the stop altogether, giving no information on whether they categorized the stop as voiced or voiceless. Thus, it was important to verify the suggestion that children sometimes spell stops after /s/ as voiced.

In experimental work on the spelling of stops after /s/ (Treiman, 1985c), I asked children to spell a relatively large number of syllables beginning with /s/-stop clusters. The procedures in the experiments were controlled to a degree that is not possible in a naturalistic study. For example, the syllables to be spelled were presented on tape to ensure that all children heard the same thing. The children were asked to repeat each syllable before spelling it, ensuring that the children correctly heard and pronounced the syllables. Most of the items in the experiments were not real words. Thus, the children could not have memorized their conventional spellings.

The results of two experiments showed that kindergarteners and first graders sometimes spell stops after /s/ as voiced (Treiman, 1985c). Children who correctly used *b* for /b'o/ and *p* for /p'o/ and who correctly spelled the second sounds of syllables like /sn'o/ and /sl'o/ sometimes spelled the second sound of /sp'o/ as if it were the voiced /b/ rather than the voiceless /p/. A few children consistently produced voiced spellings of stops after /s/. More often, however, children vacillated between voiced spellings and voiceless ones. Voiced spellings were less common among better readers than among poorer readers.

There were more voiced spellings of stops after /s/ among the first graders in the experiments than the first graders in the naturalistic study. For the first graders in my experiment, the percentage of voiced spellings relative to all voiced plus voiceless spellings was about 15%. For the first graders in the naturalistic study, the percentage was about 5%. One reason for the difference is that the children in the experiments spelled nonsense syllables rather than familiar real words. Thus, they could not rely on memorized whole-word spellings. For the kindergarteners in the experiments, the percentage of voiced spellings relative to voiced plus voiceless spellings was even higher, around 37%.

Are children's spellings of stop consonants after /s/ related in any systematic way to their pronunciations of these consonants? I addressed this issue in collaboration with Joseph Stemberger (Stemberger & Treiman, unpublished data). We chose ten kindergarteners who had participated in the second of my two experiments (Treiman, 1985c). The children were tested not long after they had completed the experiment. We asked the children to pronounce one word with each of initial /p/, /b/, /t/, /d/, /k/, and /g/ and two words with each of initial /sp/, /st/, and /sk/. The words (taken from Catts & Kamhi, 1984) were *pot, boat, top, dog, Kate, gate, spot, spoon, stop, stove, skate,* and *skin.* A picture was drawn for each word and the child was asked to name the picture. In some cases, as with a picture of a girl named *Kate,* the experimenter said the word herself when she first showed the picture. Usually, though, this was not necessary. Each child pronounced each word five times. Measurements of voice onset time or VOT were made using a Voice Identification RT 1000 real-time spectrograph.

Table 5.6 shows the average VOT values in milliseconds for voiceless stops, voiced stops, and stops after /s/. The column on the right presents the results for all ten children as a group. The other columns show the results separately for the four children who produced 50% or more voiced spellings of stops after /s/ in the experiment and the six children who produced less than 50% voiced spellings.

The VOTs show no clear differences between the children who spelled stops after /s/ as voiced a majority of the time and the children who favored voiceless spellings. To confirm this impression, an analysis of variance was performed using the factors of child's spelling (more than 50% voiced spellings versus less than 50% voiced spellings), type of stop (initial voiced, initial voiceless, stop after /s/), and place of articulation (bilabial [/p/, /b/], alveolar [/t/, /d/], velar [/k/, /g/]). There was no main effect of child's spelling and no interactions involving this factor. These results confirm that the pattern of VOT values did not differ for children who spelled stops after /s/ as voiced a majority of the time and children who did not.

The analysis of variance did show a main effect of type of stop ($F(2,16) = 65.6$, $p < .001$). VOTs for initial voiced stops were the shortest, VOTs for stops after /s/

Table 5.6. Average VOT Values in Milliseconds for Stop Consonants in the Stenberger and Treiman Experiment on Spelling and Pronunciation

Consonant	Children with More Than 50% Voiced Spellings of Stops After /s/	Children with Less Than 50% Voiced Spellings of Stops After /s/	All Children
/p/	69.3	80.3	75.9
/t/	81.0	94.0	88.8
/k/	82.7	97.5	91.5
/b/	−5.5	−13.8	−10.5
/d/	−14.8	11.0	0.7
/g/	6.4	2.4	4.0
/p/ after /s/	10.1	12.4	11.4
/t/ after /s/	20.2	20.7	20.5
/k/ after /s/	25.5	26.0	25.8

were intermediate, and VOTs for voiceless stops were the longest (all differences significant at $p < .05$ by Tukey tests). There was also a main effect of place of articulation ($F(2,16) = 8.1, p < .005$). VOTs for bilabial stops were shorter than those for alveolar and velar stops, which were statistically indistinguishable. These results mirror the findings of previous studies with adults (e.g., Klatt, 1975; Lisker & Abramson, 1964; Ohde, 1984). This convergence gives us confidence in the reliability of our measurements.

Thus, children's spellings of stops after /s/ are not closely tied to their own pronunciations. On the dimension of VOT, stops after /s/ were no more similar to voiced stops among children who favored voiced spellings than among children who favored voiceless spellings. *All* children, regardless of how they spelled stops after /s/, pronounced them with fairly short VOTs. Although the study was a small one, its findings agree with findings reported elsewhere in this book: Children's spellings do not necessarily reflect the phonetic details of their pronunciations.

In conclusion, children do not always spell stops after /s/ in the conventional way. Children who know the links between /b/ and *b* and /p/ and *p* sometimes choose *b* for the second sound of /sp/. There is no evidence that children's spellings of stops after /s/ are systematically related to the phonetic details of the children's pronunciations.

/t/ and /d/ Before /r/. The first graders in my study, like the children studied by Read, sometimes symbolized /t/ and /d/ before /r/ with letters that were more appropriate for /tʃ/ and /dʒ/. For example, they spelled *trap* as CHRAP and *drowned* as JRAD. In an experiment with kindergarteners and first graders (Treiman, 1985b), I examined these errors in more detail.

The experiment was designed to address three questions that are not answered by the naturalistic results presented in this book or the naturalistic results of Read. First, are the errors specific to /t/ and /d/ before /r/? Earlier in this chapter, I reported that affricate spellings were more frequent for /t/ and /d/ before /r/ than for /t/ and /d/ in other contexts. These other contexts were often single /t/ and /d/, as in *Tom* and *had*. Given children's difficulties in spelling consonant clusters (see Chapter 8), it would be preferable to compare /t/ and /d/ before /r/ to /t/ and

/d/ before /w/ (/w/ being the only consonant other than /r/ that may follow initial /t/ and /d/ in English). If errors like *ch* and *c* for /t/ reflect the sound of /t/ before /r/, rather than something about clusters per se, these errors should be more common on words like *trap* than words like *twin*. A second question addressed by the experiment was that of individual differences. Do children who symbolize the affrication of /t/ before /r/ tend to do the same for /d/ before /r/? Finally, the experiment also examined the link between reading ability and the spelling of /t/ and /d/ before /r/.

In the experiment, kindergarteners and first graders were asked to spell the first sounds of syllables beginning with /t/, /tr/, /tw/, /d/, /dr/, and /dw/. Syllables with initial /tʃ/ and /dʒ/ were also included; the results for these syllables are described in the following section of this chapter. The children usually spelled initial /t/ and /d/ before /r/ in the conventional way, with *t* and *d*. However, they sometimes spelled these sounds with letters that were more appropriate for affricates. The percentage of affricate spellings in the experiment was about 15%, as compared with about 9% for the first graders in the naturalistic study. This difference may reflect the fact that the majority of syllables in the experiment were not familiar to the children. Affricate spellings were most common for /t/ and /d/ before /r/. There was no reliable increase in affricate spellings for /t/ and /d/ before /w/ as compared with single /t/ and /d/. Thus, errors like *c* for /t/ before /r/ primarily reflect the sound of /t/ before /r/. They do not just reflect the fact that the consonant occurs in a cluster. As for the issue of individual differences, there was some consistency in the children's spellings. Children who produced many affricate spellings for /t/ before /r/ tended to do the same for /d/ before /r/. Finally, the nonstandard spellings were less common among better readers than among poorer readers.

/tʃ/ and /dʒ/. The first graders in the naturalistic study sometimes spelled /tʃ/ with *t* and /dʒ/ with *d*. These errors, I suggested, reflect the similarity between the affricates /tʃ/ and /dʒ/ and the stop consonants /t/ and /d/. Although /tʃ/ is usually considered to be a single phoneme, it actually contains a stop portion similar to /t/ followed by a fricative portion similar to /ʃ/. Likewise, /dʒ/ may be analyzed as /d/ followed by /ʒ/.

Because the first graders in the naturalistic study made only a few *t* and *d* errors on /tʃ/ and /dʒ/, and because such errors had not been reported previously, additional work was needed to verify that some children use *t* for /tʃ/ and *d* for /dʒ/. Another question is whether *t* and *d* spellings truly reflect the phonological characteristics of /tʃ/ and /dʒ/. It is possible, if unlikely, that children use these letters because they know how to read words like *fortune* and *credulous*. In these words, /tʃ/ and /dʒ/ are spelled with *t* and *d,* respectively. The results of the naturalistic study speak against this reading-experience hypothesis, since children used *t* for /t ʃ/ significantly more often than expected given the frequency of this correspondence in English. If *t* and *d* spellings of /tʃ/ and /dʒ/ decrease as reading skill increases, this would further support the idea that *t* and *d* spellings do not reflect knowledge of uncommon words like *fortune* and *credulous.*

In the experiment just described (Treiman, 1985b), the children were asked to spell syllables with initial /tʃ/ and /dʒ/ as well as syllables with initial /t/, /tr/, /tw/,

/d/, /dr/, and /dw/. The most common error on initial /tʃ/ was *t*. The most common error on /dʒ/ was *d*. Pooling over kindergarteners and first graders, stop spellings of /tʃ/ occurred 24.5% of the time. Stop spellings of /dʒ/ were much less common, occurring 5.9% of the time. In the naturalistic study, too, stop spellings were more frequent for /tʃ/ than for /dʒ/. The reason for this difference is probably that the most common spelling of /tʃ/ is a difficult-to-learn digraph *(ch),* whereas /dʒ/ is usually spelled with a single letter (*j* or *g*). Despite the difference in the overall rate of stop spellings for /tʃ/ and /dʒ/, children who spelled /tʃ/ as a stop also tended to spell /dʒ/ as a stop. The use of *t* and *d* for /tʃ/ and /dʒ/ was less frequent among better readers than among poorer readers. Thus, knowledge of uncommon words like *fortune* and *credulous* cannot be the major cause of stop spellings. Rather, the spellings reflect the phonological properties of /tʃ/ and /dʒ/.

Factors That Affect Children's Spellings of Consonants

In this section, I attempt to draw together my findings on children's spellings of consonant phonemes. I consider the effects of several factors on children's spellings, including experience with conventional spelling, phonological knowledge, and knowledge of letter names.

Exposure to Print

The printed words that children see and read serve as a model for their own attempts to spell. Children notice which letters are used to represent which sounds in the words that they know. When spelling a new word, they often adopt the same correspondences.

Although first graders learn a great deal about the links between phonemes and graphemes from their reading, children do not master all the correspondences to which they are exposed. For example, children often see the words *the, they,* and *there.* When spelling these words, however, they sometimes write *t* for *th.* Partial knowledge of standard spelling is also revealed in confusions of *b* and *d.* With lowercase letters, these errors suggest that children know the shapes of the letters but are unsure of their orientations.

Phonology

In an alphabetic writing system, a word's spelling reflects its sound. Thus, children's spellings are affected by their knowledge of the sounds in words. The influence of phonology on spelling may be seen in the effects of phonological similarity. Children implicitly know that /tʃ/ and /dʒ/ are more similar to one another than are /tʃ/ and /m/. Correspondingly, they are more likely to misspell /tʃ/ as *j* or *g* than to misspell /tʃ/ as *m*. The results presented in this chapter and in Chapter 3 suggest several conclusions about the kinds of similarity among consonants to which children are sensitive. For one thing, children consider consonants that differ only in voicing to be particularly close. They sometimes confuse the spellings of consonants that are alike in all respects but voicing. Also, children recognize the similarity between affricates, on the one hand, and stops and fricatives, on the other. They implicitly know that affricates share properties with both stops and fricatives.

The conclusion that children are sensitive to similarity relations among consonants parallels the conclusion reached in Chapter 4 for vowels. With both vowels and consonants, children do more than distinguish phonemes from one another. Without being formally taught to do so, children learn that some phonemes are more similar to one another than others are. The similarity relations that are revealed by children's spellings resemble the similarity relations that are recognized by linguists. Young children differ from linguists, of course, in having little *explicit* awareness of the properties of sounds.

Errors such as CHRAP for *trap* and SGIE for *sky* provide further evidence that children's spellings reflect the sounds of words. Although these spellings are usually classified as illegal, they represent the words' spoken forms in a reasonable manner.

To what level of language are children attending when they produce spellings like CHRAP for *trap* and SGIE for *sky?* If the University of Virginia researchers' use of the term phonetic is meant to parallel the use of this term by linguists, their theory implies that children at the semiphonetic and phonetic stages of spelling development attempt to depict the phonetic level of speech. I call this the *phonetic spelling hypothesis.* To explore the implications of the phonetic spelling hypothesis, recall the distinction between the phonetic and phonemic levels of language that was made in Chapter 1. Phonetic information is more detailed than phonemic information. At the phonetic level, the first sounds of *trap* and *tap* are different. The first is affricated, whereas the second is aspirated. At the phonemic level, the first sounds of *trap* and *tap* are alike. Both are members of the /t/ phoneme. In such cases, the conventional English writing system represents the phonemic similarity rather than the phonetic difference. The first sounds of *trap* and *tap* are spelled alike even thought they have different phonetic forms.

According to the phonetic spelling hypothesis, children's phonemic representations of words may well be the same as adults'. Like adults, children consider both *trap* and *tap* to begin with the phoneme /t/. The problem is that children at the semiphonetic and phonetic stages of spelling development do not represent the phonemic level in their spelling. They spell the two /t/s differently because the /t/s have different phonetic forms. Thus, during the semiphonetic and phonetic stages of spelling development, children do not yet know that spelling reflects the phonemic level (and deeper levels) of the language. They fundamentally misunderstand the nature of the English writing system. Only when children reach the transitional stage of spelling development do they realize that the writing symbolizes deeper levels of the language. With this insight, errors like CHRAP for *trap* disappear. Thus, beginning writers must learn which level of the spoken language they are to represent, just as they must learn specific links between sounds and letters. Children do not necessarily assume that letters of the alphabet stand for phonemes.

If the phonetic spelling hypothesis is correct, children are sensitive to the phonetic differences *within* phonemic categories as well as to the differences *among* phoneme categories. Just as children hear the difference between the first sounds of *tap* and *cap,* so they hear the difference between the first sounds of *trap* and *tap.*

Children sometimes misspell *trap* as CHRAP because they try to symbolize phonetic variation in their spelling.

The phonetic spelling hypothesis ascribes spelling errors like CHRAP and SGIE to children's tendency to represent speech at the phonetic level. However, there are at least two other explanations for such errors. One possibility is that children's phonemic representations differ, in some cases, from those assumed by the conventional writing system and those assumed for adults. This hypothesis may be called the *different phonemic representations hypothesis*. In this view, some children assign the first consonant of *trap* to the phoneme /tʃ/ rather than the phoneme /t/. Some children assign the second consonant of *sky* to /g/ rather than /k/. If so, CHRAP and SGIE accurately reflect the phonemic level as it exists for these children.

The different phonemic representations hypothesis maintains that beginning spellers attempt to symbolize speech at the phonemic level. Very early in the process of learning to spell, children know that letters of the alphabet represent phonemes rather than allophones. Children sometimes misspell words because their phonemic systems do not fully match those assumed by the conventional writing system. Under the different phonemic representations hypothesis, learning to read and spell may actually change certain aspects of children's phonemic systems. For example, some preliterate children may categorize the second consonant of *sky* as /g/. As children observe that this sound is spelled with *k* instead of *g*, they may reassign the consonant to /k/.

Yet a third possibility is that children do not assign the second consonant of *sky* to either /k/ or /g/. They consider it to be a separate unit, one that is neither voiced or voiceless. Trubetzkoy (1939/1969) has called such units *archiphonemes*. The archiphoneme in *sky* contains information about manner of articulation (stop) and place of articulation (velar) but no information about whether the consonant is voiced or voiceless. According to the *archiphoneme hypothesis,* children (and perhaps even adults) consider the second consonant of *sky* to be an archiphoneme. If so, children may vacillate between spellings that symbolize voiceless stops, like *k,* and spellings that symbolize voiced stops, like *g*. Or, children may arbitrarily choose one type of spelling over the other. With exposure to printed words like *skin* and *stop,* children come to spell the archiphonemes with the conventional *p, t, c,* and *k.*

To summarize the discussion to this point, there is little doubt that errors like CHRAP for *trap* and SGIE for *sky* reflect the sounds of spoken words. However, there are at least three ways in which they may do so. First—the phonetic spelling hypothesis—children may consider the first sounds of *trap* and *tap* to be allophones of /t/ but may believe that spelling represents the phonetic level rather than the phonemic level. Second—the different phonemic representations hypothesis— children may spell phonemically but their phonemic systems may not completely match those assumed by the English writing system. Third—the archiphoneme hypothesis—children may assign certain phones to archiphonemes. The existing data do not allow us to distinguish among these three hypotheses. What *is* clear is that children try to represent the sounds of words when they spell. Children's errors sometimes reflect properties of sounds that are not captured in the conventional English writing system but that are nevertheless real.

Letter Names

Children's knowledge of letter names plays some role in their spelling of consonants. For example, other things being equal, the first graders did better on phoneme-grapheme correspondences in which the name of the grapheme contains the phoneme (e.g., the correspondence between /b/ and *b*) than on phoneme-grapheme correspondences in which the name of the grapheme does not contain the phoneme (e.g., the correspondence between /w/ and *w*) (see Chapter 3). However, the effect of letter names on first graders' spelling of consonants is relatively small. For instance, even though /z/ appears in the name of the letter *z,* the children did not usually spell /z/ with *z.* Even though the children knew that *y* is named /wai/, they did not often spell /w/ with *y.*

At younger ages, the names of consonant letters may play a larger role in spelling. After all, first graders have several sources of information from which to draw when deciding how to spell a phoneme. Importantly, they know how the phoneme is spelled in certain familiar words. Younger children have less information. As a result, they may rely more heavily on their knowledge of letter names. Consider a child who does not know the conventional spelling of *any* word containing /w/. This child's only hope of spelling /w/, besides asking an adult, is to find this sound in the name of a letter. If the child's phonological awareness skills are good enough to abstract out the /w/ in the letter name /wai/, the child may spell /w/ with *y.*

Some evidence that knowledge of consonant letter names plays a role in the earliest spellings of phonologically aware children comes from my observations of my son, Joe. At the age of three and a half, Joe could recite the alphabet. He knew that /e/, /bi/, /si/, and so on were the names of letters, although he did not know the visual forms of some of the letters. Joe could analyze spoken syllables into onset and rime units. However, he knew the complete spelling of only one word, his name. When asked what letter *Wendy* began with, Joe replied that it began with *y.* This response could only have been based on analysis of the letter name /wai/. Joe also thought that *Jillian* started with *g.* This response seems also to have been based on letter-name knowledge—knowledge that the name of *g, /dʒi/,* has the onset /dʒ/. Interestingly, Joe used letter names in this case rather than his knowledge that his own name begins with *j.* Joe also said that *Sarah* began with *c.* The phoneme /s/ occurs in two different letter names, *c* and *s.* However, /s/ is more accessible in /si/, where it is the onset of the syllable, than in /ɛs/, where it is part of the rime. This may explain why Joe chose *c* rather than *s* for the first letter of *Sarah.* Systematic research is certainly needed, but these observations suggest that letter names may play an important role in the earliest spellings of some phonologically aware children.

Implications

Classification of Spelling Errors

How should children's spelling errors be classified? Two general points of view may be discerned in the literature. The first is that errors should be classified by reference to the correct spelling of the word—an orthographic system. The second is that errors should be classified by reference to the pronunciation of the word—a phonological system.

The results presented in this chapter, along with results presented elsewhere in this book, show that any classification system that is based purely on orthography cannot account for many of children's errors. For example, an orthographic classification system would have difficulty explaining why some *t*s, like those in *water* and *latter,* are sometimes replaced with *d,* while other *t*s, like those in *Tom* and *pretend,* are rarely replaced with *d.* To understand this difference, we must consider the sounds that the letters represent, not just the letters themselves. We must realize that the *t* in *water* stands for a flap, while the *t* in *pretend* does not.

Given that phonology cannot be ignored in the study of children's spellings, what sort of phonologically based classification is best? Many investigators have suggested that errors be divided into two categories—phonologically legal errors and phonologically illegal errors. This division hinges on whether the spelling may represent the sound in the conventional English writing system. Although the legal/ illegal distinction has been widely used in spelling research, it has some serious problems.

For one thing, the legal/illegal dichotomy may blind us to the logic behind certain so-called illegal errors. As an example, *ch* for /t/ before /r/ is classified as illegal because /t/ is never spelled with *ch* in English. However, this error accurately reflects certain properties of /t/ before /r/. By placing *chr* for /tr/ into the illegal category, together with *m* for /tr/, one obscures the difference between the two errors. The first error—which did occur in my collection of first-grade spellings— has a reasonable phonological basis. The second error—which did not occur—does not rest on a solid phonological foundation.

A further problem with the legal/illegal distinction is that it is adult centered. Even when a child makes a so-called legal error, the child does not necessarily know that the spelling is conventional. An example is *t* for /tʃ/. Most children who make this error do not know that *t* may spell /tʃ/ in words like *fortune.* Rather, children spell /tʃ/ as *t* because the first part of /tʃ/ sounds like /t/.

To understand the phonological basis of children's errors, it is necessary to go beyond the legal/illegal dichotomy. It is necessary, ultimately, to understand children's knowledge of phonology and of how phonology is reflected in spelling.

The Concept of Regularity

It is often assumed that if words were spelled regularly, "as they sound," children would learn to read and write with ease. On the whole, regular words *are* easier for children to spell than irregular words (see Chapter 2). However, the concept of regularity is not as simple as it first appears. What is regular to an adult is not necessarily regular to a child.

According to most linguists, adults consider the spoken forms of *to, trap, sty,* and *city* to all contain /t/. Moreover, adults take writing to represent the phonemic level (and deeper levels) of the language. From the adult's perspective, then, all of the words just listed should include a *t* in their spelling. They do, so the English writing system is regular for adults in this case.

For children, the use of *t* in *to, trap, sty,* and *city* may not be regular. Under the different phonemic representations hypothesis, some children consider *sty* to contain /d/ rather than /t/. For these children, a regular spelling of this word would contain *d. Sty,* the conventional spelling, is irregular. Under the archiphoneme hypothesis, some children consider the second sound of *sty* to be an archiphoneme that is not specified for voicing. For these children, *sdy* or *sty* would be equally regular. Finally, under the phonetic spelling hypothesis, children do not share adults' belief that the alphabet represents the phonemic level of language. Children are more sensitive to a level at which the /t/s in *to, trap, sty,* and *city* are different than to a level at which the /t/s are alike. For these children, a regular system might spell *trap* as *chrap, sty* as *sdy,* and *city* as *side.*

Any alphabetic writing system is based on a particular categorization of the sounds of the spoken language. If the user's categorizations match the categorizations assumed by the writing system, learning to spell will be relatively easy. If the user's categorizations do not match the categorizations assumed by the writing system, learning to spell will be relatively hard. My results suggest that such mismatches occur in the case of English. These mismatches contribute to children's difficulties in learning to spell.

The Teaching of Spelling

Informal Spelling Instruction. Informal instruction can play an important role in learning to spell. In this type of instruction, the teacher observes the errors that a child produces when he or she is writing. Based on these errors, the teacher makes some guesses about the child's underlying knowledge and improvises a response. Responses are tailored to the individual child and are designed to improve that child's knowledge about words.

Responses are most effective if they are based on an accurate assessment of the child's knowledge. For instance, although TESE is not said as /tʃ'iz/ when read aloud, it *is* a reasonable misspelling of *cheese.* The error probably reflects the child's knowledge that /tʃ/ sounds similar to /t/. As another example, although /t/ is never spelled with *ch* in English, CHRAP for *trap* reflects the properties of /t/ before /r/. The child who made this error probably had a good understanding of the sound structure of the spoken word.

Ironically, the very literacy skills that teachers are trying to teach sometimes make it difficult for them to appreciate errors like TESE for *cheese* and CHRAP for *trap.* In a sense, literacy conceals the way that words really sound. Many years of experience with written language have made it hard for us to think about spoken words as distinct from printed words. If adults can put themselves in the place of children who are not yet able to read—something that is made easier by training in phonetics—they will realize that certain sounds have more than one possible spelling. Children's choices, even when they do not conform to the choices made by the English writing system, may still be reasonable.

If teachers and parents appreciate the knowledge that lies behind children's misspellings, they can respond to the errors in the most helpful manner. For instance, the child who spelled *cheese* as TESE probably did not mishear or mispronounce the word. It would do little good to drill the child on the distinction between /ʧ/ and /t/. The child probably distinguishes these sounds perfectly well. Rather, the child might be told that /ʧ/ is normally spelled with two letters, *c* followed by *h*. As another example, the first grader who spelled *trap* as CHRAP could be told that he or she did a good job of trying to spell the word as it sounds. The teacher might say that the first part of the word does sound like /ʧ/ but that it also sounds similar to /t/. Thus, it is spelled with *t*.

Formal Spelling Instruction. Proponents of whole-language teaching maintain that children learn about the relations between spellings and sounds from exposure to print. These relations need not be taught in a formal manner. My results support this view to some extent. They show that many children pick up certain correspondences between sounds and spellings without formal teaching. For instance, children learn that /z/ is typically spelled with *s* from reading words like *was* and *is*. However, the fact that children grasp some things on their own does *not* mean that instruction has no role to play. Children learn more quickly and easily if given instruction that meets their needs. My results offer some suggestions about how this might be done.

When teaching children about the relations between sounds and letters, it is best to begin with the clear cases. Consider the correspondence between /t/ and *t*. To teach this correspondence at the beginnings of words, it is best to use words like *ten* (which begin with single /t/) rather than words like *trap* (which begin with /t/ before /r/). To teach this correspondence in the middles of words, one should start with words like *pretend* (which have aspirated /t/) rather than *city* (which have flapped /t/) or *sty* (which have unaspirated /t/). When first graders make errors like CHRAP for *trap* and SIDE for *city,* as some will do, these errors should not be treated as serious. In most cases, the errors do *not* mean that the children need more drill on the link between /t/ and *t*.

As I argue later in this book, many first graders can benefit from instruction in how to spell consonant clusters. It is hard for them to figure out how to spell clusters on their own. For initial clusters, it is probably best to begin with cases like /fr/ and /br/. The clusters /tr/ and /dr/ should be avoided at first because /t/ and /d/ change under the influence of a following /r/ in a way that /f/ and /b/ do not. The clusters /sp/, /st/, and /sk/ should also be avoided during the early stages of instruction. In these clusters, the identity of the stop consonant is not clear. Contrary to the suggestion of Hanna, Hodges, and Hanna (1971), /st/ is *not* a good cluster to teach first. Once children understand that consonant clusters contain more than one phoneme and are spelled with more than one grapheme, extra attention should be paid to /tr/, /dr/, /sp/, /st/, and /sk/. When first graders make errors like *chr* for /tr/ and *sb* for /sp/, as some will probably do, the errors should be corrected gently or even overlooked at first.

Spelling instruction that does not take account of children's knowledge of phonology and orthography and that is not sensitive to the logic behind children's errors may indeed be worse than no instruction at all. However, problems with existing methods should make us refine our teaching. They should not make us abandon formal instruction altogether.

Notes

1. Other uses of *d* for /t/ occurred when /t/ was a regular past tense marker, as in *jumped*. In these cases, English uses *ed* to spell /t/. The *d* errors may reflect partial knowledge of the standard *ed* spelling.

2. Although I have focused on stops after word-initial /s/, stops after syllable-initial /s/ *within* a word are also unaspirated. However, analyses of /s/-stop clusters within words are hindered by difficulties in locating syllable boundaries. Such difficulties seem to be particularly pronounced for words with medial /s/-stop clusters (Treiman & Zukowski, 1990). Thus, the analyses reported here are confined to stops after word-initial /s/.

3. Illegal substitutions on /ʒ/ are not discussed because children only attempted this phoneme four times.

4. This statement holds for the words in my collection as well as for the words in the much larger collection of Hanna et al. (1966).

5. The phonemes /θ/ and /ŋ/ were excluded from this analysis because children can make the errors *t* for /θ/ and *g* for /ŋ/ when they omit a letter from the common digraph spellings *th* and *ng*.

6

The Influence of Orthography on Children's Spelling of Vowels and Consonants

So far, the first graders' spellings have been studied from a phonological perspective. Spellings have been classified according to the phonemes they symbolize in order to examine children's knowledge of the various phoneme-grapheme correspondences of English. The results of these analyses have shown that children's spellings are built on their conceptions of phonemic structure. But orthographic influences have been visible too. As we have seen, the words that children see and read affect their own attempts to spell. In this chapter, these orthographic influences take center stage. The children's spellings are classified according to the conventional spellings of the words that they represent in order to examine children's knowledge of such orthographic features as digraphs and final *e*s. The question is whether and how the conventional spelling of a word affects children's attempts to spell the word.

The special characteristics of these children's first-grade experience make it particularly interesting to examine their learning of orthographic conventions. These children received little direct instruction in spelling. Even if they asked how to spell a word, their teacher did not tell them. The children were not explicitly taught about such orthographic conventions as the fact that *ck* occurs in the middles and at the ends of words but not at the beginnings of words. Did the children nevertheless pick up such conventions from the words they saw and read? For example, did they induce that *ck* occurs only in the middles and at the ends of words from seeing words like *package* and *sick* but not words like **ckat*? To anticipate the results presented in this chapter, the children did pick up this and other orthographic patterns on their own. Thus, the findings suggest that children can learn about certain orthographic conventions from their experiences with printed words, in the absence of direct instruction.

Vowels and Consonants Conventionally Spelled with More Than One Letter

The results presented in this book show that children often misspell graphemes such as *ai* and *sh*. Clearly, children have difficulty with graphemes in which two or more

152

letters symbolize a single phoneme. Less clear, at this point, are the sources of this difficulty and the conditions under which it occurs. To address these issues, I now examine children's performance on different types of multiple-letter graphemes. The discussion is restricted to graphemes that contain two letters, which are by far the most common type of multiple-letter grapheme in English. I first discuss vowels that are spelled with two-letter graphemes and then turn to consonants with two-letter spellings.

Vowels

Vowel Doublets. A *doublet* is a spelling such as *ee.* Two identical letters that are adjacent to one another in a printed word symbolize a single phoneme. Two different vowel doublets occurred among the conventional spellings of my collection—*ee* and *oo.* As expected, the children were much less accurate on *ee* and *oo* than on single *e* and *o* (36.2% correct versus 64.6% correct; $p < .001$ by a chi-square test).

Table 6.1 depicts how the children spelled vowel doublets. As shown, children often replaced the double vowel with the corresponding single vowel. Such errors occurred 27.1% of the time and were the most common type of error on vowel doublets. Although the children often replaced *ee* and *oo* with *e* and *o,* they rarely (1.6% of the time) replaced single *e* and *o* with the corresponding doublet ($p < .001$ for the difference by a chi-square test).

In English, only some vowel letters occur as doublets. The doublets *ee* and *oo* are common but the doublets *aa, ii,* and *uu* are rare. The latter occur only in such infrequent words as *aardvark, skiing,* and *vacuum.* The spelling lists, phonics workbook, and reading texts that were used in the first-grade classroom did not contain any words with *aa, ii,* or *uu.* The children probably saw few, if any, such words in other places. However, the fact that only certain vowel letters occur as doublets was not explicitly taught at school and was probably not taught at home either. Thus, we may ask the question posed at the outset of this chapter: Do children pick up

Table 6.1. Spellings of Vowel Doublets

Type	Example	Number	Percent
Correct (V_1V_1)	CEEPT for *keeped* [sic]	83	36.2
V_1	FLOR for *floor*	62	27.1
V_x	FUD for *food*	35	15.3
Omitted	GD for *good*	17	7.4
V_1V_x	TOUTH for *tooth*	6	2.6
V_1 & V_1	ASLEPE for *asleep*	5	2.2
V_xV_y[a]	WEED for *wood*	4	1.7
V_xV_1	DOER for *deer*	2	0.9
Other errors	TUTHE for *tooth*	15	6.6
	Total	229	100.0

Note. V_1 is the letter in the correct spelling. V_x and V_y are letters that are not in the correct spelling. & means that the letters in the spelling are not adjacent.

[a]The two letters may be the same or different.

the orthographic constraint on their own? To address this question, I examined cases in which children produced a vowel doublet that did not appear in the conventional spelling of the word. Usually (96 of 110 cases), the double vowel was *e* or *o*. Examples include LRNEE for *learning* and HOOS for *horse*. Less often (14 of 110 cases) was the double vowel *a, i,* or *u*. Examples are AAD for *and,* BIIC for *bike,* and CUUM for *come*. One would have expected many more instances of *aa, ii,* and *uu* based on the frequency of *a, i,* and *u* in the children's spelling. This difference (*p* < .001 by a chi-square test for the difference between the observed and expected values) shows that the children had begun to learn that some vowel letters may occur as doublets, but others usually do not. The children seem to have picked this up on their own from the printed words that they saw.

One might expect some spellings with the unusual doublets *aa, ii,* and *uu* at the beginning of the school year, when the children had less experience with print. These spellings might become less common as the school year progresses. However, the children avoided *aa, ii,* and *uu* during the first semester of the school year as well as the second. There was no significant difference between semesters by a chi-square test. Apparently, children are quick to notice the rarity of certain vowel doublets.

Vowel Digraphs. Doublets are one type of two-letter spelling that occurs in English. Digraphs are another. A *digraph* is a group of two different letters that, together, symbolize one phoneme. For example, *ei* represents a single vowel in *their*. The letters *e* and *i* stand for one phoneme rather than a sequence of two phonemes. This section focuses on cases in which two different vowel letters (counting *w* and *y* as vowels) represent a single vowel phoneme.

The children did better on those few digraphs that were the most common spellings of the vowels that they represented (e.g., *oy* for /oi/, as in *boy*) than on the many digraphs that were not the most common spellings of the vowels (e.g., *ey* for /i/, as in *key*) (37.5% correct versus 25.9% correct; *p* < .025 by a chi-square test). However, for all graphemes that were the most common spellings of vowels, children did worse when the grapheme was a digraph than when the grapheme was a single letter (37.5% correct versus 77.8% correct; *p* < .001 by a chi-square test). This result confirms, once again, that multiple-letter graphemes are harder than single-letter graphemes.

Table 6.2 shows the kinds of spellings that the children produced for vowel digraphs. Most of the errors were single letters. Often, these single letters were one letter of the correct digraph. Errors that were the first letter of the correct spelling outnumbered errors that were the second letter of the correct spelling by a ratio of almost 3 to 1.

There are two possible reasons for the predominance of first-letter errors over second-letter errors. One possibility—the orthographic hypothesis—is that errors like *e* for *ei* reflect partial knowledge of conventional spelling. Children have seen *ei* in words like *their* but remember the first letter of the digraph better than the second letter. A second possibility—the phonological hypothesis—is that children know nothing about the *ei* digraph. They spell *their* with *e* because *e* is a common

Table 6.2. Spellings of Vowel Digraphs

Type	Example	Number	Percent
Correct (V_1V_2)	EATR for *eater*	200	27.7
V_1	SAD for *said*	154	21.3
V_X	FRAND for *friend*	74	10.2
V_2	TRUBL for *trouble*	54	7.5
V_XV_Y[a]	ROOD for *reads*	46	6.4
Omitted	LRNING for *learning*	34	4.7
V_1V_X	STAE for *stay*	31	4.3
V_XV_2	PLOY for *play*	27	3.7
V_XV_1	DEA for *day*	9	1.2
V_1V_1	REED for *read*	8	1.1
V_2V_1	SAEC for *steak*	7	1.0
V_1 & V_2	BULE for *blue*	3	0.4
V_2V_X	KUEY for *cookie*	1	0.1
Other errors	CKUS for *own*	74	10.2
	Total	722	99.8

Note. V_1 is the first letter in the correct spelling and V_2 is the second. V_X and V_Y are letters that are not in the correct spelling. & means that the letters in the spelling are not adjacent.

[a]The two letters may be the same or different.

spelling of the vowel of this word, /ɛ/. According to the phonological hypothesis, first-letter errors outnumber second-letter errors because the first letter of a digraph by itself is often a legal spelling of the phoneme. In the example, *e* often spells /ɛ/. The second letter of a digraph is often not a legal spelling of the phoneme; /ɛ/ is never written as *i* in conventional English. Because children tend to spell phonemes in a legal manner, they sometimes produce spellings that are, by coincidence, one letter of the correct digraph.

To evaluate the orthographic and phonological hypotheses, Table 6.3 breaks down the results according to whether the individual letters of the digraph are possible spellings of the vowel on their own. When only the first letter was a legal spelling of the vowel, or when the first letter was a more frequent spelling than the second, first-letter errors significantly outnumbered second-letter errors. When only

Table 6.3. Numbers of V_1 and V_2 Errors for Different Types of Vowel Digraphs

Type of Digraph	Example	V_1 Errors	V_2 Errors	Difference (chi-square test)
V_1 possible spelling of vowel, V_2 not possible spelling of vowel	*ei* for /ɛ/	77	14	$p < .001$
V_1 not possible spelling of vowel, V_2 possible spelling of vowel	*ui* for /ɪ/	1	1	not significant
V_1 and V_2 possible spellings of vowel, V_1 more common	*ie* for /ɪ/	53	30	$p < .025$
V_1 and V_2 possible spellings of vowel, V_2 more common	*oe* for /ə/	5	8	not significant
V_1 and V_2 not possible spellings of vowel	*oy* for /oi/	18	1	$p < .001$

the second letter could spell the vowel, or when the second letter was a more frequent spelling than the first letter, first-letter errors and second-letter errors did not differ reliably. Thus, children tended to prefer common legal spellings over uncommon or illegal ones. In addition to this phonological effect, there are also signs of an orthographic effect. The children seemed to prefer first-letter spellings over second-letter spellings. This suggestion is reinforced by the finding that first-letter-of-digraph errors significantly outnumbered second-letter-of-digraph errors when *neither* letter alone could symbolize the phoneme. In other words, an orthographic effect emerged when phonological legality was not a factor.

The results just presented show that *both* orthography and phonology affect children's spellings of vowel digraphs. With respect to phonology, children are more likely to use graphemes that are possible spellings of a phoneme (legal substitutions) than graphemes that are not possible spellings of the phoneme (illegal substitutions). Once this phonological effect is taken into account, an orthographic effect appears. Children are more apt to use the first letter of an arbitrary two-letter spelling than the second.

Vowel Plus Final e Spellings. In English, vowel phonemes are sometimes spelled with a single vowel letter followed by a nonadjacent silent *e* at the end of the morpheme. For example, *a* plus final *e* represents /e/ in *came*, *e* plus final *e* represents /ɛ/ in *there*, and *o* plus final *e* represents /ə/ in *something*.

Table 6.4 shows how the children spelled these vowel plus final *e* combinations. The children were correct 38.5% of the time—significantly less than the 67.6% correct for single *a, e, i, o,* and *u* ($p < .001$ by a chi-square test). The children's most common mistake on vowel plus final *e* spellings was to omit the final *e*. The children were much more likely to omit a final *e* when one was required than to add a final *e* when none appeared in the conventional spelling (29.9% versus 0.9%; $p < .001$ by a chi-square test).

Table 6.4. Spellings of V Plus Final *e* Combinations

Type	Example	Number	Percent
Correct (V$_1$ & *e*)	BICKE for *bike*	192	38.5
V$_1$	HAT for *hate*	149	29.9
V$_X$	KER for *care*	71	14.2
V$_1$V$_X$	LIACK for *like*	23	4.6
Omitted	WR for *were*	22	4.4
V$_X$V$_{Ya}$	CUUM for *come*	10	2.0
V$_X$ & *e*	TOCE for *take*	9	1.8
V$_1$V$_1$	BIIC for *bike*	5	1.0
V$_1$ & V$_X$	CAMY for *came*	3	0.6
V$_X$V$_1$	RUOBS for *rogues*	3	0.6
V$_1$ & V$_1$	HONON for *home*	1	0.2
Other	TITIUR for *tire*	11	2.2
	Total	499	100.0

Note. V$_1$ is the letter that precedes *e* in the correct spelling. V$_X$ and V$_Y$ are letters other than V$_1$. & means that the letters in the spelling are not adjacent.

[a]The two letters may be the same or different.

To further study the children's final *e* omissions, I divided the vowel plus final *e* spellings into three categories according to the phonological status of the vowel letter before the final *e*. The first category includes cases in which this vowel letter may spell the phoneme but is not its most common spelling. To belong to this category, the letter's name may not match the vowel sound. For instance, with *o* plus final *e* for /ə/, as in *some*, *o* is a possible spelling of /ə/ but is not its most common spelling. Also, the name of *o* is not /ə/. The second category of vowel plus final *e* spellings includes cases like *e* plus final *e* for /ɛ/, as in *there*. The letter *e* is the most common spelling of /ɛ/ but the name of *e* is not /ɛ/. Finally, *a* plus final *e* for /e/, as in *ate*, belongs to the third category of vowel plus final *e* spellings. The letter *a* is the most common spelling of /e/ *and* the name of *a* is /e/.

Table 6.5 shows how the children performed on the three types of vowel plus final *e* spellings. The children produced more correct vowel spellings for words in the third category, the *ate*-type words, than for words in the other two categories, the *some*-type words and the *there*-type words ($p < .001$ by a chi-square test). However, the rate of final *e* omissions, whether expressed as a percentage of all vowel spellings or as a percentage of all vowel errors, was higher for words like *ate* than for words like *some* and *there* ($p < .001$ by a chi-square test). For words like *ate*, where the name of the vowel letter matches the phoneme, the children were almost as likely to spell the vowel with single *a* than with the correct *a* plus final *e*. That is, errors like AT were nearly as common as spellings like ATE. For words like *some* and *there*, errors like SOM and THER were less common.

Thus, all final *e* omissions are not alike. These omissions are most common when the name of the remaining vowel letter matches the sound that the children are trying to spell. Final *e* omissions are less common in other cases. These results show that children use their knowledge of the names of vowel letters when they spell.

Errors like AT for *ate* are particularly noteworthy given that both the children's phonics book and spelling lists devoted much attention to the "silent *e*" pattern. The children were taught that /e/ is spelled with *a* plus final *e;* they were taught that /æ/ is spelled with single *a*. Despite the teaching that the children received, they frequently misspelled *ate* as AT.

Although the children often left out final *e*s, they occasionally used spellings

Table 6.5. Spellings of Various Types of V Plus Final *e* Standard Spellings

Type of Spelling	Example	% Correct Vowel Spellings	*e* Omissions as % of All Vowel Spellings	*e* Omissions as % of All Vowel Errors
V possible but not most common spelling of vowel, not letter-name spelling	*some*	26.5	11.5	16.4
V most common spelling of vowel, not letter-name spelling	*there*	30.2	20.3	27.7
V most common spelling of vowel, letter-name spelling	*ate*	43.1	36.9	64.8

with final *e* when these spellings were incorrect. Some of these errors would be classified as legal substitutions, as in CHANE for *chain*. Others were illegal substitutions, as in TEME for *them*. Interestingly, certain illegal substitutions had a letter other than *e* as the second part of the spelling. Examples are HADY for *had*, where *a* plus final *y* was coded as an attempt to represent /æ/, and CONO for *corn*, where *o* plus final *o* was assumed to represent the vowel. The children produced illegal vowel spellings with nonadjacent letters 102 times—65 times with final *e*, 12 times with final *y*, and the remaining times with other final letters. Both final *e* and final *y* occurred more often than expected given the frequency of these letters in children's spellings ($p < .001$ and $p < .01$, respectively, by binomial tests). The many final *e*s among the illegal spellings suggest that the children were learning about the orthographic structure of English words. Having seen words that end with *e*s having no obvious phonological function, they sometimes used final *e*s themselves. The final *y*s may also reflect orthographic knowledge. As judged by the conventional spellings in my collection, *y* is more common at the ends of words than *a, i, o,* and, *u,* although not as common as *e*.

Supporting the idea that children's spellings with incorrect final *e* and other incorrect final letters reflect their experience with print, these spellings were more common during the second semester of the school year than during the first semester ($p < .001$ by a chi-square test). That is, errors like TEME for *them* and HADY for *had* became more common as children learned about conventional orthography.

Examination of the spellings of individual children sheds further light on the emergence of errors like TEME for *them* and HADY for *had*. Mary, for instance, did not use silent final *e* at all during the first four months of the school year. During this time, she produced spellings such as MAS for *makes*, RODS for *robes*, and GOOF for *give*. The first two errors use vowel letters to spell their names; the third error is more idiosyncratic. In January and February, Mary seemed to learn about silent *e*. Sometimes, as with ARE and TAKE, she used it correctly. During these same months, though, Mary began to make errors such as HAYSAKE for *haystack* and GARY for *care*—errors of a kind she had not produced before. Errors with final letters other than *e* disappeared by the end of February; legal substitutions with final *e* continued throughout the study.

Thus, one reason that children sometimes use incorrect final *e* and other incorrect final letters is that they have seen these patterns in printed words. Another reason may lie in an exaggerated sounding out process. For example, when testing first graders in an experiment, I observed one boy sounding out the nonword /r'æl/ as /r/, /æ/, /lə/. Thinking that the nonword ended with an unstressed vowel, he spelled it as RALA. Some children may include incorrect final vowels in their spellings for this reason.

Consonants

Consonant Doublets. Consonant doublets are two-letter spellings such as the *bb* of *rabbit* and the *gg* of *egg*. The two identical consonant letters symbolize one consonant phoneme rather than a sequence of two phonemes. Twelve doublets—*bb,*

Table 6.6. Spellings of Consonant Doublets

Type	Example	Number	Percent
C_1	KITUN for *kitten*	163	49.5
Correct (C_1C_1)	OFFS for *office*	106	32.2
Omitted	BONN for *balloon*	27	8.2
C_x	SABR for *supper*	19	5.8
C_xC_x	RQQN for *raccoon*	3	0.9
C_1C_x	HAPKE for *happy*	3	0.9
C_xC_1	ECG for *egg*	2	0.6
C_1 & C_1	CLELR for *killer*	1	0.3
Other errors	RABBRAT for *rabbit*	5	1.5
	Total	329	99.9

Note. C_1 is the letter in the correct spelling. C_x is a letter that is not in the correct spelling. & means that the letters in the spelling are not adjacent.

cc, dd, ff, gg, ll, mm, nn, pp, rr, ss, and *tt*—occurred among the standard spellings of my collection. The doublets were all relatively uncommon spellings of the phonemes that they represented. The most common spelling of the phoneme was usually the corresponding single letter.

The children did poorly on the consonant doublets, getting them correct only 32.2% of the time. In contrast, the children were 85.1% correct on the corresponding one-letter spellings. The difference in accuracy ($p < .001$ by a chi-square test) is not surprising given that the doublet spellings were longer and less frequent than the one-letter spellings.

Table 6.6 shows the types of spellings that the children produced for consonant doublets. The children replaced the doublets with the corresponding single letters 49.5% of the time—more often, in fact, than they spelled them correctly. In contrast, the children rarely (0.8% of the time) replaced one-letter spellings with doublets ($p < .001$ for the difference by a chi-square test).

In English, certain consonant letters may double and others may not. Generally, *h, j, k, q, v, w, x,* and *y* do not occur in doublets.[1] The children received no formal teaching on this point. Did they nevertheless learn which consonants may double and which may not? To address this question, I examined the 86 errors that contained a consonant doublet that did not appear in the word's conventional spelling. A mere 3 of these 86 errors—HHP for *help*, RQQN for *raccoon*, and YY for *your*—involved consonants that do not normally double. The children were less likely to use double *h, j, k, q, v, w, x,* and *y* than expected given the frequency of these letters in their spellings ($p < .001$ by a chi-square test). This pattern was apparent during both semesters of the school year. Thus, the children had begun to learn which consonants may double and which may not. They learned this early and without formal teaching.

The results for consonant doublets are similar to the results for vowel doublets presented earlier in this chapter. The children performed relatively poorly on both types of doublets. They often replaced the double letter with the corresponding single letter. Although the teacher did not point out that certain doublets occur in English and others do not, the children discovered the patterns on their own.

Consonant Digraphs. English includes consonant digraphs as well as consonant doublets. This section focuses on digraphs in which two different consonant letters represent one consonant phoneme. An example is *ph* for /f/. The letters *p* and *h* symbolize not /p/ followed by /h/ but /f/. The relation between *ph* and /f/ cannot be predicted from separate rules about *p* and *h*.

Sometimes, a digraph is the most frequent spelling of a phoneme. In these cases—*sh* for /ʃ/, *ch* for /ʧ/, *th* for /θ/, *th* for /ð/, and *ng* for /ŋ/—the children were correct 70.0% of the time. In other cases, as with *ph* for /f/, the digraph is not the most common spelling of the phoneme. Children were correct only 21.0% of the time here ($p < .001$ for the difference by a chi-square test). Although digraphs that were the most common spelling of a consonant were correct 70.0% of the time, single letters that were the most common spelling of a consonant were correct 86.7% of the time ($p < .001$ for the difference by a chi-square test). This result confirms that two-letter spellings are harder than one-letter spellings.

Table 6.7 shows how the children spelled consonant digraphs. Often, children used only the first letter of the digraph, as in *g* for *gh*. Second-letter errors, as in *g* for *ng*, were less common. Errors that contained two or more letters were less frequent than one-letter errors. When an error included several letters, however, at least one of the letters usually appeared in the conventional digraph spelling.

Errors like *g* for *gh* may arise for orthographic reasons, phonological reasons, or both. According to the orthographic hypothesis, children have seen *gh* in words like *ghost*. They sometimes use the first letter of the digraph and omit the second. According to the phonological hypothesis, children know nothing about the *gh* digraph. They make errors like GOST for *ghost* because they know that *g* usually represents /g/ in English.

To distinguish between the orthographic and phonological hypotheses, I broke

Table 6.7. Spellings of Consonant Digraphs

Type	Example	Number	Percent
Correct (C_1C_2)	KENG for *king*	707	60.3
C_1	TIK for *think*	273	23.3
C_X	FEEK for *think*	61	5.2
C_2	KIG for *king*	48	4.1
Omitted	TIUR for *teacher*	34	2.9
C_XC_2	CHE for *she*	13	1.1
C_1C_X	CKES for *cheese*	11	0.9
C_2C_1	TOHT for *tooth*	7	0.6
C_XC_Y[a]	DRUNNAY for *brother*	4	0.3
C_1 & C_2	SEH for *she*	4	0.3
C_2C_X	HSEX for *cheese*	3	0.3
C_XC_1	YTIM for *them*	3	0.3
Other errors	ELEPHFETE for *elephant*	50	0.4
	Total	1173	100.0

Note. C_1 is the first letter in the correct spelling and C_2 is the second. C_X and C_Y are letters that are not in the correct spelling. & means that the letters in the spelling are not adjacent.

[a]The two letters may be the same or different.

Table 6.8. Numbers of C_1 and C_2 Errors for Different Types of Consonant Digraphs

Type of Digraph	Example	C_1 Errors	C_2 Errors	Difference (chi-square test)
C_1 legal, C_2 illegal	*gh* for /g/	134	11	$p < .001$
C_1 illegal, C_2 legal	*kn* for /n/	3	10	$p < .06$
C_1 and C_2 legal, C_2 more common	*ck* for /k/	7	18	$p < .05$
C_1 and C_2 illegal	*th* for /θ/	129	9	$p < .001$

down the errors on digraphs according to whether the individual letters in the digraph were legal spellings of the phoneme. The results are shown in Table 6.8. When the first letter was a possible spelling of the phoneme and the second letter was not, first-letter errors reliably outnumbered second-letter errors. When only the second letter could symbolize the phoneme, or when the second letter was a more common spelling than the first, second-letter errors tended to outnumber first-letter errors. Thus, children often spell phonemes with letters that may represent these phonemes in English. These phonologically motivated spellings are sometimes, by coincidence, one letter of the correct digraph. However, phonological factors cannot explain the entire pattern of results. Common legal substitutions were more predominant when these substitutions were the first letter of the digraph than when they were the second letter of the digraph ($p < .005$ by a chi-square test). This result points to a role for orthographic knowledge. In some cases, children know something about the conventional digraph spelling. They use its first letter more often than its second letter. This suggestion is confirmed by examining those digraphs for which *neither* letter of the digraph could spell the phoneme. Here, the children sometimes used the first letter of the digraph by itself. They were more likely to use only the first letter than only the second letter.

This tendency to use the first letter of a consonant digraph rather than the second letter held whether the digraph occurred at the beginning of the word or the end of the word. For digraphs in which neither letter alone could spell the phoneme—digraphs for which effects of position could be evaluated without the influence of phonological legality—the second letter was more likely to be omitted than the first letter at both the beginnings and the ends of words ($p < .001$ by chi-square tests). Thus, TICK is a more common error than HICK on *thick*. BAT is a more common error than BAH on *bath*. This finding will become important in Chapter 8, when I compare children's errors on groups of letters that stand for two different consonants (c.g., *tr* for /tr/) with their errors on groups of letters that stand for a single consonant (e.g., *th* for /θ/).

The results for consonant digraphs are similar to the results for vowel digraphs presented earlier in this chapter. For one thing, the children were less accurate on digraphs than on one-letter spellings for both vowels and consonants. Moreover, the pattern of first-letter omission errors versus second-letter omission errors was similar for vowel digraphs and consonant digraphs. This similarity mitigates against another possible explanation for the finding that children more often misspell *th* as *t* than *h*. This explanation is based on the fact that *h* is the second letter of many consonant digraphs. Children may drop this letter because they consider it to be redundant or uninformative. With vowel digraphs, however, the second letter varies widely. The similar results for consonant and vowel digraphs suggest that children's omissions of the second letter of a digraph do not reflect its perceived redundancy. Rather, the results reflect the way in which children link two-letter sequences like *th* and *oi* to phonemes. The link between the first letter and the phoneme is stronger than the link between the second letter and the phoneme. Thus, children are more likely to use just the first letter than just the second letter.

Summary of Results on Two-Letter Spellings

The children often erred when trying to spell phonemes that were symbolized with more than one letter. This was true for both vowels and consonants. It was true whether the letters in the conventional spelling were identical to one another or not; it was true whether the letters were adjacent to one another or not. The children's difficulty with two-letter spellings was due partly to the low frequency of these spellings and partly to the fact that they contained two letters.

A common error on two-letter spellings was to omit one of the letters, typically the second. These omissions occurred for both phonological and orthographic reasons. As an example of the effect of phonological factors, consider the digraph *gh*, which stands for /g/. The letter *g* is the most common spelling of /g/. The children sometimes replaced *gh* with *g* because of their tendency to spell /g/ with *g*. As another example of the effect of phonological factors, consider BIK for *bike*. One reason for this error is that the name of the letter *i* is /ai/. Children's tendency to spell /ai/ with *i* contributed to their many BIK errors. However, phonological factors do not completely explain children's omissions of the second letters of two-letter spellings. For instance, the children made many errors like TEN for *then*. They did this even though *t* may not spell /ð/ in English. In such cases, orthographic factors must be invoked. The children had some familiarity with the *th* digraph from their exposure to words like *the* and *they*. They sometimes linked just the first letter of this two-letter sequence to the phoneme /ð/.

Finally, the children had begun to learn the restrictions on which vowel and consonant letters may double. They learned this rapidly and without formal teaching.

Graphemic Alternations

Most English phonemes may be spelled in more than one way. However, people can sometimes rule out certain of the spellings based on the position of the phoneme in the word and on other factors. For instance, adults know that English words do not usually end with *i*. Thus, they know that the final vowel of *baby* should be spelled with *y* rather than *i*. On the other hand, adults prefer *i* to *y* at the beginnings and in the middles of words, since *i* is more typical in these contexts. Patterns like the alternation between *i* and *y* are called *graphemic alternations*. One grapheme is more common in some situations, while another grapheme is more common in other situations. In this section, I ask whether the first graders knew about the graphemic alternations of English. If they did, this knowledge must have resulted from exposure to the orthographic patterns in printed words rather than from direct teaching. This is because neither the children's teacher nor their phonics book explicitly mentioned any of the graphemic alternations under study.

Alternations Involving Vowel Digraphs

Some graphemic alternations involve vowel digraphs. For example, *ay, ey,* and *oy* generally appear before vowels and at the ends of morphemes, as in *mayor* (before a vowel), *obey* (at the end of a morpheme), and *boyfriend* (at the end of a morpheme). The digraphs *ai, ei,* and *oi* are more typical before consonants within a morpheme, as in *maid, rein,* and *oil.* The only word in my collection to violate this pattern was *Ayrway* (the name of a chain of stores, where *ay* occurs before a consonant within an apparent morpheme). The same pattern applies to digraphs ending in *u* and *w.* Before vowels and at the ends of morphemes, the second letter of the digraph is usually *w,* as in *power, paw,* and *newly.* Elsewhere, the second letter of the digraph is usually *u,* as in *cause, neuter,* and *ouch.* There are more exceptions to the pattern in the case of *u/w* than in the case of *i/y.* Exceptions to the *u/w* pattern in my collection include *you, growl,* and *own.*

Did the first graders know about the alternation between digraphs ending in *i* and *y* and digraphs ending in *u* and *w?* To address this question, I examined errors that contained one of the digraphs in question and in which the digraph did not occur in the word's conventional spelling. Errors such as SEILF for *self* and PLEW for *play,* which follow the pattern of graphemic alternation just described, outnumbered errors such as AI for *a* and EWT for *it,* which violate the pattern. The children were more likely to use digraphs ending in *y* and *w* before a vowel or at the end of a morpheme than elsewhere in a word (81 cases versus 30 cases; $p < .001$ by a chi-square test). The opposite pattern held for digraphs ending in *i* and *u.* These were more common before a consonant within a morpheme than before a vowel or at the end of a morpheme (63 cases versus 18 cases; $p < .001$ by a chi-square test). Consistent with the fact that the *i/y* alternation has fewer exceptions than the *u/w* alternation, the children's adherence to the pattern was stronger for *i* and *y* than for *u* and *w* (80.7% versus 55.7% compliance, $p < .05$ by a chi-square test).

Apparently, the first graders had begun to pick up the distribution of digraphs with final *i, y, u,* and *w.* This pattern was not taught in school; it was probably not taught at home either. The children must have learned it implicitly, from their experience with printed words. That exposure to print rather than explicit teaching is the important factor is supported by the finding that children followed the pattern more strongly for digraphs ending in *i* and *y,* where there are few exceptions in English, than for digraphs ending in *u* and *w,* where there are a fair number of exceptions. Even if adults were aware of this difference, it is unlikely that they would point it out to a first grader.

The children tended to follow the pattern governing digraph alternations during both semesters of the school year. Although compliance appeared to increase from the first semester to the second semester (67.6% to 79.3%), the difference was not significant by a chi-square test.

Alternations Involving Single *i* and *y*

Just as *i* and *y* alternate in the second positions of digraphs, single *i* and *y* also alternate. The letter *y* generally occurs at the ends of morphemes, as in *myself* and *city*. The letter *i* tends to occur in other positions, as in *dinosaur*. This pattern, like most other patterns of English spelling, has exceptions. *Hi* (which has *i* at the end of a morpheme) and *encyclopedia* (which has *y* in the middle of a morpheme) deviate from the principles just described.

Did the first graders honor the alternation between *i* and *y?* To find out, I examined cases in which the children incorrectly used *i* or *y* to symbolize a vowel phoneme. There were 16 such errors in which *y* occurred at the end of a morpheme and 6 in which *y* occurred at the beginning or in the middle of a morpheme ($p < .05$ by a chi-square test). That is, errors such as UWY for *away* outnumbered errors such as LYCH for *lunch*. For *i*, the pattern was reversed. Errors with initial or medial *i*, like SIKRT for *secret*, outnumbered errors with final *i*, like SI for *see* (233 versus 47; $p < .001$ by a chi-square test). Thus, although the alternation between *i* and *y* was not taught at school, and probably was not mentioned at home, the children picked it up on their own. Compliance with the *i/y* alternation increased significantly from the first semester of the school year to the second (76.2% to 86.9%; $p < .025$ by a chi-square test).

Alternations Involving Single Consonants and Consonant Doublets

The choice between a single-letter consonant spelling and a doublet, like the choice between *ou* and *ow* or between *i* and *y*, is not totally arbitrary. As is often the case in English, certain factors help to predict the correct spelling. At least two factors affect the choice between a single consonant and a doublet—the position of the consonant in the word and the phonological structure of the word.

In English, consonant doublets may occur in the middles of words, as in *pepper*. They may also occur at the ends of words, as in *egg*. Except for a few rare words such as *llama*, English words do not begin with consonant doublets. Did the children pick up the relation between position in word and consonant doubling from their reading experience? It appears that they did. Of the 86 errors that contained an incorrect doublet consonant, the doublet was at the beginning of the word only 5 times. An example is MMNE for *money*. There were 44 cases in which the incorrect doublet occurred in the middle of the word, as in SUPRMORRKIT for *supermarket*, and 37 cases in which the doublet occurred at the end of the word, as in FASS for *face*. The distribution of incorrect doublets differed significantly from the distribution that would be expected if children were equally likely to double initial, medial, and final consonants ($p < .001$ by a chi-square test). This pattern held for both semesters of the school year. The apparent increase in compliance from the first semester to the second semester (89.2% to 98.0%) was not reliable by a chi-square test. Thus, even during the first semester of first grade, the children appreciated the rarity of initial consonant doublets. Because this pattern was not explicitly taught at school and was probably not taught at home, the children must have picked it up on their own.

The phonological structure of a word also helps to determine whether a consonant is spelled with a single or double letter. Doublets are often used to symbolize consonant phonemes that follow the stressed "short" vowels /æ/, /ɛ/, /ɪ/, /ɑ/, or /ə/ and that precede unstressed vowels. For example, the middle consonants of *pepper* and *Mommy* are spelled with doublets. Single-letter spellings are preferred after the "long" vowels /e/, /i/, /ai/, /o/, or /u/. For instance, *baby* and *Rufus* have single consonants. Although a number of words in my collection, including *chili* and *city,* had single consonants rather than doublets after short vowels, violating the pattern just described, no words used doublets after long vowels.

Did the first graders know that consonant doubling often follows from the phonological structure of the word? There are two ways to address this question. First, one may compare children's performance on words such as *pepper,* where consonant doubling is predictable based on the pattern just described, to their performance on words such as *balloon,* where consonant doubling is not predictable based on this pattern. If children appreciate the pattern, they should produce more correct doublets for words like *pepper* than for words like *balloon.* The rates of correct doublet spellings were 37.0% for the *pepper*-type words and 29.3% for the *balloon*-type words. This difference was not significant by a chi-square test.[2]

A second way to ask whether children appreciate the link between phonological structure and consonant doublets is to examine children's errors on words like *chili* and *city.* If children expect double consonants after short vowels, they should make errors like CHILLI and CITTY. Children should more often incorrectly double the middle consonants of *chili* and *city* than the middle consonants of *baby* and *Rufus.* The rates of incorrect consonant doubling were 7.4% and 2.8%, respectively, for the two types of words. The difference was not statistically reliable by a chi-square test. Thus, although there are nonsignificant trends, there is no solid evidence that the first graders as a group appreciated the relation between the phonological structure of a word and the use of single or double consonants.

Adults *do* understand the link between a word's phonological structure and the use of single or double consonants. As part of a study by Treiman and Danis (1988), college students were asked to spell real words such as *chili, critic, judo,* and *baby. Chili* and *critic* are exceptions to the rule of consonant doubling after stressed short vowels; *judo* and *baby* are consistent with the rule. If college students know the rule, they should produce more incorrect doublet spellings on the words like *chili* than the words like *judo.* The results supported these predictions. Although the overall rate of doublet errors was low, the college students made significantly more such errors on the *chili*-type words (1.3% of all spellings and 18.0% of all errors) than on the *judo*-type words (0.5% of all spellings and 4.0% of all errors; $p < .001$ for the differences by chi-square tests).

Thus, although the first graders had picked up the restriction against consonant doublets at the beginnings of words, there was no solid evidence that they appreciated the link between consonant doublets and short vowels. Why was the first pattern easier to master than the second? The answer may be that the first pattern can be learned on a purely orthographic basis, by noticing which letter sequences occur in English words and which do not. Children can rule out **ddaper* as a possible spelling of *dapper* because this spelling looks odd. No English word begins with *dd.*

In contrast, knowledge of possible and impossible orthographic patterns does not eliminate *daper* as a spelling of *dapper*. Some English words, like *paper, do* look like *daper*. The idea, then, is that children begin to learn about the kinds of letter sequences that occur in English words at an early age, before their reading skills are well developed. It takes longer for children to relate the orthographic patterns in printed words to the phonological patterns in the corresponding spoken words. To learn these links, children must have some degree of reading ability.

Alternations Involving ck

First graders know something about where consonant doublets may occur in words. Do they have similar knowledge in the case of digraphs? To address this question, I examined the digraph *ck*. This digraph may spell /k/ in the middles of morphemes, as in *package,* and at the ends of morphemes, as in *sick*. However, initial /k/ is never spelled with *ck*.

The children used *ck* 38 times when it was not a part of a word's correct spelling. They used the digraph at the beginning of a word only twice, as in CKES for *cheese*. They used it in the middle of a word 11 times, as in MRCKUT for *market,* and at the end of a word 25 times, as in BICK for *bike*. These differences suggest that the children had begun to pick up the restriction against initial *ck*. This restriction was not taught in school and was probably not mentioned at home. The children must have discovered it on their own, as a result of seeing words like *sick* and *package* but not words like **ckan*. The percentage of spellings with *ck* in which *ck* was at the beginning of the word was 12.5% during the first semester of the school year and 3.3% during the second semester. This difference was not significant by a chi-square test, although the trend was for greater compliance with the pattern during the second semester.

Summary of Results on Graphemic Alternations

First graders readily learn graphemic alternations that are based on the position of a grapheme within a word. The children in this study implicitly knew that *au* and *i* appear at the beginnings of words while *aw* and *y* appear at the ends of words. They knew that *ll* and *ck* are rare at the beginnings of words but common in the middles and at the ends of words. Children pick up these patterns by observing which letter sequences occur in printed words. This orthographic learning takes place rapidly; it does not require formal instruction. The children in this study complied with each of the orthographic patterns even during the first semester of the first-grade year, although compliance tended to increase from the first semester to the second semester. The teacher did not explicitly mention any of the patterns but the children honored them nonetheless.

Alternations that are governed by the phonological structure of words seem to be harder to learn than alternations that are governed by position. There was no clear evidence that the first graders appreciated that *Willy* stands for a word with a short vowel in the first syllable and *wily* stands for a word with a long vowel in the first syllable. Patterns of this kind, which require children to relate the orthographic patterns in printed words to the phonological patterns in spoken words, are more difficult than purely orthographic patterns.

Comparison with Results of Other Studies

Read's Research

In his study of preschoolers' spellings, Read concentrated more on phonological knowledge than on orthographic knowledge. He classified children's spellings of a word according to the phonological form of the word, not according to the word's conventional spelling. Read did not discuss children's performance on doublets, digraphs, or vowel plus final *e* combinations. Nor did he consider children's appreciation of graphemic alternations. However, the tables in Read's (1975) book suggest that his preschoolers made the same kinds of errors on consonant digraphs as my first graders. In Read's study, as in mine, *c*, *s*, and *g* were frequent errors on /ʧ/, /ʃ/, and /ŋ/, respectively. The most frequent error on both /θ/ and /ð/ was *t*. Apparently, Read's preschoolers knew something about the *ch, sh, ng,* and *th* digraphs but sometimes used just one letter of the digraph rather than both letters. Read's preschoolers, like my first graders, were generally more likely to omit the second letter of a digraph than the first.

Treiman's Orthographic Constraints Test

The results in this chapter suggest that even first graders are beginning to learn about which letter sequences may occur in English and which may not. For example, the first graders made a number of errors like FASS for *face,* using a consonant doublet to end a word. They made few errors like MMNE for *money,* using a consonant doublet to begin a word. For every orthographic pattern that I studied—and I studied each of the major patterns discussed by Venezky (1970)—children complied with the pattern even during the first semester of first grade. Compliance tended to increase from the first semester of the school year to the second, although the increase was often not significant for each orthographic pattern taken by itself.

To verify that first graders are beginning to learn about the orthographic structure of English and to study how this knowledge increases with reading experience, I developed a simple test, the *orthographic constraints test.* The test includes 16 pairs of nonwords. In each pair, one nonword conforms to the orthographic patterns of English and the other does not. Participants are asked which item looks more like a real English word. For instance, one pair includes *beff* and *ffeb. Beff* could be a word in English; it contains a consonant doublet at the end. **Ffeb* could not be a word in English; it begins with a consonant doublet. The question is whether children are able to choose *beff* over *ffeb.* For the pair *beff* and *ffeb,* as for most of the pairs on the orthographic constraints test, both items are equally easy to pronounce. Thus, the test taps knowledge of orthographic structure rather than knowledge of the relations between spellings and sounds.

Table 6.9 lists all 16 pairs in the orthographic constraints test. The table also gives the orthographic constraint that is tested by each pair. For purposes of pre-

Table 6.9. Nonword Pairs Used in Orthographic Constraints Test (within each pair, the correct response is listed second)

Nonword Pair	Constraint Tested
ffeb, beff *ddaled, dalled*	Consonant doublets do not usually occur at the beginnings of words
yikk, yinn *vayying, vadding*	*kk* and *yy* do not occur
ckun, nuck *ckader, dacker*	*ck* does not occur at the beginnings of words
vaad, vadd *muun, munt* *iit, ist*	*aa, ii,* and *uu* usually do not occur
moyl, moil *awt, aut* *bei, bey* *dau, daw*	Digraphs ending with *y* and *w* do not usually occur before consonants; those ending with *i* and *u* do not usually occur at the ends of morphemes
gri, gry *yb, ib* *chym, chim*	*i* does not usually occur at the ends of morphemes; *y* does not usually occur at the beginnings or in the middles of morphemes

sentation, the order of the 16 pairs was randomized. The order of items within each pair was also chosen randomly. The two nonwords in each pair were printed in lowercase letters, the nonwords being separated from one another by a circle. A box was drawn around each pair of items.

The orthographic constraints test was given to groups of children and adults in their classrooms. By way of introduction, the experimenter wrote *xyq* and *dap* on the blackboard. She pointed to the first of these and said that it doesn't look like a word. She then pointed to the second and said that it does look like a word. Next, the experimenter wrote *flam* and *fbcz* on the blackboard. She asked, "Which one of these looks like it could be a real word?" and pointed out the correct answer, *flam.* The third example, *ioyeu* versus *bants,* was presented in a similar manner. The participants were then given the orthographic constraints test. They were asked to circle the item within each box that looked more like a real word. The procedure was the same whether the subjects were children or college students. With college students, however, the experimenter began by saying that the experiment was designed for children and that the instructions might therefore seem simple.

The first study using the orthographic constraints test was carried out with kindergarteners, first graders, second graders, and college students. The college students were 41 students who were enrolled in an upper-level psychology course at Wayne State University in Detroit. The children attended public and parochial schools in suburban Detroit. These schools served primarily white, middle- and upper middle-class populations. There were 36 kindergarteners (mean age 6 years, 1 month; range 5,5 - 7,2), 33 first graders (mean age 7 years, 0 months; range 6,3 - 8,1), and 45 second graders (mean age 8 years, 1 month; range 7,4 - 9,4). The children were tested during the second semester of the school year, in March for the first graders and in May for the kindergarteners and second graders. On the reading subtest of the Wide Range Achievement Test—Revised or WRAT-R, the kindergarteners performed at a beginning first-grade level (Jastak & Wilkinson, 1984). The first graders' average reading level was end of first grade; the second graders' average reading level was end of second grade. Interviews with the children's teachers confirmed that none of the orthographic patterns on the test was explicitly taught in the classroom.

The average percentage of correct responses on the orthographic constraints test was 56.4% for the kindergarteners, 62.3% for the first graders, 83.2% for the second graders, and 94.5% for the adults. Statistical tests confirmed that performance differed among the four groups of subjects (F(3,151) = 93.99 in an analysis of variance by subjects; F(3,45) = 48.88 in an analysis of variance by items; $p < .001$ for both). The apparent increase in performance from kindergarten to first grade was not statistically significant. All of the other differences were reliable.

If the children were guessing randomly on the orthographic constraints test, they should have averaged 50.0% correct responses. This is because there were two choices in each case. However, *all* groups of children, even the kindergarteners, performed significantly better than chance ($p < .025$ according to one-tailed *t* tests across subjects and across stimuli). Even though the kindergarteners in this study could read only simple words like *book, eat,* and *was* on the standardized reading test, as a group they had some inkling that *nuck* is more English-like than *ckun.* Apparently, children begin to induce the orthographic regularities of their language with only a small amount of reading experience.

The results show that knowledge of orthographic structure improves from early elementary school to college. However, the results do not indicate whether this improvement reflects increasing age or, as I have proposed, increasing reading experience. To address this question, I calculated the correlation between children's performance on the orthographic constraints test and their age and the correlation between children's performance on the orthographic constraints test and their raw score on the WRAT-R reading test. If reading experience is important, the second correlation should be higher than the first. The correlation between the orthographic constraints score and age was not significant at any of the three grade levels ($r = .27, .09,$ and $-.05$ for kindergarten, first grade, and second grade, respectively; $p > .05$, one-tailed, for all). Thus, knowledge of orthographic patterns is not related to age for children at the same grade level. The correlation between the orthographic constraints score and the WRAT-R score was significant at all three grade levels ($r = .36, .60,$ and $.47$ for kindergarten, first grade, and second grade, respectively; $p < .025$, one-tailed, for all). That is, the better readers in each grade knew more about orthographic patterns. For the first and second graders, the correlation between the orthographic constraints score and the reading score was significantly higher than the correlation between the orthographic constraints score and age ($p < .025$, one-tailed). This result further supports the idea that reading skill is more important than age. For the kindergarteners, the difference between the correlation coefficients was not statistically reliable.

The results of this first experiment show that middle- and upper middle-class suburban children begin to learn about English orthographic patterns as early as May of kindergarten. Although kindergarteners do not yet perform well on the orthographic constraints test, as a group they score above chance and their performance improves with reading experience. Do other groups of children have a similar ability to learn about the orthographic constraints of their language? To address this question, a second study was carried out with a racially mixed group of urban first graders. These children were from working-class backgrounds. They were given the orthographic constraints test in November and again in May.[3] The children's average age at the time of the first test was six years, four months (range 5, 11–7, 8). Their average age at the time of the second test was six years, ten months (6, 5–8, 2). As before, none of the orthographic constraints under study was explicitly taught in the classroom.

On the November orthographic constraints test, the urban first graders performed poorly. Their average score was 49.8% correct, not above the level expected by random guessing. This performance contrasts with that of the suburban children, who scored slightly but significantly above chance even in May of their kindergarten year. However, the urban first graders' knowledge of orthographic patterns increased quickly. On the May test, their average score was 67.6% correct, which was reliably above chance ($p < .001$ by one-tailed t tests across subjects and stimuli). This performance compares favorably with that of the suburban first graders, who averaged 62.3% correct when tested in March. The improvement from November to May ($p < .001$ by one-tailed t tests across subjects and stimuli) suggests that knowledge of orthographic patterns develops rapidly with exposure to print.

Combining the results of the two experiments with the results of the naturalistic study, it is clear that children learn more about the English writing system than the relations between sounds and spellings. Children also learn the characteristics of spellings themselves. Although young children cannot necessarily say what is odd about *ckun* or *ffeb,* they suspect that these are unlikely to be English words. This knowledge is shown in their ability to judge that *nuck* is more wordlike than *ckun* and in their relatively low number of spelling errors like CKUN.

Other Studies of Orthographic Knowledge

Several previous studies have examined children's ability to discriminate well-structured strings like *hemort* or *ateditol* from poorly structured strings like *cdrtei* or *ijhbwstt* (Golinkoff, 1974; Massaro & Hestand, 1983; Niles, Grunder, & Wimmer, 1977; Rosinski & Wheeler, 1972; Zivan & Samuels, 1986). In most of these studies, children performed above the level of chance in the second half of first grade or in second grade. Performance improved with increasing reading skill. However, these earlier studies were not generally designed to test children's knowledge of *specific* orthographic constraints. A further problem is that orthographic regularity and phonological regularity were usually confounded. The orthographically regular items were easy to pronounce and the irregular items were difficult or impossible to pronounce. Thus, although the results show that children's knowledge of the properties of English words improves with reading experience, they do not tell us whether the improvement is in orthographic knowledge, phonological knowledge, or both.

University of Virginia Researchers

According to the Virginia researchers, children do not begin to follow orthographic conventions until relatively late in the process of learning to spell. During the phonetic stage of spelling development, according to Gentry (1982, p. 195), "letters are assigned strictly on the basis of sound, without regard for acceptable English letter sequence or other conventions of English orthography." Gentry's description implies that children begin to appreciate orthographic constraints only during the transitional stage, the stage that follows the semiphonetic and phonetic stages. The present results do not support this view. Instead, they suggest that children begin to learn about orthographic conventions early and in the absence of direct instruction. Children who produce what appear to be phonetic or even semiphonetic spellings—UWY for *away,* SIKRT for *secret,* FASS for *face,* and SUPRMORRKIT for *supermarket*—tend to use *y* at the ends of words and *i* in the middles of words, tend to avoid consonant doublets at the beginnings of words, and so on. Certainly, first graders' knowledge of orthographic patterns is far from perfect. First graders produce some spellings that do not conform to the orthographic constraints of English. First graders perform above chance, but not far above chance, on the orthographic constraints test. However, the present results do not support the notion that first graders spell strictly on the basis of sound with no regard for the conventions of English orthography.

According to the Virginia researchers, knowledge of the relation between consonant doubling and long versus short vowels does not emerge until one of the later stages of spelling development, what Henderson (1985) called the syllable juncture stage. Most first graders do not know that *Willy* symbolizes a word with a short vowel in the first syllable while *wily* symbolizes a word with a long vowel in the first syllable. The present results support this claim.

Implications

Exposure to Print

Just as exposure to printed words teaches children about the relations betwen phonemes and graphemes, so exposure to printed words teaches children about the letter sequences that occur in English. First graders' misspellings tend to honor certain orthographic patterns of English. Children are more likely to make errors like HOOS, PLEW, and SUMM than errors like CUUM, EWT, and MMNE. Although all of these spellings are incorrect, those in the first group *look* more like English words than those in the second group.

Knowledge of orthographic patterns begins to develop early. The first graders in this study tended to avoid spellings like CUUM even during the first semester of the school year. The children in the orthographic constraints experiments began to distinguish nonwords like *nuck* from nonwords like *ckun* by the end of kindergarten or the end of first grade, depending on their backgrounds.

Formal instruction is not required for the learning of orthographic patterns. The teacher in the naturalistic study and the teachers of the children in the experiments did not point out that *uu* is rare in English or that words do not begin with *ck*. The children's parents probably did not mention these things either. Children learn about the letter sequences that occur in English words without explicit teaching.

What *is* required for the learning of orthographic patterns is exposure to print. Children must see enough words to observe that *ck* occurs in the middles and at the ends of words but not at the beginnings; they must see enough words to note that *ee* and *oo* occur but not *uu*. For the children in the naturalistic study, this exposure to words was often in a meaningful context—within stories they were reading in their basal readers and other books. However, it is possible that seeing legal spelling patterns even in *unknown* words also has some effect. Even though first graders cannot read or understand the word *acknowledge,* simply seeing this word may provide evidence that *ck* occurs in the middles of words. Whatever the role of meaning, it is clear that exposure to printed words is critical for the learning of orthographic patterns. To deprive children of such experience as they are beginning to write—as might be done in an extreme form of the "write first, read later" approach—would be to deprive children of the raw material that enables the learning of orthographic patterns.

Although first graders know something about the orthographic structure of English words, their knowledge is far from complete. The children in the naturalistic study made some orthographically illegal errors like CUUM and EWT. The first graders in the orthographic constraints experiments were above chance, but not much above chance, at distinguishing nonwords like *nuck* from nonwords like *ckun*. Knowledge of orthographic constraints certainly improves as reading and spelling skills increase. However, the important point for present purposes is that this knowledge begins to develop at an early age.

Models of the Spelling Process

There are several ways in which knowledge of orthographic constraints could be built into the spelling system. Within a connectionist framework, links from phonemes to graphemes could vary in strength depending on the position of the phoneme in the word. Thus, the link from /k/ to *ck* would have a very low weight when /k/ is at the beginning of a word. This link would have a higher weight when /k/ is in the middle or at the end of a word. As a result, spellings like CKAP would be rare, while spellings like BICK would be more common.

Letter Names

The results in this chapter mesh with findings reported elsewhere in this book that children use the names of vowel letters as a guide to the spelling of phonemes. Children's letter-name strategy helps to explain why silent *e*s are difficult to learn for the children in this study and in other studies (e.g., Beers et al., 1977). One reason for children's difficulty with spellings like *a* plus final *e* for /e/ is that there are two letters to learn and remember. As I have shown, two-letter spellings are harder than one-letter spellings. A second problem is that the final *e* spellings often conflict with the spellings expected under a letter-name system. To first graders, AT seems an excellent way to spell *ate*. Children have difficulty giving up this spelling and learning that the word is actually spelled as *ate*.

Classification of Spelling Errors

Learning to spell involves learning about the properties of printed words and about the relations between phonemes and graphemes. To understand children's errors, then, both orthography and phonology must be considered.

A system of classifying children's spelling errors that was based *only* on the conventional spellings of words would be incomplete. Under a purely orthographic system, there is no reason why children should drop the final *e* of *came* more often than the final *e* of *some*. In both cases, the error involves the omission of the last letter of the word. To understand why final *e* omissions are more frequent for *came* than for *some*, one must consider the sounds of the words. The spoken form of *came* contains /e/, the name of the letter *a*. Because children use the names of vowel letters to guide their spelling, they often misspell *came* as CAM. Children are less likely to spell *some* as SOM because the name of *o* is not /ə/.

As another example of the shortcomings of a purely orthographic system, consider the digraphs *kn*, as in *knot*, and *gh*, as in *ghost*. From an orthographic point of view, children should make the same kinds of errors on these two digraphs. This was not the case for the first graders in this study. With *gh*, *g* errors overwhelmingly outnumbered *h* errors. This is because *g* is a common spelling of the intended sound, /g/, while *h* may not represent this sound. With *kn*, *k* errors were somewhat less common than *n* errors. The explanation is again phonological: *k* may not spell /n/, but *n* may. One cannot understand the pattern of errors without considering the phonemes that the letters represent.

On the other hand, certain regularities would be missed if one classified children's spelling errors *only* by reference to phonology. One would miss the fact that children sometimes use one letter of a digraph when there is little or no phonological basis for the error. One would miss the fact that children spell the same phoneme with one grapheme in certain positions of words but with another grapheme in other positions of words. To understand first graders' spellings, one must consider *both* the phonological form of the intended word and the word's conventional spelling.

The Concept of Regularity

If only the English writing system were regular, its critics complain, children would learn to read and write with ease. Although this position has intuitive appeal, my results suggest that it is not completely correct. Regularity is *not* the only determinant of how easy a word is to learn. Suppose that, within a given dialect, /e/ was always spelled with *ai*. *Hate* was spelled as *hait*, *gauge* was spelled as *gaij*, and so on. Even though the vowel's spelling was perfectly consistent, children would *still* have difficulty. They would make errors like HAT for *hate* and GAJ for *gauge*. Children would make these errors because they tend to spell /e/ with *a*, the letter whose name matches the phoneme. For children, a system in which /e/ was spelled with *a* would be easier to learn than a system in which /e/ was spelled in some other manner. This would be true even if both systems had one-to-one mappings from phonemes to graphemes. Regularity, helpful though it may be, is not a panacea.

The Teaching of Spelling

As I have argued throughout this book, spelling instruction should be based on a detailed understanding of the knowledge that children bring with them to the learning process. In particular, spelling instruction should be designed to counteract children's natural tendencies for error. As an example of how this might be done, consider digraphs. From children's point of view, digraphs such as the *sh* of *ship* are largely arbitrary. Children cannot figure out on their own that /ʃ/ should be spelled with *s* followed by *h*. Therefore, first graders are typically taught that /ʃ/ is spelled with *sh*, that /θ/ is spelled with *th*, and so on. One's first thought would be to give equal attention to the two letters of a digraph. However, the present results suggest that more stress should be placed on the second letter. Because children are more likely to misspell *sh* as *s* than as *h*, teachers and textbooks should pay extra attention to the *h*.

Although formal teaching is common in the case of digraphs, it is not common in the case of orthographic constraints. For example, children are rarely taught that *ck* may occur at the ends and in the middles of words but not at the beginnings of words. As a result, orthographic knowledge has been considered something that is learned implicitly, through experience with print (Cunningham & Stanovich, 1991; Stanovich & West, 1989). The present results confirm that children pick up many orthographic patterns on their own. However, children might learn these patterns more rapidly and more completely if the regularities were pointed out to them. First graders would enjoy classroom exercises like my orthographic constraints test. Moreover, these exercises would get them to reflect on the letter patterns in printed words.

Notes

1. The letter *v* does double in *divvy, flivver,* and *navvy,* but these words are surely unfamiliar to first-grade children.

2. One of the words in the so-called unpredictable category was *egg.* For this word, consonant doubling actually follows from another pattern—the tendency to limit two-letter words to a select group such as *in* and *of.* Because there were so few words like *egg,* I could not ask whether the children appreciated this pattern. In any case, the same results were obtained when the *egg*-type words were eliminated from the analysis.

3. One pair of nonwords was inadvertently omitted from the November administration of the orthographic constraints test. The percentages reported are out of all items that were presented.

7

Vowel Omissions

In this chapter and the following one, I turn to omission errors. These are errors in which children fail to represent a phoneme in their spelling. I ask which phonemes children tend to omit and why. This chapter focuses on omissions of vowels, while Chapter 8 considers omission errors on consonants. Also included in Chapter 8 is a comparison of vowel omission errors and consonant omission errors.

The study of vowel omissions takes on particular importance in light of the claim that beginning spellers are particularly likely to omit vowels (Ehri, 1986; Morris & Perney, 1984). For example, Morris and Perney (1984) state that semi-phonetic spellers often produce spellings like M or ML for *mail,* omitting the middle vowels of one-syllable words. Not until the phonetic stage, they say, do vowels begin to appear in children's spellings of such words. Do children omit the vowel of *mail* because the phoneme is in the middle of the word or do they omit it specifically because it is a vowel? To find out, it is necessary to examine words whose phonemic structure is more complex than consonant–vowel–consonant. Only then will we be able to determine whether all phonemes in the middles of words are susceptible to omission, or just vowels.

Consider the child who spelled *rainy* as RNIE. The spoken form of this word contains four phonemes—/r/, /e/, /n/, and /i/. The child who produced RNIE symbolized /r/ with r, /n/ with n, and /i/ with ie. The child failed to represent /e/ altogether, a vowel omission error. Other spellings that contain vowel omissions are HLP for *help,* in which /ɛ/ is deleted, and BLUN for *balloon,* in which the unstressed /ə/ of the first syllable is deleted. In this study, omission errors are defined by reference to the spoken form of the word, not by reference to its conventional spelling. Thus, the child who spelled *said* as SID is not considered to have made an omission error. This child *did* symbolize the vowel, albeit with i instead of with the correct *ai.*

A slight complication in the definition of omission errors arises in those (rare) cases in which a phoneme is not represented with a letter in the conventional spelling of a word. For example, *K-mart* has no separate letter for the first vowel. It is not spelled *Kamart* or *Kaimart.* If a child did not spell the first vowel phoneme when writing this word, the omission would not count as an error. I did not include such cases in the analyses of omission errors reported in this chapter or the following chapter.

Of the children's 6,693 spellings of vowels, 619 or 9.2% were omission errors.

Substitution errors constituted 32.5% of the children's vowel spellings, so omissions were not as common as substitutions. However, vowel omissions did occur a non-negligible percentage of the time. Indeed, they were fairly common in certain contexts. For instance, unstressed vowels like the first vowel of *balloon* were quite susceptible to omission.

When interpreting the results presented in this chapter, keep in mind that the omission rates are based on the number of omissions relative to *all* spellings of the vowel. Over half the words in my collection were spelled correctly. The omission rates would of course be higher if they were calculated based on incorrectly spelled words only.

My goal in this chapter is to understand which vowels children tend to omit and why. To study the factors that are associated with vowel omission errors, it is necessary to consider several different factors at once. For example, suppose that I wish to determine whether children are more likely to omit unstressed vowels than stressed vowels. If I simply compared the omission rate for all unstressed vowels with the omission rate for all stressed vowels, I would find that unstressed vowels have a significantly higher omission rate. However, this difference does not prove that stress per se is related to vowel omissions. The difference could be due entirely to word length. For words that are pronounced in isolation, unstressed vowels only occur in words that have more than one syllable. Stressed vowels occur in short words as well as in long words. As I show later in this chapter, children more often omit vowels in long words than in short words. To determine whether stress has a role in vowel omissions, above and beyond the role of word length, stress and word length must both be considered. The statistical technique of multiple regression does just this.

Another issue that arises in the study of omission errors is that of syllabification. As discussed in Chapter 1, linguists do not always agree about how spoken words are divided into syllables. These disagreements may affect my study of vowel omission errors. Consider the errors HLP for *help* and BL for *bell*. These errors suggest that children's knowledge of letter names makes them omit vowels when they spell. Children sometimes symbolize the group of phonemes /ɛl/ with the single letter *l*, the letter whose name is /ɛl/, rather than with a vowel letter followed by *l*. It is possible that letter-name spellings are more frequent when the phonemes that make up the letter name belong to the same syllable of the spoken word than when they belong to different syllables. In *help*, /ɛ/ and /l/ must belong to the same syllable since the word has but one syllable. With *elephant*, however, it is not clear whether /ɛ/ and /l/ both belong to the first syllable or whether /ɛ/ belongs to the first syllable and /l/ to the second. The widely held assumptions about syllabification that were discussed in Chapter 1 do not establish whether the /ɛ/ and /l/ of *elephant* belong to the same syllable or to different syllables.

Questions about syllabification do not arise for one-syllable words, which are the majority of words in the present collection (83.9%). However, such questions do arise for words that contain more than one syllable. Thus, when examining the relation between vowel omissions and a factor such as letter names, I analyzed the results in two different ways. In the first method, I disregarded any possible syllable boundaries within a word. I counted the /ɛl/ of *elephant* as a letter-name sequence even though the two phonemes do not necessarily belong to the same syllable by the assumptions about syllabification outlined in Chapter 1. Of course, I also counted the /ɛl/ of *help* as a letter-name sequence. In the second method of analyzing the results, I counted a group of phonemes as a letter-name sequence *only* if the phonemes belonged to the same syllable by the syllabification principles of Chapter 1.[1] Using this method, the /ɛl/ of *elephant* was not considered to be a letter-name sequence while the /ɛl/ of *help* was. The two methods turned out to give similar results.

Factors Associated with Vowel Omission Errors

The analyses uncovered a number of factors that were associated with vowel omission errors, as well as a number of factors that were not. In this section, I discuss the factors that proved to be related to vowel omissions.

Stress

For the purposes of this study, I assumed that each vowel had one of three levels of stress—primary stress, secondary stress, or no stress. For example, the first vowel of *peanut* has primary stress. The second vowel of this word has secondary stress. The first vowel of *baby* has primary stress and the second vowel of this word is not stressed.

The children omitted primary stressed vowels at a rate of 4.9%. They omitted secondary stressed vowels 8.5% of the time. The omission rate for unstressed vowels was much higher—35.4%. Table 7.1 presents examples of vowel omission errors for primary, secondary, and unstressed vowels.

The findings just reported suggest that stress is associated with vowel omission errors. However, it is possible that some other factor is responsible for the apparent effect of stress. As mentioned earlier, children may omit unstressed vowels more often than stressed vowels because unstressed vowels tend to occur in relatively long

Table 7.1. Omissions of Primary Stressed, Secondary Stressed, and Unstressed Vowels

Stress	Examples
Primary	RNIE for *rainy*
	HR for *her*
	M for *my*
	RAKN for *raccoon*
Secondary	SUMWN for *someone*
	DINOS for *dinosaur*
Unstressed	BLUN for *balloon*
	BUTR for *butter*
	MAD for *meadow*
	SIPN for *shopping*
	BIGR for *bigger*

words. Statistical analyses were performed to determine whether stress was associated with vowel omissions, above and beyond the influences of other factors. Stress was significantly related to vowel omissions even after other factors were taken into account. Thus, children do not just omit unstressed vowels because these vowels tend to occur in long words. There was no significant difference between primary stressed vowels and secondary stressed vowels in their susceptibility to omission.[2]

The relation between stress and vowel omissions implies that children do not spell only by reproducing previously memorized sequences of letters. If rote word-by-word memorization were the only process involved in spelling, children should not recall letters that represent stressed vowels better than letters that represent unstressed vowels. The effect of stress on spelling suggests that children symbolize the phonological forms of words when they spell. They construct spellings for words based on the words' sounds.

Although it is clear that stress influences children's spelling, the exact mechanisms of this influence are not clear. One idea is that children sometimes omit unstressed vowels when they spell because they sometimes omit these vowels when they speak. When speaking rapidly, children may pronounce *balloon* as /bl'un/. Perhaps they spell it as BLUN because they pronounce it this way. However, this hypothesis cannot explain my results. In rapid speech, /ə/ is deleted more often than other vowels. If vowel omissions in spelling reflected vowel omissions in rapid speech, /ə/ should be omitted more often than other vowels. However, results presented later in this chapter show that children did *not* omit /ə/ more often than other vowels once other factors related to vowel omissions were taken into account. The omission of unstressed vowels in rapid speech cannot explain children's failures to spell these phonemes.

A second hypothesis about why children sometimes fail to spell unstressed vowels appeals to acoustic properties of these vowels. Unstressed vowels are typically short: Lehiste (1975), for example, found that unstressed vowels were 82% of the length of stressed vowels. However, results presented later in this chapter show that, in general, the acoustic durations of vowels are not related to their omission rates.

Thus, children's failures to spell unstressed vowels must reflect something *other* than the dropping of vowels in rapid speech or the short durations of unstressed vowels. What could the explanation be? Stressed and unstressed vowels differ in a number of ways. Unstressed vowels are produced with less energy than stressed vowels. They tend to be softer and lower-pitched. At the phonemic level, too, stressed vowels differ from unstressed vowels. My results do not allow me to pinpoint the exact cause of children's omissions of unstressed vowels. However, it appears that as children analyze a spoken word into smaller units and generate a spelling from the phonological form, they are more likely to abstract stressed vowels from the spoken word, more likely to remember them, and more likely to symbolize them in spelling.

Letter Names

First graders are well acquainted with the names of English letters. They sometimes use their knowledge of letter names when attempting to spell words. For instance, the first graders in this study sometimes misspelled *play* as PLA and *boat* as BOT. That is, they symbolized the single phonemes /e/ and /o/ with the letters that have these names. In this section, I ask whether children do the same for *groups* of phonemes. Do first graders sometimes spell groups of phonemes such as /εl/ and /ti/ with the letters that have these names?

If children use single *l* to represent the entire sequence /εl/, they may misspell *help* as HLP. If so, omissions of the /ε/ of *help* should outnumber omissions of the /ε/ of *beds,* which does not contain a letter name. Similarly, if children use their knowledge of *t*'s name in spelling, the omission rate for the vowel of *teeth* should be relatively high.

The question, then, is whether the omission rates for vowels in letter-name sequences exceed the omission rates for vowels in non-letter-name sequences. As it turned out, the answer to this question was not the same for all letters. The answer depended on the phonological characteristics of the letter name itself. English has four letters whose names contain a vowel phoneme followed by a sonorant consonant, where sonorant consonants include liquids and nasals. These letters include *r,* whose name is the vowel-liquid sequence /ɑr/, and *l,* whose name is the vowel-liquid sequence /εl/. Also, *m* has the vowel-nasal name /ɪm/ and *n* has the vowel-nasal name /ɪn/ in the dialect of the children in this study. When a spoken word contained a vowel-sonorant consonant letter name, the children omitted the vowel significantly more often than expected given other factors. Table 7.2 shows some examples of vowel omissions for these vowel-sonorant letter names. Statistically, there were no significant differences in vowel omission rates among *r, l, m,* and *n.*

When a word contained a letter-name sequence that was *not* a vowel followed by a sonorant consonant, the children were no more likely to omit the vowel than expected on the basis of other factors. A number of English letters fall into this category. Some of these letters have names consisting of a vowel followed by an obstruent consonant, where obstruents include stops, fricatives, and affricates. For example, *f* is named /εf/ and *s* is named /εs/. The letter *x,* which is named /εks/, also belongs to the vowel-obstruent category. Letters with consonant-vowel names, such as *t, j,* and *y,* are another type of letter whose name is not a vowel followed by a sonorant consonant. In all these cases, the vowel did not show an elevated omission rate. Thus, the children were no more likely to omit the /ε/ of *Jeff,* which is

Table 7.2. Vowel Omissions in Vowel-Sonorant Letter-Name Sequences

Sequence of Phonemes	Letter Name	Examples
/ɑr/	*r*	FRM for *farm* PRCK for *park*
/εl/	*l*	HLP for *help* LEFIT for *elephant*
/ɪm/	*m*	HM for *him* JOGJM for *junglegym*
/ɪn/	*n*	WNT for *went* PTND for *pretend*

part of the vowel-obstruent letter name /ɛf/, than the /æ/ of *Jack,* which does not belong to a letter name. The children were no more likely to omit the /i/ of *teeth,* which is part of a consonant-vowel letter name, than the /u/ of *tooth,* which is not part of a letter name. In other words, the children used their knowledge of letter names for some consonant letters but not others.

The finding that only vowels in vowel-sonorant letter names showed an elevated omission rate did not depend on syllabification. The results were the same whether letter-name sequences were defined as those in which the phonemes were in the same syllable of the spoken word according to the assumptions about syllabification described in Chapter 1 or whether any sequence of phonemes that formed the name of a letter was considered a letter-name sequence, regardless of whether the phonemes belonged to the same syllable.

To get a better idea of how often the children omitted vowels in letter-name and non-letter-name contexts, examine the results in Table 7.3. Because of the strong association between stress and vowel omissions documented earlier in this chapter, the results for stressed and unstressed vowels are separated in this table. Syllable boundaries are disregarded in the definition of letter-name sequences.

For stressed vowels, the omission rates for vowels in vowel-liquid letter names and vowel-nasal letter names both exceeded 10%. The omission rates for vowels in vowel-obstruent and consonant-vowel letter names were less than 5%, as was the omission rate for vowels that were not in letter names. The children attempted few words that contained vowel-obstruent letter names, so conclusions about this category must remain tentative. Within the category of vowel-sonorant letter names, the omission rate for /ɑ/ before /r/ appeared to exceed the omission rate for /ɛ/

Table 7.3. Vowel Omissions in Letter-Name-Contexts as a Function of the Phonological Characteristics of the Letter-Name Sequence

	No. Omissions	No. Cases	% Omissions
Stressed vowels			
Letter-name context			
Vowel-/r/	17	80	21.3
Vowel-/l/	9	76	11.8
Vowel-nasal	32	315	10.2
Vowel-obstruent	0	11	0.0
Consonant-vowel	4	114	3.5
Non-letter-name context	225	5154	4.4
Unstressed vowels			
Letter-name context			
Vowel-/r/	0	0	—
Vowel-/l/	0	0	—
Vowel-nasal	1	1	100.0
Vowel-obstruent	0	0	—
Consonant-vowel	27	97	27.8
Non-letter-name context	296	810	36.5

before /l/ or /ɪ/ before /m/ and /n/. As mentioned earlier, however, the apparent differences among *r, l, m,* and *n* were not statistically reliable.

For unstressed vowels, the results in Table 7.3 do not permit any conclusions about vowel-consonant letter names such as the name of *r.* The children attempted few words that contained these sequences. However, consonant-vowel letter names occurred fairly often with unstressed vowels. For example, *happy* contains /p/ followed by unstressed /i/; /pi/, of course, is the name of the letter *p.* The omission rate for unstressed vowels in these consonant-vowel letter-name contexts did not exceed the omission rate for unstressed vowels that were not in letter-name contexts. That is, the children were no more likely to omit the /i/ of *happy,* where /i/ is in a letter-name context, than the /i/ of *Sally,* where /i/ is not in a letter-name context. However, the omission rate for unstressed /i/ was relatively high in both types of words. The children often *did* make errors like HAP for *happy.* Viewing these errors in isolation, one might be tempted to suggest that children leave out the vowel because they know that *p* stands for /pi/. However, this conclusion seems to be incorrect for the children in this study. That errors like HAP for *happy* were not more common than errors like SAL for *Sally* suggests that it is the vowel's lack of stress, not its membership in a consonant-vowel letter name, that causes children to omit it.

To summarize, children's knowledge of the names of consonant letters has limited effects on vowel omissions. The effects are confined to the letters *r, l, m,* and *n;* they do not appear to extend to letters such as *s, f, t,* and *k.* The restriction of letter-name effects to certain letters speaks against one idea about letter-name spellings—that children make errors like HLP for *help* because they are confused about the distinction between letters and the sounds that they make. If first graders did not understand this distinction, they should also have produced errors like TTH for *teeth.*

Why did children's knowledge of the names of consonant letters have such limited effects on their spelling? Surely, the first graders were not more familiar with the names of *r, l, m,* and *n* than with the names of other consonant letters. The letters were taught in alphabetical order in the children's phonics book, so no superiority for *r, l, m,* and *n* would be expected on this basis. I suggest that letter-name spellings are restricted to certain consonant letters because of the *phonological* properties of these letters' names. The names of *r, l, m,* and *n* all contain a vowel phoneme followed by a sonorant consonant phoneme. As I discuss in more detail later, vowels and following sonorants in spoken words form cohesive units. Vowels and following sonorants are more cohesive than vowels and following obstruents; they are also more cohesive than consonant-vowel units. These phonological considerations may explain why letter-name spellings are more frequent with letters like *r* and *n* than with letters like *f* and *t.*

To see why some groups of phonemes are more closely connected than others, recall the theories about English syllables that were discussed in Chapter 1. A number of linguists (Fudge, 1969, 1987, 1989; Selkirk, 1982) claim that English syllables have two main units. These units are the onset and the rime. The onset is the syllable's initial consonant or consonant cluster. The rime is the vowel and any following consonants. If English syllables are composed of onsets and rimes, the vowel is more tightly linked to the consonant that follows it than to the consonant that precedes it. This is because the vowel and the following consonant belong to the same constituent of the syllable, the rime. In contrast, the consonant that precedes the vowel belongs to a different part of the syllable, the onset. Because vowels and following consonants are grouped together in the phonology of the language, children sometimes treat these phonemes as units for spelling purposes. Because initial consonants and following vowels do not form tight units, children do not usually treat them as a group.

My finding that letter-name spellings were more common for letters like *r* than letters like *f* further suggests that vowels and following sonorants are stronger units than vowels and following obstruents. This difference, too, fits with certain linguistic theories. According to many linguists, the rime of an English syllable contains two parts. The first part of the rime, and one that all rimes must possess, is the peak. The peak generally contains a vowel. The second part of the rime, which is optional, is a consonantal coda. Selkirk (1982) claims that a sonorant consonant that follows a vowel may be part of the peak. For example, the /r/ of *farm* belongs to the syllable peak. In this word, /ɑ/ and /r/ together form the peak, while /m/ is the coda. Obstruents, in contrast, may not be part of the peak. Thus, the /ɛ/ and /f/ of *Jeff* are in different parts of the rime.

Consider a first grader who is trying to spell *farm*. To construct a spelling from the word's phonological form, the student must analyze the spoken word into smaller units and must choose a grapheme for each unit. When analyzing the spoken word, the child may have trouble dividing the /ɑr/ peak into /ɑ/ and /r/. Because these phonemes are hard to separate, and because the child has a strong link between the group of phonemes /ɑr/ and the letter *r*, the child may spell /ɑr/ with single *r*. Thus, the child spells *farm* as FRM, omitting the vowel.

The same type of error occurs with words containing vowel-/l/ and vowel-nasal letter names. Students sometimes treat the /ɛ/ and /l/ of *help* as a unit, spelling the word as HLP. Similarly, children sometimes group the /ɪ/ and /n/ of *went,* spelling the word as WNT.

Errors like JF for *Jeff* are uncommon among first graders because the /ɛ/ and the /f/ of this word are not highly cohesive. Although both phonemes belong to the syllable's rime, /ɛ/ is the peak and /f/ is the coda. Thus, first graders have little trouble breaking the sequence /ɛf/ into /ɛ/ and /f/. Having analyzed /ɛf/ as two separate phonemes, children generally spell it with a letter appropriate for /ɛ/ followed by a letter appropriate for /f/. Although children *do* associate /ɛf/ and *f,* they do not usually spell /ɛf/ as *f* because of the weak phonological bond between the /ɛ/ and the /f/.

Errors such as TTH for *teeth* are also uncommon. When analyzing the spoken word, first graders have little trouble separating /t/ and /i/. This is because /t/ is the syllable's onset and /i/ belongs to its rime. Children split the syllable at the onset/rime boundary with relatively little difficulty. Although first graders know that /ti/ is the name of *t,* they rarely spell /ti/ as a unit because the two phonemes are only loosely connected to one another.

Based on the linguistic considerations that I have discussed, children should be more likely to produce letter-name spellings with letters that have vowel-obstruent names (e.g., *f*) than with letters that have consonant-vowel names (e.g., *t*). Because a vowel and a following obstruent belong to the same constituent of the syllable—the rime—while a consonant and a following vowel do not, children might have some tendency to spell sequences like /ɛf/ as units but very little tendency to spell sequences like /ti/ as units. It is difficult to evaluate the possibility of such a difference, since the children attempted so few words containing vowel-obstruent letter-name sequences.

As discussed in Chapter 1, studies with adults suggest that the two types of English sonorants—liquids and nasals—differ in their cohesiveness with a preceding vowel. There is evidence that vowels and following liquids form tighter units than vowels and following nasals (e.g., Treiman, 1984b). There is also some evidence that vowel-/r/ units are more closely linked than vowel-/l/ units (Derwing et al., 1987). If the same is true for children, letter-name spellings should be most common for *r*, next most common for *l*, and next most common for *m* and *n*. There was a trend in this direction in the vowel omission data, but it was not significant.

To summarize, first graders sometimes spell a sequence of phonemes that matches the name of a consonant letter with that consonant letter by itself. Such errors are fairly common for *r*, *l*, *m*, and *n* but are not common for other consonants. These differences may arise for phonological reasons. Specifically, children may have difficulty analyzing the vowel-sonorant sequences /ar/, /ɛl/, /ɪm/, and /ɪn/. In this view, the ability to analyze spoken words into phonemes, or phonemic awareness, is important in learning to spell. Specific limitations in phonemic awareness, such as difficulty in dividing /ar/ into phonemes, lead to specific spelling errors.

Syllabic Consonants

Linguists disagree about the phonemic forms of words like *her, after,* and *candle.* I transcribed *her* as containing /h/, /ə/, and /r/ and *after* and *candle* as containing unstressed /ə/ in their second syllables, following Trager and Smith (1951), Prator and Robinett (1972), and many dictionaries. However, as discussed in Chapter 1, some linguists (e.g., Kenyon & Knott, 1953) consider *her* to contain two phonemes rather than three. If *her* has two phonemes, is its second phoneme a vowel or a consonant? Some linguists treat this phoneme as a vowel, an *r-colored vowel*. Others treat it as a consonant, *syllabic* /r/. The consonant is said to be syllabic because it alone occupies the peak of the syllable. There is no separate vowel.

Although linguists disagree about the phonemic status of syllabic liquids, the phonetic facts are fairly clear. Phonetically, *her* contains two segments rather than three. Phonetically, *candle* does not end with a vowel segment followed by /l/. It contains the single unit syllabic /l/.

At the phonetic level, nasals may also be syllabic in unstressed syllables. Although I coded *Jason* as having /ə/ in its second syllable, this word is usually pronounced without a vowel in the second syllable; that is, with a syllabic /n/. Liquids and nasals may be syllabic in English, but obstruents may not be syllabic. Phonemically and phonetically, the final syllable of *bandit* contains unstressed /ə/ followed by /t/. The /t/ is not syllabic.

The English writing system does not indicate the syllabicity of liquids and nasals. In words like *her, after, candle,* and *Jason,* both a vowel letter and a consonant letter are used to symbolize the syllabic liquid. Whether the vowel letter precedes the consonant letter, as in *her, after,* and *Jason,* or whether it follows the consonant letter, as in *candle* and *acre,* a vowel letter is always present.

Given this background on the nature of syllabic consonants, I now ask how the first graders spelled them. If children consider *her* to contain three segments—/h/, /ə/, and /r/—they should generally spell it with three letters. If children consider *her* to contain two segments—/h/ followed by syllabic /r/—they may spell the word with only two letters. They may leave out the vowel, spelling the word as HR. Similarly, children may produce errors like AFTR for *after,* CANDL for *candle,* and JASN for *Jason.*

With syllabic liquids, vowel omissions were indeed more frequent than expected from other factors. The children omitted the *es* of *her, after,* and *candle* more often than they omitted the vowels of comparable words without syllabic liquids. There was no significant difference between syllabic /r/ and syllabic /l/ in this regard. The results were similar whether syllabic liquids were defined with or without the assumptions about syllabification outlined in Chapter 1.

Interestingly, different results were found for syllabic nasals. For syllabic nasals, vowel omissions were *not* significantly more common than predicted on the basis of other factors. The children did not omit the *o* of *Jason* significantly more often than they omitted unstressed vowels in comparable words without syllabic consonants. Null results were obtained whether or not the linguistic assumptions about syllabification were used to define syllabic nasals.

To get a better idea of how often the children omitted vowels in these various cases, examine the results in Table 7.4. The results are presented separately for stressed and unstressed vowels. For purposes of this table, any possible syllable boundaries between the vowel and the following consonant are disregarded.

Table 7.4. Vowel Omissions for Syllabic Consonants and Comparison Cases

	No. Omissions	No. Cases	% Omissions	Examples
Stressed /ə/				
Followed by /r/	56	125	44.8	HR for *her*
Followed by /l/	0	0	—	
Followed by nasal	12	130	9.2	BRG for *brung* [*sic*]
Followed by obstruent	12	247	4.9	KLB for *club*
Unstressed /ə/				
Followed by /r/	127	196	64.8	BRUTR for *brother*
Followed by /l/	50	84	59.5	APLS for *apples*
Followed by nasal	35	95	36.8	PRSN for *person*
Followed by obstruent	82	250	32.8	RADTS for *rabbits*

In the stressed case, the children omitted stressed /ə/ nearly half the time when it was followed by /r/; that is, when /r/ was syllabic. Thus, the students often spelled words like *her* and *learn* without a vowel, as in HR and LRN. The children omitted stressed /ə/ less than 10% of the time when it was followed by a nasal or an obstruent. In these cases, the consonant is not syllabic.

In the unstressed case, the children omitted /ə/ well over half the time when it was followed by /r/ or /l/. Although the omission rate appeared to be greater for /r/ than for /l/, this difference was not significant. Errors like AFTR for *after* and LITL for *little* actually outnumbered spellings that included a vowel in the second syllable. The children omitted unstressed /ə/ about one-third of the time when it preceded a nasal or an obstruent. Children probably leave out the vowel in these cases because the vowel is unstressed and because it is in the middle of the word. Effects of vowel stress were documented earlier in this chapter; effects of position in the word will be discussed later. If one viewed errors like PRSN for *person* in isolation, one might conclude that children do represent the syllabicity of nasals in their spelling. However, this conclusion does not seem to be correct. The children were not significantly more likely to omit the second vowel of *person* than the second vowel of *bandit*.

So far, I have assumed that sonorants are always syllabic in unstressed syllables. This assumption may not be strictly correct. According to Kenyon (1950, pp. 74–75), nasals and /l/ are most likely to be syllabic when they follow a consonant that is articulated at the same place in the mouth (i.e., a homorganic consonant). For example, *little* is usually pronounced with syllabic /l/ since the tongue does not move from /t/ to /l/. However, *bacon* may have a vowel in the second syllable because /k/ and /n/ have different places of articulation. When I repeated the analyses using the stricter criterion for syllabic consonants, the same results emerged: Vowels were omitted significantly more often than expected based on other factors in the case of syllabic liquids but not in the case of syllabic nasals.

Why are children more likely to omit vowels when spelling syllabic liquids than when spelling syllabic nasals? The difference between liquids and nasals speaks against the idea that children represent the phonetic level of speech in their spelling. Phonetically, it would appear, the spoken words *after, little, Jason,* and *bandit* fall into two groups. *After, little,* and *Jason* lack a vowel in the second syllable; *bandit* has a vowel. If children's spelling reflected the phonetic level of speech, children should be as likely to spell *Jason* as JASN as to spell *after* as AFTR and *little* as LITTL. Children should omit the second vowel of *Jason* significantly more often than the second vowel of *bandit*. These predictions were not supported.

The children's spellings of syllabic consonants are consistent with the idea that children represent the phonemic level when they spell. For first graders, the phonemic form of *after* may end with syllabic /r/ rather than with /ə/ plus /r/. Likewise, first graders may consider *little* to end with syllabic /l/ rather than with /ə/ followed by /l/. In contrast, children consider *Jason* to end with unstressed /ə/ followed by /n/. Similarly, the second syllable of *bandit* contains /ə/ followed by /t/. Phonemically, then, the spoken words *after, little, Jason,* and *bandit* fall into two groups— *after* and *little* in one group and *Jason* and *bandit* in the other. If children represent the phonemic level of speech in their spelling, they should omit the second vowel of both *after* and *little* more often than the second vowel of both *Jason* and *bandit*. This was the pattern that I observed.

Linguistic evidence is compatible with the idea that liquids and nasals behave differently. Recall from Chapter 1 that vowels are the most sonorant type of phoneme, pronounced with the least degree of obstruction in the mouth. Vowels are said to rank highest on the sonority scale. They are followed in turn by glides, liquids, nasals, and finally obstruents. Because /r/ and /l/ are relatively high in sonority, they may occupy the syllable peak on their own. No vowel is needed. Thus, *after* has /r/ as the peak of the second syllable. The nasals /m/, /n/, and /ŋ/, being lower in sonority, may not occupy the peak by themselves. Thus, *Jason* contains unstressed /ə/ as the peak of the second syllable followed by an /n/. Obstruents, which rank lowest in sonority, may not belong to the peak. Thus, the second syllable of *bandit* has unstressed /ə/ as the peak and /t/ as the coda.

As mentioned earlier, linguists disagree about whether the final phoneme of *her* and *after* is a type of vowel—an *r*-colored vowel—or a type of consonant—a syllabic /r/. Children's use of *r* to symbolize the final segment of *her* and *after* suggests that they consider this segment to be more similar to the consonant /r/ than to any vowel. If children considered the segment to be a vowel, I should have seen errors like HU and AFTE instead of errors like HR and AFTR.

To summarize, first graders often spell syllabic liquids with single *r* and *l* rather than with a vowel plus *r* or *l*. Such errors are less common for syllabic nasals. The errors may arise because children consider syllabic liquids as single phonemes. In contrast, they consider syllabic nasals as sequences of a vowel plus a nasal.

Word Length

The first graders were more likely to omit vowels in long words than vowels in short words. As the number of phonemes in a spoken word increased, the probability of omission of any particular vowel within the word increased. This relation is plotted in Figure 7.1, which is based on the results for all vowel phonemes.

Why do children omit vowels in long words more often than vowels in short words? There are several possible reasons. When analyzing a long word into phonemes, children may lose track of where they are in the process of phonemic analysis. They may forget some of the phonemes while trying to spell the others. To the extent that children spell by attempting to reproduce a memorized sequence of letters, long words should also cause difficulty. The more letters there are to remember, the more likely children are to leave one out.

Another possible reason why children might omit vowels in long words is that vowels in long words are relatively short (Klatt, 1973; Lehiste, 1972). However, other findings reported in this chapter suggest that the acoustic duration of a vowel is not closely related to its omission rate in children's spelling.

Position in Word

The children were more likely to omit vowels when they occurred in certain positions within a word than when they occurred in other positions. Figure 7.2 shows

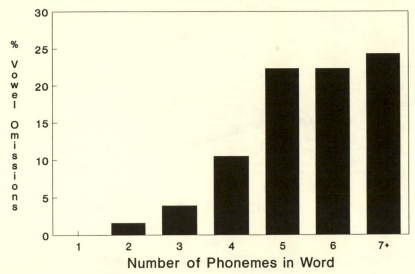

Figure 7.1. Vowel omission rate as a function of the number of phonemes in the word.

the relation between the position of a vowel in a spoken word and its omission rate for words containing various numbers of phonemes. This figure is based on the results for stressed vowels only. No figure for unstressed vowels is presented because unstressed vowels did not occur in all of the positions within a word at many word lengths. In addition, because syllabic liquids and vowels in vowel-sonorant letter names have elevated omission rates, and because such contexts are not evenly distributed across word positions and word lengths, these cases are not included in Figure 7.2.

Once other phonological effects are removed, children seem to omit vowels at the beginnings and ends of words less often than vowels in the middles of words. Statistical analyses confirmed that the omission rate for vowels in the interiors of words significantly exceeded the omission rate for vowels at the margins of words. The omission rates for vowels at the beginnings and ends of words did not differ reliably.

Why are children more likely to omit vowels in the middles of words than vowels at the beginnings and ends of words? At first glance, the effects of serial position on vowel omission rate might suggest that spelling involves the recall of letters from a previously memorized sequence. We know that people remember the first and last items of an arbitrary sequence better than they remember the middle items. However, the serial position curve found here emerged only *after* phonological factors had been taken into account. Many words do not show the typical serial position curve because of the particular phonemes that they contain. Consider *encyclopedia*. The initial *e* has a high rather than a low omission rate since it represents an unstressed vowel and since this vowel and the following consonant form the name of *n*. The final *a* is also susceptible to omission because it represents an unstressed vowel. These phonological effects suggest that the serial position curve in children's vowel omissions does not generally reflect children's memory for the string of *letters*

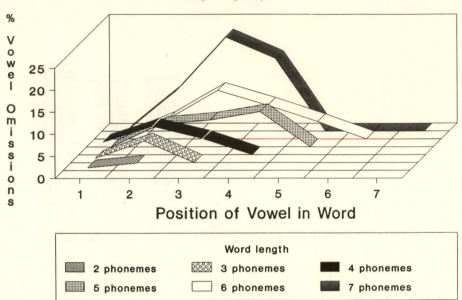

Figure 7.2. Vowel omission rate for stressed vowels as a function of the serial position of the vowel in the word. The results are shown separately for words ranging in length from two to seven phonemes. Vowels in vowel-sonorant letter-name contexts and syllabic liquids are not included.

in the written word. To the extent that the curve reflects memory factors, it primarily reflects children's memory for the string of *phonemes* in the spoken word. When children analyze a spoken word into phonemes and try to remember the phonemes, they are more apt to forget the phonemes in the middle of the sequence than the phonemes at the beginning and at the end of the sequence. Thus, they sometimes fail to spell the middle phonemes.[3]

In addition to reflecting children's ability to remember the phonemes in a spoken word, the serial position curve may also reflect children's ability to analyze the spoken word into phonemes. When analyzing a spoken word, children may find it relatively easy to isolate the phonemes at the beginning and the end of the word. This is because these phonemes must be separated from only one adjacent phoneme. Vowels in the middles of words have phonemes on both sides of them and so may be harder to isolate.

Factors Not Significantly Associated with Vowel Omission Errors

So far, I have discussed a number of factors that were significantly associated with vowel omission errors. These factors include stress, letter names, syllabic liquids, word length, and position in word. Certain other factors that might have been thought to relate to vowel omissions did not yield significant results. In this section, I consider these other factors. Of course, the finding that a particular factor did not yield statistically significant results does not necessarily mean that the factor is unrelated to vowel omissions. The null results could have arisen because my collection of spellings was too small or my data too unreliable to show a significant association. Still, some factors *did* have highly significant effects. Even given the difficulties in interpreting null results, it is worth discussing those factors that were not significantly associated with vowel omissions.

/ə/ Versus Other Vowels

Examining the results for each vowel separately, I found that the omission rate for /ə/ far exceeded the omission rates for the other vowels. The children omitted /ə/ 31.5% of the time. The omission rates for the other vowels ranged from 0.0% to 11.8%. The difference between /ə/ and the other vowels was significant by a chi-square test ($p < .001$).

Why did the students so often fail to spell /ə/? Perhaps there is something special about this particular vowel that causes children to omit it. Or, perhaps the high omission rate for /ə/ is a by-product of the factors that have already been identified. The results supported this second idea.

One reason that the children so often omitted /ə/ is that this vowel is frequently unstressed. As I showed earlier in this chapter, children omit unstressed vowels more often than they omit stressed vowels. Another reason for the high omission rate on /ə/ is that words such as *her, after,* and *little* were transcribed as including /ə/. The results suggest, however, that children do not actually consider these words to contain /ə/. Finally, as compared with other vowels, /ə/ was more likely to occur in long words and more likely to occur in the middles of words. Children often fail to spell vowels in these contexts. Taken together, these factors explain the high omission rate on /ə/. There does not seem to be anything intrinsically unusual about this particular vowel.

Vowel Duration

Vowels are measurably shorter when they occur in certain contexts than in others. For example, the /æ/ of *bat* is about two-thirds the length of the /æ/ of *bad* (e.g., Klatt, 1973; Lehiste, 1975; Peterson & Lehiste, 1960). This difference in duration reflects the voicing of the following consonant. Vowels are shorter when they precede voiceless obstruents, like /t/, than when they precede voiced obstruents, like /d/.

In English, differences in vowel length are phonetic rather than phonemic. That is, length differences do not serve to distinguish words. Although the /æ/s of *bat* and *bad* differ in acoustic duration, speakers consider them to belong to the same phoneme. A word with a long /æ/ and an otherwise identical word with a short /æ/ could not mean different things in English. In other languages, such as Danish and Korean, vowel length *is* phonemic. /b'æt/ could mean two different things depending on whether it was said with a long /æ/ or a short /æ/.

Even though vowel length is not phonemic in English, children might be sensitive to length as a phonetic characteristic. If children take spelling to represent the phonetic level of speech, they might omit the shorter /æ/ of *bat* more often than the longer /æ/ of *bad*. If so, errors like BT for *bat* should outnumber errors like BD for *bad*. My results did not support this prediction. Omission rates for vowels followed by voiceless obstruents did not differ from omission rates for vowels followed by voiced obstruents. This held even when the vowel and the following obstruent belonged to the same syllable by the syllabification assumptions of Chapter 1.

In addition to the contextually conditioned differences in vowel length just described, there are also intrinsic length differences among vowels. According to Peterson and Lehiste (1960), /ɪ/, /ɛ/, /ʊ/, and /ə/ (when not before /r/) are shorter than other English vowels. The ratio of acoustic durations for the intrinsically short vowels relative to the intrinsically long ones is about two to three. However, the children were no more likely to omit the intrinsically short vowels than the other vowels.

Thus, the spelling of English-speaking children does not seem to reflect phonetic differences in vowel duration. Children's spelling seems to represent the phonemic level of speech, a level at which vowel duration is unimportant in English. It does not seem to represent the phonetic level.

When discussing the effects of stress earlier in this chapter, I offered several possible explanations for children's high omission rate on unstressed vowels relative to stressed vowels. One idea was that children tend to omit unstressed vowels because of their short durations. The present findings speak against this notion. Moreover, the shorter duration of vowels in long words as compared with short words probably does not explain the higher vowel omission rate in long words.

Word Frequency

There was no significant relation between vowel omission rate and the frequency of the word containing the vowel. The children were no less likely to omit vowels in frequent words than vowels in infrequent words. Recall from Chapter 2 that there *was* a significant association between word frequency and correct spellings of whole words. The children spelled frequent words more accurately than infrequent words. Why, then, was word frequency not associated with vowel omissions? I suspect that such a relation exists but that it is too weak to be picked up in this study. The omission rates for different vowels within the same word vary greatly as a function of the vowels' stress, position in the word, and so on. This variation is so large that the frequency of the word itself plays only a small role.

Other Factors

The children were no more likely to omit vowels when they were part of an inflectional suffix than when they were not part of such a suffix. For example, the second vowel of *landed,* which belongs to the past tense ending, was not omitted any more often than expected on the basis of other factors.

I also examined the omission rates for vowels in derivational prefixes and suffixes. The omission rate for such vowels was not higher than otherwise expected. For example, the final vowel of *collection,* which is part of a derivational suffix, was not particularly susceptible to omission.

Within the contexts of letter-name sequences and syllabic consonants, the sonority of the consonant that followed a vowel was related to the vowel's omission rate. In general, however, the children did not omit vowels significantly more often when followed by sonorant consonants than when followed by obstruents. Nor did the omission rates differ for vowels that were at the end of a syllable according to the syllabification assumptions of Chapter 1 and vowels that were followed by one or more consonants in the same syllable.

Statistical Analyses

The results that I have described were based on multiple regression analyses. The dependent variable was the percentage of omissions for each vowel phoneme in each word of the collection. Thus, there was one line of data for the first vowel of *about,* one line for the second vowel of *about,* one line for the first vowel of *absent,* one line for the second vowel, and so on—1,286 lines of data in all. A few vowels that are not spelled with a separate letter, such as the first vowel of *K-mart,* were excluded from the analyses.

I carried out an analysis using the predictors of stressed versus unstressed vowel, vowel-sonorant letter name, syllabic liquid, number of phonemes in the spoken word, and marginal vowel (i.e., vowel at the beginning or end of a word) versus nonmarginal vowel (i.e., vowel in the interior of a word). In this analysis, all cases of stressed /ə/ before /r/ and unstressed /ə/ before /r/ and /l/ were coded as syllabic liquids, regardless of any possible syllable boundary between the vowel and the liquid. Likewise, syllabification was ignored in the definition of letter-name sequences. The regression accounted for 31.6% (31.3% adjusted) of the variance in vowel omissions ($p < .001$). All five predictors made significant contributions ($p < .001$ for stress, vowel-sonorant letter name, syllabic liquid, and number of phonemes, $p = .005$ for margin). The largest effects were for syllabic liquids and stress.

The percentage of variance explained by the regression did not increase reliably when primary and secondary stressed vowels were distinguished from one another. The effect of letter names was confined to vowel-sonorant letter names. There were no significant effects for vowel-obstruent or consonant-vowel letter names. The influence of syllabic consonants was restricted to syllabic liquids. It did not extend to syllabic nasals when syllabic nasals were defined as unstressed /ə/ before /m/, /n/, and /ŋ/. Vowels at the beginnings and ends of words did not differ significantly from one another.

In another set of analyses, letter-name sequences and syllabic liquids and nasals were coded as such only if the phonemes belonged to the same syllable by the assumptions about syllabification discussed in Chapter 1. The results were almost identical to those just described.

To further examine the relation between vowel omissions and syllabic consonants, a further analysis used a stricter definition of syllabic liquids and nasals. Here, unstressed /ə/ before nasals and /l/ was coded as syllabic only when it was preceded by a consonant with the same place of articulation. The percentage of variance accounted for by the regression declined slightly, by about 2%. As before, the syllabic consonant effect was carried by the syllabic liquids.

A factor that distinguished /ə/ from the other vowels did not add significantly to the regression. Also unsuccessful as predictors were distinctions based on the voicing of a following obstruent (voiced versus voiceless) and intrinsic vowel length (/ɪ/, /ɛ/, /ʊ/ and /ə/ not before /r/ versus all other vowels). Word frequency did not add significantly to the regression. This held true whether frequency was measured as the frequency of the word in Carroll et al. (1971), the log of Carroll et al. frequency, the number of occurrences of the word in the collection, or the log of number of occurrences. Also unsuccessful as predictors were whether the consonant after the vowel was a sonorant or an obstruent and whether the vowel was at the end of its syllable. There was no significant increase in omission rate for vowels in derivational affixes or vowels in inflectional suffixes.

Almost one-third of the variance in vowel omission rates was explained by the variables of stress, vowel-sonorant letter names, syllabic liquids, number of phonemes in the word, and marginal versus nonmarginal position. This figure is impressive given that many words only occurred once in the collection of children's spellings. For the vowels in these words, the percentage of omissions could only be 0% or 100%. When analyses were undertaken excluding vowels that occurred once, twice, and so on up to five times, the percentage of variance explained by the regression increased to a maximum of 52.3% (51.6% adjusted) when only vowels that occurred four or more times were included ($p < .001$). This analysis was based on 346 cases. As before, the variables of stress, vowel-sonorant letter names, syllabic liquids, number of phonemes, and marginal versus nonmarginal position all had significant effects. Thus, at least half of the variance in vowel omission rates seems to reflect the factors considered here, provided that relatively stable estimates of vowel omission rates are available.

Changes from First to Second Semester of the School Year

Overall, the rate of vowel omission errors declined from the first semester of the school year to the second (12.0% versus 8.2%, $p < .001$ for the difference by a chi-square test). However, the improvement was by no means uniform for the various types of vowels. Although the omission rate for stressed vowels decreased (7.9% to 3.5%, $p < .001$ by a chi-square test), the omission rate for unstressed vowels did not. The children omitted unstressed vowels 37.7% of the time during the first semester and 38.3% of the time during the second semester. This lack of improvement for unstressed vowels reflects a lack of improvement for syllabic liquids, the majority of which were unstressed. The omission rate for vowels in syllabic liquids was 61.9% during the first semester and 59.8% during the second, not a significant difference. Throughout the first grade, then, the students usually spelled syllabic liquids without vowels. These errors persisted even though most of the children could probably read words like *mother, father,* and *girl* in which syllabic /r/ is spelled with a vowel letter followed by *r.*

Although the children's spellings of syllabic liquids did not significantly improve from the first semester to the second, their spellings of vowels in letter-name contexts did improve. The children omitted vowels in vowel-sonorant letter names 18.9% of the time during the first semester of the school year and 8.9% of the time during the second semester, a significant difference ($p < .005$ by a chi-square test). Apparently, the children's tendency to treat sequences like /ɛl/ and /ɑr/ as units for spelling purposes decreased as the school year progressed.

Summary of Results

Before discussing the implications of my findings and comparing them with those of other investigators, I will briefly summarize the results. The major findings of this chapter are as follows:

1. The children were more likely to omit unstressed vowels than stressed vowels in their spellings.
2. Given a sequence of phonemes that matched the name of a letter, the children sometimes omitted the vowel when the name of the letter consisted of a vowel followed by a sonorant consonant (i.e., a liquid, /l/ or /r/, or a nasal, /m/ or /n/). Letter names had no significant effects on vowel omissions for vowel-obstruent letter names such as /ɛs/ and /ɛf/ or consonant-vowel letter names such as /pi/ and /ti/.
3. The rate of vowel omission errors was significantly higher than otherwise expected for syllabic liquids but not for syllabic nasals. Vowel omissions with syllabic liquids persisted throughout the school year.
4. The more phonemes in a word, the more likely a vowel was to be omitted.
5. The children were more likely to omit vowels when they occurred in the middles of words than when they occurred at the beginnings or ends of words.

Comparison with Results of Other Studies

Previous studies of children's spelling have concentrated more on how children spell vowels than on when and why they fail to spell them. Although there have been claims that beginning spellers are particularly likely to omit vowels (Ehri, 1986; Morris & Perney, 1984), there has been little systematic research. Thus, many of the findings reported in this chapter are new.

Read's Research

Charles Read included some discussion of vowel omissions in his book on preschoolers' invented spellings (1975). As pointed out in Chapter 3, however, Read's collection of spellings included fewer vowel omissions than my collection. In comparing Read's findings with mine, recall that the percentages of omissions that Read reports are based on the total number of incorrectly spelled words. The percentages that I report are based on all words, correctly spelled words as well as misspelled words.

Read's preschoolers often omitted the vowels in words like *her, brother,* and *candle.* My first graders made the same errors. In both Read's study and mine, there was a trend for more omissions with syllabic /r/ than syllabic /l/. This trend was not significant in my study; Read did not report a statistical test of this point.

Read claimed that children represent the syllabicity of nasals in words like *kitten* by omitting the second vowel. This statement appears to conflict with my finding that the vowel omission rate for syllabic nasals was not significantly higher than expected given other factors. Although Read did not discuss differences between syllabic liquids and syllabic nasals, his tables show that unstressed /ə/ was omitted 62.2% of the time before /r/ and 47.1% of the time before /l/, as compared with 23.5% of the time before /m/ and 21.2% of the time before /n/. (Unstressed /ə/ did not occur before /ŋ/.) As in my study, then, vowel omissions appear to be more common for syllabic liquids than for syllabic nasals. Moreover, the omission rate for unstressed /ə/ when it did *not* precede /r/, /l/, /m/, or /n/ was about 18% in Read's study. Thus, the omission rate for vowels in syllabic nasals (about 22%) was not much higher than the omission rate for other unstressed vowels (about 18%). I found a similar result. The discrepancy between the two studies in the case of syllabic nasals may be more apparent than real.

Read took children's omissions of vowels in the case of syllabic liquids and (according to his interpretation) syllabic nasals to mean that children represent the phonetic level of speech when they spell. However, the difference between syllabic liquids and syllabic nasals in both sets of data speaks against this hypothesis. I propose that children's spelling does not represent a phonetic level at which liquids and nasals may both be syllabic. Rather, it represents a level at which liquids may be syllabic but nasals may not be syllabic. Children consider liquids (perhaps especially /r/) as able to form syllable peaks on their own. Because the second syllable of *brother* contains no vowel phoneme, children often spell this word with no vowel letter in the second syllable. Nasals, being lower on the sonority scale, may not occupy a syllable peak on their own. Because the second syllable of *kitten* contains a vowel phoneme, children often include a vowel letter in their spelling.

Read observed that preschoolers often symbolized the sequence /ɑr/ with single *r* rather than with a vowel followed by *r*. Children make this error, he suggested, because they know that /ɑr/ is the name of *r*. The present findings support Read's claim. Read did not systematically examine children's spellings of other letter-name sequences, so we do not know whether his preschoolers, like my first graders, produced more letter-name spellings for some consonants than others.

University of Virginia Research

The University of Virginia researchers propose that children pass through a series of stages in learning to spell. During the first, or precommunicative stage, which was not investigated here, children string letters together in an apparently random fashion. The second, or semiphonetic stage has several important characteristics. First, students use a letter-name strategy whenever possible. If a sequence of phonemes matches the name of a letter, children use the single letter to symbolize the entire sequence. Second, it is implied that semiphonetic spellings represent the phonetic level of speech rather than the phonemic level. Third, semiphonetic spellings are abbreviated. Students do not represent all of the phones in a word. They omit some and transcribe others. Many of the spellings in my study fall into the semiphonetic category. What do the results say about the Virginia researchers' characterization of semiphonetic spelling?

My first graders produced letter-name spellings, but only for some letters. The first graders made a fair number of letter-name spellings for *r* and *l*, writing *car* as CR, *help* as HLP, and so on. However, they did not show evidence of a letter-name strategy for *s, p,* or many other letters. Although the children *did* sometimes spell *happy* as HAP, they appeared to omit the final vowel because it is unstressed, not because it is preceded by /p/. Thus, although letter names play some role in first-grade spelling, first graders do not produce letter-name spellings every time it is possible to do so. They use letter-name spellings for some consonants but not for others.

The Virginia researchers imply that semiphonetic spellings represent the phonetic level of speech rather than the phonemic level. I did not find evidence for this view. For instance, the vowel of *bat* is measurably shorter than the vowel of *bad.* Yet errors like BT for *bat* did not outnumber errors like BD for *bad.* As another example, the vowel of *kit* is measurably shorter than the vowel of *cot.* Yet vowel omissions were no more common for words like *kit* than words like *cot.* Finally, the second syllable of *Jason* does not contain a separate vowel at the phonetic level. The second syllable of *bandit* does contain a separate vowel. However, my first graders were not significantly more likely to omit the second vowel of *Jason* than the second vowel of *bandit.* Again, a difference between words at the phonetic level is not reflected in the children's spelling. Admittedly, it is difficult to draw conclusions from negative results. Perhaps vowel omission rates do differ for *bat* and *bad, kit* and *cot,* and *Jason* and *bandit* but the differences are too small to be picked up in this study. Still, none of the analyses found any evidence that first graders represent the phonetic level of speech in their spelling.

The University of Virginia researchers further state that semiphonetic spellers do not represent all the segments in a word. They spell some segments and omit others. My findings support this claim. The first graders in this study did not always represent all of the vowels in each word. But the Virginia researchers have not systematically addressed the important question of *which* vowels tend to be omitted. For example, are vowels in the middles of words more likely to be omitted than vowels at the beginnings and ends of words? Because many of the words analyzed by the Virginia researchers are monosyllables with a simple consonant-vowel-consonant phonemic structure, such as *cat* and *mail,* it is difficult to address such questions. My results show that some vowels are more susceptible to omission than others. For example, when one looks beyond consonant-vowel-consonant words to words that begin or end with vowels, one finds that vowels in the middles of words are more likely to be omitted than vowels at the beginnings or ends of words. When one looks beyond single-syllable words to words that have more than one syllable, one finds that unstressed vowels are more likely to be omitted than stressed vowels. Thus, children's vowel omissions are systematically affected by linguistic factors.

My results suggest that the University of Virginia researchers' characterization of the semiphonetic stage of spelling development is not wholly right. In some respects—the idea that letter-name spellings are used whenever possible, the idea that children represent the phonetic level of speech—it seems to be incorrect. In other respects, especially its failure to specify which types of vowels are most susceptible to omission, the theory is incomplete.

What of the phonetic stage of spelling development, which is said to follow the semiphonetic stage? According to the Virginia researchers, phonetic spellers continue to use a letter-name strategy when possible. Also, it is implied that children continue to represent speech at the phonetic level. As I have discussed, I did not find evidence for these claims.

During the phonetic stage, the Virginia researchers state, children no longer omit vowels within words (except for syllabic sonorants). Children at the phonetic stage and later stages of spelling development represent *all* the segments in each word. My results do not support this claim. Even the best of the first-grade spellers sometimes omitted vowels in vulnerable positions of words. For example, Becky would be classified as a phonetic speller during much of her first-grade year. She showed several of the hallmarks of the phonetic stage as described by Gentry (1982), including omissions of preconsonantal nasals, as in FAD for *found,* and use of *r* for syllabic /r/, as in MOTHR for *mother.* With one-syllable words, Becky never omitted vowels (except in the case of stressed syllabic /r/). With words of more than one syllable, though, Becky sometimes omitted unstressed vowels. For example, she failed to spell the unstressed second vowel of *wanted,* producing WOTD. She omitted both vowels and consonants in the unstressed syllables of *collection,* producing LAG. Becky and other children who look like phonetic spellers on one-syllable words look like semiphonetic spellers on more complex words. Thus, it may be wrong to assume, as the University of Virginia researchers do, that all of a child's productions during a given period of time are similar to one another. The same child may perform differently on words with different linguistic structures.

Implications

The findings in this chapter have implications for several important issues, including the classification of children's misspellings, the processes by which children spell, the nature of children's phonological systems, the concept of spelling regularity, and the teaching of spelling. I discuss these issues in the following sections.

Classification of Spelling Errors

If one classified children's misspellings purely orthographically, by reference to the conventional spellings of the words, many of the results in this chapter would be difficult to explain. Consider the words *pretend* and *present,* where the latter is a noun meaning a gift. The printed words are alike orthographically. They have the same number of letters, the same pattern of vowel and consonant letters, and even the same vowel letters. If children spelled by attempting to reproduce the letters in a memorized sequence, they should make similar kinds of vowel omission errors on the two words. However, the pattern of vowel omissions in the two types of words was actually quite different. In *pretend,* the children were more likely to omit the first *e* than the second. In *present,* the reverse was true. This difference makes sense only if one considers the words' phonological forms. In *pretend,* the first *e* stands for an unstressed vowel while the second stands for a stressed vowel. In *present,* the first *e* represents a stressed vowel and the second represents an unstressed vowel. The different stress patterns of the spoken words help explain the different vowel omission rates. A purely orthographic classification system could not make sense of the results.

As another example of why children's misspellings should not be classified only by reference to the conventional spellings of the words, consider *help* and *hang.* A purely orthographic classification system has trouble explaining why children are more likely to omit the vowel in *help* than *hang.* The two words have similar spellings. Both are four letters long; both have a vowel as the second letter. One cannot claim that *e* is generally more susceptible to omission than *a,* for the reverse is sometimes true. For example, children omit the *a* of *park* more often than the *e* of *pets.* To understand the pattern of vowel omission errors, one must consider the words' phonological forms. What is important is that the /ɛl/ in the spoken form of *help* and the /ɑr/ in the spoken form of *park* match the names of letters, letters whose spoken forms are difficult for first graders to analyze into phonemes. The /æŋ/ in *hang* and the /ɛt/ in *pets* do not match the names of letters. Thus, first graders are more likely to omit the *e* of *help* than the *a* of *hang.* They are more likely to omit the *a* of *park* than the *e* of *pets.*

In sum, we have little hope of understanding children's vowel omission errors unless we acknowledge that spelling is, in large part, an attempt to represent the phonological forms of words. It is not just an attempt to reproduce memorized sequences of letters.

Models of the Spelling Process

My results suggest that children spell, to a large extent, phonologically. They construct spellings for words using their knowledge of words' phonological forms and their knowledge of the links between phonemes and graphemes. As a result, children's spellings reflect the phonological characteristics of words. Children usually represent phonemes that are salient in the spoken forms of words, such as stressed vowels. They sometimes omit phonemes that are less salient in the spoken forms of words, such as unstressed vowels. When no vowel appears in the phonemic form of a word, as in the second syllable of *little,* children often include no vowel letter in their spelling.

With some familiar words, memory for the conventional spelling of the word may help children to spell the word. However, the role of visual memorization seems to be relatively small for the first graders in this study. Supporting this claim, the students did not make significantly fewer vowel omissions on frequent words than on infrequent words. Even with the common word *mother,* which is introduced in children's earliest reading materials (Harris & Jacobson, 1972), the syllabicity of /r/ leads to errors like MOTHR and MOTR. Even with *him,* which is also introduced early (Harris & Jacobson, 1972), the link between /ɪm/ and *m* causes

errors like HM. Although most first graders can read *mother* and *him,* they sometimes misspell them. The links between syllabic /r/ and *r* and /ɪm/ and *m* cause
children to overlook or to forget certain aspects of words' conventional spellings.
As these examples show, learning to read words is not always sufficient for learning
to spell them.

Given that children use phonological information to spell, does their spelling
reflect the phonemic level or the phonetic level of speech? My results suggest that
children code the phonemic forms of words in their spelling. For example, the /æ/
of *bad* is phonetically longer than the /æ/ of *bat* but the two words have the same
vowel phoneme. The first graders were equally likely to omit the /æ/ in the two types
of words, suggesting that they transcribe speech at the phonemic level. For the most
part, children use links between *phonemes* and graphemes, not links between
phones and graphemes.

To learn and use relations between phonemes and graphemes, children must
possess representations of spoken words that are segmented into phonemes. For
example, children must know that *help* is not an indivisible whole. It consists of
/h/, /ɛ/, /l/, and /p/. Some of the first graders' errors suggest that children do not
always use fully segmented representations for spelling purposes. With *help,* for
example, children may use /h/, /ɛl/, and /p/. Having failed to divide /ɛl/ into phonemes, children misspell *help* as HLP. Such errors were particularly common during the first half of first grade. Thus, phonemic awareness plays an important role
in learning to spell. Children sometimes misspell words because the phonological
representations on which their spellings are based are not fully segmented into
phonemes.

Children's Phonological Systems

Children omit vowels in their spellings more for phonological reasons, or reasons
having to do with the way words sound, than for orthographic reasons, or reasons
having to do with the way words look. Therefore, the study of vowel omissions can
shed light on which phonological properties of spoken words are salient to children
and on the nature of children's phonological forms.

The results show that children distinguish between stressed and unstressed vowels. Stressed vowels are more salient than unstressed vowels and more likely to be
represented in spelling. Within the category of stressed vowels, there was no evidence for a distinction between primary and secondary stress. As far as children's
spelling is concerned, English vowels seem to be either stressed or unstressed.

Children's spellings also shed light on their treatment of syllabic liquids and
nasals. Within linguistics, the analysis of syllabic liquids and nasals is a subject of
debate. From the phonetic and articulatory points of view, syllabic liquids and
nasals appear to be single units. At the phonemic level, some linguists treat syllabic
liquids and nasals as single phonemes. Others treat them as sequences of a vowel
followed by a consonant. Because children's spelling seems to reflect the phonemic
level, my results may shed light on children's phonemic representations. It appears
that children distinguish between syllabic liquids and syllabic nasals. Children consider syllabic liquids as single phonemes. From their perspective, *her* is /h/ followed

by syllabic /r/. It is not /h/ followed by /ə/ followed by /r/. Likewise, children consider *little* to end with syllabic /l/ rather than with /ə/ plus /l/. Children apparently treat syllabic nasals as sequences of a vowel followed by a nasal. They consider *Jason* to end with /ə/ plus /n/ rather than with syllabic /n/. In the same way, children consider *bandit* to end with a vowel followed by a consonant.

The results reported here suggest that children consider vowels and liquids to be possible syllabic peaks. Nasals and obstruents may not occupy the peak on their own. These results fit nicely with the linguistic concept of a sonority scale. On this scale, vowels and liquids rank higher than nasals and obstruents. Being higher on the sonority scale, vowels and liquids are more able to serve as peaks than nasals and obstruents.

My results further suggest that children appreciate the similarity between syllabic /r/ and /l/, as in *her* and *candle,* and nonsyllabic /r/ and /l/, as in *rear* and *lull.* Children spell syllabic /r/ and /l/ with the same letters that they use for nonsyllabic /r/ and /l/, namely *r* and *l*. Children's use of *r* to spell syllabic /r/ suggests that syllabic /r/ is a type of consonant rather than a type of vowel. Similarly, children's use of *l* to spell syllabic /l/ suggests that syllabic /l/ is a type of consonant.

As children learn to read and write, they observe that syllabic /r/ and /l/, which to them are single phonemes, are written with two letters. English uses *her, after,* and *candle* rather than **hr, *aftr,* and **candl*. Children have trouble learning to symbolize syllabic /r/ and syllabic /l/ with two letters, just as they have trouble learning to symbolize /θ/ with the digraph *th*.

Children's phonemic representations may change as they learn the conventional spellings of syllabic /r/ and /l/. In this view, children come to represent *her* as /h/ followed by /ə/ followed by /r/ rather than as /h/ followed by syllabic /r/ as a result of seeing it spelled as *her*. Such a change, if it occurs, must be slow. Even during the second half of first grade, the children often made errors like HR for *her* and BRUTR for *brother*.

It is also possible that children's representations of syllabic liquids do not change as they learn to read and write. Even adults may represent *her* as /h/ plus syllabic /r/ rather than as /h'ər/. What is learned, in this view, is a convention—the convention that syllabic liquids are spelled with two letters. Children learn this convention in much the same way that they learn the two-letter spelling of /θ/. With /θ/, learning the *th* digraph does *not* cause children to reanalyze /θ/ as a sequence of /t/ followed by /h/. Likewise, learning *er* for syllabic /r/ may not change children's representation of the phoneme itself.

Misspellings like FRM for *farm,* HLP for *help,* and HM for *him* suggest another conclusion about the nature of children's phonological representations: Children do not consider spoken words to be strings of phonemes, each phoneme equally linked to the phoneme that comes before it and the phoneme that comes after it. Rather, certain phonemes function as groups. My findings suggest that vowels and following sonorants form especially strong groups. Vowel-sonorant sequences are more cohesive than either vowel-obstruent sequences or consonant-vowel sequences. Thus, children sometimes treat /ɑr/, /ɛl/, /ɪn/, and /ɪm/ as units for purposes of spelling. They symbolize these sequences with the single letters *r, l, n,* and *m*. I did not find evidence that first graders treat groups like /ɛf/ and /ti/ as units.

These differences in the cohesiveness of various phoneme sequences may be interpreted in terms of the hierarchical theories of syllable structure discussed in Chapter 1. According to these theories, the English syllable has two main constituents, the onset and the rime. The onset is the initial consonant or consonant cluster. The rime is composed of a peak and a coda. Most of the behavioral evidence in favor of these theories has come from adults—from studies of speech errors, memory errors, and the learning of different types of word games (see Treiman, 1989). The spelling results suggest, together with other recent evidence (see Treiman, 1992), that the theories also apply to children. Children sometimes treat phonemes that belong to the same constituent of a syllable as a unit for spelling purposes. For example, the /ɛ/ and /l/ of *help* both belong to the syllable peak. Children group these two phonemes together, sometimes using *l* to spell them both.

The Concept of Regularity

Words are often divided into the two categories of regularly-spelled words and irregularly-spelled words. This division is based on *adults'* understanding of the English writing system. For example, *her* is usually classified as regular, and was so classified in the analyses reported in Chapter 2 of this book. From children's perspective, however, *her* may be irregular. The regular spelling—the one that is expected given the child's phonemic form—is *hr*. In this and other cases, spellings that are regular for adults may not always be regular for children.

Most spelling reformers have overlooked these complications in the definition of regularity. In their desire to stamp out irregular spellings, they have not seriously considered which words are regular and which words are irregular. They have not seriously considered whether adults' and children's views of regularity agree. My results suggest that, for at least some words, making the spelling system more regular for adults would not make it more regular for children.

The Teaching of Spelling

The present findings on vowel omissions can help teachers to better understand children's spelling errors and hence to respond to them more effectively. Consider the first grader who spells *her* as HR. My results suggest that this child has not misheard or mispronounced the word. Asking the child to "stretch out" the word's pronunciation so as to hear the vowel sound within it will be useless. The word does not contain a separate vowel sound. Giving the child extra drill on the letter *e* will not help either. The child probably knows very well that *e* stands for /ɛ/. The problem is that, from the child's perspective, there is no /ɛ/ in *her*. The child therefore spells the word as HR. From the child's viewpoint, HR is a fine attempt to spell *her*, just as SED is a fine attempt to spell *said*. Because children who write *her* as HR have shown that they can analyze the spoken word into phonemes and represent each phoneme with an appropriate letter, first-grade teachers might well ignore the error. If teachers *do* point out that *her* includes an *e*, the *e* should be treated as something that must be learned and remembered, just like the *ai* of *said* or the *th* of *thin*. Just as one does not expect children to figure out that *said* is spelled with *ai* based on the word's sound, so one should not expect first graders to figure out that *her* contains *e*.

With words such as *her* and *said,* a certain amount of memorization is needed for children to spell correctly. Children must memorize the *e* of *her* and the *i* of *said*. These are the kinds of words that might be included in weekly spelling lists, if such lists are used, or in children's personal collections of words. For other kinds of words, memorization is less important. Children can figure out the words' spellings from their phonemic forms. For these words, phonemic-awareness training can help children to spell correctly.

As an example of the role of phonemic-awareness instruction, consider the error HLP for *help*. Superficially, HLP for *help* seems similar to HR for *her*. Both errors involve the omission of a vowel letter, *e*. However, the two errors occur for different reasons and thus call for different responses. The child who misspells *her* as HR has successfully analyzed the spoken word into phonemes. The problem is that the child's phonemic representation does not match the one assumed by the English writing system. In contrast, the child who misspells *help* as HLP has *not* fully analyzed the spoken word into phonemes. The child has not divided the vowel-liquid unit /ɛl/ into /ɛ/ followed by /l/. In this case, unlike the case of HR for *her*, getting the child to pay careful attention to the spoken word should improve the child's spelling. The child needs help in understanding that /ɛl/ is a sequence of two sounds rather than an indivisible unit. Once the child has gained this awareness, errors like HLP should disappear. This should happen without extensive drill on the word's conventional spelling.

How should phonemic awareness skills like the segmentation of /ɛl/ into phonemes be taught? One possibility is a phoneme counting game. Children could listen for words that contain two sounds and words that contain three sounds. One could begin with relatively easy words like *say,* which contain two sounds, and *bag,* which contain three sounds. Once children have mastered the game with such words, words like *fell* could be given. At first, children might count two sounds (/f/ plus /ɛl/) rather than three sounds (/f/ plus /ɛ/ plus /l/) for this word. They could be helped to understand that /ɛl/ is divisible into two parts, so that *fell* contains three sounds.

Another game to help children analyze sequences like /ɛl/ involves comparisons of pairs of words. Teachers could introduce a puppet that likes pairs of words that sound the same in the middle. Thus, the puppet likes *bag* and *hat,* which share a vowel sound. The puppet does not like *moon* and *sit,* which do not sound the same in the middle. Once children have mastered the game with these kinds of words, they could be given pairs of words that contain sequences of a vowel followed by a liquid. For example, the puppet likes *tell* and *bet,* which sound the same in the middle. The puppet does not like *sell* and *Hal,* which do not share a vowel. To succeed with these pairs, children must analyze /ɛl/ into the vowel /ɛ/ followed by the consonant /l/.

Activities with spoken words like those just described—and good teachers can invent many others—should help children to realize that /ɛl/ is not an indivisible unit. Instead, it consists of /ɛ/ followed by /l/. Once children grasp the internal structure of /ɛl/, they should be able to spell it with a vowel grapheme followed by a consonant grapheme. Their spelling should improve as a result of the phonemic-awareness training, without memorizing the spellings of specific words.

By scrutinizing the spellings that their students produce, teachers can determine where phonemic-awareness training is needed and where it is not needed. For example, many first graders make errors like HLP for *help* and CR for *car*. These children need help in analyzing the sequences /ɛl/ and /ɑr/ into phonemes. In contrast, middle-class first graders do not often make errors like TTH for *teeth*. Training in analyzing /ti/ into /t/ and /i/ is not necessary for these children.

An analysis of first graders' spellings further reveals a weak awareness of unstressed vowels. To promote such awareness, phonemic-awareness instruction should include multisyllabic words as well as one-syllable words. Exercises could be designed to help children pay attention to the unstressed vowels in words like *meadow* and *baby*. With more awareness of unstressed vowels in speech, children should be less likely to omit these vowels in spelling.

As these examples show, phonemic-awareness training has an important role to play in the first grade. Most middle-class first graders can perform simple phonemic segmentation tasks, like dividing /ti/ into the onset /t/ and the rime /i/. Indeed, a certain level of phonemic awareness is necessary in order to begin inventing spellings at all. However, first graders have some difficulty with more complex phonemic skills, like dividing /ɛl/ into /ɛ/ and /l/. Teaching these phonemic awareness skills should improve the children's spelling.

Notes

1. Some comments about how I applied the principles of Chapter 1 are in order. I considered the maximum onset principle to hold as long as there were no conflicting units of meaning. With *bedroom,* for example, maximization of the second syllable's onset places /d/ in the second syllable. However, morphological considerations place /d/ in the first syllable. I made no assumptions about syllabification for the few words of this kind that the children attempted. With words like *estate,* which contain medial clusters beginning with /s/, adults do not always place /s/ at the beginning of the second syllable, as the usual interpretation of the maximum onset principle predicts (Treiman & Zukowski, 1990). The first graders attempted relatively few words of this kind, so disagreements about the applicability of the maximum onset principle to /s/ clusters should not substantially affect my results.

2. The omission rate is probably lower for vowels in primary-stressed syllables than for vowels in secondary-stressed syllables because of differences in word length. Words that contain secondary-stressed syllables tend to be long; children are more likely to omit vowels in long words than vowels in short words.

3. Children do not necessarily analyze a whole spoken word into phonemes at once. They may analyze and spell part of the word, then analyze and spell another part of the word. Although serial position effects would be attenuated by such a process, the first and last phonemes of the word would still be omitted less often than the middle phonemes.

8

Consonant Omissions

In this chapter, I turn from vowel omission errors to consonant omission errors. Consider the child who spelled *blow* as BOW. This child did not include any letter for /l/. Similarly, the child who spelled *tumble* as TUBOL failed to represent /m/. In this chapter, I ask when children omit consonant phonemes from their spelling and why they do so. As in Chapter 7, omission errors are defined phonologically rather than orthographically. Thus, the child who spelled *thin* as TIN symbolized each phoneme in the word's spoken form, although he did not spell /θ/ in the conventional manner. From a phonological point of view, this child did *not* make an omission error.

The study of consonant omissions is particularly important in light of the claim that beginning spellers often omit the final consonants of monosyllabic words (Morris & Perney, 1984). For example, children may misspell *back* as B or BA. Why do they do this? Is it because /k/ is the last consonant in the word, because /k/ is the last consonant in the syllable, or for both reasons? To address these questions, it is necessary to look beyond the simple consonant-vowel-consonant monosyllables that have been analyzed in much of the previous research. An examination of more complex words can also shed light on children's omissions of consonants in clusters, as in BOW for *blow*.

In the present study, consonant omission errors were not as common as consonant substitution errors. Of the children's spellings of consonants, 7.4% or 800 out of 10,831 were omission errors. In contrast, 13.3% of all consonant spellings were substitution errors. Although the percentage of consonant omission errors was relatively low overall, omissions were quite common for certain consonants. For example, omissions were relatively common for the /l/ of *blow* and the /m/ of *tumble;* they were rare for the /l/ of *love* and the /m/ of *milk*. When interpreting the omission rates reported in this chapter, remember that the percentages are out of *all* the children's spellings—correctly spelled words as well as incorrectly spelled words. Because over half of the words in the collection were spelled correctly, the omission rates are lower than they would be if only incorrectly spelled words were included.

To study the children's consonant omissions, I used the same statistical techniques that were employed in Chapter 7 for vowels. These techniques consider several different factors at once, which is important given that the factors are not independent. For example, stress is related to word length: Unstressed syllables occur only in words of more than one syllable. To determine whether syllable stress has an effect on consonant omissions, above and beyond any effects of word length, stress and word length must be considered simultaneously.

In the study of consonant omissions, as in the study of vowel omissions, it is important to know how spoken words are divided into syllables. For example, suppose that I wish to determine whether children delete consonants that belong to unstressed syllables more than consonants that belong to stressed syllables. With one-syllable words, it is probably safe to assume that all the consonants belong to the same syllable, a stressed syllable. With words of more than one syllable, complications may arise. For instance, does the middle /b/ of *baby* belong to the first syllable or the second syllable of the word? If /b/ belongs to the first syllable, it is part of a stressed syllable. If /b/ belongs to the second syllable, it is part of an unstressed syllable. Conceivably, /b/ belongs to both syllables at once and so is a part of both a stressed and an unstressed syllable. As discussed in Chapter 1, linguists do not agree about the syllabification of consonants like the middle /b/ of *baby*. Because of these disagreements, I excluded such consonants from my analyses of stress effects and other effects that may depend on syllabification.

Although the syllabification of certain multisyllabic words is controversial, the syllabification of others is relatively clear. For example, most linguists agree that *tumble* is divided between /m/ and /b/ (see Chapter 1). Thus, /m/ belongs to a stressed syllable and /b/ belongs to an unstressed syllable. When I could classify a consonant on a certain variable using the widely held assumptions about syllabification that were described in Chapter 1, I did include that consonant in my analyses.

Factors Associated with Consonant Omission Errors

Stress

In Chapter 7, we saw that stress plays an important role in vowel omissions. The first graders omitted vowels in unstressed syllables more often than they omitted vowels in stressed syllables. In this section, I ask whether the effects of stress are confined to vowels or whether they extend to consonants.

For consonants that belonged to a syllable with primary stress, the omission rate was 6.6%. The omission rate was 10.7% when the syllable had secondary stress and 14.5% when the syllable was not stressed. Table 8.1 gives examples of consonant omissions in syllables with each degree of stress.

The effect of stress on consonant omission rate was significant even after other factors were taken into account. Moreover, consonants in primary-stressed syllables and secondary-stressed syllables did not differ from one another in omission rate. The children omitted consonants in stressed syllables, whether primary or secondary stressed, significantly less often than they omitted consonants in unstressed syllables.[1]

The results for consonants mirror the results presented in Chapter 7 for vowels. Phonemes in stressed syllables are less likely to be omitted than phonemes in unstressed syllables. This is true for consonants as well as vowels. The omission

Table 8.1. Omissions of Consonants in Primary-Stressed, Secondary-Stressed, and Unstressed Syllables

Stress	Examples
Primary	HEL for *help*
	SATIMS for *sometimes*
	B for *about*
Secondary	SAMTOM for *sometimes*
	PLAYGAND for *playground*
Unstressed	LITTE for *little*
	TOLLOS for *tallest*
	APSUT for *absent*
	FAMY for *family*
	JOGJM for *junglegym*

rates for phonemes in primary-stressed and secondary-stressed syllables are statistically indistinguishable once other factors are taken into account.

The effect of stress on consonant omissions is important for at least three reasons. First, the results show that spelling is not just an attempt to reproduce memorized sequences of letters. If it were, children should not omit letters that symbolize phonemes in stressed syllables any less often than letters that symbolize phonemes in unstressed syllables. To a large extent, spelling is an attempt to represent words' phonological forms. Phonemes in stressed syllables are more salient than phonemes in unstressed syllables and, therefore, more likely to be spelled.

Second, characteristics of the syllable *as a whole,* rather than characteristics of just the vowel, are responsible for the effects of stress. For example, children's omissions of vowels in unstressed syllables cannot reflect just the short durations of these vowels. If vowel duration were the only factor, the effects of stress should be confined to vowels. They should not extend to consonants.

Finally, children's omissions of consonants in unstressed syllables do not support the idea that children's failures to spell phonemes usually reflect their failures to pronounce the phonemes. True, children and adults sometimes omit unstressed vowels when speaking rapidly. For example, they may pronounce *balloon* as /bl'un/. Consonants in unstressed syllables are not usually dropped in fast speech. Normal first graders do not pronounce *balloon* without a /b/, even when talking quickly. Although consonants in unstressed syllables are usually present in children's pronunciations, they are not always present in children's spellings. Children's spellings do not mirror their pronunciations in any simple way.

Letter Names

In Chapter 7, I showed that children's knowledge of the names of certain consonant letters affects their spelling. The children in this study pronounced the names of *r, l, m,* and *n* as /ɑr/, /ɛl/, /ɪm/, and /ɪn/, respectively. When a spoken word contained any of these phoneme sequences, the children omitted the vowel more often than expected given other factors. They made errors like FRM for *farm,* HLP for *help,* HM for *him,* and PTND for *pretend.* Importantly, these effects did not occur for all letters. They were confined to the letters just listed—letters whose names consist of a vowel followed by a sonorant (i.e., a liquid or nasal) consonant. Vowel omissions were *not* significantly elevated for sequences such as /ɛs/ *(s)*, which is a vowel followed by an obstruent, or /ti/ *(t)*, which is a consonant followed by a vowel. I interpreted these results to mean that children have trouble analyzing vowel-sonorant consonant units in spoken words. Thus, some first graders have trouble segmenting the /ɑr/ in a word like *farm*. They treat /ɑr/ as a unit for spelling purposes, symbolizing this unit with single *r* rather than with a vowel letter followed by *r*.

Results presented in Chapter 7 show that children were more likely to omit the vowel in a word like *farm*, which contains a vowel-sonorant letter name, than a word like *form*, which does not contain a vowel-sonorant letter name. I now ask whether children were less likely to delete the consonant in *farm* than *form*. That is, were errors like FAM for *farm*, which omit /r/ in the letter name /ɑr/, less common than errors like FOM for *form*, which omit /r/ in a non-letter-name sequence? Such a difference in consonant omission rates would be expected if children use *r* to symbolize the entire /ɑr/ unit.

Consonant omission errors *were* significantly less frequent for the vowel-liquid letter names /ɑr/ and /ɛl/ than expected from other factors. The effect was small but statistically reliable. In other words, the children were less likely to make errors like FAM for *farm* than errors like FOM for *form*.

The results for vowel-nasal letter names, vowel-obstruent letter names, and consonant-vowel letter names differed from the results for vowel-liquid letter names just described. Consonant omission errors were *not* less common than otherwise expected for the vowel-nasal letter names /ɪm/ and /ɪn/. The same was true for vowel-obstruent and consonant-vowel letter names, such as /ɛs/ and /ti/. For example, the children were no less likely to omit the /n/ of *went*, the spoken form of which contains the letter name /ɪn/, than the /n/ of *want*, the spoken form of which does not contain a letter name.

These results support the finding of Chapter 7 that effects of letter names on phoneme omissions do not occur for all letters. Effects are found for some letters but not for others. This outcome mitigates against the idea that children make errors like FRM for *farm* because they do not distinguish between the names of letters and the sounds that the letters make. If this were true, letter-name effects should occur for all letters.

Why are the effects of letter names on spelling so restricted? The answer may lie in the phonological characteristics of the letter names themselves. I propose that children are most likely to use a letter to spell its name when the phonemes that make up the letter's name form a strong unit, as with /ɑ/ and /r/ or /ɛ/ and /l/. When children can easily decompose a letter name into phonemes, as with /ɛ/ and /s/ or /t/ and /i/, they do *not* generally use the letter to spell its name.

The letter names of English fall into several categories with respect to phonological cohesiveness. Consider those letter names that contain a vowel phoneme followed by a liquid phoneme. English has two letters of this kind—/ɑr/ for *r* and /ɛl/ for *l*. When a word included either of these sequences, the vowel's omission rate was higher than expected on the basis of other factors. The consonant's omission rate was lower. Thus, the children sometimes misspelled *cars* as CRS, using *r* rather than a vowel grapheme plus *r* to symbolize /ɑr/. The children rarely misspelled *cars* as CAS. With /ɛl/, too, errors like HLP for *help* were relatively common, while errors like HEP were relatively rare. The significant findings for both vowel omissions and consonant omissions show that the children's knowledge of the names of *r* and *l* influenced their spelling.

Letter names in the second category consist of a vowel phoneme followed by a nasal phoneme. In English, *m* and *n* have names of this kind. Letter-name knowledge had some effects on spelling in this case, but the effects were weaker than in the vowel-liquid case. When a spoken word contained a vowel-nasal letter name, omissions of the vowel *did* increase significantly. Thus, the children sometimes spelled *went* as WNT. However, omissions of the consonant did not decline reliably. Omissions of the *n* of *went* were no less frequent than omissions of the *n* of *want*. The children's knowledge of the names of *n* and *m* affected their spelling to some extent, but the effects were not as strong as for *r* and *l*.

The names of other English letters are a vowel followed by an obstruent, as in /ɛs/ *(s)* and /ɛf/ *(f)*, or a consonant followed by a vowel, as in /ti/ *(t)* and /ke/ *(k)*. In these cases, there were *no* significant effects on either vowel omissions or consonant omissions. Although the first graders certainly knew the names of *s* and *t,* they did not spell /ɛs/ and /ti/ with single *s* and *t*. This is probably because sequences like /ɛs/ and /ti/ are relatively easy for children to analyze into phonemes.

Research with adults suggests that there is a least a three-way distinction in the cohesiveness of vowels and following consonants. Vowels and following liquids are most cohesive, vowels and following nasals are intermediate in cohesiveness, and vowels and following obstruents are least cohesive (e.g., Treiman, 1984b). As the preceding discussion shows, there are signs of a similar distinction in the spelling data. Vowels and liquids produce the clearest evidence of letter-name spellings. The effects of letter-name knowledge are weaker for vowels and following nasals and weaker still for vowels and following obstruents.

Syllabic Consonants

In Chapter 7, we saw that the first graders often omitted vowels when attempting to spell syllabic liquids. For example, the children often misspelled *her* as HR. They misspelled *little* as LITTL. Although vowel omission errors were more common than otherwise expected for the syllabic liquids /r/ and /l/, the same was not true for syllabic nasals. For instance, the second syllable of *person* contains syllabic /n/ but the children did not omit the second vowel of this word at an especially high rate.

Why were the children more likely to omit vowels in the case of syllabic liquids than in the case of syllabic nasals? The reason, I suggest, is that children's spellings reflect their phonemic representations. Many first graders consider *her* to contain /h/ followed by syllabic /r/. They do not represent it as /h/ followed by /ə/ followed by /r/. Likewise, many children consider the second syllable of *little* to contain syllabic /l/ rather than unstressed /ə/ followed by /l/. In contrast, children consider the second syllable of *person* to contain unstressed /ə/ followed by /n/. They consider the second syllable of *rabbit* to contain unstressed /ə/ followed by /t/. Because first graders classify syllabic liquids as single phonemes rather than sequences of a vowel followed by a liquid consonant, they spell syllabic liquids with single letters.

If children consider syllabic liquids to be single phonemes, are these phonemes consonants or vowels? Linguists disagree on this point. Some linguists consider syllabic /r/ to be a type of vowel, an *r*-colored vowel. Other linguists consider syllabic /r/ to be a type of consonant. Children's spellings may shed light on how they classify syllabic liquids. Suppose that children group syllabic /r/ and /l/ with the liquid consonants /r/ and /l/. If so, children should spell the syllabic liquids with *r* and *l*, the typical spellings for /r/ and /l/. They should produce many errors like HR for *her* but few errors like HE or HU for *her*. Suppose, on the other hand, that children consider syllabic liquids to be vowels. If so, children may produce errors like HE and HU for *her*, spelling syllabic liquids with letters that are appropriate for vowels.

The results in Chapter 7 suggest that children group syllabic liquids with the liquid consonants. The first graders made many errors like HR for *her*, spelling a syllabic liquid with a grapheme that is appropriate for the corresponding liquid consonant. To further test the idea that children group syllabic liquids with liquid consonants, I asked whether consonant omissions were less common for syllabic liquids than expected given other factors. That is, were errors like HE for *her* and LITTE for *little* less frequent than errors like HI for *hit* and RABBI for *rabbit?* They were. The children omitted consonants significantly less often in the case of syllabic liquids than predicted on the basis of other factors. Thus, the children often misspelled *her* as HR; they rarely misspelled it as HE or HU. This result suggests that first graders consider syllabic liquids to be single units at the phonemic level. They group these units with the liquid consonants rather than the vowels. Hence, they often spell syllabic /r/ with *r* and syllabic /l/ with *l*.

Inflected Words

The final consonants of some English words are inflectional endings or parts of inflectional endings. For instance, the final /d/ of *killed* is an inflectional suffix which indicates that the verb is past tense. The final /z/ of *dishes* is part of the plural marker. *Killed* and *build*, although similar phonologically, differ in their morphological structure. The final /d/ of *killed* is an inflectional ending; the final /d/ of *build* is not. In this section, I ask whether children's omission rate differed for final consonants that belonged to inflectional suffixes and final consonants that did not.

Consider, first, those consonants that are regular inflectional suffixes on their own, like the /d/ of *killed*. (I included in this category the final consonants of regularized irregular forms, as when a child said /k'ipt/ rather than *kept* when dictating a story to the teacher.) The children omitted final consonants that were regular inflectional suffixes significantly more often than expected given other factors. Thus, the children more often failed to spell the /d/ of *killed* than the /d/ of *build*. Table 8.2 gives some examples of these omissions.

Consider, next, consonants that are *part* of a regular inflectional ending. For example, the /z/ of *dishes* belongs to the plural suffix but is not an inflectional ending on its own. The children were more likely to omit the /z/ of *dishes* than to omit a final consonant that was not part of an inflectional suffix. Table 8.2 shows some

Table 8.2. Omissions of Final Consonants in Inflected and Noninflected Words

Word Type	Examples	Final Consonant Omission Rate (%)
Inflected		
Final consonant is regular or regularized inflectional suffix	SAV for *saved* SCEEN for *screams* CEEP for *keeped* [*sic*] CAW for *shows*	13.1
Final cononant is part of regular or regularized inflectional suffix	LRNEE for *learning* TOLLOS for *tallest* SLID for *slided* [*sic*]	19.1
Final consonant is final phoneme of irregularly inflected form	FAWN for *found* GE for *got*	4.6
Noninflected	PLAN for *plant* PAY for *please*	4.8

examples of omissions of consonants belonging to regular inflectional suffixes. The results presented so far indicate that the final consonants of regularly inflected words have elevated omission rates, whether the consonants are inflectional suffixes on their own or whether they are parts of inflectional suffixes.

Are the final consonants of *irregularly* inflected words also subject to omission? Consider the final consonants of the irregular past tense forms *found* and *thought* and the final consonant of the irregular plural *feet*. The results in Table 8.2, together with the results of statistical analyses, show that the children were less likely to omit the final /d/ of the irregularly inflected *found* than the final /d/ of the regularly inflected *killed*. The children did not omit the final consonants of irregular words more often than anticipated based on other factors. Thus, children do not omit the final consonants of plurals and past tense forms *in general*. Omissions are most common when the suffix can be predicted from the stem; that is, when the word is inflected in a regular manner.

The results in this section may be compared with the results for vowels in Chapter 7. With vowels, the omission rate was not higher when the vowel was part of an inflectional ending like /əz/ or /ɪŋ/ than when the vowel did not belong to an inflectional ending. With consonants, the omission rate was higher when the consonant was part of an inflectional ending than when it was not. It is not clear why different results were obtained for consonants and vowels in this case.

What *is* clear is that first graders are more likely to omit final consonants that are inflectional suffixes on their own than to omit other final consonants. Why do children sometimes drop inflectional endings? Perhaps they do so because adding an inflectional suffix to a word often yields a consonant cluster, as when *love* becomes *loved*. However, as I show later in this chapter, the first graders did not omit word-final consonants significantly more often when the consonants belonged to clusters than when they did not. Thus, the presence of clusters does not explain the children's failures to spell inflectional suffixes.

Nor does the duration of consonants in inflectional suffixes appear to explain children's tendency to omit them. In adult speech, consonants are actually longer when they are inflectional suffixes than when they are not. For example, /s/ is almost 10% longer when it is an inflectional suffix, as in *laps,* than when it is not a suffix, as in *lapse* (Walsh & Parker, 1983; see also Guy, 1980). If children's spelling reflected the acoustic duration of the consonant, there should be fewer omissions of /s/ when it is an inflectional ending than when it is not—the opposite of the observed pattern.

Watching children write suggests one thing that may contribute to children's failures to symbolize inflectional endings like the /d/ of *loved,* although it may not be a complete explanation. Because children write slowly, they may sometimes forget that they are using the past tense. When writing about something that happened yesterday, for example, a child may begin with the past tense but then switch to the present tense, writing LOVE instead of *loved.* When reading back what he or she has written, the child goes more quickly and therefore says *loved.* Thus, LOVE is scored as an attempt to write *loved*—a final consonant omission. The same phenomenon may occur with plurals. This explanation is compatible with the finding that final consonant omissions were more common for regularly inflected words than irregularly inflected words. With irregular forms, errors that result from forgetting about verb tense or plurality do not involve final consonant omissions. For example, a child might write GET but read it back as *got.* GET would thus be scored as an attempt to represent *got,* as actually occurred in my collection of spellings. The error would appear as a vowel substitution, not a final consonant omission.

Position in Syllable

In this section, I ask whether the position of a consonant in its syllable affects the consonant's omission rate. To anticipate the results, strong effects of syllable position were found. The first graders often failed to spell consonants in certain positions of syllable-initial clusters. For example, the children made errors like BOW for *blow,* omitting the second consonant of an initial cluster. The children also made errors on final consonant clusters. They misspelled *lets* as LAS, omitting the first consonant of the final cluster. In addition, consonants at the ends of syllables were more susceptible to omission than consonants at the beginnings of syllables.

My discussion of syllable position effects has several parts. First, I present the results for consonant clusters at the beginnings of syllables and discuss some possible explanations of the findings. Next, the findings for clusters at the ends of syllables are presented and interpreted. Finally, I compare omissions of consonants at the beginnings of syllables to omissions of consonants at the ends of syllables.

Syllable-Initial Consonant Clusters: Results. In English, syllables may begin with clusters of two consonants, as in *blow.* Syllables may also begin with clusters of three consonants. Three-consonant initial clusters in English always begin with /s/, as in *scratch* and *splint.* Syllable-initial consonant clusters are complex onsets. In the examples just given, the onset clusters are at the beginnings of words. Onset clusters also occur in the middles of words, as in *afraid.* Here, /f/ and /r/ form the onset of the second syllable by the assumptions about syllabification presented in Chapter 1.

Table 8.3. Spellings of Syllable-Initial Two-Consonant Clusters

Type	Example	Number	Percent
Correct (C_1C_2)	ARPLENE for *airplane*	269	63.6
C_1	TEE for *tree*	85	20.1
$C_{1x}C_2$	PLO for *blow*	31	7.3
C_{1x}	TOAT for *throw*	17	4.0
C_1C_{2x}	SGIE for *sky*	5	1.2
C_1 & C_2	BULE for *blue*	5	1.2
C_2	WRWF for *dwarf*	2	0.5
Omitted	RD for *scared*	2	0.5
C_1VC_2	AFURINT for *afraid*	2	0.5
Other errors	RERING for *treat*	5	1.2
	Total	423	100.1

Note. C_1 and C_2 are correct spellings of the first and second phonemes of the cluster. C_{1x} and C_{2x} are incorrect spellings of the first and second phonemes. V is a vowel that is not present in the word's phonemic form. The symbol & indicates that the letters are not adjacent.

Table 8.3 shows how the first graders spelled onset clusters containing two consonants. The results are based on clusters at the beginnings of words (e.g., the /bl/ of *blow)* and those clusters in the middles of words that are clearly at the beginning of a syllable by Chapter 1's assumptions about syllabification (e.g., the /fr/ of *afraid)*. In a majority of cases, the children spelled the cluster correctly. This is not surprising given that over half of the words in the collection were correctly spelled. When children misspelled the cluster, their most common error was to represent the first consonant of the cluster and omit the second. Overall, the omission rate for the second consonants of clusters was 24.6%. Although the children omitted the second consonant of the cluster almost a quarter of the time, they rarely omitted the first consonant. The omission rate for the first consonant of an onset cluster was only 0.9%.

Most of the consonant clusters in Table 8.3 were at the beginnings of words. Clusters at the beginning of a syllable within a word, like the /fr/ of *afraid,* were not common in the words that the children chose to spell. Thus, the effects in Table 8.3 may reflect the position of the consonant in the *word* rather than the position of the consonant in the *syllable.* The second phonemes of words may be more susceptible to omission than the first phonemes. Some evidence against this claim is provided by a look at those 33 clusters that were at the beginning of a syllable but not the beginning of a word by my assumptions about syllabification. The /fr/ of *afraid* is one such cluster. The pattern of results for these clusters mirrored the pattern for other onset clusters. The children omitted the first consonant of the cluster (e.g., the /f/ of *afraid)* at a rate of 6.1%. They omitted the second consonant of the cluster (e.g., the /r/ of *afraid)* significantly more often—a rate of 30.3% ($p < .005$ for the difference by a binomial test). This difference between first-consonant omissions and second-consonant omissions suggests that the second consonants of two-consonant onsets are more susceptible to omission than the first consonants. This is true regardless of the onset's position in the word. However, the results are not conclusive. Some of the words with an onset cluster in the middle were compound words like *playground.* If children consider *playground* to be two words rather than one (Tunmer, Bowey, & Grieve, 1983), /gr/ is at the beginning of a word rather than in the middle. Stronger evidence that the pattern of omission errors for onsets in the middles of words is similar to the pattern of omission errors for onsets at the beginnings of words comes from the results of an experiment reviewed in a later section of this chapter describing previous research on children's spelling of syllable-initial consonant clusters. These results support the idea that the position of a consonant in the syllable onset is important.

Although the pattern of omission errors for the /f/ and /r/ of *afraid* appeared similar to the pattern of omission errors for the /f/ and /r/ of *friend*, the omission rates were higher in the first case than in the second. For two-consonant onsets in the middles of words, the omission rates for the first and second consonants were 6.1% and 30.3%, respectively. For two-consonant onsets at the beginnings of words, the omission rates for the first and second consonants were 0.5% and 24.1%, respectively. Apparently, children are more apt to omit consonants in the middles of words than consonants at the beginnings of words. Further evidence for this claim is provided later in this chapter. Thus, the position of a consonant in the syllable and the position of a consonant in the word *both* affect the omission rate for the consonant.

I turn now to the case of three-consonant initial clusters. Three-consonant initial clusters were less common than two-consonant initial clusters among the words that the children chose to spell, just as they are less common in English generally. Almost all of the three-consonant clusters that the children attempted were at the beginnings of words.

Table 8.4 shows how the children spelled three-consonant initial clusters. As with two-consonant onsets, correct spellings were the single most common type. However, the children sometimes failed to spell one or more consonants of the cluster. Although the children never omitted the first consonant of a three-consonant cluster (omission rate 0.0%), they sometimes omitted the second consonant, the third consonant, or both. The omission rate for the second consonant was 25.0% and the omission rate for the third consonant was 41.7%.

Comparing the results for two-consonant and three-consonant initial clusters, a consistent pattern appears: The *interior* phoneme or phonemes of the cluster are most susceptible to omission. The children tended to omit the second consonants

Table 8.4. Spellings of Syllable-Initial Three-Consonant Clusters

Type	Example	Number	Percent
Correct ($C_1C_2C_3$)	BISTRY for *destroy*	12	33.3
C_1C_{2x}	SDN for *spring*	6	16.7
C_1C_3	SRAG for *string*	4	11.1
C_1C_2	SCEEN for *screams*	4	11.1
C_1	SET for *street*	4	11.1
$C_1C_{2x}C_3$	SKRACH for *scratch*	3	8.3
Other errors	SHKWTUD for *squirted*	3	8.3
	Total	36	99.9

Note. C_1, C_2, and C_3 are correct spellings of the first, second, and third phonemes of the cluster. C_{2x} is an incorrect spelling of the second phoneme.

of two-consonant initial clusters and the second and third consonants of three-consonant initial clusters. In contrast, the children rarely deleted the *exterior* phoneme of a cluster, which is the first phoneme of its syllable.

As I discuss in more detail later in this chapter, I carried out statistical analyses in which syllable-initial and syllable-final consonant clusters were analyzed together. The results confirmed that the interior phonemes of clusters were omitted more often than otherwise expected. However, the exterior phonemes of clusters did *not* show an elevated omission rate. In other words, the children sometimes omitted the /l/ of *blow;* they did not often omit the /b/. Thus, what is critical for spelling is not whether a consonant belongs to a cluster. More important is the position of the consonant within the cluster. Consonants that are in the interiors of clusters have a relatively high omission rate; consonants that have an exterior position show a relatively low omission rate.

Syllable-Initial Consonant Clusters: Reasons for the Omissions. So far, I have shown that first graders sometimes fail to spell the /l/ of *blow,* the /r/ of *afraid,* and the /k/ and /r/ of *scratch.* Having documented these errors, I now ask why they occur. In this section, I consider some possible reasons for the errors.

One hypothesis is that children's omissions of the interior phonemes of syllable-initial clusters reflect the sonority of these phonemes. Recall that the phonemes of English may be arranged on a scale according to their degree of sonority or openness. Obstruents, which include stops and fricatives, are low in sonority. They are followed in turn by nasals, liquids, glides, and vowels. In English, as in other languages, the exterior and interior phonemes of onset clusters usually differ in sonority. The exterior phonemes of onset clusters are low in sonority. For example, the first phonemes of /pr/ and /fl/ are obstruents, which are low in sonority. The interior phonemes of initial clusters are usually more sonorous than the exterior phonemes. This is true for /pr/ and /fl/. Perhaps children are more likely to omit sonorant consonants than obstruent consonants in general. They omit the interior phonemes of onset clusters because these phonemes are usually sonorants.

However, my results do not support the sonority hypothesis just described. Other things being equal, the children did *not* omit sonorant consonants significantly more often than obstruent consonants. The position of the consonant in an onset cluster (exterior versus interior) is a more important determinant of omission rate than the nature of the consonant itself (sonorant versus obstruent).

Further evidence against the sonority hypothesis comes from those clusters that have an atypical sonority profile. With /sp/, /st/, and /sk/, the second consonant of the cluster is *not* more sonorous than the first. If sonority is critical, children should omit the second consonants of /s/-stop clusters less often than the second consonants of other clusters. This was not the case. In the first-grade spellings, as in the experimental work reviewed later in this chapter, /s/-stop clusters show the same pattern as the other clusters—more omissions of the stop than the /s/.

Supporting the idea that omissions of the interior consonants of initial clusters occur for all types of consonants, Table 8.5 presents additional examples of these omissions. As the examples show, the first graders omitted both sonorants and obstruents when they were the second or third consonants of onset clusters.

Table 8.5. Omissions of Interior Consonants of Syllable-Initial
Consonant Clusters

Consonant Type	Examples
Glide	COURDR for *quarter*
	SET for *sweat*
Liquid	BOTTSRIS for *brontosaurus*
	AFAD for *afraid*
	SCEEN for *screams*
Nasal	SUKC for *snake*
	SAK for *snake*
Obstruent	SRA for *sprayed*
	SAEC for *steak*
	SUNCK for *skunk*

If sonority does not explain why children sometimes fail to spell the /l/ of *blow,* perhaps children's pronunciations are responsible. Perhaps children delete the /l/ of *blow* when spelling the word because they do not pronounce the /l/ when saying the word. However, as with most attempts to derive children's spellings directly from their pronunciations, this explanation is implausible. Although children who are just learning to talk sometimes fail to pronounce consonants in clusters, at least as judged by the adult ear, such omissions are largely gone by the first grade for normal children (e.g., Kornfeld, 1978; Smith, 1973). Although I do not have information on how each child in this study pronounced each word, I can be fairly sure that the children pronounced both phonemes of onset clusters.

Further evidence against the idea that omissions of consonants in spelling usually reflect misarticulation comes from the results of experiments reviewed later in this chapter. The children in the experiments were asked to repeat words and nonwords with initial clusters before spelling them, and were given several chances to do so. The children almost always repeated the stimuli correctly. Even so, they sometimes failed to spell the second consonants of the clusters.

Another blow to the mispronunciation hypothesis is that the pattern of consonant deletions in preschoolers' speech does not match the pattern of consonant omissions in first graders' spelling. Two- and three-year-olds who simplify consonant clusters in speech typically drop the second phonemes of obstruent-sonorant clusters like /bl/ and /gr/. To the adult ear, their pronunciation of *blow* sounds like /b'o/. However, the same children may drop the *first* phonemes of /s/-stop clusters like /sp/, pronouncing *spoon* as /p'un/ or /b'un/ (e.g., Kornfeld, 1978; Smith, 1983). If first graders' cluster omissions in spelling mirrored younger children's cluster deletions in speech, as suggested by Hoffman and Norris (1989), first graders should fail to spell the second consonants of clusters like /bl/ and the first consonants of clusters like /sp/. I did not find such a result in the first-grade study or in the experimental work described later in this chapter. In spelling, /s/-stop initial clusters show the same pattern as other onsets—more omissions of the second consonant than the first consonant.

If mispronunciation cannot explain most of first graders' misspellings of initial clusters, perhaps the short duration of the consonants can. Consonants in clusters are shorter than single consonants, at least for adults (e.g., Haggard, 1973; Klatt, 1974; Umeda, 1977). Perhaps children sometimes omit the interior consonants of onset clusters because these consonants are short. However, *both* the first and second consonants of two-consonant clusters are shortened. If children's failures to spell consonants in clusters reflected the short durations of the consonants, I should have found many omissions of the exterior phonemes of onset clusters as well as the interior phonemes of these clusters.

Thus, the children's omissions of consonants in syllable-initial clusters do not reflect the sonority profile of the clusters, the children's current or previous pronunciations of the clusters, or the short durations of the consonants. Why, then, do children sometimes fail to spell consonants in clusters at the beginnings of syllables? These errors, I propose, stem from a lack of phonemic awareness. Some first graders are not fully aware of the internal structure of onset clusters. They have difficulty analyzing the initial cluster of a word like *blow* into /b/ and /l/. Consequently, they have difficulty spelling the cluster.

The idea that the consonants of initial clusters are cohesive units fits with many linguistic theories of syllable structure (e.g., Clements & Keyser, 1983; Fudge, 1969, 1987, 1989; Selkirk, 1982). According to these theories, initial consonant clusters form a constituent of the syllable, the onset. Psycholinguistic evidence supports the idea that the consonants of initial clusters are grouped together. Adults often treat these clusters as units when perceiving, producing, and manipulating speech (see Treiman, 1989). Although adults *can* divide cluster onsets into phonemes when required to do so, they often prefer to keep them intact. Children are even more likely to treat onsets as units (Treiman, 1992). They have trouble segmenting these units into phonemes and paying attention to or manipulating one phoneme at a time.

Children's difficulty in analyzing a cluster like /bl/ into phonemes may cause them to spell the cluster with a single letter rather than with the correct sequence of two letters. There are two slightly different hypotheses about why children more often spell /bl/ with *b* than with *l*. The first hypothesis assumes that the exterior consonants of onset clusters are more accessible or more salient than the interior consonants. Evidence for this assumption is provided by Bruck and Treiman (1990). Because the /b/ of /bl/ is more accessible than the /l/, children sometimes symbolize only the /b/ in spelling. A second hypothesis about why children misspell /bl/ as *b* is that /bl/, as a unit, is more similar to /b/ than to /l/. Stemberger and Treiman (1986) found evidence from adults' speech errors to support this claim. When deciding how to spell /bl/, children use *b* rather than *l* because the cluster, as a whole, is similar to /b/. In this view, errors like BOW for *blow* are one example of children's tendency to use the same grapheme to represent similar sounds. In this case, children use *b* for both /b/ and /bl/.

Syllable-Final Consonant Clusters: Results. In English, consonant clusters may occur at the ends of syllables as well as at the beginnings. Clusters of two consonants occur at the ends of spoken words like *old* and *fox*. Words like *apartment* contain clusters that, by virtue of the assumptions about syllabification in Chapter 1, form the end of a syllable within a word. The /rt/ cluster in *apartment* must be at the end

Table 8.6. Spellings of Syllable-Final Two-Consonant Clusters

Type	Example	Number	Percent
Correct (C_1C_2)	PRT for *part*	466	51.7
C_2	OD for *old*	172	19.1
C_1	FRAN for *friend*	75	8.3
C_1C_{2x}	BRDDAY for *birthday*	48	5.3
C_{2x}	FUOS for *fox*	36	4.0
$C_{1x}C_2$	BETS for *bakes*	23	2.6
Omitted	FE for *feeds*	19	2.1
$C_{1x}C_{2x}$	STAPT for *stepped*	19	2.1
C_1 & C_2	HNOT for *hunt*	18	2.0
C_{1x}	ANN for *and*	11	1.2
C_2C_1	MEKL for *milk*	7	0.8
Other errors	PLAD for *pulled*	7	0.8
	Total	901	100.0

Note. C_1 and C_2 are correct spellings of the first and second phonemes of the cluster. C_{1x} and C_{2x} are incorrect spellings of the first and second phonemes. The symbol & indicates that the letters are not adjacent.

of the second syllable because no other division of the word produces legal sequences at both the end of the second syllable and the beginning of the third syllable.

Table 8.6 shows how the first graders spelled two-consonant clusters at the ends of syllables. The children produced correct spellings slightly over half the time. Their most common error was to omit the first consonant of the cluster and spell the second. Overall, the children omitted the first consonant of the cluster just over one quarter of the time—a 25.2% omission rate. They omitted the second consonant of the cluster less than half as often—11.8%. This is the mirror image of the pattern of omission errors on syllable-initial consonant clusters. Many of the children's second-consonant omission errors were on inflected words. As I showed earlier in this chapter, consonants that were inflectional endings, such as the /d/ of *killed,* were more often omitted than consonants that were not inflectional endings, such as the /d/ of *build.* The omission rate for the second consonants of final clusters would be lower if inflected words were excluded. Because the results in Table 8.6 include few two-consonant clusters that are not at the ends of words (e.g., the /rt/ of *apartment*), no conclusions can be drawn for this type of cluster separately.

English allows final clusters of three consonants as well as final clusters of two consonants. For example, the spoken forms of *next* and *finds* end with three-consonant clusters. Table 8.7 shows how the children spelled these three-consonant final clusters, all of which were at the ends of words. As with two-consonant final clusters, correct spellings were the single most common type. However, the children sometimes failed to spell one or more consonants of the cluster. Overall, the omission rate for the first consonants of final clusters was 25.0%. The omission rate for the second consonants was 28.9%. The omission rate for the third consonants was substantially lower, 3.9%.

Combining the results for two- and three-consonant final clusters, we see a consistent trend: The interior phonemes of final clusters are most vulnerable to omission. These interior phonemes include the first phonemes of two-phoneme final

Table 8.7. Spellings of Syllable-Final Three-Consonant Clusters

Type	Example	Number	Percent
Correct ($C_1C_2C_3$)	JOURFS for *dwarfs*	20	26.3
$C_1C_2C_{3X}$	HELPT for *helped*	7	9.2
C_1C_3	GIENS for *giants*	6	7.9
C_3	SES for *cents*	5	6.6
C_1C_{3X}	TORD for *turned*	5	6.6
C_2C_{3X}	HPT for *helped*	4	5.3
$C_{2X}C_{3X}$	PUTHT for *punched*	4	5.3
C_{3X}	TAT for *thanked*	3	3.9
$C_1C_{2X}C_3$	WRCSE for *works*	2	2.6
$C_{1X}C_{2X}C_3$	SRLES for *squirrels*	2	2.6
$C_1C_{2X}C_{3X}$	BORDT for *barks*	2	2.6
C_2C_3	JUPS for *jumps*	2	2.6
$C_{1X}C_3$	WRRS for *works*	2	2.6
Other errors	HAPL for *helps*	12	15.8
	Total	76	99.9

Note. C_1, C_2, and C_3 are correct spellings of the first, second, and third phonemes of the cluster. C_{1X}, C_{2X}, and C_{3X} are incorrect spellings of the first, second, and third phonemes.

clusters and the first and second phonemes of three-phoneme final clusters. The exterior phonemes of clusters have a lower omission rate. Statistical analyses confirmed that children omitted the interior phonemes of clusters significantly more often than expected based on other factors. The exterior phonemes of clusters did not show an elevated omission rate.

Having shown that the interior consonants of syllable-final consonant clusters are susceptible to omission, I now ask whether omissions of interior consonants are more common for some types of final clusters than for others. There turned out to be substantial differences among final clusters in this regard. The omission rate for the interior phonemes of final clusters was especially high—50.0%—for nasals that were immediately followed by voiceless obstruents. For example, the children omitted the /n/ of /nt/ and the /ŋ/ of /ŋk/ at high rates. Nasals that were followed by voiced obstruents, as in /nd/ and /mz/, were omitted substantially less often than nasals followed by voiceless obstruents. When all nasal-voiced obstruent sequences were included, the omission rate for the nasal was only 11.3%. One reason that this figure is so low is that the common word *and* falls into the nasal-voiced obstruent category. The omission rate for the /n/ of *and* was fairly low. When *and* was not considered, the omission rate for nasals before voiced obstruents was 27.4%. This is still substantially lower than the 50.0% omission rate for nasals before voiceless obstruents. The 27.4% omission rate for nasals before voiced obstruents is now similar to the 23.0% omission rate for liquids in the interior positions of final clusters, such as the /l/ of *milk*. It is also similar to the 24.2% omission rate for obstruents in the interior positions of final clusters, such as the /s/ of *mist*.

To summarize, nasals before voiceless obstruents are especially vulnerable to omission. Nasals before voiced obstruents have lower omission rates, as do liquids and obstruents before other consonants. Table 8.8 shows some examples of omissions of the interior phonemes of final clusters for various cluster types.

Statistical analyses confirmed that the children omitted nasals before voiceless

Table 8.8. Omissions of Interior Consonants of Syllable-Final
Consonant Clusters

Type of Interior Consonant	Examples
Nasal before voiceless obstruent	BUTH for *bunch*
	ELEPHAT for *elephant*
	DOWT for *don't*
	PLAS for *plants*
	JUT for *jumped*
	TACK for *thank*
	THEECK for *think*
Nasal before voiced obstruent	AAD for *and*
	MOOS for *moms*
	STAD for *stand*
Liquid	HOS for *horse*
	GRAOD for *growled*
	HAPT for *helped*
Obstruent	LAS for *lets*
	NEST for *next*
	FORET for *forest*

obstruents at a particularly high rate. Once these omissions were taken into account, the omission rate for sonorants (i.e., liquids and nasals) did not differ significantly from the omission rate for obstruents. That is, the children omitted liquids like the /l/ of *milk* about as often as obstruents like the /s/ of *mist*.

These results imply that children omit the /n/ of a word like *plant* for at least two reasons. The first reason relates to the position of the /n/ in its syllable. This /n/ is the interior consonant of a consonant cluster. Children omit the interior phonemes of consonant clusters at elevated rates, whether the cluster is at the beginning of the syllable or the end of the syllable and whether the interior phoneme is an obstruent or a sonorant. The second reason that children often omit the /n/ of *plant* relates to the specific phonemes in this word. The /n/ is a nasal that precedes a voiceless obstruent. Omissions of the interior phonemes of final clusters are especially common when the cluster is a nasal followed by a voiceless obstruent.

Although two factors—position in syllable and cluster type—promote the omission of the /n/ of *plant,* only one factor—position in syllable—promotes the omission of the /n/ of *stand.* The /n/ of *stand,* being the interior phoneme of a cluster, is vulnerable to omission. However, it is not followed by a voiceless obstruent. As a result, children are less likely to omit the /n/ of *stand* than of *plant.*

Syllable-Final Consonant Clusters: Reasons for the Omissions. Now that I have described the pattern of omissions on final consonant clusters, I must seek out the reasons for this pattern. In trying to understand why children sometimes fail to spell consonants in final clusters, one must consider both of the factors just described. First, one must ask why children sometimes omit the interior consonants of clusters at the ends of syllables. Second, one must also ask why children have a specific problem with nasal-voiceless obstruent clusters. I will discuss each of these questions in turn.

Children's omissions of the interior consonants of syllable-final clusters, like their omissions of the interior consonants of syllable-initial clusters, may reflect a difficulty in segmenting syllables into phonemes. To spell a word (at least a word whose conventional spelling they have not previously memorized), children must analyze the spoken word into phonemes and must symbolize each phoneme with a grapheme. If children do not fully analyze a word into phonemes, they may misspell it. Consider *milk*. Some first graders may segment this word into the onset /m/, the peak /ɪl/, and the coda /k/. They treat /ɪl/ as a unit; they do not segment it into /ɪ/ and /l/. Children who analyze the spoken word in this way may spell the peak with just *i* rather than with *i* followed by *l*. With *mist*, some children may divide the word into the onset /m/, the peak /ɪ/, and the coda /st/. These children may spell /st/ with a single letter rather than with the correct two-letter sequence.

In the examples just given, children's misspellings reflect a lack of awareness of the separate phonemes in spoken words. For most first graders, the spelling errors do not reflect faulty pronunciations of the words. Nor do the errors reflect phonemic representations that do not match those of adults. The /l/ of *milk* and the /s/ of *mist* are present in the children's pronunciations and in their phonemic representations. However, some children do not spell these phonemes because they do not treat them as separate units.

Why is there an additional increase in omission rate for nasals before voiceless obstruents, over and above the rate expected from the position of the nasal in the syllable? That is, why do children omit the /n/ of *plant* more often than the /n/ of *stand*? One hypothesis is that children's spelling represents the phonetic level of speech (Gentry, 1982; Read, 1975). According to this phonetic spelling hypothesis, children consider the spoken forms of both *plant* and *stand* to contain /n/. However, the two /n/s differ in their phonetic forms. The /n/ of *plant* is shorter than the /n/ of *stand* (Malécot, 1960; Raphael, Dorman, Freeman, & Tobin, 1975). Children may notice this phonetic difference and attempt to indicate it in their spelling. As a result, children omit the /n/ of *plant* more often than the /n/ of *stand*. In this view, differences at the phonetic level of speech are reflected in children's spelling.

My results provide little support for the hypothesis that children typically represent the phonetic level of speech when they spell. In particular, children do *not* seem to indicate differences in the durations of phones in their spelling. As discussed earlier in this chapter, consonants are shorter when they occur in clusters than when they occur singly. Shortening occurs for the exterior consonants of clusters as well as for the interior consonants. However, children do not omit the exterior consonants of clusters significantly more often than expected given other factors. As another example, although the /æ/ of *back* is measurably shorter than the /æ/ of *bag*, children do not omit the /æ/ of *back* any more often. In general, children's spelling does not seem to reflect the durations of phones.

One might argue in favor of the phonetic spelling hypothesis for nasal-voiceless obstruent clusters by claiming that this case is different from the others. The shortening of nasals before voiceless obstruents is more extreme than the shortening in the other cases. True, nasals are very short before voiceless obstruents. But if children's spelling reflected the phonetic level of speech, and if durational differences caused the large jump in omission rate for nasals before voiceless obstruents, one

one would expect at least some effects in the other cases. Thus, there is no good evidence that children's failures to spell nasals before voiceless obstruents reflect the children's attention to the phonetic level of speech.

Another hypothesis about why children are especially likely to omit nasals in nasal-voiceless obstruent final clusters is that the nasal and the following obstruent are articulated at the same place in the mouth. That is, the nasal and the following consonant are *homorganic*. For example, the /n/ and /t/ in *went* both have an alveolar place of articulation. With nasal-voiced obstruent clusters, the nasal and the following voiced obstruent are not necessarily homorganic. For example, the /m/ and /z/ of /mz/, as in *comes*, are not articulated at the same point in the mouth. Although nasal-voiceless obstruent and nasal-voiced obstruent clusters differ in homorganicity, this difference cannot explain the difference in omissions. As I show later in this chapter, the children did not omit consonants in homorganic clusters more often than consonants in nonhomorganic clusters.

Given the lack of support for the phonetic spelling hypothesis and the homorganicity hypothesis, why do children omit nasals in nasal-voiceless obstruent final clusters? I propose another hypothesis—the different phonemic representations hypothesis. This hypothesis assumes that children attempt to represent speech at the phonemic level. Children sometimes misspell words because their phonemic representations do not always match those assumed by the conventional English writing system. Recall that I proposed a similar hypothesis for words like *her*. Here, I argued, there is a mismatch between children's phonemic form (/h/ followed by syllabic /r/) and conventional spelling *(h, e, r)*. Consequently, children often misspell *her* as HR. There may be a similar mismatch between children's phonemic representations and the representations assumed by the English writing system for words like *plant*. Some first graders may represent this word as /pl'æ̃t/ rather than /pl'æ̃nt/. The ~ over the vowel indicates that it is a *nasalized vowel,* or a vowel in which some of the air escapes through the nose. In this view, children's representation of *plant* does not contain a separate /n/ phoneme. In contrast, children represent *stand* as /st'ænd/. This word contains a vowel followed by /n/.

According to the different phonemic representations hypothesis, the phonemic systems of at least some English-speaking children include both nasalized and nonnasalized vowels. For example, children distinguish between /æ/ and /æ̃/. They consider these to be distinct, although similar, vowel phonemes. Phonemic analyses of adult English do not distinguish between nasalized and nonnasalized vowels. However, other languages have such systems. For example, French has pairs of words that differ from one another only in that one contains a nasalized vowel and the other contains the corresponding nonnasalized vowel. The present hypothesis assumes that the phonetic properties of the spoken word *plant*—the shortness of /n/ and the nasalization of /æ/—cause some children to code it as /pl'æ̃t/ in the first place. When spelling the word, however, children focus on the phonemic level rather than the phonetic level.

If children represent *plant* as /pl'æ̃t/, why exactly do they spell it as PLAT? Children must consider the nasalized vowel /æ̃/ to be similar to the nonnasalized vowel /æ/. They use *a*, which they know to be appropriate for /æ/, to spell /æ̃/. This use of *a* for /æ̃/ is another example of the general principle that children do more than distinguish among different phonemes. They also know that some phonemes are similar to one another, while other phonemes are less similar. Children group similar phonemes together for spelling purposes. In this case, children group the nasalized vowel /æ̃/ with the nonnasalized vowel /æ/ and spell them both with the same letter.

A possible problem for the nasalized vowel hypothesis is that children do not often omit the nasal when spelling words like *plan.* They rarely misspell *plan* as PLA or PA. The relatively low omission rate for nasals at the ends of syllables suggests that children consider *plan* to contain /æ/ followed by /n/ rather than /æ̃/. Apparently, children who represent *plant* as /pl'æ̃t/ also represent *plan* as /pl'æn/. They consider *plant* and *plan* to contain the same number of phonemes. Adults, in contrast, consider *plant* to contain more phonemes than *plan.*

To summarize the results for consonant clusters at the ends of syllables, children sometimes omit the interior phonemes of these clusters when they spell. These omissions are particularly common for nasals in nasal-voiceless obstruent clusters. The general increase in omissions for the interior consonants of final clusters relative to single consonants reflects the position of the consonant in the syllable. The additional increase in omissions for nasals before voiceless obstruents has a different explanation. I proposed that at least some children do not consider nasals before voiceless obstruents to be separate phonemes. Rather, the nasalization is part of the vowel; there is no following nasal consonant. If children code *plant* as /pl'æ̃t/ rather than /pl'ænt/, if they group /æ̃/ with /æ/, and if they represent the phonemic level in spelling, it follows that they would often spell *plant* as PLAT.

Onsets Versus Rimes: Results. As I have shown, consonants in different positions of the syllable are omitted at different rates. The interior consonants of syllable-initial clusters and the interior consonants of syllable-final clusters are especially susceptible to omission. In this section, I ask whether consonants in onsets and consonants in rimes also differ in their omission rates.

Consonants like the /b/ of *bag* and the /r/ of *brand* belong to the syllable onset. The /b/ of *bag* is a single initial consonant; the /r/ of *brand* is part of an onset cluster. By virtue of the assumptions about syllabification that I have adopted, the /b/ of *tumble* is also a syllable onset. This /b/ must be the onset of the word's second syllable because it is not legal at the end of the first syllable.

The consonants that follow the syllable's peak are part of the rime. For example, the /g/ of *bag* and the /n/ and /d/ of *brand* belong to the rime. The /m/ of *tumble* is part of the first syllable's rime by the present assumptions about syllabification; /mb/ may not be the onset of a syllable in English. The middle /p/ of *Pepsi* must also be in the rime of the first syllable.

Overall, the children omitted consonants in rimes at a rate of 11.4%. The omission rate for consonants in onsets was 3.3%. Statistical analyses confirmed that, other things being equal, the children were more likely to omit a consonant when it was part of a rime than when it was part of an onset.[2]

Does the difference between onsets and rimes reflect a tendency to omit consonants at the ends of words more often than consonants at the beginnings of words? After all, consonants in rimes are often at the ends of words, whereas consonants in onsets are often at the beginnings of words. To address this question, I looked at consonants in the middles of words. Specifically, I examined consonants that were neither in the onset of the first syllable nor the rime of the last syllable and that belonged to either an onset or a rime by the syllabification assumptions of Chapter 1. For example, the /b/ of *tumble* is an onset and the /m/ is a rime. For the consonants in question, the omission rate was 8.4% for onsets and 34.0% for rimes. This difference shows that the higher omission rate for rimes than for onsets does *not* just reflect a difference between consonants at the ends of words and consonants at the beginnings of words.

Table 8.9 presents some spellings in which consonants in rimes are omitted. In these examples, the consonants are in the middle of the word rather than at the end. As the examples show, the omissions occurred for both sonorant and obstruent consonants.

Thus, the position of a consonant in its syllable affects its omission rate. In general, children are more apt to omit consonants in rimes than consonants in onsets. The position of a consonant in the word is also influential. To see this, observe that the omission rate for consonants in rimes in the middles of words (34.0%) exceeded the omission rate for consonants in rimes at the ends of words (10.2%). Also, the omission rate for consonants in onsets in the middles of words (8.4%) exceeded the omission rate for consonants in onsets at beginnings of words (3.0%). Results presented later in the following section confirm that the position of a consonant in the word affects its omission rate.

Onsets Versus Rimes: Reasons for the Omissions. Having shown that children are more apt to omit consonants in rimes than in onsets, I must now discuss the reason for this difference. Children's omissions of consonants in rimes may stem from their problems in analyzing spoken syllables into phonemes. Consider the initial /b/ of *back* and the middle /b/ of *tumble*. In both cases, /b/ is a constituent of the syllable on its own, an onset. It does not form a strong unit with the phonemes that follow it. Because children have relatively little difficulty separating the /b/ from the following phonemes, they generally represent it in their spelling. In contrast, the /k/ of *back* belongs to the /æk/ rime and the /m/ of *tumble* belongs to the /əm/ rime. The /k/ and /m/ are not syllable constituents on their own. They belong to a group of phonemes, the rime. Because the /k/ of *back* is linked with the preceding /æ/ and the /m/ of *tumble* is linked with the preceding /ə/, children do not always treat the /k/ and /m/ as separate units. Consequently, children may not spell these consonants.

Table 8.9. Examples of Omissions of Consonants in Rimes in the Middles of Words

TUBOL for *tumble*
SATIMS for *sometimes*
UWESE for *always*
PESEI for *pepsi*
ATR for *after*
PESU for *pizza*

My proposal, then, is that children's failures to spell consonants in rimes are due to a lack of phonemic awareness. These errors do *not* reflect mispronunciation: First graders almost always pronounce the /k/ of *back*. Nor do the spelling errors reflect phonemic forms that do not match those assumed by the English writing system: First graders consider *back* to contain /k/, as adults do. My hypothesis, rather, is that some first graders are not aware of the separate /k/ within *back*. As a result, they sometimes fail to spell the /k/.

Word Length

The results presented in Chapter 7 documented an association between word length and spelling omissions for vowels. Children were more likely to omit a vowel in a long word than a short word. In this section, I ask whether word length is also associated with consonant omissions.

Figure 8.1, which is based on the results for all consonants, shows the relation between word length and consonant omission errors. As the figure shows, and as statistical analyses confirmed, word length was associated with consonant omissions. As the number of phonemes in the word increased, the likelihood of omission of any particular consonant increased.

Why were children more apt to omit a consonant when it occurred in a long word than a short word? There are several possible explanations, which are not mutually exclusive. Children may have more difficulty analyzing long words into phonemes than analyzing short words into phonemes. As a result, children may more often omit phonemes in long words. Even if children successfully analyze a long word into phonemes, they may forget one phoneme while trying to spell the others. To the extent that children rely on memory to spell, long words should also

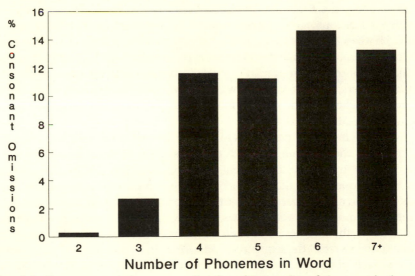

Figure 8.1. Consonant omission rate as a function of the number of phonemes in the word.

be harder than short words. Each of these explanations applies equally well to consonants and vowels. Thus, it is not surprising that word length was important for both types of phonemes.

Position in Word

I have shown that children are more likely to omit consonants in certain positions of the syllable than other positions of the syllable. In this section, I ask whether the position of the consonant in the *word* has effects above and beyond those of the position of the consonant in the syllable. Findings presented earlier in this chapter suggest that position in the word does have an effect. For example, the children were more likely to omit consonants in onset clusters when the cluster was in the middle of the word, as with the /fr/ of *afraid,* than when the cluster was at the beginning of the word, as with the /fr/ of *friend.*

Statistical analyses confirmed that the position of a consonant in the word was related to the consonant's omission rate. Once other factors were taken into account, the children were less likely to omit consonants at the margins of words (i.e., consonants in the first or last position of a word) than consonants in the middles of words (i.e., consonants in any other position of a word). There was no significant difference in omission rate between the first and last consonants of words. The pattern of results for consonants parallels the pattern of results for vowels reported in Chapter 7.

In the case of consonants, it would be misleading to depict the effects of word position by presenting serial position curves that show the omission rates for consonants in various positions of words of different lengths. This is because the position of a consonant in the word is confounded with other factors, such as the position of the consonant in the syllable. However, one can get some idea of the effect of serial position on consonant omissions by examining the results for consonants in onsets and rimes. Consider those consonants that are onsets on their own or that are the exterior consonants of onset clusters. The omission rate for these consonants was 0.5% when the consonants were in the first position of the word. In the middles of words, the omission rate for these same consonants was 5.3%. The results were similar for consonants in rimes. For single consonants and the exterior consonants of final clusters, the omission rate was 6.0% when the consonants were at the end of the word. The omission rate was much higher, 34.4%, when the consonants were in the middle of the word.

Why were the children more apt to omit phonemes in the middles of words than phonemes at the beginnings or ends of words? Several explanations may be proposed, which are not mutually exclusive. When children are analyzing a spoken word into phonemes for the purpose of spelling it, phonemes at the beginnings and ends of words may be easier to isolate than phonemes in the middles of words. Phonemes at the margins of words must be separated from only one adjacent phoneme; phonemes in the middles of words have other phonemes on both sides of them. When trying to recall the sequence of phonemes in a spoken word and to assign a letter to each phoneme, children may forget the phonemes in the middle of the sequence. We know that items in the middle of a list are harder to remember than items at the beginning or end of a list. Memory factors should also play a role when children try to spell words by recalling their conventional spellings. The middle letters of a sequence are harder to recall than the first or last letters. Each of these explanations applies to consonants as well as to vowels. Thus, it is not surprising that similar effects of word position were found for the two types of phonemes.

Factors Not Significantly Associated with Consonant Omission Errors

So far, I have discussed the factors that, according to the results of my statistical analyses, were reliably associated with consonant omission errors. In this section, I consider those factors that did not have significant effects. As always, null results must be interpreted with caution. A larger study might find significant effects for certain variables that were not significant here. Despite the problems in the interpretation of null results, I will discuss those factors that were not reliably associated with consonant omission errors in this study.

Sonorant Versus Obstruent Consonants

The consonants of English may be divided into two main categories—sonorants and obstruents. As discussed in Chapter 1, sonorants include liquids, nasals, and glides. Obstruents include fricatives, affricates, and stops. Overall, there was a substantial difference in the omission rates for these two types of consonants. The omission rate for sonorant consonants was 11.8%. The omission rate for obstruents was 4.8%. What is the reason for this difference?

One possibility is that the higher omission rate for obstruents stems from factors that have already been identified. For example, in English and other languages, sonorant consonants are often the interior phonemes of syllable-initial and syllable-final consonant clusters. English contains initial clusters like /fr/, in which an obstruent precedes a sonorant, but not initial clusters like /rf/. English contains final clusters like /lt/, in which a sonorant precedes an obstruent, but not final clusters like /tl/. As I showed earlier in this chapter, the children sometimes failed to spell consonants in the interior positions of initial and final clusters. The omission rate for sonorants may be relatively high because sonorants often occur in these positions. If so, the factor of sonorant versus obstruent would not add significantly to the prediction of consonant omissions once other factors, such as those related to the position of the consonant in the syllable, were taken into account.

Another possibility is that there is something special about sonorant consonants per se that makes them vulnerable to omission. If so, a factor that distinguished between sonorants and obstruents *would* contribute to the prediction of consonant omissions, even when factors related to position in the syllable were considered.

When a factor distinguishing between sonorants and obstruents was added to the regression, the percentage of variance that was explained did not increase. This result suggests that the high omission rate for sonorants as compared with obstruents reflects the different distributions of the two types of phonemes in syllables and words rather than intrinsic properties of the phonemes per se.

Homorganic Clusters

Phonemes that have the same place of articulation are said to be *homorganic*. For example, /s/ and /t/ are homorganic because both are formed by contact between the tongue and the alveolar ridge. If segmentation of spoken words into phonemes has an important kinesthetic component; that is, if children use changes in the position of the tongue to decide where one phoneme ends and the next one begins, they might not realize that a cluster like /st/ contains two phonemes. The results did not support this idea. The interior phonemes of syllable-initial and syllable-final homorganic clusters were not more likely to be omitted than the interior phonemes of nonhomorganic clusters. Apparently, children do *not* have more difficulty analyzing a cluster into phonemes when the phonemes are articulated at the same place in the mouth than when the phonemes are articulated at different places.

Word Frequency

Are children less likely to omit consonants in frequent words than consonants in infrequent words? In Chapter 2, I reported that misspellings are less common for frequent words than infrequent words. However, there was no significant effect of word frequency on consonant omission rate: Children were not more likely to omit consonants in infrequent words than in frequent ones. A similar result for vowels was reported in Chapter 7: Children were not more likely to omit vowels in infrequent words than in frequent ones.

There may have been no word frequency effect because omissions of phonemes vary greatly within a word as a function of the phoneme's position in the word and the syllable and other factors. For example, even though *want* is introduced in children's earliest reading materials (Harris & Jacobson, 1972), children often omit /n/ when spelling this word because it is a nasal before a voiceless obstruent. In contrast, children rarely omit /w/ or /t/. In comparison with the variation *within* words, the variation *between* words due to word frequency is very small. These between-word differences were probably too small to be detected in this study.

Other Factors

Consonants were no more likely to be omitted when they were part of a derivational suffix or prefix than when they were not. For example, the final /n/ of *collection*, which is part of a derivational suffix, did not show an elevated omission rate. Chapter 7 reported similar results for vowels in derivational prefixes and suffixes.

Statistical Analyses

Multiple regression was used to analyze the consonant omission data. The dependent variable was the percentage of omissions for each consonant phoneme in each word of the collection. Thus, there were 2,526 lines of data, one for each consonant in each word. A few consonants that are not symbolized in the conventional spellings of the word were excluded from the analyses.

A first analysis attempted to predict the omission rate for each consonant from ten characteristics of the consonant and the word in which it occurred. The predictors were stress, vowel-liquid letter name, syllabic liquid, regular or regularized inflectional suffix, part of a regular or regularized inflectional suffix, interior consonant of cluster, nasal before voiceless obstruent, rime, number of phonemes in word, and margin of word. A consonant was coded as stressed if it belonged to a primary- or secondary-stressed syllable according to the assumptions about syllabification discussed in Chapter 1. A consonant was part of a vowel-liquid letter name if it was /r/ preceded by /ɑ/ or /l/ preceded by /ɛ/. Syllabic liquid consonants were /r/s that were preceded by stressed or unstressed /ə/ in my phonemic transcriptions and /l/s that were preceded by unstressed /ə/. Regular or regularized inflectional suffixes included final /s/, /z/, /t/, and /d/ when they functioned as regular inflectional suffixes or inflectional suffixes that were regularized by the child. The consonants in the inflectional endings /əd/, /əz/, /ər/, /əst/, and /iŋ/ were coded as part of an inflectional suffix. A consonant was the interior consonant of a cluster if it was the second or third consonant of a clear syllable-initial cluster or the next-to-last or third-to-last consonant of a clear syllable-final cluster. Nasals followed by voiceless obstruents in the same syllable were coded as nasals before voiceless obstruents. A consonant was part of a rime if it followed a vowel within a syllable. Number of phonemes was the number of phonemes in the spoken word. Word-marginal consonants were those at the beginning or the end of a word.

The analysis just described relied on the assumptions about syllabification discussed in Chapter 1. Missing values were coded when the status of a consonant with respect to a certain variable was unclear due to ambiguities about syllabification. For instance, the middle /b/ of *baby* was not coded for stress or for rime because it is not clear whether this consonant belongs to the first or second syllable of the word. As another example, the /f/ of *after* must belong to the word's first syllable by the syllabification assumptions. However, it is not certain whether /f/ is the interior phoneme of the syllable-final cluster /ft/ or whether it is a syllable-final single consonant. Thus, /f/ was coded as belonging to a stressed syllable and as being part of a rime but it received a missing value on the interior phoneme of cluster variable. Because some consonants were not coded for certain variables, the number of cases in the regression (2,183) was less than the total number of cases (2,526).

The regression accounted for 16.9% of the variance (16.5% adjusted) in consonant omissions ($p < .001$). The variables of stress ($p = .005$), vowel-liquid letter name ($p < .05$), syllabic liquid ($p < .001$), inflectional suffix ($p < .025$), part of inflectional suffix ($p = .05$), interior consonant of cluster ($p < .005$), nasal before voiceless obstruent ($p < .001$), rime ($p < .001$), number of phonemes ($p < .01$), and margin of word ($p < .001$) made significant contributions. The largest effects were for nasal before voiceless obstruent and margin of word.

The percentage of variance explained by the regression did not increase reliably when syllables with primary and secondary stress were distinguished from one another. The effect of letter names was specific to vowel-liquid letter names. Vowel-nasal letter names, vowel-obstruent letter names, or consonant-vowel letter names did not add significantly to the prediction. The final consonants of irregularly inflected words were not omitted more often than otherwise expected, nor were there significant differences between consonants at the beginnings and ends of words. Also unsuccessful as predictors were whether the consonant was a sonorant or an obstruent and whether the consonant belonged to a derivational affix. Measures of word frequency, including the frequency of the word in Carroll et al. (1971), the number of times the word occurred in my collection, or the log transforms of these measures, did not contribute additionally to the regression. An analysis that was restricted to the interior consonants of clusters found no significant difference between homorganic and nonhomorganic clusters. Finally, the results were virtually identical when the variables of vowel-liquid letter name, syllabic liquid, and nasal before voiceless consonant were defined using the syllabification assumptions, as in the analyses just reported, and when they were defined without regard to syllabification.

The percentage of variance explained by the regression was relatively low, less than 17%. Contributing to this low figure may be the fact that many words occurred just once in my collection. For the consonants in these words, the percentage of omissions could be only 0% or 100%. The analyses were therefore repeated, successively eliminating words that occurred once, twice, and so on, up to five times. When words that occurred five times or fewer were excluded from the analysis, the percentage of variance explained by the regression reached 49.6% (48.3% adjusted, $p < .001$; this analysis included 389 cases). Thus, the variables that have been identified here may explain at least half of the variance in consonant omission rates.

Changes from First to Second Semester of the School Year

Overall, the rate of consonant omission errors declined from the first semester of the school year (10.1%) to the second semester (5.9%; $p < .001$ for the difference by a chi-square test). Even during the second semester, though, the first graders frequently omitted consonants that occurred in certain positions of words and syllables. For example, the omission rate for the interior consonants of syllable-initial and syllable-final clusters was 20.8% in the second semester. Although this figure is lower than the 36.0% observed during the first semester ($p < .001$ by a chi-square test), it is still relatively high. In the case of nasals before voiceless obstruents at the ends of syllables, the omission rate was 41.1% in the second semester as compared with 57.3% in the first semester. Although there was a significant decrease from the first semester to the second ($p < .05$), children often omitted nasals in nasal-voiceless obstruent clusters even during the second semester of the school year.

Summary of Results

Before discussing the implications of the findings, I will briefly summarize the results presented in this chapter.

1. The first graders more often failed to spell consonants in unstressed syllables than consonants in stressed syllables.
2. When a word contained /ɑr/ (the name of *r)* or /ɛl/ (the name of *l)*, the chil-

dren were less likely to omit the consonant than expected on the basis of other factors. There were no significant effects for other letter names.

3. Syllabic liquids, as in *little,* were less likely to be omitted than otherwise expected. The same was not true for syllabic nasals, as in *person.*

4. The children were more likely to omit consonants that were regular inflectional endings, such as the /d/ of *killed,* than consonants that were not inflectional endings, such as the /d/ of *build.*

5. The interior consonants of syllable-initial consonant clusters (e.g., /l/ of /bl/, /p/ and /r/ of /spr/) showed elevated omission rates. So did the interior consonants of syllable-final consonant clusters (e.g., /l/ of /ld/). However, the exterior consonants of clusters (e.g., /b/ of /bl/, /d/ of /ld/) were not omitted significantly more often than single consonants.

6. For clusters at the ends of syllables, the omission rate for nasals followed by voiceless obstruents was particularly high. For example, /n/ was more likely to be omitted when it preceded the voiceless /t/ than when it preceded the voiced /d/.

7. The first graders more often omitted consonants in rimes than consonants in onsets.

8. The more phonemes in a word, the more likely a given consonant was to be omitted.

9. The children were more apt to omit consonants in the interiors of words than consonants at the beginnings or ends of words.

Comparison of Consonant Omissions and Vowel Omissions

Now that I have summarized the results on consonant omissions, it is important to compare the findings on consonant omissions reported in this chapter with the findings on vowel omissions reported in Chapter 7. It has sometimes been implied that children are especially likely to omit vowels (e.g., Ehri, 1986). If so, one would expect vowel omissions to consistently outnumber consonant omissions, regardless of the type of word that children are attempting. One might further expect that different factors would relate to vowel omissions and consonant omissions. As I discuss in this section, these expectations were not confirmed.

Many of the same factors were related to both consonant omissions and vowel omissions. One factor that was associated with both consonant and vowel omissions, and in the same way, was stress. The children were less likely to omit phonemes in primary-stressed and secondary-stressed syllables than phonemes in unstressed syllables. This held true whether the phonemes were vowels or consonants. Even though stress is sometimes thought to be a property of the syllable's vowel or the syllable's rime, the effects of stress on spelling were *not* confined to vowels. Nor were the effects confined to rimes. A regression analysis that was limited to consonants in syllable onsets found a significant effect of stress, as did the regression that included all consonants. In its effects on spelling, then, stress is a property of the entire syllable.

The students' knowledge of letter names affected their omissions of both consonants and vowels. When a spoken word contained either of the vowel-liquid sequences /ɑr/ or /ɛl/, the children sometimes spelled the two-phoneme sequence with single *r* or *l* rather than with a vowel grapheme followed by a consonant grapheme. The children apparently used single *r* or *l* because of their difficulty in analyzing vowel-liquid sequences into phonemes. Consonant-vowel letter names such as /ti/ and vowel-obstruent letter names such as /ɛf/ did not reliably affect vowel omissions or consonant omissions. Apparently, first graders have little trouble segmenting consonant-vowel sequences and vowel-obstruent sequences. As a result, they do not often spell these sequences as units.

Only for the vowel-nasal letter names *m* and *n* did the vowel omission results and the consonant omission results disagree. For these letters, vowel omissions were significantly higher than otherwise expected but consonant omissions were not significantly lower. These conflicting results may reflect the intermediate degree of cohesiveness of vowel-nasal sequences. Vowel-nasal sequences may be harder to analyze than consonant-vowel or vowel-obstruent sequences but easier to analyze than vowel-liquid sequences. Children have some tendency to use letter-name spellings for *m* and *n,* but this tendency is not as strong as with *r* and *l.*

With syllabic liquids, as in *her, brother,* and *little,* the consonant omission results and the vowel omission results again pointed to similar conclusions. The children often symbolized syllabic liquids with only consonants, omitting the vowel that appears in conventional English. I argued that some first graders represent a word like *her* as containing two phonemes, /h/ followed by syllabic /r/. They do not represent it as containing three phonemes, /h/ followed by /ə/ followed by /r/. Hence, children often misspell the word as HR.

For syllabic nasals, the vowel omission data and the consonant omission data again agreed. The pattern of vowel and consonant omissions in the second syllable of a word like *Jason* did not differ reliably from the pattern of omissions in the second syllable of a word like *bandit.* I argued that children's phonemic representations of both words end with an unstressed vowel followed by a consonant. When spelling *Jason,* children represent this phonemic level rather than a phonetic level at which /n/ is syllabic. Because both *Jason* and *bandit* contain a vowel phoneme in the second syllable, children are no more likely to omit the second vowel of *Jason* than the second vowel of *bandit.*

For both consonants and vowels, the length of the word and the position of the phoneme within the word were important determinants of omissions. Children were more likely to omit phonemes in long words than in short words. Moreover, once other factors were taken into account, children were more likely to omit phonemes in the middles of words than phonemes at the beginnings and ends of words. The omission rate did not differ significantly for initial and final phonemes. All of these results held for both vowels and consonants.

For consonants, the position of the phoneme within a cluster also affected omissions. Omissions were relatively common when a consonant was an interior phoneme of a syllable-initial or syllable-final cluster, particularly when it was the interior phoneme of a nasal-voiceless obstruent final cluster. Omissions were relatively uncommon when a consonant was the exterior phoneme of a cluster or when it was a singleton. Because vowels do not participate in clusters within a syllable, these results are specific to consonants.

The omission rate for consonants in rimes exceeded the omission rate for consonants in onsets. This difference, I suggested, reflects a limitation in children's ability to analyze spoken syllables into phonemes. Some first graders have difficulty abstracting a consonant from the rime of the syllable. However, the children did *not* seem to have difficulty abstracting the vowel from the rime. Vowels at the ends of syllables, which form the rime of the syllable on their own, were no less likely to be omitted than vowels that were followed by one or more consonants. Thus, first graders do not have a general problem in analyzing rimes into phonemes. The problem seems to be specific to consonants.

Consonants that were inflectional endings on their own, such as the final /d/ of *killed,* were more likely to be omitted than consonants that were not inflectional endings. Because the only one-phoneme inflections in English are consonants, this result is necessarily specific to consonants. An apparent discrepancy between the consonant results and the vowel results emerged for phonemes that were parts of inflectional endings. Consonants that were part of an inflectional ending, such as the /z/ of *dishes,* showed an elevated omission rate. However, the omission rate was not significantly higher than expected for vowels such as the second vowel of *dishes.* The reason for this discrepancy is not clear.

With derivational prefixes and suffixes, the results for consonants and vowels again converged. The first graders were no more likely to omit a phoneme when it belonged to a derivational affix than when it did not. The null effects for derived words must be interpreted with caution, however, since the first graders in this study attempted relatively few derived words.

Other negative findings were also consistent for both vowels and consonants. In neither case was acoustic duration related to omission rate. Nor did the frequency of the word have a significant impact on phoneme omissions.

So far, in Chapters 7 and 8, I have analyzed the results for vowels and consonants separately and compared the results of the two sets of analyses. Another way to compare consonant omissions and vowel omissions is to examine the omission rates for consonants and vowels in particular types of words. Table 8.10 presents such an analysis. This table shows the percentage of omissions for each consonant and vowel in words with various phonological structures.

The most common type of word attempted by the children had the phonological structure C'VC, as in *big* and *mail.* For these words, vowel omissions were most common, final consonant omissions were next most common, and initial consonant omissions were least common. This pattern fits with the findings of this chapter and of Chapter 7. It also fits with the observations of previous researchers (e.g., Ehri, 1986; Morris & Perney, 1984), who have reported that children often omit vowels and final consonants in one-syllable words that begin and end with consonants. The vowel's high omission rate in C'VCs appears to reflect its position in the word rather than its phonological category per se. Because the vowel is in the middle of the word, it is more vulnerable to omission than the consonants at either end. The final consonant, being part of the rime, is more susceptible to omission than the initial consonant.

Table 8.10. Consonant and Vowel Omissions in Words with the Most Common Types of Phonological Structures

Structure	No. of Cases	Percent Omissions
C'VC	1,536	C: 0.4 V: 4.5 C: 3.1
C'V	912	C: 0.3 V: 2.0
C'VCC	503	C: 0.4 V: 11.1 C: 33.2 C: 9.7
'VC	414	V: 1.4 C: 0.4
'VCC	204	V: 1.0 C: 3.4 C: 9.3
C'VCVC	190	C: 0.0 V: 8.4 C: 6.8 V: 49.5 C: 18.4
CC'VC	125	C: 0.0 C: 24.0 V: 4.0 C: 3.2
C'VCV	98	C: 1.0 V: 9.2 C: 3.1 V: 7.1
C'VCCVC	79	C: 0.0 V: 19.0 C: 32.9 C: 5.1 V: 53.2 C: 16.5
CC'V	58	C: 0.0 C: 31.0 V: 0.0

Note. 'V words, although common, are not included in the table because no omissions occurred on these words.

Although children omitted the vowel more often than the consonants in C'VC words, vowel omissions did not always outnumber consonant omissions. With C'VCC words such as *want* and *lets,* the second-to-last consonant of the word—the interior consonant of the final cluster—had the highest omission rate of any phoneme. The omission rate for this consonant exceeded the omission rate for the vowel. With CC'VC words such as *flat,* the second consonant of the word—the interior consonant of the initial cluster—had the highest omission rate. Again, the omission rate for this consonant exceeded the omission rate for the vowel. Thus, the balance between vowel omissions and consonant omissions varies with the phonological structure of the spoken word. Children do not always omit vowels more than they omit consonants.

The results presented in this section speak against the idea that vowels, because of their phonological properties, are particularly susceptible to omission. In C'VC words, it is true, children are more likely to omit the vowel than to omit either of the consonants. However, this is largely because the vowel is in the middle of the word. With other types of words, vowel omissions do not necessarily outnumber consonant omissions.

Recall that the children in this study, like other children learning to spell in English, produced more correct spellings for consonants than for vowels. In Chapter 3, I asked whether this difference reflects intrinsic phonological differences between consonants and vowels. The results suggested that it does not. Instead, it reflects differences in the ways in which these two types of phonemes are conventionally spelled in English. In this chapter, likewise, I asked whether the higher omission rate for vowels than consonants in certain types of words, notably consonant-vowel-consonant words, reflects intrinsic phonological differences between the two types of phonemes. The results suggest that it does not. Thus, many of the differences between consonants and vowels in the spelling of English-speaking children reflect the characteristics of the writing system and the positions in which consonants and vowels tend to occur in words.

Comparison with Results of Other Studies

Read's Research

Read's collection of spellings included fewer consonant omissions than my collection. The only type of consonant omission that Read discussed in any detail was the omission of nasals in final clusters. Read found, as I did, that children sometimes failed to spell nasals that immediately preceded another consonant. For example, Read's preschoolers misspelled *stamps* as STAPS and *want* as WOT. The children rarely omitted nasals in other contexts. They almost always symbolized the /n/ of *night* and the /m/ of *Sam.* Read also found, as I did, that nasal omissions were more common before voiceless stops than before voiced stops. Thus, both preschoolers and first graders omit nasals in words like *stamps* and *want.*

Why do beginning spellers sometimes fail to symbolize the /m/ of *stamps,* the /n/ of *want,* and the /ŋ/ of *bank?* Read suggested three possible explanations. First, children may represent the phonetic level of speech in their spelling. Especially before voiceless stops, nasals are very short (Malécot, 1960; Raphael et al., 1975). The vowel of *want* is nasalized; the nasal segment itself is short or nonexistent. Children who consult the phonetic level of speech as they spell may therefore spell *want* as WOT. The phonetic spelling hypothesis predicts a close relation between the durations of nasals and children's tendency to spell the nasals. The hypothesis further predicts that children group the nasal of *want* with the vowel.

A second explanation for errors like WOT for *want* follows from the fact that, at least within a morpheme, a nasal and the following consonant are homorganic, or articulated at the same place in the mouth. Because the /n/ and /t/ of *want* share their place of articulation, children may identify them as a single unit. They may spell this unit with *t* rather than *n.* The homorganicity hypothesis predicts that children should represent the nasals in words like *comes.* In such two-morpheme words, the nasal and the following consonant are not homorganic. The homorganicity hypothesis further predicts that children should omit other types of consonants in homorganic clusters, not just nasals. For example, children should often omit the /l/ of the homorganic cluster /ld/. They should rarely omit the /l/ of the nonhomorganic cluster /lk/. Finally, the homorganicity hypothesis predicts that children group the /n/ of *want* with the final consonant.

Read suggested yet a third hypothesis for children's failures to spell nasals in final clusters. In this environment, the nasal is partially redundant. Knowing that a morpheme's final consonant is /t/ and knowing that this consonant is preceded by a nasal, one can predict that the nasal is /n/. Similarly, if the final consonant is /p/, the nasal must be /m/. This redundancy hypothesis claims that children treat the nasal as an aspect of the consonant. They therefore ignore the nasal when they spell. The redundancy hypothesis, like the homorganicity hypothesis, predicts that children group the nasal with the final consonant. The redundancy hypothesis also predicts that children should rarely omit the nasals in words like *comes.* Here, the identity of the nasal is not predictable. Finally, the redundancy hypothesis predicts that beginning spellers should omit *all* segments that are partially redundant, not just nasals. For example, if the second consonant of an initial cluster is /p/, /t/, or

/k/, the first consonant must be /s/. The /s/, like a preconsonantal nasal, is partially redundant. Children should therefore omit the /s/ of *steak*.

Read favored the first hypothesis for the omission of preconsonantal nasals—the hypothesis that children represent the phonetic level of speech when they spell. As evidence, Read noted a relation between nasal duration in speech and nasal omissions in children's spelling. Phonetically, nasals are shorter before voiceless stops than before voiced stops (Malécot, 1960; Raphael et al., 1975). Correspondingly, Read's preschoolers (and my first graders) more often omitted nasals before voiceless stops than before voiced stops. Phonetically, nasals are shorter after /ɪ/, /ə/, and /æ/ than after other vowels (Malécot, 1960). In Read's study, too, children omitted nasals more often after /ɪ/, /ə/, and /æ/ than after other vowels. However, the ranking of the three vowels was not the same as in Malécot's study. Malécot reported that nasals are shortest after /æ/; Read reported most omissions after /ɪ/.

Read found further support for the phonetic spelling hypothesis in the results of several experiments (Read, 1975, pp. 108–112). These results suggest that children who spell *bent* as BET consider the spoken words *bent* and *bet* to differ in the vowel, as the phonetic spelling hypothesis predicts. They do not consider the two words to differ in the final consonant, as the homorganicity and redundancy hypotheses predict.

Read noted two problems for the hypothesis that children's spelling of nasals before voiceless obstruents represents the phonetic forms of these nasals. One problem comes from the results of another experiment (Read, 1975, pp. 112–115). For this experiment, Read used a computer to lengthen the nasals in the spoken words *can't, hunt,* and *mint.* Thirty first graders were asked to spell both the original and the modified versions of each word. The children were no less likely to omit the nasal when its duration was long than when its duration was normal. On the surface, this result does not support the hypothesis that children represent the durations of nasals in their spelling. As Read pointed out, however, hearing a few words with long preconsonantal nasals may not be enough to change children's ideas about the phonetic forms of nasals.

The second problem that Read noted for the phonetic spelling hypothesis is that nasals preceding voiced stops are relatively long. If duration were the only important factor, children should rarely omit nasals before voiced stops. For instance, they should rarely omit the /n/ of *stand.* Yet Read's preschoolers omitted nasals almost a quarter of the time in these contexts. I, too, observed many omissions of nasals before voiced stops. The short duration of nasals in certain contexts cannot be the *only* cause of nasal omissions in spelling.

The present findings allow me to further evaluate the three hypotheses proposed by Read. My results, even more strongly than Read's, speak against the homorganicity and redundancy hypotheses. The homorganicity hypothesis predicts that beginning spellers should omit consonants in all types of homorganic clusters. Omissions should be rare in nonhomorganic clusters. However, I did not find a significant difference between consonant omissions in homorganic and nonhomorganic clusters. The redundancy hypothesis predicts that children should omit the /s/ of initial /sp/, /st/, and /sk/. The first graders in the present study did not do this.

To the contrary, they often omitted the second consonants of /s/-stop clusters, spelling *steak* as SAEC rather than as TAEC.

What do my findings have to say about Read's preferred hypothesis for the omission of nasals in final clusters—the phonetic hypothesis? According to a strong version of this hypothesis, omissions of consonants in clusters should be confined to final clusters that consist of a nasal followed by a voiceless consonant. This is because nasals before voiceless consonants show a degree of shortening that is not observed for other consonants. However, first graders' consonant omissions are *not* confined to nasals before voiceless consonants. Children also omit nasals before voiced consonants, as in MOOS for *Moms*. They omit liquids and obstruents before voiced and voiceless consonants, writing *called* as CAD and *lets* as LAS. Nor are omissions confined to final clusters. Children also omit nasals, liquids, obstruents, and glides in initial clusters. They spell *snake* as SAK, *afraid* as AFAD, *steak* as SAEC, and *sweat* as SET. One cannot explain the omission of so many types of consonants in both initial and final clusters by appealing to phonetic properties that are specific to nasals in final clusters. A more general explanation must be invoked—one that applies to different types of consonant phonemes and to different types of clusters. Phonemic awareness is a likely candidate. In this view, beginning spellers sometimes omit consonants in clusters because they have difficulty segmenting syllables into phonemes. Segmentation difficulties occur for both final clusters and initial clusters, for both clusters that contain nasals and clusters that do not. Segmentation difficulties even occur, to some degree, for rimes that contain a vowel and a consonant, with no cluster at all. To a large extent, omissions of nasals in final clusters are a manifestation of a larger phenomenon.

Although children's difficulties in segmenting syllables into phonemes may explain many of their misspellings of nasal clusters, segmentation difficulties do not explain *all* of the misspellings. After all, omissions of nasals before voiceless obstruents were much more common than omissions of nasals before voiced obstruents and more common than omissions of liquids and obstruents in comparable positions of the syllable. These differences suggest that children have specific problems with final clusters of nasals and voiceless obstruents. These problems exist in addition to their general difficulties with clusters. What makes clusters like /nt/ and /ŋk/ especially difficult to spell?

Perhaps children's extra problems with nasal-voiceless obstruent final clusters stem from the phonetic properties of these clusters. In this view, Read's phonetic hypothesis is partially correct. Although children's errors on initial clusters and many of their errors on final clusters reflect a general difficulty in segmenting syllables into phonemes, the additional errors on nasal-voiceless obstruent final clusters reflect the very short duration of the nasals in these clusters. However, two pieces of evidence mitigate against even this weak form of the phonetic hypothesis. First, my results do not show a close relation between the duration of the nasal in a nasal-voiceless obstruent final cluster and children's tendency to omit it. According to Malécot (1960), nasals are shortest after /ɪ/, /ə/, and especially /æ/ in the speech of adults. Read found a similar pattern: Nasal omissions were more frequent after /ɪ/, /ə/, and /æ/ than after other vowels, although the ranking of /ɪ/, /ə/, and /æ/ was not the same as in Malécot's study. My results show even less agreement with Malécot's. Omissions of nasal before consonants were, if anything, more frequent after /i/ and /au/ (52.6%) than after /ɪ/, /ə/ and /æ/ (40.4% when *and* was eliminated from consideration, $p < .05$ for the difference by a chi-square test). Thus, children do not necessarily omit nasals most often when the nasals are shortest. A second problem with even a weak form of the phonetic spelling hypothesis is that, if children's spelling reflected the durations of segments at the phonetic level, effects of duration should not be confined to nasals. They should also occur for other phonemes. I did not find such effects. For example, vowels are shorter before voiceless stops than before voiced stops. However, the first graders did not omit vowels before voiceless stops any more often than vowels before voiced stops. There is no clear support for the hypothesis that children code the phonetic level of speech when they spell.

To understand why children omit nasals before voiceless obstruents more often than they omit the interior phonemes of other final clusters, it may be necessary to consider the nature of children's *phonemic* representations. Many first graders may consider a word like *bent* to contain three phonemes—/b/, /ɛ̃/ (i.e., nasalized /ɛ/), and /t/. They do not code the word with four phonemes, as adults do and as the conventional English writing system assumes. In contrast, children represent *bend* with the four phonemes /b/, /ɛ/, /n/, and /d/. If children's phonemic representations are as I have described, the spelling results follow nicely. Children often spell *bent* with the three letters *b, e,* and *t,* one for each phoneme. They use *e* for /ɛ̃/ because this phoneme is similar to /ɛ/. Children generally spell *bend* with four letters—*b, e, n,* and *d.* My different phonemic representation hypothesis fits with Read's finding that children who spell *bent* as BET consider the spoken words *bent* and *bet* to differ in the vowel. According to this hypothesis, children code the words as /b'ɛ̃t/ and /b'ɛt/. The two words differ only in their vowel phoneme. The phonemic hypothesis also fits with Read's finding that lengthening the /n/ of a word like *bent* does not make children any more likely to spell it with *n.* For purposes of spelling, children consult their internal phonemic representations of words. They do not consult the words' phonetic forms. Provided that children identify the word they hear as *bent,* its phonetic characteristics do not influence their spelling.

As children learn to read and write, they observe that *bent* is spelled with *n, jump* is spelled with *m,* and so on. Children's phonemic systems may change as a result. Children begin to represent the /ɛ̃/ of *bent* as /ɛ/ plus /n/ rather than as a single nasalized vowel.

The different phonemic representation hypothesis does not deny the importance of phonetic factors. The short duration of the /n/ of *bent* is what causes children to code the word as /b'ɛ̃t/ in the first place. According to the hypothesis, though, the influence of phonetic factors on spelling is *indirect.* When children are spelling a word, they consult the phonemic representation of the word as it is stored in their mental dictionary. Although the phonetic form that they hear determines which word is identified, this phonetic information is no longer active at the time that children spell the word. After all, phonetic information is ephemeral. It fades quickly from memory. It would be surprising if children relied on phonetic information to spell.

University of Virginia Research

According to the University of Virginia researchers, the earliest spellings in my study should belong to the semiphonetic stage of spelling development. At this stage, it is thought, children provide a partial mapping of the word's phonetic form. They represent some phones and omit others. Later in the school year, more of the spellings should belong to the phonetic stage and to higher stages of spelling development. During these stages, the Virginia researchers claim, omissions no longer occur.

If the Virginia researchers' use of the term phonetic parallels the use of this term by linguists, the implication is that beginning spellers represent speech at the phonetic level. This implication, I have argued, is not correct. The present results suggest that even beginners transcribe speech at the phonemic level rather than the phonetic level. Errors occur when the children's phonemic representations do not match those assumed by the conventional writing system. Errors also occur when children treat their representations wholistically, without parsing them into individual phonemes.

The Virginia researchers have not systematically addressed the question of *which* consonants and vowels are omitted during the semiphonetic stage of spelling development. My results show that the omissions are far from random. Certain consonants—those in stressed syllables, those in short words, and the first consonants of syllable onsets, to name a few—are usually represented. Other consonants—including those in unstressed syllables and those in the interior positions of clusters—are more often omitted. Children's early spellings are abbreviated, to be sure, but in a highly systematic manner.

A further problem for the Virginia theory is that omissions do not disappear at a certain point in spelling development. They persist for the most vulnerable consonants. Consider Becky, who would be a phonetic speller by the University of Virginia scheme during much of her first-grade year. She symbolized almost all of the segments in the many C'V, 'VC, and C'VC words she attempted, spelling *she* as HSE, *it* as IT, and *when* as WIN. With consonant clusters, however, Becky sometimes omitted the interior segments. She spelled *from* as FOM, *horse* as HOS, and *tried* as CID. The use of *c* for /t/ before /r/ is a hallmark of the phonetic stage according to Gentry (1982). Also, Becky sometimes omitted consonants in unstressed syllables, producing LAG for *collection*. Becky shows that a child who looks like a phonetic speller on simple words may look like a semiphonetic speller on more complex words.

According to the Virginia researchers, young children use their knowledge of letter names to help them spell words. Children at the semiphonetic and phonetic stages of development represent any sequence of sounds that matches the name of a letter with the corresponding letter. My findings do not support this claim. Here and in Chapter 7, I found differences among letters in the prevalence of letter-name spellings. Children are more likely to produce letter-name spellings for some letters than for others, and these differences reflect the linguistic properties of the letters' names.

Other Research on Children's Spelling of Syllable-Initial Consonant Clusters

An important question in the study of consonant omissions is whether children's omissions of nasals in final clusters are specific to nasals or whether they are one sign of a more general difficulty in segmenting spoken words into phonemes. To address this question, it is necessary to determine whether children omit other phonemes in clusters besides nasals. Do children omit consonants in initial clusters? Do children omit nonnasal consonants in final clusters? In this section, I discuss the research on initial clusters. The following section takes up the research on final clusters.

Read did not systematically address children's spelling of consonant clusters at the beginnings of syllables. However, several other investigators have done so, including Bruck and Treiman (1990), Marcel (1980), Miller and Limber (1985), and Treiman (1991). Their results show that children sometimes fail to spell the second consonants of two-consonant clusters at the beginnings of words. Omissions occur whether the second consonant is a sonorant or an obstruent and whether it is voiced or voiceless (Treiman, 1991). Importantly, children sometimes misspell a word like *blow* as BOW even when they have just pronounced it correctly.

In one experiment (Treiman, 1991, Study 5), I asked whether omissions of the second consonants of initial clusters occur only for clusters at the beginnings of words or whether they occur for all onset clusters. As discussed earlier in this chapter, the spellings of the first graders in the naturalistic study are not well suited for addressing this question. This is because the children attempted few one-morpheme words like *patrol* or *Madrid*—words that contain clusters that form the onset of a syllable within the word but not the onset of the word itself. In the experiment, first graders were asked to spell a number of words like *patrol*. These words contain a consonant cluster that, given our knowledge of syllabification, forms the onset of a syllable within the word.[3] The question is whether children sometimes misspell *patrol* as PATOL or PACOL, just as they sometimes misspell *troll* as TOL or COL. Errors like PATOL and PACOL for *patrol did* outnumber errors like PAROL. Apparently, first graders are more likely to omit the second consonant of an onset than the first consonant. This holds whether the onset is at the beginning of the word or in the middle of the word.

Other Research on Children's Spelling of Syllable-Final Consonant Clusters

Several researchers have replicated Read's finding that children sometimes fail to spell nasals in final consonant clusters (see Read, 1986). Most of the studies have examined only final clusters that contain nasals. There has been little research on whether English-speaking children also omit other types of consonants in final clusters.

Marcel (1980) did find that children and adults who had serious difficulties in spelling sometimes omitted liquids in liquid-stop final clusters. For example, these people sometimes spelled *help* as HAP; they sometimes spelled the nonword /dɛlp/ as DEP.

Extending Marcel's research to normal children, Zukowski and Treiman (1989) studied children in the second half of first grade. These children sometimes failed to spell liquids and obstruents that were the first consonants of final clusters. For example, children spelled the nonword /n'ɪld/ as NID and the nonword /p'æft/ as PATE. We also examined nonwords with final clusters containing nasals. Like previous researchers, we found that nasal omissions were more common before voiceless obstruents than before voiced obstruents. We also found that nasal omissions before voiceless obstruents were more common than omissions of liquids and obstruents before final consonants. The omission rate was 61% for nasals before voiceless obstruents; it was at least 20% lower for the first consonants of other final clusters. The children in the Zukowski and Treiman (1989) study were more likely to omit the first consonant of a final cluster when this consonant was a liquid (about 41% omissions) than when it was an an obstruent (about 13% omissions). The first graders in the naturalistic study did not show such a difference. Resolution of this discrepancy awaits further research.

Although questions remain, it is now clear that omissions of consonants in final clusters are not restricted to nasals. Children omit other types of consonants in word-final clusters, sometimes at fairly high rates. It is also clear that there is something about the nasals of nasal-voiceless obstruent clusters that makes them especially vulnerable to omission. This "something" could be the phonetic properties of nasals before voiceless obstruents, as Read and the Virginia researchers suggest. It could alternatively be the lack of a nasal phoneme in children's phonemic representations of words like *want,* as the phonemic hypothesis proposed here suggests. Additional research is needed to distinguish between these two proposals.

Other Research on Children's Omissions of Inflectional Suffixes

The first graders in this study sometimes misspelled *saved* as SAV or *screams* as SCEEN. The children were more likely to omit final consonants that were inflectional suffixes than final consonants that were not inflectional suffixes. Rubin (1988) reported similar results for final /t/ and /d/ in a spelling dictation test with kindergarteners and first graders. Specifically, children were more likely to omit /t/ and /d/ when they represented the past tense, as in *messed,* than when they did not represent the past tense, as in *dust.* Sterling (1983) found omissions of inflectional /t/, /d/, and /s/ in the compositions of twelve-year-old children. Thus, it appears that children sometimes omit inflectional suffixes. The omissions are not confined to first graders. The reasons for these omissions are not yet clear. Earlier, I suggested that children may make these errors when they forget about past tense or plurality as they are writing stories. However, this does not seem to be a complete explanation, since the same kinds of errors occurred in the single-word dictation test of Rubin (1988).

Other Research on Position Effects

In this study, children were less likely to omit phonemes at the beginnings or ends of syllables than phonemes in the middles of syllables. These position effects were seen for both vowels and consonants. Likewise, Stage and Wagner (1992) found that children in kindergarten through third grade were less likely to misspell phonemes at the beginnings and ends of syllables than phonemes in the middles of syllables. Stage and Wagner analyzed children's spellings as correct or incorrect; they did not distinguish between omission errors and substitution errors. In the Stage and Wagner study, errors were also more common for syllable-final consonants than for syllable-initial consonants. The majority of the items in the Stage and Wagner study were monosyllabic, so it is difficult to distinguish between effects of position in syllable and position in word based on the results of this study.

Implications

Classification of Spelling Errors

These results underline the importance of phonology in the classification of children's spelling errors. Consider the words *with* and *silk*. From a purely orthographic perspective, children should make the same kinds of errors on these two words. This is because the words are similar orthographically. Both begin with a consonant letter followed by a vowel letter and two more consonant letters. In fact, the first graders made different errors on words like *with* and words like *silk*. For words like *with,* errors like WIT (omissions of the last letter, from an orthographic point of view) outnumbered errors like WIH (omissions of the second-to-last letter). For words like *silk,* errors like SIK (omissions of the second-to-last letter) outnumbered errors like SIL (omissions of the last letter). The differences between the two types of words show that one must consider the sounds that the letters represent, not just the letters themselves. In particular, one must consider that the last two letters of *with* represent a single phoneme ($/\theta/$), whereas the last two letters of *silk* represent two separate phonemes ($/lk/$). As this example shows, one must classify children's spelling errors phonologically, not just orthographically.

Many researchers who have attempted to classify children's spelling errors from a phonological point of view have distinguished between phonologically legal spellings and phonologically illegal spellings. Many of the errors discussed in this chapter, such as SAEC for *steak* and HAPT for *helped,* fall into the illegal category. Although these spellings do not symbolize all the phonemes in the spoken words, they are almost surely attempts to represent the words' sounds. They are not attempts to reproduce the letters in the words' written forms. As these examples show, errors that are classified as illegal, like those that are classified as legal, may reflect a phonological approach to spelling. Children who produce illegal spellings do not necessarily rely on rote memory.

Children's Phonological Systems

Children's spellings reflect their knowledge of the sounds of English words. Thus, spelling can provide a window into children's phonological systems. In this section, I discuss what we can learn about children's phonological representations through examination of their spellings.

Stress. For purposes of spelling, children seem to distinguish two levels of stress—stressed syllables and unstressed syllables. In spelling, children do not differentiate syllables with primary stress and syllables with secondary stress. This finding is of interest in light of a debate within linguistics on the nature of English stress. Some linguists (e.g., Ladefoged, 1982) argue that there are only two levels of stress. Other linguists (e.g., Chomsky & Halle, 1968; Gleason, 1961; Kenyon, 1969) claim that there are more than two levels of stress. My findings suggest that, as far as children's spelling is concerned, English syllables are either stressed or unstressed. Although children distinguish primary and secondary stress when they speak, they consider this distinction too subtle or too low-level to be reflected in spelling.

Children's spellings further suggest that they consider stress to be a property of the syllable as a whole, not a property of just the vowel or just the rime. As a result, children omit both consonants and vowels in unstressed syllables. This finding is of interest in light of a debate within linguistics on the carrier of word stress. According to some linguists (e.g., Chomsky & Halle, 1968), stress is a property of the vowel. According to many other linguists (e.g., M. Liberman & Prince, 1977), stress is carried by the syllable. My results support the latter view.

Affricates. Linguists disagree on the status of the English affricates /tʃ/ and /dʒ/. Some linguists consider these affricates to be single phonemes. Others consider them to be sequences of a stop consonant followed by a fricative consonant. My results suggest that at least some first graders are sensitive to the two-part nature of affricates. The children in this study sometimes symbolized only the first (or stop) portion of an affricate, as in TESE for *cheese* (see Chapter 5). They rarely symbolized only the second (or fricative) portion of an affricate. This difference suggests that the first part of the stop-fricative "cluster" is more salient than the second part.

Children's spellings of onset clusters are similar, in some ways, to their spellings of affricates. Children sometimes spelled the onset cluster /tw/ with just *t* but rarely spelled it with just *w*. The first part of the cluster seems to be more salient than the second part, just as it is for affricates.

Although children's spellings of both affricates and onset clusters point to a greater salience for the first element of the sequence than the second, children's spellings of affricates and of onset clusters are not completely alike. With affricates, the first graders never produced two-part spellings like *tsh* for /tʃ/, which represent both the stop and the fricative. With clusters like /tw/, two-part spellings like *tw* were common. A major reason for this difference is that spellings like *tsh* for /tʃ/ never occur in English, whereas spellings like *tw* for /tw/ do. Children produce sequences like *tw* because they have seen such spellings. Another reason, however, may lie in phonological differences between the stop-fricative "clusters" that make up affricates and clusters like /tw/. The stop and fricative elements of the /tʃ/ and /dʒ/ "clusters" form a tighter unit than the two phonemes of onset clusters such as /tw/. Research with kindergarten and first-grade children supports this claim. In a previous study (Treiman, 1985b), I found that children have more difficulty deleting the /t/ of /tʃ'o/, forming /ʃ'o/, than deleting the /t/ of /tw'o/, forming /w'o/. Thus, although at least some first graders appreciate the two-part nature of affricates, the two parts of an affricate form a strong unit.

Children's Phonemic Representations. Children's phonemic representations sometimes differ from those assumed by the conventional English writing system. I discuss two such cases here—syllabic liquids and nasals before voiceless obstruents.

Some first graders seem to represent syllabic liquids as single phonemes rather than as sequences of two phonemes. These children consider *her* to be /h/ followed by syllabic /r/ rather than /h/ followed by /ə/ followed by /r/. Children classify the syllabic liquids /r/ and /l/ as similar to the nonsyllabic liquids /r/ and /l/. When spelling *her* and *little,* therefore, they often write HR and LITL. Children symbolize the syllabic liquid with a single grapheme, a grapheme that is appropriate for /r/ or /l/, rather than with two graphemes.

Although first graders seem to represent syllabic liquids as single phonemes, they do not seem to represent syllabic nasals in this way. Children consider syllabic nasals to be sequences of two phonemes—an unstressed /ə/ followed by a nasal consonant. Thus, the second syllable of *Jason* contains /ə/ followed by /n/. Because children's phonemic representations match those assumed by the English writing system in this case, children have less difficulty learning the conventional spelling of *Jason* than the conventional spelling of *little* or *brother.*

Another case in which some first graders' phonemic representations seem to differ from those assumed by the English writing system is that of nasals before voiceless obstruents. Some first graders, it appears, consider *jump* to be /dʒʌ̃p/ rather than /dʒəmp/. They classify the nasalized vowel /ʌ̃/ as similar to the nonnasalized vowel /ə/. Thus, the children often misspell *jump* as JUP, using *u* for /ʌ̃/.

With syllabic liquids and nasalized vowels, exposure to print may change children's phonemic representations. Before they learn to read and write, children may consider the phonemic form of *jump* to contain an initial consonant, a nasalized vowel, and a single final consonant. For them, this word contains three phonemes rather than four. As children learn that this word and others like it are spelled with four letters, they add a nasal phoneme to their representation. Similarly, prereaders may consider *her* to contain two phonemes rather than three. As they learn that this and similar words are spelled with a vowel letter and *r,* rather than with just *r,* they may add a vowel to their phonemic representations.

Alternatively, learning to read and write may teach children certain orthographic conventions but may not change their phonemic representations. In this view, children learn that syllabic /r/ is spelled with a vowel letter and *r* but continue to think of it as a single phoneme. In the same way, children learn that /θ/ is spelled with *t* followed by *h* but still consider it a single phoneme.

Access to Phonemes. In the cases just discussed—syllabic liquids and nasalized vowels—children may misspell words because their phonemic representations do not match those assumed by the English writing system. In other cases, there is no such mismatch. Yet children still misspell words because of a difficulty in accessing certain phonemes. Children treat some groups of phonemes as units rather than as sequences of separate segments. In these cases, misspellings reflect incomplete phonemic awareness rather than unconventional phonemic representations.

The first graders' spellings suggest that several phoneme groups are difficult for them to analyze. One such group consists of a vowel phoneme followed by a liquid. When a word contains such a sequence, and when the sequence matches the name of an English letter, first graders sometimes use this letter to spell the entire sequence. Thus, children sometimes symbolize the /ɛl/ of *help* with *l* rather than *el.* Because /ɛl/ is difficult to segment, and because they already have a strong link between /ɛl/ and *l,* children sometimes spell /ɛl/ with *l.*

Another unit that is difficult for first graders to analyze is a two- or three-consonant cluster at the beginning of a syllable. Some first graders treat syllable-initial /bl/ as a unit. They spell it with a single *b* instead of *b* followed by *l.* In addition, some first graders have difficulty abstracting consonants from vowel-final consonant rimes. As a result, children are more likely to omit the final consonant of a syllable than the initial consonant of a syllable.

Children's difficulty in analyzing certain sequences of phonemes may be interpreted in light of hierarchical theories of syllable structure. Phonemes that belong to the same constituent of the syllable form a unit and so are difficult to separate. Initial consonants and consonant clusters are one constituent of the syllable, the onset. Some first graders have difficulty segmenting cluster onsets into phonemes. Vowels and following consonants are another constituent of the syllable, the rime. Some first graders have difficulty abstracting consonants from rimes. Within rimes, vowel-liquid sequences cause special difficulty. This may be because vowels and following liquids form a subunit of the rime, the peak.

The Teaching of Spelling

There are at least two reasons why a child may fail to spell a phoneme. First, the child's phonemic representation of the word may not match the representation assumed by the English writing system. Second, the child may represent a word in the conventional manner but may treat certain groups of phonemes as units for spelling purposes. Analyses of spelling errors can suggest their underlying causes and, in turn, suggest what type of feedback will be most effective.

Consider, first, those errors that reflect mismatches between the phonemic system of the child and the phonemic system assumed by the conventional system. One such error, I have suggested, is WAT for *want.* To a child, this word contains three phonemes—an initial consonant, a nasalized vowel, and a final consonant. It does *not* contain a separate nasal consonant. If the child's phonemic representation is /wãt/, the child who produces WOT possesses many of the skills that are required for spelling. The child accurately perceives the spoken word, analyzes it into phonemes, and symbolizes each phoneme with an appropriate grapheme. The only problem is that the phonemic form being analyzed is the child's own. It is not the form assumed by conventional English.

Given the knowledge revealed in errors like WAT for *want,* first-grade teachers can find much to praise in these errors. Corrections, if made at all, should be made gently. For example, one might say that WAT is a good attempt to spell *want* but that this word happens to contain *n.* It would be unwise to imply that the child should have known to include *n* based on the word's sound. After all, the child who spells *want* as WAT is in the same boat as the child who spells *been* as BIN. In both cases, the child has symbolized each phoneme in his or her representation of the word—the /w/, the /ã/ and the /t/ of *want* and the /b/, /ɪ/, and /n/ in the American pronunciation of *been*. Based on the words' sounds, the child has no reason to include *n* in *want* and no reason to include two *e*s in *been*. These aspects of conventional spelling must be memorized; they cannot be inferred from the words' sounds. Just as one would not ask a child to listen for the double *e* in *been*, knowing full well that this word does not contain the typical long *e* sound, so one should not ask a child to listen for the *n* in *want*.

Other consonant omissions occur when children treat groups of phonemes as units for spelling purposes. Here, the problem lies in the grouping of phonemes within children's phonemic representations rather than in unconventional phonemic representations. At some level, first graders probably represent *blow* as /bl'o/, as adults do. However, many first graders treat /b/ and /l/ as a unit. Consequently, they may spell the word as BOW. These children need help in segmenting the spoken word into phonemes. They need to learn that the /bl/ cluster consists of /b/ and /l/. That errors like BOW for *blow* continue into the second half of first grade suggests that the analysis of clusters does need to be taught. Some children do not develop this ability quickly and easily on their own.

Children's skill at analyzing clusters in spoken words can be improved through games with spoken words. For instance, children can be introduced to a puppet that "talks funny." The puppet says *cat* as *at*, *pin* as *in*, and so on. First graders can master such items with little difficulty (Bruck & Treiman, 1990). Once children succeed with words like *cat* and *pin*, they can play the same game with words like *blow*. Children's first response may well be *oh*—a deletion of the entire onset (Bruck & Treiman, 1990). Children can be told that, if just a small part of the word's beginning is deleted, the answer is *low*. After playing the phoneme-deletion game with words like *blow, bread*, and *play*, children will begin to learn that /bl/, /br/, and /pl/ consist of two phonemes. They will learn that the phonemes can be manipulated independently, that they do not have to be treated as a unit. Once children can access the individual phonemes of clusters like /bl/, they should begin to spell the clusters correctly.

Most first graders who misspell blow as BOW do not need extra drill on the correspondence between /l/ and *l*. After a few months in first grade, most children know perfectly well that /l/ is spelled with *l*. When /l/ occurs in an accessible position within a spoken word, as in *love* and *alone*, children almost always spell it with *l*. The reason that children sometimes fail to spell the /l/ of /bl/ is that they lack awareness of the /l/ in the /bl/ onset. The cure is phonemic-awareness training, not drill on letter-sound correspondences.

Errors like BOW for *blow* show that learning correspondences between phonemes and graphemes is just one part of learning to spell. For some words, it is a relatively small part. Children must also learn to segment spoken words into phonemes. For example, in addition to learning that /l/ is spelled with *l*, children must learn to recognize /l/ when it occurs within a word. This phoneme is fairly easy to recognize in *love* and *alone* but is hard to recognize in *blow* and *milk*. We cannot teach children how to spell isolated phonemes and expect them to spell new words. We must also teach children how to segment spoken words into phonemes.

Notes

1. The omission rate is probably higher for consonants in secondary-stressed syllables than for consonants in primary-stressed syllables because words that contain secondary-stressed syllables are relatively long. Children are more likely to omit consonants in long words than in short words.

2. The reader may have noticed that the omission rates for the interior consonants of syllable-final clusters did not appear to exceed the omission rates for the interior consonants of syllable-initial clusters, as would be expected if consonants are more often omitted in rimes than in onsets. However, the results are skewed by the many instances of the word *and*. The children made few omissions on the phonemes of this word. When the results for *and* were removed from consideration, the omission rate for the interior consonants of syllable-final clusters was higher than the omission rate for the interior consonants of syllable-initial clusters.

3. The experiment also included words like *April,* with a "long" vowel followed by a consonant cluster that is legal at the beginning of a syllable. In an experiment by Treiman and Zukowski (1990), adults generally treated such clusters as syllable-initial. There was evidence that the children in the experiment did the same.

9

Reversals

So far, in studying how children spell phonemes, I have discussed three kinds of spellings that children may produce. First, children may spell the phoneme correctly. Second, children may use an incorrect spelling in place of the correct spelling. Third, children may fail to spell the phoneme altogether. In this chapter, I consider yet another type of error. This error, a reversal error, involves a *pair* of phonemes. In a reversal error, a child symbolizes both phonemes in a pair, either correctly or incorrectly. The error arises because the child transcribes the phonemes in the wrong order. For example, the child who spelled *and* as NAD presumably intended *n* to symbolize /n/ (a correct spelling), *a* to symbolize /æ/ (a correct spelling), and *d* to symbolize /d/ (also a correct spelling). Although the child represented each phoneme in the word, she placed the letter for /n/ before the letter for /æ/. That is, she reversed /æ/ and /n/. In this chapter, I ask when and why such errors occur.

The study of reversals takes on particular significance given the importance that has sometimes been attached to such errors. Reversals of letter sequence as in NAD for *and,* like reversals of individual letters as in DAT for *bat,* have often been seen as symptoms of spelling and reading disability. For example, Orton (1937) viewed these errors as signs of brain dysfunction. He claimed that the errors reflect a failure to establish normal hemispheric dominance for language. Contrary to Orton's claims, it appears that reversals in reading are better explained in terms of orthographic knowledge than in terms of minimal brain dysfunction (I.Y. Liberman, Shankweiler, Orlando, Harris, & Berti, 1971). Misreadings like *was* for *saw* are not limited to disabled readers. They also occur among normal beginners. In this chapter, I ask whether the same holds true for spelling. Do normal beginning spellers sometimes make reversal errors? If so, when do these errors occur?

Traditionally, reversal errors have been defined orthographically, with regard to the letters in the word's conventional printed form. Children are said to make a reversal error when they use the right letters but place the letters in the wrong order. This definition of reversal errors is based on a view of spelling as the reproduction of letters from a memorized sequence. The present view of spelling is rather different. In this view, spelling is largely an attempt to represent the phonological forms of words. Therefore, reversal errors are defined with regard to the sequence of *pho-*

nemes in the spoken word rather than with regard to the sequence of *letters* in the printed word.

Sometimes, as with NAD for *and,* a reversal of two phonemes from the spoken form of the word (/æ/ and /n/) gives the same result as a reversal of two letters from the printed form of the word (*a* and *n*). However, this is not always true. Consider the error MI for *am.* I assume that *m* represents /m/ (a correct spelling) and that *i* represents /æ/ (a substitution error). The child who spelled *am* as MI reversed /æ/ and /m/. However, this child did *not* make a reversal error according to the traditional orthographic definition. Indeed, only 14% of all the errors that were reversals from the phonemic point of view were also reversals from the orthographic point of view.

The phonemic transcriptions described in Chapter 1 were used to define reversal errors. For example, because I coded *her* as containing /ə/, HRE involves a reversal of /ə/ and /r/. HRE was therefore included in the tally of reversal errors. I argue later, however, that HRE may *not* actually be a phoneme reversal from the child's viewpoint.

In this chapter, I focus on cases in which the conventional spelling of the word does not include a phoneme reversal. For example, LITLE for /lɪtəl/ *(little)* was not counted as a reversal error because the conventional spelling of /əl/ in this word is *le* rather than *el* or *ul.* The rates of reversal errors reported in this chapter are based on the number of reversals relative to the number of cases in which the conventional spelling of the word does not contain a reversal.

Although the first graders made some reversal errors, these errors were not very common. My collection of 5,617 spellings, which included 2,740 misspelled words, contained only 105 reversal errors. Eighty-eight of the reversals involved a pair of adjacent phonemes. In NAD for *and,* for example, the reversed phonemes /æ/ and /n/ are adjacent to one other in the spoken word. The remaining reversals involved nonadjacent phonemes or were ambiguous.

Although reversal errors were not all that common, the significance that has been attached to these errors in the learning disabilities literature makes it important to understand when and why these errors occurred. If the errors typically represent the reversal of phonemes, as I propose, they should be affected by the phonological properties of words. For instance, reversals may be more common with some types of phoneme pairs than with others. If reversals typically represent the misordering of letters from a memorized sequence, then the phonemes that these letters represent should be of little importance. As I show, reversal errors were more common with some types of phonemes than with others, suggesting that these errors are largely phonological in nature.

Factors Associated with Reversals of Adjacent Phonemes

In this section, I discuss the factors that were associated with reversal errors. The discussion focuses on reversals of adjacent phonemes, which were the most common type of reversal error.

VC Reversals Versus Other Reversals

In the reversal errors presented so far, including NAD for *and* and MI for *am,* the child reversed a vowel phoneme and a following consonant phoneme. NAD and MI may be called VC reversals. Other reversal errors are also possible. In a CV reversal, the child misorders a consonant and a following vowel. In PEPIS for *Pepsi,* for example, the child symbolized /s/ and /i/ in the wrong order. CC reversals are also possible, as in LEST for *lets.* Here, the consonants /t/ and /s/ were misordered. VV reversals are a final possibility, as in JEO for *Joey.*

If reversal errors represent the misordering of letters from a memorized sequence, then it should not matter whether the letters represent vowels or consonants. Relative to their opportunity for occurrence, VC, CV, CC, and VV reversals should all be about equally common. On the other hand, if reversal errors represent the misordering of phonemes from a spoken form, some types of reversals may be more frequent than others. This is what I found. VC reversals were more common than CV, CC, or VV reversals. VC reversals occurred 72 times, representing 1.5% of the children's spellings of vowel-consonant sequences that were conventionally spelled with a vowel grapheme followed by a consonant grapheme. CV reversals occurred 8 times, which corresponds to 0.2% of the children's spellings of consonant-vowel sequences. CC reversals were also quite rare. The 8 CC reversals in my collection represented only 0.4% of the children's spellings of consonant-consonant sequences. Finally, the children made no VV reversals. The rates of CV, CC, and VV reversals did not differ reliably from one another. However, VC reversals were significantly more common than the CV, CC, and VV types ($p < .001$ by chi-square tests). That VC reversals were more frequent than other reversals supports the idea that reversals are not solely an orthographic phenomenon. These errors are affected by the phonological forms of words.

Why were children more likely to reverse a vowel and a following consonant than to reverse other pairs of adjacent phonemes? Part of the answer is that many VC reversals involved syllabic liquids. Returning to the example given earlier, HRE for *her* was coded as a reversal of /ə/ and the following /r/ because /ə/ and /r/ were transcribed as separate phonemes. However, findings reported elsewhere in this book suggest that children consider /ə/ and /r/ to be a single unit, syllabic /r/. Children make errors like HRE because they sometimes spell syllabic /r/ with *r* followed by a vowel letter rather than with a vowel letter followed by *r.* For children, HRE for *her* does *not* involve a reversal of two phonemes. Similar errors occurred with syllabic /l/, as in ANMLOS for *animals.* The children reversed /ər/ and /əl/ in 8.7% of their attempts to spell syllabic liquids that were conventionally spelled with a vowel grapheme followed by a consonant grapheme. They misordered other VC sequences 0.9% of the time—significantly less according to a chi-square test ($p < .001$) and according to the results of statistical analyses discussed later in this chapter. I discuss reversals with syllabic liquids in more detail later.

Thus, one reason that VC reversals outnumbered other types of reversals is that many VC reversals involved syllabic liquids. However, reversal errors on syllabic liquids do not explain the *entire* difference between VC reversals and other reversals. Even when syllabic liquids were not considered, the rate of VC reversals, at

0.9%, exceeded the 0.2% average rate for CV, CC, and VV reversals ($p < .001$ by a chi-square test).

Why were VC reversals more common than CV, CC, and VV reversals even when syllabic liquids were discounted? The reason may lie in the structure of the English syllable. Recall that, according to many linguists and psycholinguists, spoken syllables contain two main units (see Fig. 1.6). These are the onset and the rime. The onset of a syllable is its initial consonant or consonant cluster; the rime contains the vowel and any following consonants. The rime itself has two parts, the peak and the coda. The peak includes the vowel. According to Selkirk (1982), the peak may also contain a sonorant (i.e., liquid or nasal) consonant that follows the vowel.[1] Any other consonants form the syllable's coda. Thus, *milk* has the onset /m/ and the rime /ɪlk/. The peak is /ɪl/ and the coda is /k/.

How might the grouping of phonemes such as the /ɪ/ and /l/ of *milk* lead to misspellings like MLIK? There are at least two ways in which this could occur. The first possible source of the misspellings lies in the analysis of the spoken word into phonemes. If the /ɪ/ and /l/ of *milk* form a unit, children may have difficulty segmenting this unit into phonemes and ascertaining the order of the phonemes within it. Children may sometimes analyze the word into /m/, /l/, /ɪ/, and /k/ and so spell the word as MLIK. A second possible explanation for the reversals lies in children's ability to remember the phonemes in the spoken word. Suppose that a child has correctly segmented *milk* into /m/, /ɪ/, /l/, and /k/. When placing the phonemes into short-term memory, the child codes them as three groups—/m/, /ɪ/ plus /l/, and /k/. Because the phonemes /ɪ/ and /l/ are encoded together, the two phonemes may sometimes be misordered at recall. A child who recalls the phonemes in the order /m/, /l/, /ɪ/, and /k/ may misspell the word as MLIK.

That VC reversals were more common than other types of reversals is consistent with the hypothesis that reversals tend to involve phonemes from the same unit of the syllable. Except when a syllable boundary intervenes, a vowel and a following consonant belong to the same unit of the syllable, the rime. In some cases, as with the /ɪ/ and /l/ of *milk,* the vowel and consonant both also belong to the peak. Although VC sequences often belong to the same constituent of the syllable, CV sequences and VV sequences never do. Even when a consonant and a following vowel are part of the same syllable, the consonant is in the onset and the vowel is in the rime. And when two vowel phonemes follow one another in a spoken word, they always belong to different syllables. (The case of CC reversals is discussed presently.)

As a more stringent test of the idea that reversals tend to involve phonemes from the same unit of the syllable, I examined reversals in one-syllable words that did not contain syllabic liquids. In a one-syllable word, no syllable boundaries separate any of the phonemes. To compare VC and CV reversals within a syllable, I focused on words that presented the same number of opportunities for the two types of reversals. In this restricted sample of words, all VC reversals are reversals of phonemes from the rime. In some cases, they may also be reversals of phonemes from the peak. All CV reversals involve a phoneme from the onset and a phoneme from the rime. In the sample of words under consideration, the children made 17 VC reversals. Examples are HLAP for *help* and HROS for *horse.* The children made only 2

CV reversals, as in FORM for *from*. Although the numbers are small, the difference between VC reversals and CV reversals was significant ($p < .001$ by a chi-square test). The predominance of VC reversals suggests that the reversed phonemes generally belong to the same constituent of the syllable.

But to *which* syllable constituent do the vowels and following consonants that participate in VC reversals belong? In all cases in the foregoing analysis, the vowel and the consonant that were reversed belonged, by definition, to the syllable's rime. In every case, it turned out, the two phonemes also belonged to the syllable's peak, where the peak is defined as a vowel and a following sonorant consonant. Thus, the VC reversals observed here may actually be reversals of phonemes from the syllable peak.

Further evidence that peaks are critical comes from the finding that, in general, children were more likely to reverse vowels and following sonorant consonants than vowels and following obstruents ($p < .001$ by a chi-square test and also significant by regression analyses described later in this chapter). The reversal rate for vowel-sonorant sequences was 1.8% when syllabic liquids were eliminated from consideration. An example is HROS for *horse*, which involves a reversal of a vowel and a sonorant, specifically a vowel and a liquid. The reversal rate for vowel-obstruent sequences was lower, only 0.2%. One of the few examples is CRSMSE for *Christmas*, in which a vowel (the /ə/ of the second syllable) and a following obstruent (/s/) are misordered. The higher reversal rate for vowel-sonorant sequences than vowel-obstruent sequences suggests that reversals tend to involve phonemes from the syllable's peak.

Given other evidence that vowels and following liquids are more strongly linked than vowels and following nasals, it is of interest to compare the reversal rates for these two types of vowel-sonorant sequences. The reversal rates were 3.1% for liquids and 1.3% for nasals; this difference was not significant according to analyses reported later in this chapter.

If phonemes from the syllable's peak sometimes participate in reversal errors, does the same hold true for phonemes from other constituents of the syllable? For example, do children sometimes reverse pairs of consonants from the coda or pairs of consonants from the onset? Although the overall rate of CC reversals was low, not all CC sequences belong to an onset or to a coda. Sometimes two adjacent consonants belong to separate syllables; sometimes one consonant belongs to the peak of a syllable and the other to the coda. To determine whether children reverse consonants within codas and consonants within onsets, it is necessary to examine cases in which both consonants belong to a coda or an onset.

To study reversals of consonants within the coda, I looked at words that ended with VCC sequences and that did not contain syllabic liquids. In such words, the VCC is the rime of the syllable. Also, there are the same number of opportunities for VC reversals and CC reversals. Table 9.1 shows the numbers and percentages of VC and CC reversals in these rimes, broken down by the type of consonant after the vowel. When the consonant that followed the vowel was a sonorant, reversals generally involved the VC, which may be the syllable's peak. In this case, there were 14 VC reversals and only 2 CC reversals. When the consonant after the vowel was an obstruent, only three reversals occurred. All three involved the obstruent and

Table 9.1. Numbers of VC and CC Reversals as a Function of Type of Consonant After Vowel in Word-Final VCC Rimes that do not Contain Syllabic Liquids (error rate as a percentage of opportunities for error is in parentheses)

	Type of Reversal	
	VC	CC
First graders' classroom spellings		
Type of consonant after vowel		
Sonorant	14 (2.4)	2 (0.3)
Obstruent	0 (0.0)	3 (1.8)
Experiment with CVCCs (Zukowski & Treiman, 1989)		
Type of consonant after vowel		
Sonorant	12 (0.8)	4 (0.3)
Obstruent	0 (0.0)	10 (2.8)
Experiment with CVCCs (unpublished)		
Type of consonant after vowel		
Sonorant	10 (1.1)	0 (0.0)
Obstruent	0 (0.0)	2 (1.1)

the consonant that followed it, which was also an obstruent. These two consonants belong to the syllable's coda. Examples are LEST for *lets* and OSG for *hogs*. Although the numbers are small, the association between type of reversal (VC versus CC) and type of consonant after the vowel (sonorant versus obstruent) was significant ($p = .01$ by a Fisher exact test). The CC reversals in rimes like /ɛts/ and /ɔgz/ suggest that children occasionally reverse consonants from a syllable's coda.

The children did not make any reversals that involved two phonemes from the onset of a syllable. For example, the children never misspelled *blue* as LBOO or *afraid* as ARFAD. For all of the CC reversals in which syllabification was clear, both consonants belonged to the syllable's rime. Because of the small numbers involved, however, the lack of reversals within the onset could have been an accidental gap.

The results on within-rime reversals suggest that different English rimes have different linguistic properties and different effects on spelling. For rimes like /ɪlk/, which contain a vowel, a sonorant consonant, and a final consonant, the vowel and the sonorant form the stronger unit. A reversal, if it occurs, will probably involve these two phonemes. For rimes like /ɔgz/, which contain a vowel followed by two obstruents, the obstruents have the tighter bond. If a reversal occurs, it will involve these two consonants. These results may be interpreted in light of hierarchical theories of syllable structure such as that of Selkirk (1982). According to Selkirk, a vowel and a following sonorant may form a unit, the syllable peak. Any other consonants in the rime make up the coda. Thus, the two strongest bonds within the rime are that between the vowel and a following sonorant consonant and that between the consonants in an obstruent-obstruent final cluster. The other bonds between phonemes in the rime are weaker.

To summarize, the children were more likely to reverse vowels and following consonants than other pairs of phonemes. This held true even when syllabic liquids were eliminated from consideration. The consonants involved in VC reversal errors were likely to be sonorants. Children probably represent a word like *horse* as containing four phonemes—/h/, /o/, /r/, and /s/. However, /o/ and /r/ form a unit in children's phonemic representations. Children have some difficulty segmenting /or/ into phonemes and ascertaining or remembering the order of the phonemes within the unit. This difficulty causes them to sometimes misspell the word as HROS.

Syllabic Liquids

If children spell by reproducing previously memorized strings of letters, errors like HNE for *hen* should be as common as errors like HRE for *her*. After all, both errors reverse the second and third letters of a three-letter word. The phonemes that the letters symbolize should not matter. The results do not support this orthographic hypothesis. The children misordered the *e* and *r* of words like *her* (i.e., words with syllabic liquids) much more often than they misordered the *e* and *n* of words like *hen* (i.e., words with other VC sequences). The reversal rate was 8.7% for syllabic liquids as compared with 0.9% for other VC sequences. Some additional examples of reversal errors on syllabic liquids are shown in Table 9.2. The different results for words like *her* and words like *hen* imply that spelling involves more than the rote memorization of letter sequences. To understand why errors like HRE for *her* outnumber errors like HNE for *hen,* one must consider the sounds of the words, not just their conventional spellings.

Although *hen* and *her* are similar orthographically, they are different phonologically. The spoken form of *hen* contains three phonemes—/h/, /ɛ/, and /n/. For children, *her* probably contains only two phonemes—/h/ followed by syllabic /r/. If so, HRE does not actually involve a reversal of two separate phonemes. In contrast, HNE for *hen* is a true phoneme reversal.

Children's different phonemic representations for words like *her* and *hen* can explain why they spell these two types of words differently. Because children have no separate vowel phoneme in *her,* they are not sure whether the printed form of this word should contain a vowel grapheme. Even if they remember that the printed word contains a vowel, they may forget where the vowel goes. Thus, children may misspell the word as HR, without a vowel letter, or as HRE, with the vowel in the wrong place. Because children *do* have a vowel phoneme in their representation of *hen,* they usually include a vowel grapheme in their spelling. Because the vowel phoneme in the spoken word is surrounded by two consonant phonemes, children

Table 9.2. Reversal Errors Involving Syllabic Liquids

Type of Syllabic Liquid	Examples
Stressed syllabic /r/	HRE for *her* BRID for *bird* WRIK for *work*
Unstressed syllabic /r/	TETRE for *teacher* SALRE for *cellar* ATRE for *other*
Unstressed syllabic /l/	ANMLOS for *animals* ANLIS for *animals*

usually place the vowel grapheme in the middle of the printed word, surrounded by two consonant graphemes. Children do not often make errors like HN or HNE for *hen*.

As shown in Chapters 7 and 8, children often use *r* or *l,* without a vowel letter, to symbolize a syllabic liquid. Indeed, almost half of the children's spellings of syllabic /r/s and /l/s whose conventional spelling contained a vowel grapheme followed by *r* or *l* were single *r* or single *l.* The children's next most common spelling, occurring about a quarter of the time, was a vowel grapheme followed by *r* or *l.* Reversal errors were the third most common type of spelling, occurring about 9% of the time. These results suggest that children prefer to symbolize each phoneme in a spoken word with a single letter. Because *her* contains /h/ followed by syllabic /r/, children often spell the word as HR. When children *do* use two letters to represent syllabic /r/, they are not always sure whether the vowel letter should precede the consonant letter or vice versa.

One would expect errors like HRE for *her* to emerge gradually, as children learn about the conventional English writing system. Children who at first spell *her* as HR may begin to include a vowel letter as they see that almost all English words contain a vowel. Words like **hr* and **grl* do not occur. Because children's phonological knowledge does not specify the location of the vowel, they sometimes put the vowel in the wrong place, spelling *her* as HRE. To test the hypothesis that errors like HRE for *her* emerge as children learn about the conventional English writing system, I compared the rate of these errors during the two semesters of the school year. The rate of reversal errors on syllabic liquids was 6.8% during the first semester and 9.4% during the second semester, a small increase. For VCs that were not syllabic liquids, the reversal rate was 1.2% during the first semester and 0.8% during the second semester, a slight decrease. The interaction between type of sequence (syllabic liquid versus other VC) and semester (first versus second) was significant ($p < .05$ by a chi-square test). These results suggest that errors like HRE for *her* are in some sense more advanced than errors like HR. Moreover, the different patterns for syllabic liquids as compared with other VCs confirm that reversal errors on syllabic liquids are different from other VC reversals.

I have argued that errors like HRE for *her* outnumber errors like HNE for *hen* for phonological reasons. Children represent the first word as containing two phonemes and the second word as containing three phonemes. Because the words' phonological forms differ, children spell them differently. However, there is another possible interpretation of the results. Children may make errors like HRE for *her* because they have seen printed words like *acre* and *little*—words in which syllabic /r/ and /l/ are spelled with *re* and *le* rather than with a vowel followed by *r* or *l.* In this view, children rarely make errors like HNE for *hen* because sequences like /ɛ/ plus /n/ are never spelled with *n* followed by *e.*

If children spell syllabic liquids with a consonant followed by a vowel because of their familiarity with words like *acre* and *little,* these errors should be most common for syllabic /l/. This is because *le* spellings are fairly widespread, as in *little, table,* and *uncles.* Reversals should be less common for unstressed syllabic /r/, which is occasionally spelled as *re*, as in *acre.* They should be least common for stressed syllabic /r/, which to my knowledge is never spelled as *re.* The results did not support these predictions. The rate of reversal errors was 5.4% for unstressed syllabic /l/, 7.7% for unstressed syllabic /r/, and 11.2% for stressed syllabic /r/. These figures did not differ significantly from one another by a chi-square test. Clearly, children's reversals are not confined to cases in which reversals occur in conventional English. Although exposure to printed words like *acre* may contribute to errors like SALRE for *cellar,* it cannot be the only cause of these errors. Children's phonological representations are also important.

Stress

Another linguistic factor that was associated with reversal errors was stress. Consider VC reversals. These errors occurred at a rate of 1.0% when the vowel had primary or secondary stress. When the vowel was not stressed, the rate was 4.5%, significantly higher ($p < .001$ by a chi-square test and also significant according to the results of regression analyses described later in this chapter). VC reversals in unstressed syllables occur in CRSMSE for *Christmas,* where the vowel and final consonant of the unstressed second syllable are misordered, and GONI for *going,* where a reversal also occurs in the unstressed second syllable.

Why were children more likely to reverse phonemes in unstressed syllables than phonemes in stressed syllables? Perhaps children have more trouble analyzing syllables into phonemes when the syllables are not stressed than when the syllables are stressed. As a result, children more often omit phonemes in unstressed syllables than phonemes in stressed syllables (Chapters 7 and 8). When children *do* symbolize the phonemes in unstressed syllables, they sometimes spell them in the wrong order.

The effect of stress on reversal errors supports the idea that most reversals reflect the misordering of phonemes. If reversals represented the misordering of letters from a memorized sequence, the errors should be no more common when the letters stand for phonemes in unstressed syllables than when the letters stand for phonemes in stressed syllables. As I argue throughout this book, one cannot understand children's spelling errors without considering the phonological forms of words.

Word Length

There was a reliable effect of word length on VC reversals. Once other factors were taken into account, VC reversals were more common on short words than on long words. The reasons for this difference are not clear. Perhaps omissions are so common on long words (Chapters 7 and 8) that reversals—which may only occur if neither phoneme of a pair is omitted—are less common. This would be the opposite of the explanation just proposed for stress effects and as such is not completely satisfactory.

Statistical Analyses

Statistical support for the findings comes, in part, from the results of multiple regression analyses. In these analyses, I attempted to predict the reversal rate for each VC sequence in each word in my collection in which the sequence was spelled with a vowel grapheme followed by a consonant grapheme. The total number of VC sequences in the analysis was 1,128.

A multiple regression analysis using the four predictors of syllabic liquid, type of consonant (sonorant versus obstruent), stress (primary or secondary stress versus no stress), and number of phonemes in the word explained 4.3% (4.0% adjusted) of the variance in reversal rate. This figure is very low, probably because the overall rate of reversals was so low. For the great majority of VC sequences, the reversal rate was zero. However, the regression did explain a statistically significant percentage of the variance ($p < .001$). There were reliable effects for each predictor—syllabic liquid ($p < .001$), type of consonant ($p < .01$), stress ($p < .01$), and word length ($p < .05$). Other variables did not add significantly to the prediction. In particular, although the reversal rate was significantly higher for vowel-sonorant sequences than for vowel-obstruent sequences, the rate for vowel-liquid sequences did not reliably exceed the rate for vowel-nasal sequences. Nor did the reversal rate differ for letter-name sequences and non-letter-name sequences or for VC sequences at the ends of words and VC sequences in the middles of words.

Comparison with Results of Other Studies

Traditionally, reversal errors have been defined with respect to the conventional spellings of words. They have not been defined with respect to the words' phonemic forms. A child who misspelled *her* as HRE, it was thought, remembered the letters in the word's spelling but did not correctly remember the order of the letters. As a result, the child placed two of the letters in the wrong sequence. Because reversals have been considered an orthographic phenomenon, researchers who study the phonological bases of children's spelling errors, like Charles Read, have largely ignored these errors.

In two experiments, Andrea Zukowski and I did examine reversal errors. One experiment was reported in Zukowski and Treiman (1989); the second is unpublished. In these studies, we asked first-grade pupils to spell CVCC nonwords such as /dʒ'ɪlk/ and /n'ɑps/. The syllables were dictated to the children and the children had three chances to repeat each syllable before trying to spell it. In this way, we could ensure that reversals of phonemes in spelling do not reflect reversals of phonemes in pronunciation. Children who misspelled /n'ɑps/ as NOSP, for example, almost always pronounced it correctly. They did not pronounce the word as /n'ɑsp/. With reversal errors, as with most spelling errors produced by normal first graders, misspelling does not imply mispronunciation.

The first graders in the experiments, like the first graders in the naturalistic study, made few reversals. In the first experiment, only 1.4% of all spellings contained a reversal. In the second experiment, the figure was 1.1%. These figures are similar to the percentage of reversals in the naturalistic study, which was 1.9%. In general, first graders do not often misorder phonemes when they spell.

Even though reversals were infrequent in each study, one can ask whether the same phonological factors that were associated with reversals in the naturalistic study were also associated with reversals in the experiments. This is an important question. Because so few reversals occurred in each case, suggestions that are based on a single study must remain tentative. If similar results are found in three different studies, stronger conclusions can be drawn.

The results of the experiments do not permit any inferences about the effects of syllabic liquids, stress, or word length on reversal errors. None of the stimuli in the experiment contained syllabic liquids. All of the phonemes belonged to primary-stressed syllables and all of the stimuli contained the same number of phonemes. However, one can examine the types of phonemes that were reversed in the experiments, asking whether the findings parallel those for the first graders' classroom spellings.

The children in the Zukowski and Treiman (1989) experiment made 27 reversals of adjacent phonemes. Of these, 12 involved VCs, 14 involved CCs, and only one involved a CV. In the second (unpublished) experiment, there were 12 reversals of adjacent phonemes. Ten of these involved VCs, two involved CCs, and none involved CVs. Thus, CV reversals were rare in both experiments, as in the naturalistic study. The rarity of CV reversals, I hypothesize, reflects the linguistic structure of the syllable. Children are unlikely to misorder one phoneme from the syllable's onset and another phoneme from the syllable's rime. Reversed phonemes usually belong to the same unit of the syllable.

Given that most reversals in the experiments involved phonemes from the rime, what is the nature of the within-rime reversals? Table 9.1 shows, for each experiment, the numbers and percentages of VC and CC reversals as a function of whether the consonant after the vowel was a sonorant or an obstruent. The association between type of reversal (VC or CC) and type of consonant (sonorant or obstruent) was significant for each experiment ($p < .001$ for the first experiment and $p < .025$ for the second experiment by Fisher exact tests). The pattern was similar to that in the classroom data. With rimes like /ɪlk/, where a sonorant followed the vowel, reversals were more likely to involve the vowel and the following sonorant than the sonorant and the final consonant. With rimes like /ɑps/, where an obstruent followed the vowel, reversals always involved the two final consonants, both of which were obstruents. VC reversals never occurred when an obstruent came after the vowel.

These results confirm that reversals are not purely an orthographic phenomenon. Phonology plays an important role. With syllables like /dʒɪlk/, reversals tend to involve the second and third phonemes, as in JLOK. The reason, I suggest, is that /ɪ/ and /l/ form a strong unit—the syllable peak according to hierarchical theories of syllable structure such as Selkirk's (1982). With syllables like /nɑps/, reversals tend to involve the third and fourth phonemes, as in NOSP. Here, /p/ and /s/ form a unit—the syllable coda according to the hierarchical theories. Reversals that involve phonemes from the same unit of the syllable are more common than reversals that involve phonemes from different units.

Summary of Results

In this chapter, I asked whether normal beginning spellers sometimes reverse the order of phonemes in their spelling. Reversal errors do occur among first graders, although they are not one of the more frequent types of error. Even though reversal errors are less common than other spelling errors, they—like other spelling errors—are influenced in a predictable way by linguistic factors. There is no evidence that reversal errors are a unique category of error that is affected by different factors than other errors and that might signify a specific brain dysfunction (Orton, 1937).

Reversals are most frequent with syllabic liquids. Children sometimes misspell *her* as HRE and *work* as WRIK. Children make these errors because they consider the spoken words to contain syllabic /r/s rather than sequences of a vowel followed by /r/. Because the words' phonemic forms do not contain a separate vowel, children often misspell the words as HR and WRK. When children *do* include a vowel in their spelling, having learned that virtually all English words contain vowels, their phonemic representations do not indicate whether the vowel letter should precede the *r* or vice versa. Thus, children sometimes misspell the words as HRE and WRIK.

Reversals are more common with vowel-liquid and vowel-nasal sequences than with vowel-obstruent sequences. Although children probably consider both *horse* and *hogs* to contain four phonemes, the /o/ and /r/ of *horse* form a tighter unit than the /ɔ/ and /g/ of *hogs*. Children may have difficulty dividing /or/ into phonemes and ascertaining the order of the phonemes within it. They have less difficulty segmenting /ɔg/. Also, children may group /o/ and /r/ together when trying to remember the string of phonemes in the spoken word. They are less likely to encode /ɔ/ and /g/ as a unit. Because of these effects on phonemic awareness, short-term memory, or both, children more often misspell *horse* as HROS than *hogs* as HGOS.

CC reversals, when they occur, tend to involve obstruent-obstruent final clusters such as the /g/ and /z/ of *hogs*. Apparently, phonemes such as /g/ and /z/ form a unit when they occur at the end of a word or syllable and are subject to reversal. Finally, reversals seem to be more common in unstressed syllables than in stressed syllables and in short words than in long words.

Implications

The results in this chapter support the central thesis of this book—that children's spelling is, to a large extent, an attempt to represent the phonological forms of words. It is not just an attempt to reproduce memorized sequences of letters. To understand many of the errors that children make, one must consider the sounds of words.

The findings provide evidence for two specific ideas about children's phonological systems, ideas that are also supported by findings reported elsewhere in this book. First, children represent a word like *her* as having two phonemes—/h/ followed by syllabic /r/. They do not represent it as /h/ followed by a vowel followed by /r/. Second, children organize the phonemes in spoken syllables into groups or units. These units include onsets, peaks, and codas. The phonemes within a unit are linked together and children sometimes have difficulty accessing their correct order.

If first graders' reversal errors represented reversals of letters from the memorized spellings of words, as traditionally thought, the prescription for these errors would be obvious. Children who make reversal errors need drill on the conventional spellings of words. They especially need drill on the correct order of the letters. However, if first graders' reversal errors are not usually orthographic in nature, memorization of words' conventional spellings may not be the best cure for the errors. With some kinds of words, it may be more helpful for children to focus on the words' sounds than on their conventional spellings. Consider the child who misspells *milk* as MLIK. This child needs aid in analyzing /ɪl/ into phonemes and ascertaining and remembering the order of the phonemes within this unit. Because the spelling of *milk* closely reflects its sound, increasing the child's awareness of the phonemes within the word should improve the child's spelling. This should happen without extra drill on the word's conventional spelling.

Although having children focus on the sounds of words may often help to eliminate reversal errors, this is not always so. Consider the child who spells *her* as HRE. This child probably considers syllabic /r/ to be a single phoneme. It makes little sense to tell the child that an /ə/ comes before the /r/ in the spoken form of the word, as I have heard people say. It makes little sense to do what I have heard other people do—say the word slowly in hopes that the child will hear separate /ə/ and /r/ sounds within it. The child cannot deduce from the word's pronunciation that syllabic /r/ should be spelled with *er*. Rather, the child must memorize the conventional two-letter spelling of syllabic /r/. With syllabic liquids, memorization is more important than phonemic awareness in promoting correct spelling.

In many ways, learning to spell syllabic liquids is like learning to spell digraphs such as *th* and *sh*. Children must learn the conventional two-letter spellings of syllabic liquids just as they must learn the conventional two-letter spellings of /θ/ and /ʃ/. With digraphs, the need for memorization is clear to adults. Children who spell *thin* as TIN are not told to listen for the /h/ in the spoken word. Adults do not say *thin* slowly, hoping that children will hear /h/ within it. Children are told, instead, that *thin* happens to contain the letter *h*. This is something that they must simply learn and remember. Textbooks, too, recognize the need for instruction on digraphs. The phonics book used in this first grade devoted several pages to *th* and to other digraphs. With syllabic liquids, in contrast, the need for instruction is not so obvious to adults and to textbook publishers. Given their many years of experience with printed words like *her*, some adults understandably believe that the spoken word contains a separate vowel. They expect children to deduce that the printed word *her* contains a vowel letter in the same way that they can deduce that the printed word *hen* contains a vowel letter. Some phonics books, including the one used in this classroom, do not teach spellings like *er* for syllabic /r/. As I have shown, errors on syllabic liquids are a major problem among first graders. I recommend that children be taught how to spell syllabic liquids in the same way that they are taught how to spell digraphs.

Notes

1. In Selkirk's (1982) theory, a sonorant may belong to the peak only when the vowel is "short." Because of the small number of reversals in my study, I did not investigate the effect of vowel length.

10

Inflected and Derived Words

In this chapter, I discuss the first graders' spellings of inflected and derived words. The children in this study often misspelled inflected words (Chapter 2). One type of error that has already been documented is the omission of inflectional endings like the /s/ of *books* (Chapter 8). This chapter considers the children's spellings of inflected and derived words in more detail.

Before beginning the discussion, some definitions and examples are in order. In English, inflections are added to the ends of words to mark such things as tense and number. For example, *helped* contains the verb stem *help* plus the past tense inflectional suffix. I refer to the past tense suffix as *-D. Helped* contains two morphemes or units of meaning, *help* and *-D*. The inflected word *books* also contains two morphemes, the stem *book* and the plural suffix *-Z*. As these examples show, the addition of an inflectional suffix does not change a word's part of speech.

Derivations differ in several ways from inflections. For one thing, English derivational morphemes may be either prefixes or suffixes. One derivational prefix is *re-*, which may be added to the verb *read* to form *reread*. Derivational suffixes include *-ion* and *-ly*. Unlike inflections, derivations may change a word's part of speech. For example, the noun *vacation* is derived from the verb *vacate* by the addition of *-ion;* the adjective *facial* is derived from the noun *face* by the addition of *-ial*. The relation in meaning between a stem and a derived form is often less transparent than the relation in meaning between a stem and an inflected form. For instance, one cannot predict the full meaning of *vacation* from the meaning of its parts.

As discussed in Chapter 1, the spellings of inflected and derived words in English often represent the words' morphemic forms rather than their phonemic forms. For example, the past tense suffix is /t/ in words like *helped,* whose stem ends with a voiceless consonant, but /d/ in words like *cleaned,* whose stem ends with a voiced consonant. The phonemic forms of stems, too, sometimes change when inflectional or derivational morphemes are added. Thus, the final consonants of *vacate* and *relate* change from /t/ to /ʃ/ when adding *-ion*. The English writing system often ignores these predictable phonemic variations. Morphemes are spelled in a consistent fashion. Thus, both *helped* and *cleaned* end with *ed* even though *ed* sounds different in the two words. Both *relate* and *relation* include *t,* even though *t* sounds different in the two words. The similar spelling of the stem signals that aspects of its meaning are retained in the derived form despite changes in phonemes and in stress.

This tendency to preserve the spellings of morphemes in the face of changes in their pronunciations means that the English writing system is not strictly phonemic. In a strictly phonemic system, *helped* would end with *pt* and *cleaned* would end with *nd*. The different final phonemes of the two words would be signaled with different letters. In its spelling of many inflected and derived words, English deviates systematically from the phonemic principle.

In this chapter, I ask how the first graders spelled words like *helped* and *cleaned*. Did they grasp the morphological nature of the English writing system, writing the past tense of both words with *ed?* Or did they spell phonemically, writing *helped* with final *t* and *cleaned* with final *d?* Such questions take on particular importance in light of these first graders' classroom experience. The children in this study saw many inflected words in their reading materials. However, they were taught very little about the morphological basis of English spelling. None of the words in their spelling lists had regular inflections or derivations and only two pages in their phonics book dealt directly with such words (specifically, with the *ed* and *ing* inflections). The children's teacher, consistent with her educational philosophy, did not offer any teaching about the spelling of inflected and derived words beyond the small amount provided by the phonics exercises. Thus, we can ask whether these first graders grasped the morphological basis of English spelling on their own, as a result of their exposure to printed words.

In Chapter 6, a similar question was asked regarding children's knowledge of orthographic constraints. The first graders in this study were not explicitly taught about such orthographic patterns as the restriction of *ck* to the middles and ends of words. Nonetheless, the children picked up these orthographic patterns on their own from their exposure to printed words. They rarely produced spellings beginning with *ck*. To anticipate the results presented in this chapter, the findings are different in the case of morphology. As a group, the first graders had a poor grasp of the morphological basis of the English writing system. They often spelled *helped* as HLPT and *cleaned* as CLEND. Apparently, exposure to words like *helped* and *cleaned* is not usually sufficient for first graders to induce the morphological basis of English writing. This is an area in which teaching has an important role to play.

Children's Spellings of Inflected Words

The first graders attempted several different types of inflected words—verbs like *helped, helps,* and *helping,* nouns like *books* and *fox's,* and adjectives like *bigger* and *biggest.* I discuss their spellings of the various inflectional suffixes and then their spellings of the stems.

-D

Consider the past tense verbs *helped, cleaned,* and *lifted.* Each past tense verb contains a stem followed by the -*D* suffix. The form of the suffix differs in the three cases, being /t/ in *helped,* /d/ in *cleaned,* and /əd/ in *lifted.* This variation is not arbitrary.

The form of the suffix may be predicted from the final phoneme of the stem. For regular English verbs, the past tense is /t/ when the stem ends with any voiceless consonant but /t/. Thus, *help* forms its past tense by adding /t/. The morpheme -*D* is realized as /d/ when the stem ends with a vowel or any voiced consonant except /d/. Therefore, *clean* adds /d/ to form the past tense. Finally, -*D* has the form /əd/ when the stem ends with /t/ or /d/. This rule applies to *lift*. Even though -*D* corresponds to different phonemes in *helped, cleaned,* and *lifted,* it is spelled as *ed* in all three cases.

Although most verbs make their past tense by adding /t/, /d/, or /əd/, with no change in the stem, some common verbs are irregular. For example, the past tense of *keep* is *kept* and the past tense of *find* is *found.* Irregular past tense forms are spelled in accord with their phonemic form, rather than morphologically, with final *ed.* Thus, *kept* is not spelled as **keped* or **keeped,* and *found* is not spelled as **founed* or **finded.*

Table 10.1 shows how the first graders spelled the past tense morpheme in regular verbs. The results for /t/, /d/, and /əd/ are presented separately. Spoken forms that were regularized by the child, as when a child said /kʼipt/ rather than /kʼɛpt/ for the past tense of *keep,* are included in this table. Correct *ed* spellings occurred only 12.4% of the time pooling over the /t/, /d/, and /əd/ forms. This low value indicates that the children had trouble learning the conventional *ed.*

Instead of spelling -*D* morphologically, with *ed,* the children often spelled it in accord with its phonemic form. When the past tense was realized as /t/, the children symbolized it as *t* over half the time. They used *t* significantly more often when -*D* had the form /t/ than when -*D* was /d/ or /əd/ ($p < .001$ by a chi-square test). When the past tense suffix was /d/, the children spelled it with *d* in a majority of cases. Spellings with *d* were significantly more frequent when the past tense suffix was /d/ than when it was /t/ or /əd/ ($p < .001$ by a chi-square test). Finally, when -*D* was realized as /əd/, over a third of the children's spellings were legal representations of /əd/. These spellings included the correct *ed* as well as *id, ide,* and *ud.* Legal spellings of /əd/ were significantly more frequent when -*D* appeared as /əd/ than when it appeared as /t/ or /d/ ($p < .01$ by a chi-square test). Several other spellings of /əd/ may also have been attempts at phonemic spellings in that they consisted of *e* followed by *b* or *t,* the two most frequent illegal substitutions for /d/. Thus, phonemic spellings of the regular past tense marker were common. Correct morphological spellings were not common.

Although phonemic spellings of the regular past tense marker predominated, omissions were also fairly common (see Chapter 8). Omissions occurred at a rate of 22.1%, actually outnumbering correct *ed* spellings.

A few errors suggest that some of the first graders knew something of the conventional *ed.* The children occasionally used single *e* and single *d* for past tense /t/. Once, a child used *e* for past tense /d/. Children may make these errors because they remember one of the letters of the conventional *ed,* just as they make errors like *t* and *h* for /θ/ because they remember one of the letters of the *th* digraph. However, the small number of single *e* and single *d* errors, together with the relatively low percentage of correct *ed* spellings, suggests that many first graders knew little or nothing about the conventional *ed* ending.

To further study the children's spelling of past tense forms, I now ask how they

Table 10.1. Spellings of -*D* in Regular and Regularized Verbs

Child's Spelling	Example	Number	Percent
-*D realized as* /t/			
Spelled as *ed*			
t	JUMT for *jumped*	30	56.6
omitted	CEEP for *keeped* [*sic*]	9	17.0
ed	CHOPED for *chopped*	7	13.2
e	HALPE for *helped*	2	3.8
d	JUPD for *jumped*	2	3.8
other	WYTHER for *washed*	3	5.7
	Total	53	100.1
-*D realized as* /d/			
Spelled as *ed*			
d	CLEND for *cleaned*	39	54.9
omitted	CIL for *killed*	18	25.4
ed	CALLED for *called*	7	9.9
b	SOB for *showed*	2	2.8
e	SRFE for *served*	1	1.4
t	PLT for *pulled*	1	1.4
other	CLC for *called*	3	4.2
	Total	71	100.0
-*D realized as* /əd/			
Spelled as *ed*			
omitted	FLOOW for *floated*	5	23.8
ed	WUNED for *wanted*	4	19.0
e	SCRDE for *squirted*	2	9.5
id	SQRDID for *squirted*	2	9.5
d	WOTD for *wanted*	1	4.8
ide	FLOTIDE for *floated*	1	4.8
eb	LIFTEB for *lifted*	1	4.8
ud	SHKWTUD for *squirted*	1	4.8
et	BAEBSTET for *babysitted* [*sic*]	1	4.8
eteta	BAEBSTETETA for *babysitted* [*sic*]	1	4.8
do	TRGTDO for *treated*	1	4.8
a	SIDA for *slided* [*sic*]	1	4.8
	Total	21	100.2

spelled final /t/ and /d/ in words that were phonemically similar to regular past tense verbs but that were not past tense verbs. For instance, *fast* ends with a voiceless consonant followed by /t/ and thus is similar to *passed*. *Fast,* however, is not a past tense verb. As another example, *brand* ends with a voiced consonant followed by /d/ but is not a past tense verb. The results for words like *fast* and *brand* appear in Table 10.2.[1]

A comparison of the results in Table 10.1 and Table 10.2 reveals that *t* and *d* spellings were more frequent for noninflected words like *fast* and *brand* than for inflected words like *passed* and *banned* ($p < .001$ by a chi-square test). Conversely, *ed* spellings were less frequent for noninflected words like *fast* and *brand* than for inflected words like *passed* and *banned* ($p < .001$ by a chi-square test). Indeed, the

Table 10.2. Spellings of Final /t/ and /d/ in Words Not Ending in *-D* that are Phonemically Similar to Regular Past Tense Verbs Ending in *-D*

Child's Spelling	Example	Number	Percent
Final /t/ after voiceless consonant			
Spelled as *t*			
t	FRST for *first*	21	75.0
omitted	FAS for *fast*	7	25.0
Total		28	100.00
Final /d/ after voiced consonant or vowel			
Spelled as *d*			
d	BOAD for *board*	309	85.6
omitted	BAN for *brand*	31	8.6
b	BRB for *bird*	5	1.4
t	GOT for *gold*	2	0.6
other[a]	SLIEBBIESEF for *slide*	14	3.9
Total		361	100.1

[a]No *ed* or *e* spellings occurred in this category.

children *never* extended *ed* to words like *fast* and *brand*. In addition, when /t/ was not a past tense marker the children never spelled it with *e* or *d* and when /d/ was not a past tense marker the children never spelled it with *e*. The children's occasional use of *ed* (and of its component letters, when these were not legal spellings) was restricted to past tense verbs. Thus, once children did learn the conventional *ed*, they realized that *ed* marks the past tense. They did not extend the *ed* spelling to words like *fast* and *brand*.

Turning from regular past tense verbs to irregular past tense verbs, Table 10.3 shows how the children spelled the final phonemes of irregular past tense verbs that ended with /t/ and /d/. Examples are *kept* and *found*. The children usually used the conventional *t* to represent the final /t/ of verbs like *kept*. Likewise, the children generally symbolized the final /d/ of verbs like *found* with the correct *d*. There was only one case, representing less than 1% of the total, in which a child spelled an irregular past tense form with the regular *ed* while pronouncing the irregular past tense form correctly. This was SAIED for *said*. This may be a regularization error in spelling, just as /k'ipt/ for *kept* is a regularization error in speech.

How did the children spell irregular past tense forms that did not end with /t/ or /d/? The children never used final *ed* here. They never produced regularizations in spelling like KNOWED for *knew* or TAKED for *took*, although they *did* occasionally produce regularizations in speech like /n'od/ for *knew*. Thus, regularizations of the regular past tense pattern are more common in children's speech than in their spelling. The principles that govern the phonemic realization of the past tense morpheme are fairly strong in children's spoken language. Even first graders sometimes extend the regular pattern to irregular spoken forms, saying /n'od/ instead of *knew*. Such regularizations are often interpreted to mean that children have a solid operational knowledge of morphology, although this knowledge may not be explicit. In contrast, the rule about the *ed* spelling of the past tense morpheme is weak. First graders rarely extend this spelling to irregular printed forms.

Table 10.3. Spellings of Final /t/ and /d/ in Irregular Verbs

Child's Spelling	Example	Number	Percent
Final /t/			
Spelled as *t*			
t	THOT for *thought*	131	87.3
omitted	LIS for *lost*	13	8.7
d	WEND for *went*	2	1.3
tt	BITT for *bit*	1	0.7
other	WSES for *went*	3	2.0
	Total	150	100.0
Final /d/			
Spelled as *d*			
d	FAWD for *found*	93	81.6
omitted	FAW for *found*	7	6.1
t	DET for *did*	4	3.5
b	MAB for *made*	3	2.6
ed	SAIED for *said*	1	0.9
dd	ADD for *had*	1	0.9
vd	HAVD for *had*	1	0.9
vb	HAVB for *had*	1	0.9
other	HN for *had*	3	2.6
	Total	114	100.0

Correct spellings of regular past tense verbs were quite rare during the first semester of the school year (1.3%). They were more common (25.0%) during the second semester ($p < .001$ for the difference by a chi-square test). These children, then, needed at least half a year's experience in first grade to even begin to grasp the *ed* ending.

I could not track individual children's progress over the course of the school year in detail, because most children did not attempt many past tense verbs. However, I did examine the spellings produced by Mark, the child who wrote the largest number of past tense forms. During the first semester of the school year, Mark never spelled regular -*D* correctly. Some of his errors on -*D* were phonemic, as in DRAST for *dressed,* JRAD for *drowned,* and DROWNDID for *drownded* [sic]. Elsewhere he omitted the past tense marker altogether, as in LIKE for *liked.* In late March, Mark began to produce correct *ed* spellings for the /t/, /d/, and /əd/ variants of -D. The *ed* spelling emerged at about the same time for all three forms. Throughout the school year, Mark spelled irregular past tense forms ending in /t/ with final *t* and irregular past tense forms ending in /d/ with final *d,* with the occasional omission. Throughout much of first grade, then, Mark was a phonemic speller. Not until fairly late in the school year did he begin to spell regular past tense forms with *ed,* ignoring predictable variations in their phonemic forms.

-Z

Consider the plural nouns *books, bags,* and *dishes.* The phonemic form of the plural marker differs in the three cases, being /s/ after voiceless consonants (except for

/s/, /ʃ/, and /tʃ/), /z/ after voiced consonants (except for /z/, /ʒ/, and /dʒ/) and after vowels, and /əz/ after /s/, /z/, /ʃ/, /ʒ/, /tʃ/, and /dʒ/. Possessive nouns follow a similar pattern (e.g., *Matt's, Sally's, fox's),* as do third person singular present tense verbs (e.g., *eats, lives, washes).* For present purposes, the plural morpheme, the possessive morpheme, and the third person singular present tense morpheme are all called -*Z.*

In English, plural and third person singular -*Z* are usually spelled as *s* when they are realized as /s/ or /z/. The only exception are words that end with *y;* here -*Z* is spelled as *es* and the *y* of the stem changes to *i,* as when *baby* becomes *babies.* Plural and third person singular -*Z* are spelled as *es* when they have the form /əz/. Thus, the spelling of plural and third person singular -*Z* usually ignores the predictable variation between the voiceless /s/ and the voiced /z/. It *does* represent the difference between these forms and /əz/. Possessive -*Z* is spelled alike whether it is realized as /s/, /z/, or /əz/. For singular nouns, *'s* is added to form the possessive; for plural nouns, an apostrophe is added to the plural form.[2] Because I did not include apostrophes when coding the spellings, it was not usually possible to distinguish possessive forms from other forms with final -*Z.*

Table 10.4 shows how the first graders spelled -*Z* in regular nouns and verbs. This table includes spoken forms that were regularized by the child, as when a child said the plural of *sheep* as *sheeps.* When -*Z* was /s/ or /z/, the children generally spelled it as *s.* This was usually correct. The percentage of *s* spellings when -*Z* had the form /s/ was statistically indistinguishable from the percentage of *s* spellings when -*Z* had the form /z/. However, both of these were significantly greater than the percentage of *s* spellings when -*Z* had the form /əz/ ($p < .001$ by chi-square tests). Although the children generally spelled -*Z* as *s* when it was realized as /z/, they *did* use *z* 4.6% of the time in these cases. Because the children never used single *z* for the /s/ or /əz/ forms of -*Z,* *z* spellings were significantly more frequent for the /z/ form than for /s/ and /əz/ ($p < .05$ by a chi-square test). Finally, when -*Z* appeared as /əz/, 40% of the children's spellings were legal representations of /əz/. These included *is, es,* and *az.* Legal spellings of /əz/ were significantly more common for -*Z* as /əz/ than for -*Z* as /s/ or /z/ ($p < .001$ by a chi-square test).

Thus, the children generally used *s* for both the /s/ and /z/ forms of -*Z.* One might interpret this result to mean that the children knew that the /s/ and /z/ variants of -*Z* should be spelled alike because they both represent the same morpheme. However, this interpretation is undermined by findings presented in Table 10.5. This table shows how children spelled final /s/ and /z/ in words that did *not* contain the -*Z* morpheme but that were phonemically similar to words that did.[3] For example, *triceratops* ends with a voiceless consonant followed by /s/ but is not a plural noun; *because* ends with a vowel followed by /z/ but /z/ does not represent the -*Z* morpheme. For all the words in Table 10.5, the conventional spelling of both final /s/ and final /z/ was *s.* Correspondingly, the children usually symbolized both final /s/ and /z/ with *s.* The children used *s* for /z/ because *s* is the most common spelling of /z/ in English (see Chapter 3). There was no significant difference in the percentage of *s* spellings for /s/ and /z/ as a function of whether /s/ and /z/ represented the -*Z* morpheme (as in Table 10.4) or not (as in Table 10.5). Thus, the children usually spelled the final sound of *bags* with *s* because they knew that /z/ is usually

Table 10.4. Spellings of -*Z* in Regular and Regularized Nouns and Verbs

Child's Spelling	Example	Number	Percent
-*Z realized as /s/*			
Spelled as *s*			
s	BUKS for *books*	74	86.0
omitted	ET for *eats*	6	7.0
us	PATUS for *plants*	1	1.2
other	WRKSH for *works*	5	5.8
	Total	86	100.0
-*Z realized as /z/*			
Spelled as *s*			
s	BARS for *bears*	115	82.7
omitted	KED for *kids*	15	10.8
z	WAZ for *weighs*	6	4.3
other	ALGADRY for *alligators*	3	2.2
	Total	139	100.0
Spelled as *es* (after *i*)			
s	STORRYS for *stories*	6	50.0
omitted	GRRY for *groceries*	2	16.7
ss	PENSS for *puppies*	2	16.7
es	STORIES for *stories*	1	8.3
z	PNNEZ for *pennies*	1	8.3
	Total	12	100.0
-*Z realized as /əz/*			
Spelled as *es*			
is	BOXIS for *boxes*	4	30.8
s	BXS for *boxes*	3	23.1
e	DERE for *dishes*	2	15.4
es	ONGES for *oranges*	1	7.7
ues	SAMUCHUES for *sandwiches*	1	7.7
az	DISAZ for *dishes*	1	7.7
ce	DESCE for *dishes*	1	7.7
	Total	13	100.1
Spelled as *s*			
s	FOXS for *fox's*	2	100.0
	Total	2	100.0

transcribed with *s*. They did not spell the final sound of *bags* with *s* because they knew that the /s/ and /z/ variants of the -*Z* morpheme should be spelled alike.

The children attempted only a handful of irregular plurals. Children who pronounced the irregular forms correctly never spelled them with final *s* or *es*. Rather, they spelled the plurals in line with their phonemic forms, as in FET for *feet* and CHILLDREN for *children*. Irregular third person singular verbs attempted by the children included *does, has,* and *is*. The final /z/ of these forms is spelled with *s* rather than *z*, consistent with the general tendency to spell /z/ with *s* in English. Once a child spelled *has* as HAVES while saying it correctly. This may be a true spelling regularization involving -*Z*, but it is the only one. In this case, the child spelled the third person singular verb as the infinitive plus *s*, extending the spelling rule for regular verbs to an irregular verb.

Table 10.5. Spellings of Final /s/ and /z/ in Words Not Ending in -Z that are Phonemically Similar to Regularly Inflected Words Ending in -Z

Child's Spelling	Example	Number	Percent
Final /s/ after voiceless consonant			
Spelled as *s*			
s	TRIYTERITOPS for *triceratops*	3	100.0
	Total	3	100.0
Final /z/ after voiced consonant or vowel			
Spelled as *s*			
s	BECUSE for *because*	123	73.7
z	CEZ for *cheese*	20	12.0
omitted	PAY for *please*	10	6.0
other	HSEX for *cheese*	14	8.4
	Total	167	100.1

The percentage of correct spellings of regular -Z was significantly higher during the second semester than during the first semester—82.8% versus 61.1% ($p < .001$ by a chi-square test). Even during the first semester, though, a majority of children's spellings of -Z were correct. Examining the -Z spellings produced by Mark, the child whose spellings of -D were discussed earlier, I found that most were correct. However, two errors during the first semester included *z*—ROGZ for *rogues* and DISAZ for *dishes.*

Comparison of -D and -Z

Now that I have discussed children's spellings of -D and -Z, I may compare the results for the two morphemes. In terms of how the English writing system treats them, regular -D and regular -Z seem to be quite similar. In both cases, predictable variations in the morphemes' forms are not symbolized in print. Specifically, variation between a voiced consonant and the corresponding voiceless consonant (/t/–/d/ or /s/–/z/) is ignored. The English writing system often uses the same letter(s)—*ed* for -D and *s* for -Z—to represent the voiced and voiceless versions of each morpheme. Despite this superficial similarity between -D and -Z, the children performed quite differently on the two morphemes. They did much better on -Z than -D. The percentage of correct spellings was 76.6% for regular -Z as compared with only 12.4% for regular -D ($p < .001$ by a chi-square test).

Why were the students so much better at spelling -Z than -D? One reason, and probably the most important one, is that children need not grasp the morphological basis of the English writing system to be correct on -Z. Children who spell phonemically, representing /s/ and /z/ with the letters that typically symbolize these phonemes, will generally be right. This is because both /s/ and /z/ are usually spelled with *s*. To produce correct spellings for -D, children must learn a new spelling, *ed.* Children who spell final /t/ and /d/ of regular verbs with the letters that typically represent these phonemes—*t* for /t/ and *d* for /d/—will be incorrect. Thus, only -D offers children a real choice between phonemic and morphological spellings. Only -D provides a true test of children's ability to spell an inflectional morpheme in a consistent manner despite changes in its phonemic form.

The main reason that children are more accurate on -*Z* than -*D*, I have suggested, is that children can spell -*Z* correctly without truly understanding that morphemes retain their spellings across changes in their phonemic forms. In addition, a second factor may contribute to children's greater success on -*Z* than -*D*. Irregular forms with -*D* are more common than irregular forms with -*Z*. Indeed, irregular verbs like *went* and *did* appear in children's earliest reading materials (Harris & Jacobson, 1972). These words may give children the idea that past tense forms ending in /t/ and /d/ are to be spelled with final *t* and *d* rather than with *ed*.

-ING

To form the present progressive of a verb, -*ING* is added to the infinitive. This morpheme is always spelled as *ing,* as in *thinking* and *ending.* Its phonemic form does not vary with the form of the stem, as do those of -*D* and -*Z*. Table 10.6 shows how the children spelled -*ING*. Although Read (1971) reported many *ig* and *eg* errors for -*ING* (see also Beers & Henderson, 1977), no such errors occurred here. Rather, many errors included *n,* perhaps because inflectional -*ING* is often pronounced with /n/ rather than /ŋ/.

-ER and -EST

Adjectives add -*ER* to form the comparative, as in *bigger.* The morpheme -*EST* is used for the superlative, as in *biggest.* These morphemes have the phonemic forms /ər/ and /əst/, respectively; their realizations are not affected by the nature of the stem. The morphemes are spelled as *er* and *est.* Few inflected adjectives occurred among the words that the children chose to spell. When the children did spell -*ER* they used *r,* consistent with findings reported elsewhere in this book on the spelling of syllabic /r/.

Children's Spellings of the Stems of Inflected Words

For most regularly inflected words, the spelling of the stem does not change when an inflectional ending is added. For example, *help* is retained in the past tense

Table 10.6. Spellings of -*ING*

Spelling	Example	Number	Percent
ing	TAEKING for *thinking*	33	48.5
omitted	SUP for *shopping*	8	11.8
en	CHOPEN for *shopping*	5	7.4
n	CIDN for *shopping*	5	7.4
e	INDE for *ending*	3	4.4
on	GOON for *going*	2	2.9
ene	GRADENE for *grading*	2	2.9
ni	GONI for *going*	2	2.9
other	GOWNG for *going*	8	11.8
	Total	68	100.0

helped; tall is retained in the superlative *tallest.* For some stems, there are minor spelling changes. Stems ending with a so-called silent *e* drop the *e* when adding a suffix beginning with a vowel. *Trade* becomes *traded* and *ride* becomes *riding.* Stems ending with *y* preceded by a consonant change the *y* to *i* when adding a suffix with an initial *e. Try* becomes *tried* and *baby* becomes *babies.* Also, one-syllable words and multisyllabic words that have stress on the last syllable and that end with a single consonant preceded by a single vowel generally double the final consonant when adding a suffix that begins with a vowel. Thus, the final consonant is doubled in *chopped* and *biggest.*[4]

Although stems generally maintain their spelling in the case of regularly inflected words, the same is not true for irregularly inflected words. For example, the vowel of *kept* is spelled with *e*, befitting its phonemic form. It is not spelled with *ee*, as in the stem *keep.* The *v* of *have* does not appear in *has.*

Do children understand that stems generally maintain their spellings when inflectional suffixes are added? To find out, I looked at words such as *can* (morphemes that end with a single consonant) and *canned* (regularly inflected forms that end with a two-consonant cluster). If children understand the morphological nature of English writing, they should maintain the spelling *can* when adding an inflectional suffix. If children spell phonemically, they may not maintain the *can* spelling. Instead, they may make many errors like CAD for *canned*, befitting their tendency to omit the interior consonants of final clusters (Chapter 8). The omission rate for consonants like the /n/ of *can* was very low, 0.9%. The omission rate for consonants like the /n/ of *canned* was much higher, 22.3% ($p < .001$ by a chi-square test). Indeed, the 22.3% omission rate for consonants like the /n/ of *canned* was statistically indistinguishable from the 23.6% omission rate for consonants like the /n/ of *band* (the penultimate consonant of a single-morpheme word ending with a two-consonant cluster). Thus, even though the children rarely omitted the /n/ of *can*, they often omitted the /n/ of *canned.* The children did not seem to spell stems in a consistent manner.

The results were similar for stems that ended with two-consonant clusters. The omission rate for the final consonant of a morpheme that ended with a cluster of two consonants, such as *jump*, was 8.8%. When -*D* or -*Z* was added, as in *jumped*, the critical consonant, /p/, was now in the second-to-last position of the word. That is, it was the interior consonant of a final cluster. The omission rate for the consonant more than tripled, rising from 8.8% to 30.6% ($p < .001$ by a chi-square test). Thus, errors like JUMT for *jumped* were fairly common while errors like JUM for *jump* were not especially common. Children who symbolize the /p/ of *jump* but omit the /p/ of *jumped* are children who fail to maintain the spelling of the stem when adding -*D.* These children's spelling is more affected by the phonemic context of the stem than by a tendency to spell the stem in a consistent fashion.

Inflected words containing flaps provide another way to ask whether children spell stems consistently. Consider the word *squirted.* Although the final /t/ of *squirt* does not flap when the word is pronounced alone, it *does* flap when a suffix that begins with a vowel is added. Similarly, the /d/ of *read* flaps when -*ING* is added. As shown in Chapter 5, the first graders often misspelled flaps. They misspelled flapped /t/ as *d* or *dd* just over 20% of the time; they misspelled flapped /d/ as *t* or *tt* about equally often. If children spell stems consistently, errors on flaps should be more common for some flaps than for others. Children should often err on the flaps of words like *water* and *garden*. This is because no stems *wat and *gard exist in English. In contrast, children should rarely err on the flaps of words like *squirted* and *reading*. This is because children rarely (less than 1% of the time) confuse *t* and *d* when spelling the final consonants of words like *squirt* and *read*. If children spell stems in a consistent fashion, confusions of *t* and *d* should be equally rare on words like *squirted* and *reading*. The results did not support these predictions. Confusions of *t* and *d* occurred at a 21.3% rate on words that were not inflected or derived (e.g., *water*) and at a 19.0% rate on inflected words (e.g., *squirted)*. The very small numerical superiority for inflected words was not significant by a chi-square test. Thus, although the children rarely misspelled *squirt* as SQRD, they sometimes misspelled *squirted* as SQRDID. This result suggests, once again, that the children felt no particular pressure to retain the spelling of the stem when spelling an inflected word.

Yet another piece of evidence that children do not necessarily spell stems consistently comes from an examination of final consonant doubling. As mentioned earlier, the final consonant of a stem may double when a suffix that begins with a vowel is added. Thus, the past tense of *chop* is *chopped* rather than *choped*. When a stem ended with a single consonant that normally doubles before inflectional *ed, ing, er,* or *est,* the children usually failed to produce the correct double consonant. They often used a single consonant, as in CHOPED for *chopped*. How does the rate of correct doublet spellings compare for words like *chopped,* where the stem ends with a single consonant, and words like *called,* where the stem ends with a double consonant? If some children know that *chop* ends with *p* and that *call* ends with *ll,* and if these children spell the stems in a consistent manner, there should be more correct doublet spellings for words like *called* than for words like *chopped*. The children produced 4 out of 23 (17.4%) correct doublet spellings for words like *called* and 1 out of 18 (5.6%) correct doublet spellings for words like *chopped*. The difference did not approach significance by a chi-square test. Although this evidence is weak on its own, due to the small number of cases involved, there is again no clear sign that first graders spell morphemes consistently in inflected and noninflected words.

Together, the results suggest that most of the first graders did not spell stems in a consistent manner. Most had not yet grasped the morphological basis of English spelling. They did not know that many morphemes are spelled the same way in inflected and noninflected words.

Although most of the first graders had a poor understanding of the morphological character of English spelling, there *were* a handful of cases in which children appeared to maintain the spelling of a stem when adding an inflectional ending. Examples are RIDEING for *riding,* TRYED for *tried,* and STORYS for *stories*. Several times, too, children kept the letters of the stem in an irregularly inflected form. In addition to HAVES for *has,* the error that was mentioned earlier, children also produced HAVD and HAVB for *had*. These errors may have been attempts to retain the stem *hav(e)* and to add a past tense marker. Thus, some of the children were starting to learn about the morphological basis of English spelling.

Despite the few cases just mentioned, the main influence on children's spellings of inflected words was the phonological properties of the words. The meaning relations between inflected words and stems had relatively little effect. When the phonological characteristics of a word changed—as when /n/ moved from final position in *can* to the interior position of a final cluster in *canned*, or when /t/ moved from nonflapped in *squirt* to flapped in *squirted*—the children's spellings changed accordingly. As a result, the children did not usually spell morphemes in a consistent fashion.

Children's Spellings of Derived Words

In the case of inflected words, the English writing system is not purely phonemic. Morphemes are often symbolized in a consistent fashion even when their phonemic forms change. For example, the past tense morpheme is realized as /t/, /d/, or /əd/, depending on the context, but is spelled as *ed* in all three cases. With derived words, too, the spellings of morphemes often stay the same. When *vacation* is formed from *vacate*, for example, the letter *t* remains even though the phoneme becomes /ʃ/. *Courage* is preserved in *courageous* despite the change in pronunciation. Although morphemes are often spelled consistently in derived words, this is not always true. For example, English uses *vacancy* rather than **vacanty* and *profundity* rather than **profoundity*.

In their spellings of inflected words, the first graders focused more on the phonological characteristics of individual words than on the meaning relations among sets of words. Children who fail to spell morphemes consistently in the case of inflected words would be expected to do the same in the case of derived words. Indeed, one might expect even *fewer* morphologically based spellings for derived words than for inflected words. This is because the meaning relations among derived words are usually less obvious than the meaning relations among inflected words.

One way to ask whether children display meaning relations in their spellings of derived words is to examine words like *eater*. The /t/ of *eater* is flapped; the /t/ of *eat* is not flapped. If children spell the stem consistently, they should misspell the flap of *eater* less often than the flap of *water*. This is because there is a root word *eat* but no root word **wat*. If children do not spell the stem consistently, they should be as likely to spell the flap of *eater* with *d* or *dd* as to spell the flap of *water* with *d* or *dd*. The results supported this latter prediction. Confusions of *t* and *d* were as common on derived words (27.3%) as on words that were not inflected or derived (21.3%; difference not significant by a chi-square test).

Another way to ask whether children's spellings of derived words are based on morphology is to examine words like *Mommy*. If children spell the stem *Mom* consistently, they should make many errors like MOMY. They should produce fewer correct doublet spellings for words like *Mommy* than for words like *Terry*, which are not related to a stem that ends in a single consonant. These predictions were not confirmed. The children produced 55.6% correct doublet spellings for words like *Mommy* and 51.6% correct doublet spellings for words like *Terry*. The difference was not significant by a chi-square test.[5] Again, it does not appear that children spell morphemes in a consistent manner.

Other than the cases already discussed, the first graders attempted few derived words that were diagnostic of the tendency to spell morphemes consistently in spite of variations in their phonemic forms. One of the handful of such words was *vacation*, which two children attempted. Their spellings, VAYCAYSHAWN and VACASN, symbolized /ʃ/ with *sh* or *s* (a common substitution for /ʃ/) rather than with the *t* of *vacate*. Words like *office* also test children's ability to spell morphemes in a consistent manner. Although the second vowel of *office* is unstressed /ə/, the vowel is pronounced as /ɪ/ and spelled as *i* in *official*. If one knows the word *official* and *if* one appreciates the relation in meaning between *office* and *official*, which many first graders do not, one should be able to infer that *office* contains an *i*. The first graders did not seem to make such inferences on the few such words they tried. For example, one child spelled *office* as OFFS, omitting the unstressed vowel of the second syllable (a common error, as shown in Chapter 7) rather than spelling it with *i*.

Comparison with Results of Other Studies

Read's Research

In their spelling of inflected and derived words, the first graders studied here resemble the younger children studied by Read (1975). With the inflectional suffix *-D*, the children in Read's study predominantly used *t* for the /t/ variant, *d* for the /d/ variant, and *id* for the /əd/ variant. My first graders made similar errors, although the use of *id* for /əd/ was not as prominent here as in Read's study. Also like the children studied by Read, the first graders usually spelled irregular past tense forms in accord with their phonemic forms. Both studies agree, then, that beginning spellers have difficulty learning to use *ed* for regular *-D*. For the most part, they spell phonemically rather than morphologically.

An apparent difference between the two studies concerns children's progress from a three-way distinction among /t/, /d/, and /əd/ to the use of *ed* for all regular past tense forms. Read reported that children often passed through an intermediate stage in which they used *d* for both /t/ and /d/ but continued to spell /əd/ with a vowel followed by *d*. The first graders studied here showed little evidence of such an intermediate stage. They spelled regular past tense /t/ as *d* only 3.8% of the time. As noted, however, there were not enough data to track the progress of most individual first graders. The sequence observed by Read may occur among a few first graders, as among some younger children.

My results for the *-Z* morpheme also agree in most respects with those of Read. Read observed that children usually spelled the /z/ form of *-Z* with *s*, as in POS for *paws*. There were some *z* spellings, as in OWSENZ for *oceans*, but they were not all that common. I found the same thing. Although my results are similar to Read's, my interpretation is quite different. Read attributed children's tendency to spell /s/ and /z/ alike to the fact that /s/ and /z/ differ only in voicing as well as to the predictability of the voicing alternation for the *-Z* morpheme. I suggest that children's exposure to printed words is more important. Having noticed that /z/ is usually spelled with *s*, as /s/ is, children generally spell /s/ and /z/ alike. Thus, they correctly spell the *-Z* of words like *paws* at the same time that they incorrectly spell the *-D* of words like *jumped* and *cleaned*. In my view, children's spelling of -*Z* does *not* provide a true test of their knowledge that regular inflectional morphemes are spelled in a consistent manner despite changes in their phonemic forms.

Read also examined children's spellings of derived words. With the apparent exception of some children in a Montessori school, Read found that beginning spellers do not display meaning relations among derived words. My results point to the same conclusion.

Other Investigators

The first graders in this study did not spell the flaps of words like *reading* and *eater* significantly more accurately than the flaps of words like *garden* and *water*. Apparently, the children did not consult the root words *read* and *eat* when deciding how to spell *reading* and *eater*. If they had, they should have performed better on *reading* and *eater*, which are formed from the smaller parts *read* and *eat*, than on *garden* and *water*, which are not formed from smaller parts *gard and *wat. Ehri and Wilce (1986) found a similar result when they studied children's judgments about the sounds in spoken words. In their study, first graders, second graders, and fourth graders heard sentences that contained words like *fatter* and *letter*. The children were asked whether each word contained a *t* sound or a *d* sound in the middle. The children performed no better on words like *fatter*, which are formed from a stem ending with /t/, than on words like *letter*, which are not formed from such a stem. This pattern of results held at each of the three grade levels. Ehri and Wilce's findings suggest that, at least in this oral task, even children in the fourth grade (about 9 and 10 years old) do not spontaneously analyze inflected and derived words into morphemes. Ehri and Wilce did not ask children to spell the words, so it is not clear whether the lack of morphological analysis that characterized the children's judgments about sounds would also characterize the children's spellings.

Some apparent evidence that young children do understand the morphological basis of English spelling comes from results reported by Rubin (1988). Rubin asked kindergarteners and first graders to spell inflected words like *pinned* and *hummed* and noninflected words like *band* and *tent*. If children think of *pin* when spelling *pinned*, they should be less likely to omit the /n/ of *pinned* than the /n/ of *band*. If children do not use morphological information in spelling, nasal omissions should be equally common with inflected words like *pinned* and noninflected words like *band*. Rubin reported that nasal omissions were less common with the inflected words than the noninflected words. This result suggests that even kindergarteners take advantage of the relation between *pinned* and *pin* when they spell. However, there is a problem with Rubin's stimuli that calls her results into question. All six of the inflected words that Rubin analyzed ended with a nasal-voiced obstruent cluster such as /nd/. Three of the six noninflected words had the nasal-voiceless obstruent final cluster /nt/; the other three words had a nasal-voiced obstruent final cluster. As shown in Chapter 8, children are more likely to omit nasals in clusters like /nt/ than clusters like /nd/. The children in Rubin's study may have performed better on the inflected words than the noninflected words because of this failure to equate the stimuli for type of final cluster.

Other findings indicate that difficulty in appreciating the morphological consistencies of English spelling persists into later childhood (Sterling, 1983; Waters, Bruck, & Malus-Abramovitz, 1988) and, for poor spellers, into adulthood (Fischer, Shankweiler, & I. Y. Liberman, 1985). For example, good adult spellers can deduce that the second vowel of *inspiration* is *i* by relating *inspiration* to *inspire.* Similarly, they can relate *office* to *official.* Many children and poor adult spellers do not to do this.

Summary and Implications

For the most part, the first graders in this study did not expect morphemes to be spelled in a consistent fashion. Having been taught very little about the morphological basis of English spelling, these children spelled phonemically rather than morphologically. Supporting this claim, the children usually spelled the regular past tense suffix in accord with its phonemic form. Although the variation among the /t/, /d/, and /əd/ versions of the past tense marker is completely predictable, the children did not usually spell all three versions with *ed.* In addition, the children often failed to spell stems in a consistent fashion. Although they almost always spelled *eat* with *t,* they sometimes spelled *eater* with *d.* Although they rarely omitted the /p/ of *help* or *keep,* they sometimes omitted the /p/ of *helped* or *keeps.* There *were* a handful of errors like HAVES for *has* and TRADEED for *traded* in which the children spelled stems and inflectional suffixes in a consistent manner. However, such errors were not common. During much of their first-grade year, many of the children did not yet realize that morphemes often retain their spellings across inflected and derived forms. The children's spellings were more influenced by words' phonological characteristics than by their morphological characteristics. The children's widespread failure to display meaning relations in spelling is all the more striking given that they were writing meaningful stories rather than isolated words. Even though the children must have been thinking about the meanings of the words they wrote, they did not usually signal aspects of meaning in their spellings of inflected and derived words.

The slowness with which children learn about the morphological basis of English spelling is particularly apparent when comparing the results presented in this chapter with the results presented in Chapter 6. Chapter 6 focused on children's learning of orthographic constraints. Although the children in this study were not explicitly taught that *ck* may occur in the middles and at the ends of words but not at the beginnings of words, they learned this pattern from exposure to words like *package* and *sick.* Even during the first semester of the school year, the children generally avoided spellings like CKAT. In the case of morphology, the first graders received a very small amount of instruction on the *ed* spelling of the past tense. They saw many regular past tense verbs in their reading materials. Despite this exposure, it was not until the second semester of the school year that some of the children began to grasp that the past tense is spelled with *ed* despite variations in its phonemic form.

Why do first graders have such difficulty appreciating the morphological basis of English spelling? The answer to this question may be different for derived words and inflected words. In the case of derived words, children may not grasp the meaning relations among words that are represented in conventional English spelling. For example, first graders may consider *vacation* to be a semantically unanalyzable unit. Even if *vacate* is in their spoken vocabulary, which it probably is not, first graders do not know that *vacation* is related to *vacate*. Thus, there is no reason for children to spell *vacation* with a *t*. Similarly, first graders may not know the word *official* or may not know that its meaning is related to that of *office*. As a result, children have no particular reason to use *i* in the second syllable of *office*. Moreover, derived words are uncommon in the reading materials of first graders. First graders rarely see words like *vacation* and *vacate* or *office* and *official*. With derived words, then, children's failure to display morphological relations in spelling reflects their limited vocabularies, their lack of knowledge of the meaning relations among derived words, and their lack of exposure to the spellings of these words.

The explanations just proposed are less plausible in the case of inflected forms such as *helped*. Regularly inflected words are common in the reading materials of first graders. Children often see words like *helped, liked,* and *played*. They have many opportunities to learn the *ed* spelling of the past tense. Despite these opportunities, children learn the *ed* spelling more slowly than they learn other aspects of the conventional writing system. Moreover, both *helped* and *help* are in the speaking vocabulary of first graders. Children surely know at some level that *helped* consists of a stem, *help*, plus a past tense marker. They know that *helped* is related in meaning to *help*. Thus, the necessary morphological knowledge exists at an implicit level in the case of inflected words. The problem lies in explicit awareness of morphology and of how it is reflected in spelling.

Children's slowness in understanding the morphological basis of English spelling may reflect the assumptions that they bring with them to the task of learning to spell. Early on, children assume that letters symbolize phonemes (or groups of phonemes that are so closely bound as to be almost equivalent to single phonemes, such as /ɑr/). Most children grasp those aspects of the English writing system that conform to the phonemic principle with relative ease. Thus, they have little trouble learning to spell /æ/ with *a*, since /æ/ is almost always so spelled in English. Children have more difficulty with those aspects of the English writing system that deviate from a strict phonemic principle. Thus, children have trouble learning to use *ed* at the ends of both *jumped* and *cleaned*. They have trouble learning to use *t* in *vacation* and *relation*. To learn these things, children must go beyond their original assumptions, something that is difficult for them to do.

Some have argued that the tendency of the English language to spell morphemes in a consistent manner is helpful to writers and readers. For example, Chomsky and Halle (1968, p. 49) claim that "conventional orthography is . . . a near optimal system for the lexical representation of English words." But for whom is the system optimal? Adults know that *reread* is related to *read* and that *vacation* is related to *vacate*. When reading, adults may grasp the meaning of *vacation* more quickly because it is spelled *vacation* rather than *vacashun*. When spelling, adults may include a *t* in *vacation* because they know that it is related to *vacate*. Children, however, may not know that *vacation* has anything to do with *vacate*. For children, a system in which *vacation* was spelled as *vacashun* and *helped* was spelled as *helpt* might be easier and more natural than the present system. Children's frequent failures to spell morphemes in a consistent fashion mean that the morphological aspects of the English writing system are not "near optimal," in Chomsky and Halle's (1968) words, for beginners. Although meaning relations among words ease the spelling challenge for adults, they are of little help to untutored children.

The results in this chapter suggest that teaching has a critical role to play in helping children understand that morphemes are often spelled in a consistent manner. Exposure to inflected and derived words is not enough. The very small amount of teaching provided to the children in this study—two pages of exercises in a phonics workbook—was not enough either. For children to understand the morphological basis of English spelling, more systematic and extensive instruction must be provided.

Notes

1. The children did not attempt any words that ended with /əd/ that were not past tense verbs.

2. There are a few exceptions to these generalizations but no exceptional cases occurred among the words that the children attempted.

3. Words ending in /ks/ spelled as *x* (e.g., *fox*) and the word *Mrs.* are not included in the data of Table 10.5. Other than *Mrs.*, the children did not attempt any words ending with /əz/ in which /əz/ did not represent the *-Z* morpheme.

4. Although there are some unsettled cases—for example, *busses* and *buses* are both possible spellings for the plural of *bus* according to many dictionaries—the first graders did not attempt any such words.

5. The children produced more correct doublet spellings for the words in this analysis than for other words containing consonant doublets because many of the words in this analysis were proper names. As shown in Chapter 2, children were more accurate on proper names than otherwise expected.

11

Conclusions and Implications

Classification of Spelling Errors

Traditionally, spelling errors have been classified orthographically, by reference to the correct spelling of the word (see Spache, 1940). For example, the child who spells *read* as RED is said to have omitted the letter *a*. Orthographic classification schemes are based on the idea that children spell by recalling the letters in printed words that they have seen and memorized. Children may err by omitting a letter, reproducing the letters in the wrong order, substituting one letter for another, and so on. Orthographic classification schemes contrast with phonological classification schemes, in which errors are viewed by reference to the word's sound.

My results show that orthographic classification schemes are not sufficient to explain first graders' spellings. Consider BAD for *bed* and SHA for *she*. From an orthographic viewpoint, the two errors should be about equally common. Both involve the substitution of *a* for *e*. However, the first graders were more likely to substitute *a* for *e* when *e* represented /ɛ/, as in *bed,* than when *e* represented /i/, as in *she*. This difference cannot be understood if one considers only the letters in the printed words. One must also consider the phonemes that the letters represent. The phoneme /æ/ is more similar to /ɛ/ than it is to /i/. This is one reason why children more often use *a* to spell /ɛ/ than to spell /i/.

To make the same point in another way, consider the errors HR for *her* and HN for *hen*. From an orthographic perspective, both errors involve the omission of an *e* in the middle of a three-letter word. The two errors should be about equally common. In fact, the first graders were much more likely to omit the *e* of *her* than the *e* of *hen*. This difference does not make sense on purely orthographic grounds. It can be understood only if one considers the phonological forms of the two words. From the child's point of view, the spoken form of *her* contains /h/ followed by a syllabic liquid. The spoken form of *hen* contains /h/ plus /ɛ/ plus /n/. Because *her* contains only two segments for the child, the child often spells it as HR.

Examples of the kinds just given—and I could list many more—show that any purely orthographic classification scheme cannot fully capture the intricacies of children's spellings. Although it *is* important to consider the correct spelling of words, as shown in Chapter 6 of this book, it is also important to consider the words' sounds.

One way to invoke phonology in the classification of children's errors is to determine whether an error is a "phonologically legal" representation of the spoken word. For example, TAIP is a legal spelling of *tape* since *ai* is sometimes used to spell /e/ in English. TOOP is not a legal spelling of *tape* since *oo* is never used for /e/. The distinction between legal and illegal errors has been widely employed in spelling research.

By classifying errors as legal or illegal, one captures the notion that children try to symbolize the sounds of words when they spell. However, there are several problems with the legal/illegal classification scheme. For one, it is usually assumed that children who use a legal correspondence between a phoneme and a grapheme know that this correspondence occurs in the conventional spellings of at least some words. But children who spell *cheese* as TESE probably do *not* know that *t* symbolizes /ʧ/ in words like *fortune*. They make this error for other reasons, reasons having to do with the similarity between /ʧ/ and /t/. As another example, children who misspell *bed* as BAD may not know that *a* symbolizes /ɛ/ in words like *Mary*. They make this error for other reasons, reasons having to do with the similarity between /ɛ/ and /æ/ and /ɛ/ and /e/.

In addition, researchers who classify errors as legal or illegal usually assume that children's phonological representations of words are the same as adults'. Thus, SGY is an illegal spelling of *sky* since /k/ is never spelled as *g* in English. However, if children consider *sky* to contain /g/ rather than /k/, SGY is *not* an illegal error for children. As this example shows, any classification of errors as legal or illegal rests on assumptions about children's phonological representations. If children's phonological representations do not always agree with adults', errors that are illegal for adults may not always be illegal for children.

Errors like BETS for *bakes* and PAY for *play,* although classified as illegal, are probably attempts to generate spellings from words' phonological forms. In the case of BETS for *bakes,* the child symbolized /k/ with *t,* a letter that is used for the similar-sounding phoneme /t/. In the case of PAY for *play,* the child symbolized the /pl/ onset with single *p*. Although these errors are illegal, they seem to reflect phonological processes rather than rote visual memorization.

To summarize, many of children's spelling errors are attempts to represent the sounds of words. These errors are not limited to the set of "legal" misspellings like TAIP for *tape.* Errors like SGY for *sky,* BETS for *bakes,* and PAY for *play,* although illegal by traditional criteria, are also based on phonology. The a priori division between legal and illegal errors obscures this important point. Rather than mechanically dividing errors into legal and illegal categories, one must scrutinize the errors themselves to determine how children derive spellings from sounds and why their errors do not always appear reasonable to adults.

Models of the Spelling Process

Traditionally, learning to spell was thought to be a purely visual process. In this view, children memorize the sequence of letters in a word just as they memorize the items in an arbitrary list. Children learn one word at a time in a rote manner. When it comes time to write a word, children try to reproduce the letters in the memorized sequence.

I have argued that this visual memorization view of spelling is incorrect. For beginning spellers who are encouraged to write on their own, spelling is more an attempt to represent a word's sound than it is an attempt to recall a word's memorized spelling. Current theoretical frameworks, including both dual-route models and connectionist models, capture this insight by granting an important role to phonology. Each framework incorporates a phonological spelling process by which people construct or assemble spellings for words from the words' phonological forms.

To determine how children generate spellings from words' phonological forms, it is useful to distinguish between children's stored knowledge of the relations between phonemes and graphemes and the processes by which children put this knowledge to use while spelling. In what follows, I consider the implications of my results for each of these issues.

Even first graders seem to have a fairly sophisticated knowledge of the relations between phonemes and graphemes in English. They know that many phonemes have more than one possible spelling. They know that some spellings of a particular phoneme are more common than others. Moreover, children know that the spelling of a phoneme may depend on the phoneme's context. Having observed that English includes words like *pack* but not words like **ckap*, children infer that /k/ may be spelled with *ck* at the ends of words but not at the beginnings of words. Having observed that English includes words like *miss* but not words like **ssim*, children infer that final /s/ may be spelled with *ss* but that initial /s/ may not.

Children's knowledge of the relations between phonemes and graphemes could be captured in a connectionist model. In such a model, there are links from phonemes to graphemes. These links are not one-to-one for English. In English, most phonemes are linked to more than one grapheme. For example, /k/ is linked to both *k* and *c*. Many graphemes are linked to more than one phoneme, as when *c* is linked to both /k/ and /s/. Each connection has a weight which indicates its strength. For instance, the link from /e/ to *a* is very strong. The link from /e/ to *ai* is relatively weak. In some cases, the weights depend on the phonemes' contexts. For /k/ at the ends of words, the weight for *ck* is relatively high. For /k/ at the beginnings of words, this correspondence has a low weight.

The weights on connections between phonemes and graphemes are affected by several factors. One important factor is the words to which children are exposed; more specifically, the phoneme-grapheme relations that are embodied in these words. The more often children encounter a grapheme in combination with a particular phoneme, the stronger the connection between the phoneme and the grapheme. The weights are also affected by whatever formal instruction the children receive. For example, teaching children that /e/ is spelled as *ai* increases the strength of the link from /e/ to *ai*. My results further suggest that the connection between a phoneme and the first letter of a two-letter grapheme (e.g., the connection from /θ/ to *t*) is stronger than the connection between a phoneme and the second letter of a two-letter grapheme (e.g., the connection from /θ/ to *h*). Finally, the knowledge that children bring with them to the task of learning to spell is important. Most middle-class American children learn the names of letters when they are four or five years old. Even before children begin to read and write words, they have links between phonemes and sequences of phonemes and the letters that have those names. Thus, preschoolers already have a link from /e/ to *a*. When these children begin to read, this link is strengthened by exposure to words like *baby*. As a result, children often spell /e/ with *a*.

How do children put their knowledge of phoneme-grapheme links to use when they spell? At least three processes seem to be involved in spelling a word—analyzing the spoken word into smaller units, remembering the identity and order of the units, and assigning a grapheme to each unit. Once children have generated the spelling of a word, still other processes are required to produce the spelling physically, processes that are beyond the scope of this book.

It is useful to consider the nature of the three processes just discussed. The first process involves the analysis of spoken words. Children must analyze the word to be spelled into smaller units. They must treat the word as a sequence of parts rather than as an indivisible whole. Given the nature of the English writing system, children should be able to analyze words into morphemes and morphemes into phonemes. For example, if children analyze *spelled* into the morphemes *spell* and -*D*, and if they analyze the morpheme *spell* into /s/, /p/, /ɛ/, and /l/, they stand a good chance of spelling the word correctly.

The second process involves memory. Whatever the nature of the units, children must store the units in short-term memory while carrying out the other processes involved in spelling. Children must remember both the identity of the units and their order. If children code two or more segments together, as a "chunk," they must remember the order of the segments within the chunk.

The third process involves the assignment of spellings to units. Children must transcribe each unit with a letter or group of letters. To do so, they use their stored knowledge of the correspondences between sounds and spellings, which was discussed earlier.

The processes of analysis, memory, and spelling assignment need not be carried out in sequence. With a two-syllable word, for instance, a child may analyze the first syllable into phonemes and assign graphemes to the phonemes before beginning to analyze the second syllable.

If assembling a spelling involves several processes, different spelling errors may involve different processes. Some misspellings reflect a lack of explicit morphological analysis. For example, the child who spells *spelled* as SPELD or *jumped* as JUMPT seems to have bypassed the step of morphological analysis. The child analyzed the spoken words into phonemes. The child did not analyze the words morphologically, into a stem plus a past tense marker.

Other errors reflect an incomplete analysis into phonemes. Consider BL for *bell*. The child who produced this error does not seem to have analyzed the spoken word into the phonemes /b/, /ɛ/, and /l/. Instead, the child divided the word into the onset /b/ and the rime /ɛl/. The child used B to symbolize the onset and L to symbolize the rime. As another example, the child who spelled *play* as PAY seems to have analyzed the spoken word into the onset /pl/ and the rime /e/. The child spelled the /pl/ onset as a unit. As these examples show, difficulties in achieving a complete phonemic breakdown of a spoken word may cause children to misspell the word.

Errors like BL for *bell* and PAY for *play* seem to reflect an analysis that does not go far enough—an analysis that inappropriately stops with groups of phonemes rather than proceeding to individual phonemes. In theory, there is another possible type of error—an error based on an analysis that goes too far. Children may go beyond analyzing words at the phonemic level to analyzing words at a detailed phonetic level. With a phonetic analysis, children would analyze *bad* as containing a longer /æ/ than *bat*. However, I found no clear evidence that first graders symbolize the phonetic level of speech when they spell.

Other spelling errors may reflect failures of memory for the segments in a word. For instance, the child who spells *cat* as GAT may have correctly analyzed the word into phonemes but may have misremembered /k/ as the similar-sounding /g/. Another possible explanation for this error, however, is that the child abstracted the wrong initial phoneme in the first place. BLE for *bell* may also be a memory error. The child may have correctly analyzed the syllable into /b/, /ɛ/, and /l/ but reversed the order of /ɛ/ and /l/ in short-term memory. These phonemes, because they form a unit of the syllable, may have been remembered as a chunk. However, there are other possible explanations for the BLE error.

Still other errors arise in the process of assigning spellings to units. Consider the child who spells *said* as SED. This child, it seems, successfully analyzed the spoken word into /s/, /ɛ/, and /d/ and successfully remembered the order and identity of the phonemes. The error occurred because the child spelled /ɛ/ with the grapheme that usually represents this vowel, *e*, rather than with the correct *ai*. As another example, TAIP for *tape* reflects an error during the process of spelling assignment. The child used *ai* rather than *a* followed by final *e* to represent the vowel.

Children's Phonological Systems

Because children's spellings are, to a large extent, attempts to represent the phonemic forms of words, the study of children's spellings can shed light on the nature of children's phonological systems. Children's spellings tell us about the nature of their phonemic representations and about the similarities and differences that they perceive among phonemes.

The Segments in Children's Phonemic Representations

Children's spellings suggest that the segments in their phonemic representations do not always agree with the segment in adults' phonemic representations. To a child, the spoken form of the word *her* probably contains two units, /h/ followed by syllabic /r/. It does not contain a vowel. Thus, children often misspell *her* as HR. As another example, children may consider the spoken form of *want* to contain three units—/w/, /ɑ̃/, and /t/. They may not consider it to contain /n/. Thus, children spell the word as WAT. Finally, some children may consider *sky* to contain /g/ rather than /k/. They therefore spell the word with *g*. In each case, children's phonemic representations differ from those embodied in the conventional English writing system and from those typically assumed for adults. Thus, even children who perform the processes of phonemic analysis and spelling assignment without a flaw, as judged from the perspective of their own phonemic systems, produce errors from the perspective of standard English.

In the cases just discussed, learning to read and write may change children's phonemic representations. For instance, children see that syllabic /r/ is spelled with a vowel grapheme followed by *r* in *her, butter, girl, learn,* and so on. As a result, children may begin to categorize syllabic /r/ as a sequence of /ə/ followed by /r/. Similarly, children may assign the second phone of *sky* to /k/ rather than /g/ as a result of seeing it spelled with *k* (in words like *sky*) and *c* (in words like *scare*).

The notion that reading experience shapes children's phonemic representations is consistent with the idea that phoneme-level representations grow and change during children's early years (see Fowler, 1991). A two-year-old who can say only a small number of words may not represent these words in terms of phonemes. Instead, the child may code each word in terms of a few articulatory gestures. The ordering of these gestures may change each time the child says the word, causing the child to pronounce the word differently on different occasions. As children's vocabularies increase, they must distinguish more and more different words. Thus, a phonemic level of representation gradually emerges. Although phoneme-level representations are surely in place by the time children enter school, these representations may not be fully formed. Still malleable, children's phonemic representations may be "fine tuned" by exposure to print.

Alternatively, exposure to the English writing system may teach children spelling conventions but may not alter their phonemic systems. In this view, children learn that syllabic /r/ is spelled with a vowel grapheme plus *r* but they continue to think of syllabic /r/ as a single unit. They learn that the second sound of *sky* is spelled with *k* but they continue to think of it as /g/. Further research will be needed to determine the extent to which learning to spell shapes children's phonemic representations versus the extent to which it teaches them spelling conventions.

The Grouping of Phonemes into Larger Units

So far, I have discussed the segments in children's phonemic representations. Children's spellings further reveal that they organize these segments into groups or units. Certain sequences of phonemes "stick together," forming cohesive units. These include consonant-consonant groups like /pl/ and vowel-liquid groups like /εl/ and /ɑr/. Children sometimes spell these sequences with single letters. Thus, they may spell /pl/ with single *p* rather than with *p* followed by *l,* making errors like PAY for *play.* They may spell /εl/ with single *l* and /ɑr/ with single *r,* making errors like BL for *bell* and FRM for *farm.* In these and other cases, an incomplete phonemic analysis of spoken words causes children to misspell the words.

The results support the idea that there are phonological units intermediate in size between the syllable and the phoneme and that these units play a role in language behavior (see Treiman, 1989). Of most importance here, intrasyllabic units are critically involved in the development of linguistic awareness and the development of spelling. By the time they enter the first grade, most middle-class children have some ability to analyze spoken words into smaller units. They can segment words into syllables; they can segment syllables into smaller units to some extent.

However, many first graders have difficulty achieving a *complete* phonemic breakdown of the syllable. Children sometimes treat groups of phonemes like /pl/ and /ɛl/ as units. These difficulties lead to spelling errors like PAY for *play* and BL for *bell*. The current findings reinforce previous suggestions that intrasyllabic units play a role in the development of linguistic awareness (Bowey & Francis, 1991; Kirtley et al., 1989; Treiman, 1985a; Treiman, 1992; Treiman & Zukowski, 1991). Moreover, the results show that *specific* problems in phonemic segmentation lead to *specific* misspellings.

The findings about intrasyllabic units may be interpreted within two different linguistic frameworks. One framework—the one on which I have relied to this point in the book—is that of hierarchical theories of syllable structure (e.g., Fudge, 1969, 1987, 1989; Selkirk 1982). According to these theories, the English syllable is made up of a hierarchy of units. Its two main units are the onset and the rime. The rime is in turn broken into a peak and a coda. In such theories, cohesion among phonemes is imposed by the superordinate units, such as onsets and rimes. Phonemes within the same higher-level unit are sometimes treated as a group. Because children have difficulty segmenting intrasyllabic units into phonemes, they sometimes spell these units with single letters.

My results on children's spelling correspond fairly well with the units postulated by hierarchical theories of syllable structure. For example, children are more likely to symbolize a sequence of phonemes with the letter that has the matching name for sequences like /ɛl/ (where the phonemes /ɛ/ and /l/ form the syllable peak) than sequences like /ti/ (where /t/ belongs to the syllable onset and /i/ to the rime). However, my results are not fully consistent with the constituents postulated by the hierarchical theories. For example, there was some evidence that letter-name spellings like BL for *bell* (use of a letter name for a vowel-liquid unit) are more common than letter-name spellings like BN for *Ben* (use of a letter name for a vowel-nasal unit). The linguistic theories just cited do not predict such a difference. According to Selkirk (1982), for example, both liquids and nasals may occupy the peak with the vowel. One would not expect more letter-name spellings with liquids than with nasals.

Further questions about the hierarchical view of syllable structure arise from work with adults. With adults, too, vowel-liquid sequences are more likely to behave as units than vowel-nasal sequences (e.g., Derwing et al., 1987; Treiman, 1984b). In addition, there is some evidence that vowel-/r/ sequences are more cohesive than vowel-/l/ sequences (e.g., Derwing et al., 1987). These graded effects are difficult to interpret within the hierarchical framework.

A different framework for explaining cohesiveness among phonemes has been suggested by Vennemann (1988). Vennemann proposes that there are bonds between the phonemes of spoken words. These bonds vary in strength. For example, a tight bond, called the onset bond, links the consonants of a syllable-initial cluster. The bond between a vowel and the following consonant(s) within the syllable is generally stronger than the bond between a vowel and the preceding consonant(s). The vowel-consonant bond is especially close when the consonant is a liquid. It may be closer when the liquid is /r/ than when it is /l/. The bond between a vowel and a following nasal is stronger than the bond between a vowel and a fol-

lowing obstruent. In this view, cohesiveness among phonemes reflects properties of
the phonemes themselves. It is not imposed from above, as in the hierarchical
model.

As yet, theories based on phoneme bonds are not fully elaborated for English or
any other language. However, these theories may be able to handle the spelling
results as well as, and quite possibily better than, the hierarchical theories. If the
bond between a vowel and a following liquid is stronger than the bond between a
vowel and a following nasal, which is in turn stronger than the bond between a
vowel and a following obstruent, letter-name spellings like BL for *bell* should outnumber letter-name spellings like BN for *Ben,* which should in turn outnumber
letter-name spellings like JF for *Jeff.* My results are consistent with these predictions. If the bond between a vowel and a following /r/ is stronger than the bond
between a vowel and a following /l/, one might see more letter-name spellings with
r than with *l.* I found a trend in this direction, although it was not significant. Thus,
bonds among phonemes that vary continuously in strength may provide a good
way of explaining the graded effects that are seen in the children's spelling and in
the research with adults. Theories that include such bonds may turn out to be preferable to theories in which cohesiveness is imposed from higher-level units with
discrete boundaries.

Whichever theoretical framework is adopted—that based on a hierarchy of syllable constituents or that based on phoneme bonds—it is clear that children do not
consider syllables as simple strings of phonemes. Some groups of phonemes are
closely linked in children's representations, forming cohesive units. Other groups
of phonemes are less tightly bound. When attempting to analyze spoken syllables
into smaller units for spelling purposes, first graders do not always reach the level
of individual phonemes. Children treat some sequences of phonemes as units. Children's failures to fully analyze spoken syllables into phonemes lead to specific spelling errors.

One Phoneme or Two?

Linguists have often argued about whether certain segments are one phoneme or
two phonemes. For example, are the affricates at the beginnings of *chill* and *Jill*
single phonemes or are they sequences of /t/ followed by /ʃ/ and /d/ followed by
/ʒ/, respectively? Are the diphthongs at the ends of *boy, buy,* and *bough* single vowels or sequences of two vowels? The spelling results shed light on these questions.

Some first graders show by their spelling that they appreciate the two-part
nature of affricates and of vowel diphthongs. Children who spell *out* as AOT apparently analyze /au/ into two parts, the first part similar to /æ/ and the second part
similar to /u/. The children use *a* to represent the first part of the diphthong and *o*
to represent the second part. Similarly, some first graders show by their spelling that
they recognize the similarity between the affricate /ʧ/ and the stop /t/. Thus, the
two-part nature of diphthongs and of affricates is not a linguistic fiction. It is not
too subtle or too low-level to be available to ordinary people.

The phoneme bond theories that were discussed in the preceding section provide a nice account of these results. Consider the case of /ʧ/. Children (and adults)

may represent /ʧ/ as a sequence of two segments, /t/ followed by /ʃ/. However, these segments are joined by such a strong bond that they usually behave as a unit. The affricate bond that joins the /t/ and /ʃ/ of *chill* is stronger than the onset bond that joins the /t/ and /w/ of *twill,* as shown, for example, by the results of Treiman (1985b). Because the affricate bond is so strong, children usually spell affricates as single units. However, they do not always do so. Within the bond framework, the question of whether a segment is one unit or two need not have a clear-cut answer. Intermediate answers are also possible.

Similarities and Differences Among Phonemes

Children who speak and understand distinguish among the phonemes of their language. For example, they differentiate between /g/ and /k/ and between /ɛ/ and /æ/. However, as also emphasized by Read (1975), children do much more than this. Children tacitly recognize the similarities and differences among the phonemes that they classify as different. For example, children consider pairs of consonants that are the same in all respects but voicing (e.g., /g/ and /k/) to be similar to one another. They sometimes use a letter that is appropriate for one consonant of the pair for the other consonant, as in *g* for /k/. As another example, children place both /ɛ/ and /æ/ in the category of front, unrounded vowels. As a result, they sometimes use *a* to spell /ɛ/. Such findings imply that part of language development is learning to recognize the similarities among phonemes that one has previously learned to treat as different.

What Kind of Writing System is Easiest to Learn?

Alphabetic writing systems differ from one another in many ways. The most obvious difference, perhaps, is in the regularity of the relations between phonemes and graphemes. In some writing systems, such as Finnish, virtually every phoneme is represented with the same grapheme each time it occurs. That is, there are one-to-one relations from phonemes to graphemes. In other writing systems, such as English, phonemes generally have more than one possible spelling. That is, there are one-to-many relations from phonemes to graphemes. Systems of the former sort are thought to be easier to learn than systems of the latter sort (e.g., Downing, 1973; Kyöstiö, 1980; Lindgren et al., 1985).

My results support the commonsense belief that regularity is important in learning to spell. The first graders in this study were more accurate on regular words such as *plan* than on irregular words such as *plaid.* They were more accurate on phonemes that had only a few spellings than on phonemes that had many spellings. These results imply that, other things being equal, a writing system in which each phoneme was spelled in only one way would be easier to master than a more complex writing system.

However, the concept of regularity is not as simple as it might first seem. Consider the words *tape, sty,* and *city.* From an adult's perspective, the *t* in all these words is regular. All three words contain a /t/ phoneme; /t/ is spelled with *t* in all three cases. Children, however, may consider *sty* to contain /d/ rather than /t/. If so, the *t* in *sty* is not regular from their point of view. What is regular for adults may not always be regular for children.

Although English is often considered highly irregular, it *does* have a number of regularities at a morphological level. Consider the words *jumped* and *cleaned.* On the basis of sound alone, these words are irregularly spelled. *Jumped* should end with *pt; cleaned* should end with *nd.* When meaning is taken into account, the spellings become more regular. Both words contain the past tense morpheme; this morpheme is spelled as *ed* in both cases. Many first graders do not yet understand that morphemes tend to be spelled in a consistent manner. As a result, these children misspell *jumped* as JUMPT or JUPT and *cleaned* as KLEND or KLED. The problem, in this case, is not that the English writing system is irregular. Regularities exist, but at the level of meaning rather than the level of sound. As this example shows, one should not be too quick to ascribe all of children's spelling errors to the irregularity of the English writing system.

Another case in which even very regular words are difficult for children to spell is that of digraphs. Although *thin* and *ship* are regular by any imaginable criterion, first graders often misspell these words. They make errors like TIN or HIN for *thin* and SIP for *ship.* The problem lies in the digraphs *th* and *sh.* Children have difficulty segmenting the printed word *thin* into graphemes because there is no visual clue that the letters *t* and *h* belong together. Even if children segment the printed word correctly, into *th, i,* and *n,* they have difficulty learning the link between the phoneme /θ/ and the group of letters *th.* My results imply that, other things being equal, a writing system with few or no digraphs would be easier to learn than a writing system with many digraphs.

Words whose spoken forms contain consonant clusters are also difficult for first graders to spell, even when the words are regular. For example, children misspell *play* as PAY, *snake* as SAK, and *milk* as MIK. These errors, I have argued, reflect children's problems in segmenting the spoken words into phonemes. In the case of *play,* children treat /pl/ as a unit rather than dividing it into the separate phonemes /p/ and /l/. My results imply that, other things being equal, children would learn to spell more easily in a language that had few or no consonant clusters than in a language that had many consonant clusters.

When comparing children's performance in different languages, one must also consider the names that are given to letters. In English, the names of letters are not always a good guide to the spelling of words. For example, *tape* is not spelled *tap; rain* is not spelled *ran.* Children use the names of letters to help them spell, especially when, like middle-class American children, they learn letter names at an early age. Other things being equal, a writing system in which the letters' names consistently indicated the letters' sounds would be easier to master than a writing system in which they did not.

Thus, the irregularity of the English writing system is one source of difficulty for children learning to spell in English. However, it is not the only problem. Other trouble spots include the morphological basis of the English writing system, its use of digraphs, the consonant clusters in the spoken language, and the fact that English letter names are not always a good guide to spelling. If children learning to write and read in English have more difficulty than children learning to write and read in some other language, we cannot ascribe the difference to regularity alone. We must consider other aspects of the writing systems, including their use of digraphs and their system of letter names. We must also consider aspects of the spoken languages, including their use of consonant clusters.

Although it is possible to distinguish between the orthographic complications of a particular writing system—for example, its use of digraphs—and the linguistic complications of a spoken language—for example, its use of consonant clusters—orthography and phonology are closely related. For instance, digraphs are one possible response to a situation in there are fewer letters in the written language than phonemes in the spoken language. English has such a mismatch, with 26 letters and about 38 phonemes. If only single-letter graphemes were allowed, many letters would have to symbolize more than one phoneme. That is, there would be many-to-one mappings from phonemes to graphemes. In response to this problem, English has chosen to use letter groups such as *sh* to stand for single phonemes. The use of digraphs increases the regularity of the English writing system. Unfortunately, digraphs also cause difficulty for beginning spellers. It is not clear whether the benefits of increased regularity outweigh the costs.

Another possible response to a mismatch between letters and phonemes is to use *diacritical marks,* or marks that are added to letters. For example, *š* could be used to symbolize /ʃ/, while unadorned *s* is used for /s/. The symbol *ē* could be used for /i/, with *ĕ* being used for /ɛ/. Like digraphs, diacritics increase the regularity of the system by effectively increasing the number of letters. However, diacritics may be easier for children to handle than digraphs. This is because diacritics are easier to parse. It is clear, in the spelling *šin* for /ʃ'ɪn/, that the symbol ˘ goes with the symbol *s*. It is less clear in *shin* that *h* goes with *s*. Not surprisingly, teachers have long used diacritics such as ‾ and ˘ to mark "long" and "short" vowels.

The Relation between Spelling and Reading

How are spelling and reading related to one another? Children who read well usually spell well too (e.g., Gough et al., 1992). However, the correlation between spelling and reading is not perfect. Some children (and some adults) read well but spell appallingly. In addition, Bryant and Bradley (1980) have suggested that the *activities* of spelling and reading are not closely connected for young children. For instance, children may spell a word but then be unable to read it.

My results suggest that reading and spelling are related in some ways but different in other ways. Spelling and reading are related in that the store of knowledge that children use for spelling is similar to the store of knowledge that they use for reading. Supporting this claim, the words that children know how to read influence their spelling. For example, the first graders in this study often spelled /ɑ/ as *a* even though this correspondence was not formally taught in their classroom. The children must have done this because they had seen words like *water* and *garden*. As another example, the first graders rarely produced spellings like CKAP or SSIM.

This was true even though the children had not been taught that words may not begin with *ck* or *ss*. Children must avoid spellings like CKAP and SSIM because they have seen words like *pack* and *miss* but not words like **ckap* and **ssim*. Ehri and Robbins (1992) have provided further evidence that information remembered from reading words affects children's spelling. Thus, spelling and reading draw on a similar fund of knowledge.

For young children, the activities of spelling and reading are less closely connected. Children do not typically check their spellings by determining whether what they have produced, when read back, matches what they intended to write. Indeed, the goal of spelling is more to get something down on paper than to get something down that can later be read back by the child or by another person. Thus, children often produce spellings that they themselves would not pronounce as the intended word. For example, some first graders spell *play* as PAY even though they say *pay* when asked to read PAY. Moreover, first graders sometimes produce identical spellings for words that sound different. For example, they may spell *bed, bad,* and *bade* as BAD. They may spell both *play* and *pay* as PAY. Even when shown that they have spelled different-sounding words alike, first graders do not necessarily change their spellings or show signs of puzzlement (Read, 1975; Treiman, 1991). Thus, although spelling and reading draw on a similar fund of knowledge, and the processes involved in the two activities are not the same for first graders.

For adults, spelling and reading are more similar. They are similar in the store of knowledge on which they draw and they are similar in the processes by which they are carried out. Thus, adults often write a word and then determine whether what they have written, when read back, matches what they meant to write. In this way, the reading process becomes a part of the spelling process for adults.

The Teaching of Spelling

The Place of Spelling in the First-Grade Classroom

If spelling and reading do not involve precisely the same processes, spelling cannot be ignored in the elementary-school classroom. We cannot assume that skill in spelling will follow directly from skill in reading. Although learning to read words certainly helps children learn to spell, it is not always sufficient. Thus, it is not advisable to postpone writing until children have achieved a fair amount of skill in reading—a practice that, until recently, was common in American schools. Children should write from the very beginning.

It is sometimes argued that young children should not be encouraged to write because they will misspell words. Children will read and learn these incorrect spellings, the argument goes, and so have trouble learning the correct spellings. My results suggest that this should not be a major concern at the first-grade level. True, the spellings that people see and read influence their attempts to spell. My findings attest to this, as do the results of other research with children (Ehri & Robbins, 1992) and adults (Jacoby & Hollingshead, 1990). However, first graders do not always read back the spellings that they produce. They pay more attention to the process of spelling than to the product. Moreover, first graders feel little need for consistency in their spelling. If they misspell a word once, they will not necessarily misspell it the same way again.

For first graders, the many benefits of independent writing outweigh the costs. Writing requires children to think about the sounds and meanings of spoken words, to observe the characteristics of printed words, and to form hypotheses about the relations between sounds and letters. All of these activities are of great value in helping children grasp the alphabetic nature of the English writing system.

I suspect, along with Frith (1985), that writing is actually *more* potent than reading in forcing children to come to grips with the alphabetic principle. When reading a word, beginners can focus on one characteristic of the word that distinguishes it from all of the other printed words they know (see Gough et al., 1992). For example, they can recognize *dog* by virtue of the "tail" at the end of the word. They can recognize *camel* by virtue of the two "humps" on the *m*. Beginning readers who rely on this logographic approach do not process all of the letters in printed words. They pay attention to only the word's most salient features. Although the logographic approach eventually breaks down as children learn more and more words, many children rely on it when they first start to read. Indeed, children can get by for some time as purely logographic readers. When writing, there is less room for such shortcuts. Children must pay attention to each letter in a word as they write it. Unless they have memorized the word's complete spelling, they must also pay attention to the spoken word and its phonemes in order to spell the word. Thus, practice in spelling may be even more important than practice in reading for acquisition of the alphabetic principle.

In addition, writing has benefits beyond the word level. It forces children to reflect upon and organize their ideas and to express their thoughts. These benefits, important though they are, are beyond the scope of this book.

Research supports the idea that first graders profit from producing their own spellings. Clarke (1988) compared two groups of children—those whose teacher encouraged them to invent their own spellings and those whose teacher encouraged conventional spelling. When the children's spelling and reading skills were tested in March of first grade, the inventive spellers performed better than the traditional spellers on most measures.

Recognizing the benefits of writing and spelling, some experts have suggested that children should start to write *before* they begin to read (e.g., Chomsky, 1979; Montessori, 1966). My results suggest that, although writing is important, the "write first, read later" view should not be pushed to extremes. Much of the raw material that children use to form and test hypotheses about the links between sounds and spellings and about the properties of printed words comes from their experience with reading. Children benefit from their reading experience to learn things they have not been explicitly taught. To deny children exposure to printed words would be to cripple their spelling. Thus, although there is room for debate about the relative emphasis that should be placed on spelling and reading during the beginning stages of instruction, both skills are important. Children should write from the beginning, but they should read too.

If first graders are to write independently or semi-independently, what attitude should teachers take toward correct spelling? There are good reasons to downplay correct spelling at the first-grade level. Children who feel free to invent spellings for unknown words produce longer stories containing a greater variety of words than children who feel constrained to produce only words whose spellings they already know (Clarke, 1988). Children who feel free to invent their own spellings find that their writing, even when it contains errors, can be read by other people. Writing, they learn, serves to communicate. Although first graders should not be expected to spell all words correctly, they should learn that every word has a conventional spelling. They should learn that, even if they do not yet know a word's conventional spelling, they will learn it when they get older. I disagree with the practice, followed by the teacher in this study, of not telling children the conventional spelling of a word when the children ask for it. Given the speed and ease with which children learn from exposure to conventional spelling, it seems wrong to deny children the information they seek.

Letter Names

There is little doubt that familiarity with the letters of the alphabet provides a basic foundation for learning to spell and read. As Adams (1990, p. 361) states, "solid familiarity with the visual shapes of the individual letters is an absolute prerequisite for learning to read." But to what extent does knowledge of letter names help spellers generate the correct spellings of specific words? According to some investigators, letter names are quite useful in this regard. For example, Durrell and Murphy (1963, p. 5) state:

> Since most letter names contain the sounds of the letter, the ability to name letters should aid in establishing relations between the phonemes of the spoken word and the printed form of the word. The child who knows letter names has an excellent first step in phonics.

My findings provide only limited support for this view for children learning to spell in English. Letter names *do* provide helpful clues to the spellings of some words. For example, knowledge of letter names helps children to spell the /o/ of *both* and the /e/ of *baby*—vowel phonemes that are symbolized with the letters that have those names. Knowledge of letter names (coupled with ability to divide spoken syllables into onsets and rimes) helps children to learn the links between /b/ and *b* and /t/ and *t*—letters whose names contain the phonemes that they represent. In other cases, however, reliance on letter names alone can cause children to misspell words. One reason for this is that phonemes and groups of phonemes that match the name of a letter are not always spelled with that letter in English. For instance, the /ai/ of *bike* is spelled with *i* followed by final *e* rather than with single *i*. The /a/ and /r/ of *car* are spelled with *a* followed by *r* rather than with single *r*. Children who use a letter-name strategy may misspell these words as BIK and CR. A second reason why letter names are not always helpful for English-speaking children is that some phonemes do not appear in the name of the letter that typically represents the phoneme. For example, /g/ is not found in the name of *g*. Children cannot rely on their knowledge of letter names to remember the link between /g/ and *g*.

My results confirm that children who know the names of letters before they begin to write and read use this knowledge to suggest the spellings of specific pho-nemes. The problem, for English, is that letter names are not always good clues to spelling. For children who are already familiar with letters when they enter first grade, additional drill on letter names is probably unnecessary. Rather than trying to improve children's spelling *indirectly,* by drilling children on the names of letters, we should focus more *directly* on spelling.

Informal Instruction

Spelling instruction falls into two general categories—informal instruction and for-mal instruction. There is little debate in the educational community on the value of informal spelling instruction. Such instruction is compatible with a phonics approach and is encouraged by those who also advocate formal spelling instruction (e.g., Henderson, 1985). Informal spelling instruction also fits with the language-experience and whole-language philosophies. This is because the teacher responds on the spot to a child's errors. Words and sound are discussed within a meaningful context; the instruction is tailored to the child's needs.

Given the value of informal spelling instruction, how can such instruction be most effective? Three things are needed. First, it is helpful if the teacher can look at a child's spellings and figure out what the child meant to write. If time has passed, the child cannot always remember. Second, the teacher must make a good guess about why the child spelled the word in the way that he or she did. Third, the teacher must determine what help the child needs in order to spell better.

Experienced teachers are good at interpreting children's errors. They do fairly well even when the errors are taken out of context (Chapter 2). No doubt, they do much better when the errors are in context. However, adults cannot always figure out what children meant to write. The more teachers know about the sounds of the English language and about the common spelling errors of young children, the bet-ter they will be. Teachers' ability to decipher children's errors will also improve if they realize that many errors do not match the intended word when read aloud.

It is also important to understand why children produce the spellings they do and how they can be helped to improve. My results suggest that different errors arise for different reasons and call for different responses.

Some errors arise in the assignment of spellings to sounds. For example, chil-dren may misspell *been* as BIN, symbolizing /ɪ/ with its typical spelling, *i,* rather than with *ee.* With irregular words such as *been,* children have no choice but to memorize the conventional spelling of at least part of the words. Errors like MIN for *men,* among children who speak a dialect like the one in this study, occur for similar reasons. Children who speak such a dialect code the spoken word as /mɪn/; they spell /ɪ/ with the letter *i.* These children must learn that the /ɪ/ of /mɪn/ is spelled with *e.*

Children sometimes misspell words because their phonemic categories do not match those assumed by the English writing system. For example, first graders may consider *her* to contain two phonemes, /h/ followed by syllabic /r/. As a result, they often spell it with two letters, HR. These errors are similar to the BIN and MIN errors just discussed in that children who misspell *her* as HR have accurately analyzed the spoken word into smaller segments and have used reasonable graphemes to represent the segments. The only problem is that the spoken form being analyzed is the children's own, not the one assumed by the conventional writing system.

Other errors arise in the analysis of spoken words into phonemes. For example, children may analyze *play* into /pl/ and /e/ rather than into /p/, /l/, and /e/. They spell the unit /pl/ with *p,* producing PAY. Errors like FRM for *farm* and SL for *spell* also reflect incomplete analysis of syllables into phonemes. In these cases, children need help in phonemic analysis. Phonemic-analysis training should improve their spelling, even without drill on the conventional spellings of the words.

Still other errors reflect a lack of explicit morphological analysis. For example, children who spell *jumped* as JUMPT need to become aware that this word ends with the past tense morpheme. They need to know that this morpheme is spelled with *ed* even when it is pronounced as /t/.

Finally, some errors reflect children's experience with printed words. For instance, children who have observed that virtually all printed words contain a vowel letter may spell *her* as HRE. They know that there must be a vowel letter in this word but their phonemic representation of the word, /h/ followed by syllabic /r/, does not tell them where the vowel letter should go. As another example, children who have seen *th* for /θ/ in words like *thing* may remember one letter of the digraph but forget the other. Or, the children may place the two letters in the wrong order.

Formal Instruction

If children are to be given formal instruction in spelling—and I believe that they should—my results offer some suggestions about what types of instruction are most needed at the first-grade level.

It makes sense to allot more time and effort to things that children find difficult than to things that children find easy. Children will learn the easy things on their own. They will have trouble with the difficult things unless the difficulties can be overcome through teaching. As one example, the correspondence between /ε/ and *e* is hard for children to learn. The main reason is that /ε/ sounds similar to other vowels that are spelled differently. The correspondence between /æ/ and *a* is comparatively easy for children to learn. This is because /æ/ is spelled so consistently in English and because /æ/ is not similar to many other vowels. Instead of spending equal time on the correspondence between /ε/ and *e* and the correspondence between /æ/ and *a,* as most spelling programs do, why not spend more time on the link between /ε/ and *e?*

Phonemic-awareness training, although not typically considered part of the spelling curriculum, is crucial for young children. A certain level of phonemic awareness is necessary for children to even begin inventing their own spellings. For those first graders who do not write at all or who persist in producing letter sequences like ACR for "I like swings and I like slides. And I like the sun," instruction in phonemic awareness is vital. Potentially, it can prevent these children from experiencing the ever-increasing spiral of difficulties in reading, spelling, and overall school performance that they would otherwise face. Phonemic-awareness training is important, too, for average first graders. Although many middle-class first graders can divide spoken syllables into onsets and rimes, they have difficulty subdividing these units into phonemes. Exercises with spoken words can help children perform such analyses. If children can learn to recognize the /l/ in the spoken words *play* and *milk,* they will know to use *l* when spelling these words. If children are not aware of the /l/ in the spoken forms of *play* and *milk,* no amount of drill on the correspondence between /l/ and *l* will eliminate spelling errors like PAY and MIK.

Appendix I

These results show the children's spellings of each phoneme broken down by the conventional spellings of the phoneme. The results are for *all* words in the collection, including words that the children spelled correctly and words that the children spelled incorrectly. The symbol & indicates that the letters or groups of letters in a spelling are not adjacent. For example, *a&e* is the conventional spelling of /e/ in the word *came*. When a letter is enclosed in parentheses, this means that the letter represents a phoneme in addition to the one in question. For example, *x* represents both /k/ and /s/ in *fox*.

/i/

1138 Total Occurrences

Standard spelling = *e* (e.g., *he, rodeo*)		Standard spelling = *i* (e.g., *king, pizza*)	
e	526	*i*	84
omitted	16	*e*	49
ee	7	omitted	27
a	7	*a*	8
u	7	*ee*	7
y	6	*ei*	7
ey	5	*e&e*	5
ie	4	*u*	3
i	4	*e&i*	3
ea	2	*a&e*	3
ai	1	*o*	2
n	1	*a&y*	2
en	1	*ai*	2
iy	1	*ea*	1
w	1	*ey*	1
iey	1	*y*	1
ar	1	*ae*	1
is	1	*ay*	1
Total	592	*i&e*	1
		i&i	1
		eey	1
		ei&e	1
		igi	1
		ikei	1
		i&u	1
		t	1
		iyee	1
		u&e	1
		e&ie	1
		Total	218

Standard spelling = *y*
(e.g., *happy, city*)

y	39
e	34
omitted	14
ey	4
ie	4
a	2
ye	2
ee	1
n	1
ys	1
eys	1
Total	103

Standard spelling = *ee*
(e.g., *asleep, three*)

e	34
ee	33
i	6
e&e	5
e&i	3
omitted	2
ea	1
a	1
i&e	1
ee&e	1
he	1
Total	88

Standard spelling = *ea*
(e.g., *eat, clean*)

e	38
ea	24
ee	6
i	2
omitted	2
e&e	2
el	2
y	1
a	1
ie	1
ae	1
e&u	1
oo	1
ear	1
g	1
Total	84

Standard spelling = *ee&e*
(*cheese*)

e	12
e&e	2
omitted	1
are&e	1
Total	16

Standard spelling = *ie*
(e.g., *babies, stories*)

omitted	3
e	3
y	2
ie	1
ey	1
i	1
Total	11

Standard spelling = *ey*
(e.g., *Joey, key*)

ey	3
e	3
y	2
oe	1
Total	9

Standard spelling = *a*
(e.g., *villagers, oranges*)

a	2
e	2
omitted	1
Total	5

Standard spelling = *ay*
(*always*)

e	2
e&e	1
ia	1
Total	4

Standard spelling = *eo*
(*people*)

e	3
Total	3

Standard spelling = *e&e* (creme, Charlene)		Standard spelling = *i&e* (machines)	
e&e	1	ee	1
e	1	Total	1
Total	2		

Standard spelling = *ea&e* (please, leave)	
e	1
ay	1
Total	2

/e/

486 Total Occurrences

Standard spelling = *a* (e.g., *a, baby*)		Standard spelling = *ay* (e.g., *birthday, playing*)	
a	211	ay	34
a&e	6	a	25
ai	3	ae	4
ae	3	ew	2
ay	2	a&e	1
omitted	2	ey	1
e	2	ea	1
ak	1	aye	1
uo	1	y	1
Total	231	o	1
		aey	1

Standard spelling = *a&e* (e.g., *came, face*)		iay	1
		iy	1
a&e	41	au	1
a	41	oy	1
ae	4	Total	76
e	3		
ea	3		
omitted	2		
ai	2		
aa	1		
e&e	1		
oo	1		
a&y	1		
i&e	1		
ao	1		
iey	1		
u	1		
o&e	1		
Total	105		

Standard spelling = *ey*
(they)

ey	9
ay	8
a	3
ea	3
y	3
e	2
aye	2
omitted	1
en	1
eye	1
uay	1
Total	34

Standard spelling = *ai*
(e.g., *Kool-Aid, rain*)

a	9
a&e	4
i	3
ay	2
ae	2
ai	1
e	1
omitted	1
aye	1
o	1
renm	1
Total	26

Standard spelling = *e*
(eggs, legs)

e	3
a	2
Total	5

Standard spelling = *ea*
(e.g., *steak, great*)

a	2
a&e	1
ae	1
Total	4

Standard spelling = *eigh*
(weighs)

a	1
a&e	1
o	1
Total	3

Standard spelling = omitted
(K-Mart)

omitted	1
i	1
Total	2

/ai/

825 Total Occurrences

Standard spelling = *i*
(e.g., *I, dinosaur*)

i	418
ia	8
i&e	6
y	2
e	2
iy	1
ii	1
ai	1
im	1
in	1
ooie	1
ir	1
Total	443

Standard spelling = *y*
(e.g., *my, by*)

y	122
i	38
omitted	8
iy	6
ie	5
e	2
i&e	1
ii	1
a	1
aoy	1
ay	1
ee	1
ig	1
uy	1
ei	1
iiy	1
ya	1
Total	192

Standard spelling = *i&e*
(e.g., *wife, nice*)

i&e	93
i	49
ie	7
o	5
ii	3
ia	2
a	2
il&e	2
e	1
ie&e	1
il	1
ide	1
oe&e	1
ae	1
itiy	1
Total	170

Standard spelling = *igh*
(e.g., *high, night*)

i	7
i&e	1
ie	1
iy	1
o	1
Total	11

Standard spelling = *uy*
(*buy, buys*)

iy	3
i	1
oiy	1
Total	5

Standard spelling = *ie*
(*fries, cries*)

i	2
iy	1
Total	3

Standard spelling = *eye*
(*eyes*)

iey	1
Total	1

/o/

232 Total Occurrences

Standard spelling = *o*
(e.g., *both, go*)

o	76
ow	8
omitted	5
oo	2
uo	2
o&e	1
owe	1
a	1
u&e	1
eo	1
Total	**98**

Standard spelling = *o&e*
(e.g., *home, hope*)

o	34
o&e	11
omitted	3
e	3
oo	1
uo	1
a	1
oa	1
eo	1
oy	1
ou	1
oi	1
o&o	1
ao	1
oneo	1
Total	**62**

Standard spelling = *ow*
(e.g., *blow, followed*)

o	19
ow	12
omitted	3
owe	3
l	3
oe	3
oat	2
o&e	1
oo	1
uo	1
oow	1
oy	1
u	1
aw	1
cku	1
ll	1
le	1
rd	1
oyo	1
Total	**57**

Standard spelling = *oa*
(e.g., *coach, board*)

o	6
oa	1
ow	1
oo	1
a	1
oow	1
Total	**11**

Standard spelling = *oo*
(*door, floor*)

o	2
Total	**2**

Standard spelling = *oh*
(*oh*)

o	1
Total	**1**

Standard spelling = *ough*
(*though*)

oupt	1
Total	**1**

/u/

290 Total Occurrences

Standard spelling = *o*
(e.g., *do, who*)

o	111
oo	14
ow	5
u	2
a	2
oh	2
e	1
uo	1
ee	1
w	1
Total	140

Standard spelling = *oo*
(e.g., *food, kangaroo*)

oo	23
o	15
omitted	8
u	6
ou	4
o&e	3
u&e	2
e	2
a	1
r	1
u&y	1
oon	1
qe	1
g	1
oi	1
ooy	1
Total	71

Standard spelling = *ou*
(e.g., *groups, you*)

ou	10
u	4
uo	2
oow	1
ay	1
oou	1
Total	19

Standard spelling = *ue*
(e.g., *blue, Sue*)

ue	13
u&e	2
ow	1
uw	1
oey	1
Total	18

Standard spelling = *oo&e*
(e.g., *goose, loose*)

oo	4
o	3
o&e	2
oo&e	1
u	1
ou	1
omitted	1
ooe	1
io	1
oe	1
o&ee	1
r&y	1
Total	18

Standard spelling = *ew*
(e.g., *flew, knew*)

ow	4
oo	3
ew	2
u	1
ou	1
oow	1
iew	1
uv	1
Total	14

Standard spelling = *u*
(*supermarket, Rufus*)

omitted	3
u	1
oo	1
Total	5

Standard spelling = *ui*
(*fruit, fruits*)

o	1
u	1
Total	2

Standard spelling = *u&e*
(*rule, used*)

u&e	1
oo	1
Total	2

Standard spelling = *oe*
(*shoe*)

oow	1
Total	1

/ɑ/

335 Total Occurrences

Standard spelling = *o*
(e.g., *got, fox*)

o	187
i	13
omitted	8
a	6
e	4
u	3
r	2
o&e	2
oo	2
uo	1
Total	228

Standard spelling = *a*
(e.g., *garden, water*)

a	29
o	28
omitted	17
u	6
i	4
e	3
a&e	2
ah	1
un	1
Total	91

Standard spelling = *a&e*
(*are*)

a&e	9
a	1
Total	10

Standard spelling = *ou*
(*our*)

ou	1
o	1
a	1
a&e	1
u	1
ie	1
Total	6

/ɔ/

302 Total Occurrences

Standard spelling = *o*
(e.g., *dog, corn*)

o	131
oo	7
a	6
omitted	4
i	4
o&e	4
r	3
u&e	2
o&o	2
u	1
ou	1
oa	1
e	1
a&e	1
w	1
a&ye	1
Total	170

Standard spelling = *a*
(e.g., *all, wash*)

o	13
a	10
oo	5
omitted	4
ou	3
oa	2
i	2
ol	1
oe	1
u	1
e	1
y	1
w	1
ao	1
iu	1
r&e	1
os	1
uos	1
h	1
uo	1
ro	1
Total	53

Standard spelling = *au*
(e.g., *dinosaur, auction*)

au	13
o	7
omitted	3
u	3
a	1
a&i	1
oy	1
Total	29

Standard spelling = *aw*
(e.g., *saw, sawing*)

ol	7
o	1
oi	1
lel	1
od	1
oley	1
ow	1
rl	1
relae	1
ole	1
Total	16

Standard spelling = *ough*
(*bought, thought*)

o	8
omitted	1
i	1
o&e	1
ur	1
auy	1
Total	13

Standard spelling = *au&e*
(because, Claude)

o	2
u	2
au&e	1
a	1
oo	1
omitted	1
ou	1
u&e	1
oi	1
Total	11

Standard spelling = *al*
(e.g., *walk, sidewalk*)

o	2
al	1
oe	1
a	1
oo	1
a&e	1
ol	1
Total	8

Standard spelling = *augh*
(caught)

o	1
ae	1
Total	2

/au/

161 Total Occurrences

Standard spelling = *ou* (e.g., *mountain, about*)		Standard spelling = *ou&e* (e.g., *blouse, house*)	
ou	18	a	5
a	16	ou&e	3
o	10	omitted	3
aw	6	al	2
omitted	4	o&e	2
ow	3	w	2
ao	3	oue	2
ae	2	ou	1
al	1	o	1
ou&e	1	ao	1
o&e	1	i	1
i	1	a&y	1
alo	1	ia&e	1
a&o	1	oa	1
oe	1	ol	1
uo	1	ouo	1
Total	**70**	ouo&e	1
		e	1
		Total	**30**

Standard spelling = *ow* (e.g., *cow, growled*)	
ow	23
a	8
al	6
o	5
aw	5
omitted	1
ao	1
ae	1
ai	1
aal	1
aoe	1
as	1
ay	1
u	1
owl	1
oow	1
aol	1
wen	1
ah	1
Total	**61**

/oi/

44 Total Occurrences

Standard spelling = *oy* (e.g., *boy, destroy*)	
oy	24
oe	3
o	2
al	1
auy	1
ay	1
ey	1
y	1
oi	1
oowe	1
ooy	1
ou	1
ow	1
ue	1
ooeye	1
oye	1
Total	42

Standard spelling = *oi* (*coin*)	
o	1
Total	1

Standard spelling = *oi&e* (*noise*)	
oy	1
Total	1

/ɪ/

765 Total Occurrences

Standard spelling = *i* (e.g., *him, it*)	
i	392
e	58
omitted	41
a	18
o	3
e&e	2
ai	2
ea	2
i&e	1
ia	1
oi	1
ei	1
eeeh	1
e&a	1
ew	1
i&u	1
r	1
io	1
Total	528

Standard spelling = *e* (e.g., *end, pretty*)	
i	65
e	59
omitted	17
a	16
e&e	6
i&e	3
o	3
ia	2
(*o&e*)	2
oi	1
e&y	1
se	1
Total	176

Standard spelling = *ie*
(*friend, friends*)

e	7
a	4
e&e	3
i	2
omitted	2
i&e	1
u	1
e&i	1
Total	21

Standard spelling = *i&e*
(e.g., *give, lived*)

i	5
i&e	2
e	2
omitted	1
a	1
e&e	1
e&i	1
oo	1
Total	14

Standard spelling = *ee*
(*been, deer*)

omitted	3
e	2
ee	1
i	1
oe	1
Total	8

Standard spelling = omitted
(*Mrs.*)

i	4
omitted	2
o	1
Total	7

Standard spelling = *a*
(*any, anything*)

i	2
ei	1
e	1
Total	4

Standard spelling = *ea*
(*year, really*)

i	2
e	1
Total	3

Standard spelling = *ui*
(*building*)

u	1
i	1
Total	2

Standard spelling = *y*
(*junglegym*)

omitted	1
Total	1

Standard spelling = *ai*
(*again*)

e	1
Total	1

/ɛ/

255 Total Occurrences

Standard spelling = *e*
(e.g., *best, help*)

e	82
a	47
omitted	10
i	8
o	2
u	2
a&e	1
a&a	1
eu	1
ei	1
ee	1
ia	1
Total	157

Standard spelling = *ea*
(e.g., *meadow, bread*)

a	15
e	9
omitted	2
i	2
o	1
ea	1
Total	30

Standard spelling = *e&e*
(e.g., *there, where*)

a	13
e	4
e&e	3
omitted	1
o	1
Total	22

Standard spelling = *ai*
(e.g., *said, hairy*)

a	5
ai	3
i	2
a&e	2
i&e	2
e	1
u	1
ae	1
ae&e	1
ai&e	1
Total	19

Standard spelling = *a&e*
(care, scared)

a	4
a&e	2
e	2
a&y	2
omitted	1
iuv	1
ay	1
Total	13

Standard spelling = *a*
(e.g., *Mary, carrots*)

a	3
omitted	2
o	2
u	1
Total	8

Standard spelling = *ei*
(their)

e	2
a	1
omitted	1
Total	4

Standard spelling = *ay* (*Ayrway*)		Standard spelling = *ey&e* (*they're*)	
a&y	1	*e*	1
Total	1	Total	1

/æ/

614 Total Occurrences

Standard spelling = *a* (e.g., *had, brand*)		Standard spelling = *a&e* (*have*)	
a	518	*a&e*	12
omitted	16	*a*	3
i	12	omitted	1
a&e	10	Total	16
e	10		
o	9	Standard spelling = *au*	
aa	4	(*aunt*)	
ae	2	*e*	1
ao	2	Total	1
ai	1		
au	1		
c	1		
d&e	1		
ea	1		
a&y	1		
al	1		
aoo	1		
t	1		
oa	1		
odi	1		
u	1		
ah	1		
ay	1		
Total	597		

/ʊ/

102 Total Occurrences

Standard spelling = *oo* (e.g., *book, wood*)		Standard spelling = *oul* (e.g., *could, would*)	
oo	26	*oo*	2
o	9	*o*	2
u	8	omitted	1
omitted	4	*i*	1
i	2	*ua*	1
ua	2	*a*	1
e	2	Total	8
a	1		
r	1	Standard spelling = *o* (*woman*)	
ouru	1	*u*	2
g	1	*o*	1
h	1	*i*	1
o&e	1	Total	4
ee	1		
Total	60		

Standard spelling = *u* (e.g., *put, pushed*)	
u	7
omitted	7
o	6
oo	3
(*u*)	2
a	1
ow	1
en	1
e&e	1
ou	1
Total	30

/ə/

1144 Total Occurrences

Standard spelling = e (e.g., *bigger, dishes*)		Standard spelling = u (e.g., *peanut, us*)	
omitted	200	u	104
e	120	o	19
u	17	omitted	13
i	17	i	7
o	11	a	6
a	5	e	3
y	3	u&e	2
ei	2	ou	1
ue	1	y	1
e&e	1	a&e	1
i&e	1	ue	1
e&ee	1	ie	1
io	1	eu	1
al	1	yi	1
oy	1	Total	161
Total	382		

Standard spelling = a (e.g., *asleep, elephant*)		Standard spelling = o (e.g., *brother, dinosaur*)	
		o	50
a	88	u	32
omitted	48	omitted	29
u	40	e	6
o	22	a	5
e	17	i	4
i	10	u&e	2
oi	2	ou	1
o&e	1	a&e	1
y	1	aa	1
ue	1	or	1
uo	1	aw	1
e&e	1	Total	133
ae	1		
o&y	1		
ui	1		
uts	1		
oo	1		
r&e	1		
r	1		
Total	239		

Standard spelling = *i*
(e.g., *birthday, animals*)

omitted	44
i	19
e	9
u	5
a	5
o	2
ue	1
l	1
oe	1
Total	87

Standard spelling = *o&e*
(e.g., *come, love*)

u	15
o&e	13
omitted	5
a	5
o	5
e	4
u&e	3
a&e	2
ou&e	1
uu	1
Total	54

Standard spelling = *ou*
(e.g., *curious, trouble*)

omitted	8
ou	7
o	4
u	2
ou&o	2
a	1
y	1
uo	1
ou&e	1
Total	27

Standard spelling = omitted
(e.g., *didn't, fire*)

omitted	22
u	3
a	1
Total	26

Standard spelling = (*o&e*)
(e.g., *one, someone*)

u	5
(*o&e*)	4
a	1
(*o*)	1
omitted	1
Total	12

Standard spelling = *e&e*
(e.g., *were, serve*)

omitted	7
o	2
u	1
e	1
i	1
Total	12

Standard spelling = *ea*
(*learning*)

omitted	3
Total	3

Standard spelling = *u&e*
(*treasure, fortune*)

uo	1
o	1
oa	1
Total	3

Standard spelling = *ai*
(*mountain, mountains*)

i	1
ia	1
Total	2

Standard spelling = *i&e*
(*favorite*)

i	1
Total	1

Standard spelling = *oe*
(*does*)

e	1
Total	1

Standard spelling = *y*
(*tyrannosaurus*)

omitted	1
Total	1

/p/

380 Total Occurrences

Standard spelling = *p* (e.g., *poke, help*)		Standard spelling = *pp* (e.g., *chopped, pepper*)	
p	303	*p*	23
omitted	18	*pp*	10
b	6	*d*	2
d	2	*n*	2
m	2	omitted	1
pp	1	*b*	1
pw	1	*pk*	1
hr	1	Total	40
t	1		
q	1		
o	1		
pc	1		
g	1		
p&p	1		
Total	340		

/t/

1208 Total Occurrences

Standard spelling = *t*
(e.g., *to, cat*)

t	950
omitted	83
d	24
tt	7
th	5
s	3
r	3
ch	2
c	2
i	2
d&nd	1
nd	1
t&n	1
tr	1
n	1
st	1
gt	1
ded	1
nt	1
re	1
ng	1
h	1
dt	1
Total	1094

Standard spelling = *tt*
(e.g., *little, getting*)

t	25
tt	15
omitted	6
d	4
ff	1
tn	1
ht	1
Total	53

Standard spelling = *ed*
(e.g., *dressed, jumped*)

t	30
omitted	9
ed	7
d	2
e	2
s	1
to	1
er	1
Total	53

Standard spelling = *tw*
(*two*)

t	4
Total	4

Standard spelling = *z*
(*pizza*)

omitted	2
z	1
Total	3

Standard spelling = *d*
(*used*)

t	1
Total	1

/k/

810 Total Occurrences

Standard spelling = *k* (e.g., *key, bike*)		Standard spelling = *ck* (e.g., *back, chickens*)	
k	266	k	18
c	52	ck	17
ck	31	c	7
omitted	16	omitted	3
t	6	kt	1
g	2	ct	1
kl	2	xck	1
d	2	t	1
b	1	gr	1
cv	1	Total	50
hn	1		
kd	1	Standard spelling = *q* (e.g., *queen, squirrels*)	
f	1		
nk	1	q	9
(k)	1	c	7
kc	1	omitted	4
cgth	1	k	2
sc	1	qu	2
cst	1	ck	1
nr	1	g	1
s	1	Total	26
Total	390		
		Standard spelling = *(x)* (e.g., *fox, boxes*)	
Standard spelling = *c* (e.g., *care, because*)		(x)	15
c	223	x	2
k	58	omitted	2
omitted	6	c	2
g	4	ck	1
q	2	Total	22
ck	1		
x	1	Standard spelling = *ch* (*Christmas, school*)	
n	1		
cr	1	c	10
kch	1	ch	4
chc	1	k	3
w	1	Total	17
Total	300		
		Standard spelling = *cc* (*raccoon*)	
		k	3
		cc	1
		qq	1
		Total	5

/b/

399 Total Occurrences

Standard spelling = *b* (e.g., *brother, grab*)		Standard spelling = *bb* (e.g., *rabbits, stubby*)	
b	365	*bb*	5
d	13	*b*	5
p	2	*d*	4
bb	1	*bbr*	1
l	1	*dd*	1
r	1	Total	16
Total	383		

/d/

844 Total Occurrences

Standard spelling = *d* (e.g., *deer, friend*)		Standard spelling = *ed* (e.g., *called, tried*)	
d	641	*d*	30
omitted	79	omitted	8
b	23	*ed*	5
t	19	*b*	2
ed	3	*t*	1
dd	3	*r*	1
r	2	*ded*	1
a	2	*c*	1
dt	2	Total	49
s	2		
nd	2	Standard spelling = *dd*	
j	2	*(teddy)*	
nt	1	*d*	1
teta	1	Total	1
db	1		
d&ne	1		
vb	1		
vd	1		
n	1		
tt	1		
k	1		
ds	1		
bbiesef	1		
e	1		
p	1		
ll	1		
Total	794		

/g/

306 Total Occurrences

Standard spelling = g (e.g., *got, hungry*)	
g	279
omitted	3
gg	2
b	1
gr	1
c	1
Total	287

Standard spelling = gg (e.g., *egg, bigger*)	
g	5
omitted	3
gg	2
cg	1
cgh	1
Total	12

Standard spelling = gu (e.g., *guessed, rogues*)	
g	4
b	1
Total	5

Standard spelling = gh (*ghost*)	
g	2
Total	2

/f/

275 Total Occurrences

Standard spelling = f (e.g., *fox, after*)	
f	238
omitted	4
v	1
fenaef	1
s	1
Total	245

Standard spelling = ph (e.g., *elephant, phonic*)	
f	12
ph	6
ff	1
omitted	1
v	1
phf	1
hp	1
Total	23

Standard spelling = ff (e.g., *stuff, office*)	
ff	4
f	2
j	1
Total	7

/θ/

161 Total Occurrences

Standard spelling = *th* (e.g., *think, tooth*)			
th	93	*ft*	1
t	45	*v*	1
f	7	*s*	1
omitted	4	*l*	1
ht	3	*ts*	1
h	2	*r*	1
d	1	Total	161

/s/

694 Total Occurrences

Standard spelling = *s* (e.g., *some, blouse*)		Standard spelling = *ss* (e.g., *Missy, across*)	
s	549	*s*	17
omitted	14	*ss*	4
ss	4	*st*	1
t	3	*sts*	1
sh	3	Total	23
c	2		
st	1	Standard spelling = (*x*) (e.g., *fox, next*)	
z	1	(*x*)	15
sg	1	*s*	6
g	1	omitted	1
y	1	Total	22
ch	1		
s&s	1	Standard spelling = *st* (*listen, Christmas*)	
fs	1	*s*	13
us	1	*st*	2
io	1	omitted	2
w	1	Total	17
Total	586		

Standard spelling = *c* (e.g., *city, cellar*)	
s	21
c	6
ss	3
st	1
t	1
Total	32

Standard spelling = *ce* (e.g., *Alice, dance*)		Standard spelling = *z* (*pizza, Putzi*)	
s	7	s	3
ss	2	z	1
ce	1	Total	4
Total	10		

/ʃ/

105 Total Occurrences

Standard spelling = *sh* (e.g., *sheet, wash*)		Standard spelling = *c* (*grocery, groceries*)	
sh	39	omitted	3
s	30	Total	3
ch	4		
h	4	Standard spelling = *ch* (*machines, Charlene*)	
c	2	ch	1
r	2	sh	1
s&h	2	Total	2
st	2		
omitted	1	Standard spelling = *ci* (*special*)	
hs	1		
ss	1	ci	1
sw	1	Total	1
th	1		
y	1		
Total	91		

Standard spelling = *ti* (e.g., *caution, auction*)	
sh	3
s	3
ch	1
omitted	1
Total	8

/h/

415 Total Occurrences

Standard spelling = *h*
(e.g., *had, behind*)

Standard spelling = *wh*
whole)

4

2

6

pelling = *f*

13

12

1

1

1

1

1

1

31

5.

St

(e.

th

t

v

omi

h

ht

y

hn

1

1

1

1

1

1

1

1

512

/z/

429 Total Occurrences

Standard spelling = *s* (e.g., *was, pounds*)		Standard spelling = *es* (e.g., *cookies, stories*)	
s	329	s	6
z	28	omitted	2
omitted	27	ss	2
ss	6	es	1
l	3	z	1
c	2	Total	12
y	2		
t	2	Standard spelling = omitted *(Mrs.)*	
v&s	1		
rf	1	omitted	6
x	1	s	1
n	1	Total	7
sk	1		
v	1	Standard spelling = *z* *(zoo)*	
zie	1		
s&n	1	z	1
sz	1	Total	1
zz	1		
Total	409		

/ʒ/

4 Total Occurrences

Standard spelling = *ge* (*garage*)		Standard spelling = *s* (*treasure*)	
h	1	omitted	2
t	1	Total	2
Total	2		

/ʧ/

79 Total Occurrences

Standard spelling = *ch* (e.g., *cheese, bunch*)		Standard spelling = *tch* (e.g., *watch, kitchen*)	
ch	28	ch	4
c	8	s	2
t	8	g	2
s	5	tch	1
th	3	ck	1
ck	2	omitted	1
omitted	2	k	1
j	2	tstg	1
k	1	st	1
hs	1	Total	14
h	1		
rh	1	Standard spelling = *t*	
sh	1	*(fortune)*	
tc	1	ch	1
Total	64	Total	1

/ʤ/

47 Total Occurrences

Standard spelling = *j* (e.g., *jungle, jam*)		Standard spelling = *ge* (*orange*)	
j	30	ge	2
d	2	Total	2
Total	32		

Standard spelling = *g* (e.g., *giants, stage*)	
j	5
g	4
s	2
ck	1
ch	1
Total	13

/m/

729 Total Occurrences

Standard spelling = *m* (e.g., *my, jam*)		Standard spelling = *mm* (e.g., *Tommy, hammering*)	
m	652	*mm*	13
omitted	26	*m*	9
mm	5	omitted	2
n	5	Total	24
b	1		
s	1	Standard spelling = *nd* (grandma, grandpa)	
md	1	omitted	3
o	1	*nd*	1
h	1	Total	4
n&n	1		
mml	1	Standard spelling = *mb* (climbed)	
nm	1	*m*	1
a	1	Total	1
mn	1		
p	1		
ms	1		
Total	700		

/n/

972 Total Occurrences

Standard spelling = *n* (e.g., *snake, seen*)		Standard spelling = *kn* (e.g., *know, knew*)	
n	798	*n*	6
omitted	122	*kn*	1
nn	6	*k*	1
m	4	Total	8
ng	4		
t	4	Standard spelling = *nn* (e.g., *dinner, running*)	
nd	4	*nn*	4
r	2	*n*	2
nt	2	omitted	1
nh	2	Total	7
mn	1		
npu	1		
s	1		
mp	1		
ns	1		
p	1		
nr	1		
w	1		
h	1		
Total	957		

/ŋ/

208 Total Occurrences

Standard spelling = *ng* (e.g., *king, going*)		Standard spelling = *n* (e.g., *think, angry*)	
ng	54	omitted	57
n	26	n	33
omitted	15	ng	4
g	11	g	1
cg	2	s	1
s	1	Total	96
n&ng	1		
n&g	1		
nk	1		
Total	112		

/r/

951 Total Occurrences

Standard spelling = *r* (e.g., *brother, for*)		Standard spelling = *rr* (e.g., *carrots, married*)	
r	781	r	11
omitted	125	rr	7
rr	8	omitted	2
m	2	Total	20
l	2		
c	2		
n	2		
ur	1		
ratave	1		
rn	1		
y	1		
r&n	1		
rr&r	1		
rt	1		
rw	1		
rirs	1		
Total	931		

/l/

674 Total Occurrences

Standard spelling = *l* (e.g., *look, milk*)		Standard spelling = *ll* (e.g., *ball, bulletin*)	
l	430	*l*	63
omitted	84	*ll*	41
ll	16	omitted	12
t	3	*i*	2
i	2	*l&l*	1
r	1	*llr*	1
n	1	*lmbl*	1
j	1	Total	121
lj	1		
lt	1	Standard spelling = *el* (squirrel, squirrels)	
il	1		
(k)	1	*l*	7
lil	1	*el*	1
Total	543	omitted	1
		g	1
		Total	10

/w/

447 Total Occurrences

Standard spelling = *w* (e.g., *was, away*)		Standard spelling = *u* (e.g., *quarter, queen*)	
w	290	omitted	16
wh	7	*u*	5
omitted	5	*w*	5
v	3	Total	26
h	3		
m	1	Standard spelling = *(o&e)* (e.g., *one, someone*)	
y	1		
Total	310	*w*	5
		(o&e)	4
Standard spelling = *wh* (e.g., *when, where*)		*o*	2
		(o)	1
w	78	Total	12
wh	17		
(o&e)	2		
v	1		
o	1		
Total	99		

/j/

51 Total Occurrences

Standard spelling = *y* (e.g., *your, backyard*)		Standard spelling = (*u*) (*curious, used*)	
y	40	omitted	6
n	1	(*u*)	2
hw	1	*u*	1
Total	42	Total	9

Appendix II

These results show the children's spellings of each phoneme. The results are for *only* those words that the children spelled incorrectly. These tables may therefore be compared with the tables presented by Read (1975), which are also based on incorrectly spelled words. Spellings that occurred at a rate of less than 1.0% each are grouped together in these tables under the "other" category.

/i/			/e/		
Spelling	Number	Percent	Spelling	Number	Percent
e	202	38.8	a	108	46.0
omitted	66	12.7	ay	25	10.6
i	62	11.9	a&e	21	8.9
ee	32	6.1	ae	14	6.0
y	25	4.8	e	10	4.3
a	19	3.6	ea	7	3.0
e&e	15	2.9	omitted	6	2.6
ey	12	2.3	ai	6	2.6
u	10	1.9	aye	4	1.7
ie	9	1.7	i	4	1.7
ea	7	1.3	y	4	1.7
ei	7	1.3	o	3	1.3
e&i	6	1.2	other	23	9.8
other	49	9.4	Total	235	100.2
Total	521	99.9			

329

/ai/

Spelling	Number	Percent
i	125	52.1
i&e	25	10.4
ie	13	5.4
iy	12	5.0
ia	10	4.2
omitted	8	3.3
y	6	2.5
o	6	2.5
e	5	2.1
ii	5	2.1
a	3	1.3
other	22	9.2
Total	240	100.1

/u/

Spelling	Number	Percent
oo	35	24.0
o	23	15.8
u	16	11.0
omitted	12	8.2
ow	10	6.8
ou	6	4.1
o&e	5	3.4
u&e	4	2.7
a	3	2.1
e	3	2.1
oow	3	2.1
uo	3	2.1
oh	2	1.4
other	21	14.4
Total	146	100.2

/o/

Spelling	Number	Percent
o	98	56.3
ow	12	6.9
omitted	11	6.3
oo	5	2.9
o&e	4	2.3
owe	4	2.3
uo	4	2.3
e	3	1.7
l	3	1.7
oe	3	1.7
a	3	1.7
oa	2	1.1
oow	2	1.1
eo	2	1.1
oy	2	1.1
oat	2	1.1
other	14	8.0
Total	174	99.6

/ɑ/

Spelling	Number	Percent
o	54	38.3
omitted	25	17.7
i	17	12.1
a	15	10.6
u	10	7.1
e	7	5.0
a&e	3	2.1
r	2	1.4
o&e	2	1.4
oo	2	1.4
other	4	2.8
Total	141	99.9

/ɔ/

Spelling	Number	Percent
o	68	36.4
a	15	8.0
oo	14	7.5
omitted	13	7.0
ol	9	4.8
u	7	3.7
i	7	3.7
ou	5	2.7
o&e	5	2.7
u&e	3	1.6
oa	3	1.6
r	3	1.6
o&o	2	1.1
e	2	1.1
a&e	2	1.1
oi	2	1.1
oe	2	1.1
w	2	1.1
other	23	12.3
Total	187	100.2

/oi/

Spelling	Number	Percent
oe	3	14.3
o	3	14.3
oy	2	9.5
al	1	4.8
auy	1	4.8
ay	1	4.8
ey	1	4.8
y	1	4.8
oi	1	4.8
oowe	1	4.8
ooy	1	4.8
ou	1	4.8
ow	1	4.8
ue	1	4.8
ooeye	1	4.8
oye	1	4.8
Total	21	100.5

/ɪ/

Spelling	Number	Percent
i	169	40.2
e	94	22.4
omitted	67	16.0
a	39	9.3
e&e	12	2.9
o	7	1.7
i&e	5	1.2
other	27	6.4
Total	420	100.1

/au/

Spelling	Number	Percent
a	29	24.0
o	16	13.2
aw	11	9.1
al	9	7.4
omitted	8	6.6
ow	6	5.0
ao	5	4.1
ae	3	2.5
o&e	3	2.5
ou	2	1.7
w	2	1.7
i	2	1.7
oue	2	1.7
other	23	19.0
Total	121	100.2

/ɛ/

Spelling	Number	Percent
a	86	42.8
e	56	27.9
omitted	17	8.5
i	12	6.0
o	6	3.0
a&e	4	2.0
u	4	2.0
a&y	3	1.5
other	13	6.5
Total	201	100.2

/æ/

Spelling	Number	Percent
a	148	64.9
omitted	17	7.5
i	12	5.3
e	11	4.8
a&e	10	4.4
o	9	3.9
aa	4	1.8
other	17	7.5
Total	228	100.1

/ʊ/

Spelling	Number	Percent
o	18	22.5
u	14	17.5
oo	12	15.0
omitted	12	15.0
i	4	5.0
ua	3	3.8
a	3	3.8
(u)	2	2.5
e	2	2.5
r	1	1.3
ouro	1	1.3
g	1	1.3
ow	1	1.3
en	1	1.3
e&e	1	1.3
ou	1	1.3
h	1	1.3
o&e	1	1.3
ee	1	1.3
Total	80	100.6

/ə/

Spelling	Number	Percent
omitted	370	39.8
u	175	18.8
e	117	12.6
o	84	9.0
a	66	7.1
i	50	5.4
other	68	7.3
Total	930	100.0

/p/

Spelling	Number	Percent
p	242	83.7
omitted	19	6.6
b	7	2.4
pp	4	1.4
d	4	1.4
other	13	4.5
Total	289	100.0

/d/

Spelling	Number	Percent
d	320	65.3
omitted	87	17.8
b	25	5.1
t	20	4.1
ed	6	1.2
other	32	6.5
Total	490	100.0

/t/

Spelling	Number	Percent
t	548	74.9
omitted	100	13.7
d	30	4.1
tt	15	2.0
other	39	5.3
Total	732	100.0

/g/

Spelling	Number	Percent
g	133	89.9
omitted	6	4.1
gg	3	2.0
b	2	1.4
other	4	2.7
Total	148	100.1

/k/

Spelling	Number	Percent
k	239	41.4
c	207	35.9
ck	40	6.9
omitted	31	5.4
q	9	1.6
g	7	1.2
t	7	1.2
other	37	6.4
Total	577	100.0

/f/

Spelling	Number	Percent
f	179	91.8
omitted	5	2.6
ph	2	1.0
ff	2	1.0
v	2	1.0
other	5	2.6
Total	195	100.0

/b/

Spelling	Number	Percent
b	231	89.2
d	17	6.6
bb	5	1.9
other	6	2.3
Total	259	100.0

/θ/

Spelling	Number	Percent
th	57	45.6
t	45	36.0
f	7	5.6
omitted	4	3.2
ht	3	2.4
h	2	1.6
other	7	5.6
Total	125	100.0

/s/

Spelling	Number	Percent
s	491	89.9
omitted	17	3.1
ss	9	1.6
other	29	5.3
Total	546	99.9

/ʃ/

Spelling	Number	Percent
s	33	45.8
sh	12	16.7
ch	5	6.9
omitted	5	6.9
h	4	5.6
c	2	2.8
r	2	2.8
s&h	2	2.8
st	2	2.8
hs	1	1.4
ss	1	1.4
sw	1	1.4
th	1	1.4
y	1	1.4
Total	72	100.1

/h/

Spelling	Number	Percent
h	181	92.3
omitted	9	4.6
w	2	1.0
other	4	2.0
Total	196	99.9

/v/

Spelling	Number	Percent
v	69	75.8
f	10	11.0
omitted	3	3.3
der	1	1.1
ft	1	1.1
t	1	1.1
vn	1	1.1
v&d	1	1.1
l	1	1.1
n	1	1.1
vw	1	1.1
y	1	1.1
Total	91	100.0

/ð/

Spelling	Number	Percent
th	57	45.6
t	46	36.8
v	4	3.2
omitted	3	2.4
h	2	1.6
ht	2	1.6
y	2	1.6
other	9	7.2
Total	125	100.0

/z/

Spelling	Number	Percent
s	202	68.9
omitted	35	11.9
z	29	9.9
ss	8	2.7
l	3	1.0
other	16	5.5
Total	293	99.9

/ʒ/

Spelling	Number	Percent
omitted	2	50.0
h	1	25.0
t	1	25.0
Total	4	100.0

/tʃ/

Spelling	Number	Percent
ch	31	40.8
c	8	10.5
t	8	10.5
s	7	9.2
ck	3	3.9
th	3	3.9
omitted	3	3.9
g	2	2.6
j	2	2.6
k	2	2.6
tstg	1	1.3
hs	1	1.3
h	1	1.3
rh	1	1.3
sh	1	1.3
tc	1	1.3
st	1	1.3
Total	76	99.6

/dʒ/

Spelling	Number	Percent
j	24	70.6
g	4	11.8
d	2	5.9
s	2	5.9
ck	1	2.9
ch	1	2.9
Total	34	100.0

/m/

Spelling	Number	Percent
m	313	84.8
omitted	31	8.4
mm	7	1.9
n	5	1.4
other	13	3.5
Total	369	100.0

/n/

Spelling	Number	Percent
n	402	71.2
omitted	123	21.8
nn	8	1.4
other	32	5.7
Total	565	100.1

/ŋ/

Spelling	Number	Percent
omitted	72	41.9
ng	42	24.4
n	39	22.7
g	12	7.0
cg	2	1.2
s	2	1.2
other	3	1.7
Total	172	100.1

/r/

Spelling	Number	Percent
r	611	79.6
omitted	127	16.5
rr	13	1.7
other	17	2.2
Total	768	100.0

/l/

Spelling	Number	Percent
l	362	70.7
omitted	97	18.9
ll	34	6.6
other	19	3.7
Total	512	99.9

/j/

Spelling	Number	Percent
y	19	63.3
omitted	6	20.0
(*u*)	2	6.7
n	1	3.3
hw	1	3.3
u	1	3.3
Total	30	99.9

/w/

Spelling	Number	Percent
w	285	84.6
omitted	21	6.2
wh	12	3.6
v	4	1.2
other	15	4.5
Total	337	100.1

Bibliography

Adams, M. J. (1990). *Beginning to read: Thinking and learning about print*. Cambridge, MA: MIT Press.

Agard, F. B., & DiPietro, R. J. (1965). *The sounds of English and Italian*. Chicago: University of Chicago Press.

Barron, R. W. (1980). Visual and phonological strategies in reading and spelling. In U. Frith (Ed.), *Cognitive processes in spelling* (pp. 195–213). London: Academic Press.

Barton, D., Miller, R., & Macken, M. A. (1980). Do children treat clusters as one unit or two? *Papers and Reports on Child Language Development, 18*, 93–137.

Beers, J. W., Beers, C. S., & Grant, K. (1977). The logic behind children's spelling. *Elementary School Journal, 77*, 238–242.

Beers, J. W., & Henderson, E. H. (1977). A study of developing orthographic concepts among first-grade children. *Research in the Teaching of English, 11*, 133–148.

Bissex, G. L. (1980). *Gnys at wrk*. Cambridge, MA: Harvard University Press.

Bloomer, R. H. (1961). Concepts of meaning and the reading and spelling difficulty of words. *Journal of Educational Research, 54*, 178–182.

Bloomer, R. H. (1964). Some formulae for predicting spelling difficulty. *Journal of Educational Research, 57*, 395–401.

Bond, G. L., & Dykstra, R. (1967). The cooperative research program in first-grade reading instruction. *Reading Research Quarterly, 2*, 5–142.

Bowey, J. A., & Francis, J. (1991). Phonological analysis as a function of age and exposure to reading instruction. *Applied Psycholinguistics, 12*, 91–121.

Brown, R., & McNeill, D. (1966). The "tip of the tongue" phenomenon. *Journal of Verbal Learning and Verbal Behavior, 5*, 325–337.

Bruck, M., & Treiman, R. (1990). Phonological awareness and spelling in normal children and dyslexics: The case of initial consonant clusters. *Journal of Experimental Child Psychology, 50*, 156–178.

Bruck, M., & Waters, G. (1988). An analysis of the spelling errors of children who differ in their reading and spelling skills. *Applied Psycholinguistics, 9*, 77–92.

Bryant, P. E., & Bradley, L. (1980). Why children sometimes write words which they do not read. In U. Frith (Ed.), *Cognitive processes in spelling* (pp. 355–370). London: Academic Press.

Burns, J. M., & Richgels, D. J. (1989). An investigation of task requirements associated with the invented spellings of four-year-olds with above average intelligence. *Journal of Reading Behavior, 21*, 1–14.

Cahen, L. S., Craun, M. J., & Johnson, S. K. (1971). Spelling difficulty—a survey of the research. *Review of Educational Research, 41*, 281–301.

Caisse, M. (1981, December). *Pitch perturbations induced by voiceless unaspirated stops*. Paper presented at the meeting of the Acoustical Society of America, Miami, FL.

Campbell, R. (1985). When children write nonwords to dictation. *Journal of Experimental Child Psychology, 40*, 133–151.

Carroll, J. B., Davies, P., & Richman, B. (1971). *Word frequency book.* Boston: Houghton Mifflin.

Catts, H. W., & Kamhi, A. G. (1984). Simplification of /s/ + stop consonant clusters: A developmental perspective. *Journal of Speech and Hearing Research, 27,* 556–561.

Chall, J. S. (1967). *Learning to read: The great debate.* New York: McGraw-Hill.

Chomsky, C. (1979). Approaching reading through invented spelling. In L. B. Resnick & P. A. Weaver (Eds.), *Theory and practice of early reading (Vol. 2)* (pp. 43–65). Hillsdale, NJ: Erlbaum.

Chomsky, N., & Halle, M. (1968). *The sound pattern of English.* New York: Harper & Row.

Clarke, L. K. (1988). Invented versus traditional spelling in first graders' writings: Effects on learning to spell and read. *Research in the Teaching of English, 22,* 281–309.

Clements, G. N. (1990). The role of the sonority cycle in core syllabification. In J. Kingston & M. E. Beckman (Eds.), *Between the grammar and physics of speech* (pp. 283–333). New York: Cambridge University Press.

Clements, G. N., & Keyser, S. J. (1983). *CV phonology: A generative theory of the syllable.* Cambridge, MA: MIT Press.

Coltheart, M. (1978). Lexical access in simple reading tasks. In G. Underwood (Ed.), *Strategies of information processing* (pp. 151–216). London: Academic Press.

Cunningham, A. E., & Stanovich, K. E. (1991). Tracking the unique effects of print exposure in children: Associations with vocabulary, general knowledge, and spelling. *Journal of Educational Psychology, 83,* 264–274.

Davis, S. (1989). On a non-argument for the Rhyme. *Journal of Linguistics, 25,* 211–217.

Derwing, B. L., Nearey, T. M., & Dow, M. L. (1987, December). *On the structure of the vowel nucleus: Experimental evidence.* Paper presented at the meeting of the Linguistic Society of America. San Francisco, CA.

Dodd, B. (1980). The spelling abilities of profoundly pre-lingually deaf children. In U. Frith (Ed.), *Cognitive processes in spelling* (pp. 423–440). London: Academic Press.

Downing, J. (Ed.). (1973). *Comparative reading.* New York: Macmillan.

Durrell, D. D., & Murphy, H. A. (1963). Boston University research in elementary school reading. *Boston University Journal of Education, 146,* 3–53.

Ehri, L. C. (1983). A critique of five studies related to letter-name knowledge and learning to read. In L. M. Gentile, M. L. Kamil, & J. Blanchard (Eds.), *Reading research revisited* (pp. 143–153). Columbus, OH: C. E. Merrill.

Ehri, L. C. (1986). Sources of difficulty in learning to spell and read. In M. L. Wolraich & D. Routh (Eds.), *Advances in developmental and behavioral pediatrics (Vol. 7)* (pp. 121–195). Greenwich, CT: JAI Press.

Ehri, L. C., & Robbins, C. (1992). Beginners need some decoding skill to read words by analogy. *Reading Research Quarterly, 27,* 13–26.

Ehri, L. C., & Wilce, L. S. (1986). The influence of spellings on speech: Are alveolar flaps /d/ or /t/? In D. B. Yaden & S. Templeton (Eds.), *Metalinguistic awareness and beginning literacy* (pp. 101–114). Portsmouth, NH: Heinemann.

Ehri, L. C., Wilce, L. S., & Taylor, B. B. (1987). Children's categorization of short vowels in words and the influence of spellings. *Merrill-Palmer Quarterly, 33,* 393–421.

Eimas, P. D. (1975). Distinctive feature codes in the short-term memory of children. *Journal of Experimental Child Psychology, 19,* 241–251.

Fallows, D. (1981). Experimental evidence for English syllabification and syllable structure. *Journal of Linguistics, 17,* 309–317.

Ferreiro, E., & Teberosky, A. (1982). *Literacy before schooling.* New York: Heinemann.

Fischer, F. W., Shankweiler, D., & Liberman, I. Y. (1985). Spelling proficiency and sensitivity to word structure. *Journal of Memory and Language, 24,* 423–441.

Fitts, P. M., & Posner, M. I. (1967). *Human performance.* Belmont, CA: Brooks/Cole.

Fowler, A. E. (1991). How early phonological development might set the stage for phoneme awareness. In S. A. Brady & D. P. Shankweiler (Eds.), *Phonological processes in literacy: A tribute to Isabelle Y. Liberman* (pp. 97–117). Hillsdale, NJ: Erlbaum.

Fowler, C. A., Liberman, I. Y., & Shankweiler, D. (1977). On interpreting the error pattern in beginning reading. *Language and Speech, 20,* 162–173.

Fowler, C. A., Shankweiler, D., & Liberman, I. Y. (1979). Apprehending spelling patterns for vowels: A developmental study. *Language and Speech, 22,* 243–252.

Fox, R. A. (1983). Perceptual structure of monophthongs and diphthongs in English. *Language and Speech, 26,* 21–60.

Frith, U. (Ed.) (1980). *Cognitive processes in spelling.* London: Academic Press.

Frith, U. (1985). Beneath the surface of developmental dyslexia. In K. E. Patterson, J. C. Marshall, & M. Coltheart (Eds.), *Surface dyslexia: Neuropsychological and cognitive studies of phonological reading* (pp. 301–330). Hillsdale, NJ: Erlbaum.

Fudge, E. C. (1969). Syllables. *Journal of Linguistics, 5,* 253–286.

Fudge, E. (1987). Branching structure within the syllable. *Journal of Linguistics, 23,* 359–377.

Fudge, E. (1989). Syllable structure: A reply to Davis. *Journal of Linguistics, 25,* 219–220.

Gentry, J. R. (1982). An analysis of developmental spelling in GNYS AT WRK. *The Reading Teacher, 36,* 192–200.

Gibson, E. J., & Levin, J. (1975). *The psychology of reading.* Cambridge, MA: MIT Press.

Gleason, H. A. (1961). *An introduction to descriptive linguistics.* New York: Holt, Rinehart and Winston.

Glushko, R. J. (1979). The organization and synthesis of orthographic knowledge in reading aloud. *Journal of Experimental Psychology: Human Perception and Performance, 5,* 674–691.

Golinkoff, R. (1974, February). *Children's discrimination of English spelling patterns with redundant auditory information.* Paper presented at the meeting of the American Educational Research Association.

Goodman, K. S. (1986). *What's whole in whole language.* Portsmouth, NH: Heinemann.

Goswami, U., & Bryant, P. (1990). *Phonological skills and learning to read.* Hillsdale, NJ: Erlbaum.

Gough, P. B., Juel, C., & Griffith, P. L. (1992). Reading, spelling, and the orthographic cipher. In P. B. Gough, L. C. Ehri, & R. Treiman (Eds.), *Reading acquisition* (pp. 35–48). Hillsdale, NJ: Erlbaum.

Gough, P. B., & Hillinger, M. L. (1980). Learning to read: An unnatural act. *Bulletin of the Orton Society, 30,* 179–196.

Goyen, J. D., & Martin, M. (1977). The relation of spelling errors to cognitive variables and word type. *British Journal of Educational Psychology, 47,* 268–273.

Groff, P. (1982). Word frequency and spelling difficulty. *Elementary School Journal, 83,* 125–130.

Groff, P. (1984). Word familiarity and spelling difficulty. *Educational Research, 26,* 33–35.

Groff, P. (1986). The spelling difficulty of consonant letter clusters. *Educational Research, 28,* 139–141.

Guy, G. R. (1980). Variation in the group and the individual: The case of final stop deletion. In W. Labov (Ed.), *Locating language in time and space* (pp. 1–36). New York: Academic Press.

Haggard, M. (1973). Abbreviation of consonants in English pre- and post-vocalic clusters. *Journal of Phonetics, 1,* 9–24.

Hanna, P. R., Hanna, J. S., Hodges, R. E., & Rudorf, E. H. (1966). *Phoneme-grapheme cor-*

respondences as cues to spelling improvement. Washington, DC: U.S. Government Printing Office.

Hanna, P. R., Hodges, R. E., & Hanna, J. S. (1971). *Spelling: Structure and strategies.* Boston: Houghton Mifflin.

Harris, A. J., & Jacobson, M. D. (1972). *Basic elementary reading vocabulary.* London: Macmillan.

Henderson, E. (1985). *Teaching spelling.* Boston: Houghton Mifflin.

Henderson, E. H., & Beers, J. W. (Eds.) (1980). *Developmental and cognitive aspects of learning to spell: A reflection of word knowledge.* Newark, DE: International Reading Association.

Hoard, J. W. (1971). Aspiration, tenseness, and syllabification in English. *Language, 47,* 133–140.

Hoffman, P. R., & Norris, J. A. (1989). On the nature of phonological development: Evidence from normal children's spelling errors. *Journal of Speech and Hearing Research, 32,* 787–794.

Hooper, J. B. (1972). The syllable in phonological theory. *Language, 48,* 525–540.

Humphreys, G. W., & Evett, L. J. (1985). Are there independent lexical and non-lexical routes in word processing? An evaluation of the dual-route model of reading. *Behavioral and Brain Sciences, 8,* 689–740.

Jacoby, L. L., & Hollingshead, A. (1990). Reading student essays may be hazardous to your spelling: Effects of reading incorrectly and correctly spelled words. *Canadian Journal of Psychology, 44,* 345–358.

Jared, D., McRae, K., & Seidenberg, M. S. (1990). The basis of consistency effects in word naming. *Journal of Memory and Language, 29,* 687–715.

Jastak, S., & Wilkinson, G. (1984). *The Wide Range Achievement Test—Revised.* Wilmington, DE: Jastak Associates.

Jensen, A. R. (1962). Spelling errors and the serial-position effect. *Journal of Educational Psychology, 53,* 105–109.

Jespersen, O. (1904). *Lehrbuch der phonetik.* Leipzig and Berlin.

Jorm, A. F. (1977). Children's spelling processes revealed by transitional error probabilities. *Australian Journal of Psychology, 29,* 125–130.

Juel, C., Griffith, P. L., & Gough, P. B. (1984). Reading and spelling strategies in first-grade children. In J. A. Niles & R. Lalik (Eds.), *Issues in literacy: A research perspective* (pp. 306–309). Rochester, NY: National Reading Conference.

Just, M. A., & Carpenter, P. A. (1987). *The psychology of reading and language comprehension.* Boston: Allyn and Bacon.

Kahn, D. (1976). *Syllable-based generalizations in English phonology.* Bloomington: Indiana University Linguistics Club.

Kavanagh, J. F., & Mattingly, I. G. (Eds.). (1972). *Language by ear and by eye: The relationships between speech and reading.* Cambridge, MA: MIT Press.

Kenyon, J. S. (1950). *American Pronunciation (10th ed.).* Ann Arbor, MI: George Wahr Publishing Company.

Kenyon, J. S., & Knott, T. A. (1953). *A pronouncing dictionary of American English.* Springfield, MA: Merriam.

Kirtley, C., Bryant, P., Maclean, M., & Bradley, L. (1989). Rhyme, rime, and the onset of reading. *Journal of Experimental Child Psychology, 48,* 224–245.

Klatt, D. H. (1973). Interaction between two factors that influence vowel duration. *Journal of the Acoustical Society of America, 54,* 1102–1104.

Klatt, D. H. (1974). Duration of [s] in English words. *Journal of Speech and Hearing Research, 17,* 51–63.

Klatt, D. H. (1975). Voice onset time, frication, and aspiration in word-initial consonant clusters. *Journal of Speech and Hearing Research, 18,* 686–706.

Kornfeld, J. R. (1978). Implications of studying reduced consonant clusters in normal and abnormal child speech. In R. N. Campbell & P. T. Smith (Eds.), *Language development and mother-child interaction (pp. 413–423)*. New York: Plenum Press.

Kreiner, D. S., & Gough, P. B. (1990). Two ideas about spelling: Rules and word-specific memory. *Journal of Memory and Language, 29,* 103–118.

Kyöstiö, O. K. (1980). Is learning to read easy in a language in which the grapheme-phoneme correspondences are regular? In J. F. Kavanagh & R. L. Venezky (Eds.), *Orthography, reading, and dyslexia* (pp. 35–49). Baltimore: University Park Press.

Ladefoged, P. (1982). *A course in phonetics* (2nd ed.). San Diego: Harcourt Brace Jovanovich.

Lehiste, I. (1972). Timing of utterances and linguistic boundaries. *Journal of the Acoustical Society of America, 51,* 2018–2024.

Lehiste, I. (1975). Some factors affecting the duration of syllable nuclei in English. In G. Drachman (Ed.), *Salzburge beitrage zur linguistik* (pp. 81–104). Tübingen, W. Germany: Verlag Gunter Narr.

Liberman, A. M., Cooper, F. S., Shankweiler, D., & Studdert-Kennedy, M. (1967). Perception of the speech code. *Psychological Review, 74,* 431–461.

Liberman, I. Y., Rubin, H., Duques, S., & Carlisle, J. (1985). Linguistic abilities and spelling proficiency in kindergarteners and adult poor spellers. In D. B. Gray & J. F. Kavanagh (Eds.), *Biobehavioral measures of dyslexia* (pp. 163–176). Parkton, MD: York Press.

Liberman, I. Y., Shankweiler, D., Fischer, F. W., & Carter, B. (1974). Explicit syllable and phoneme segmentation in the young child. *Journal of Experimental Child Psychology, 18,* 201–212.

Liberman, I. Y., Shankweiler, D., Orlando, C., Harris, K. S., & Berti, F. B. (1971). Letter confusions and reversals of sequence in the beginning reader: Implications for Orton's theory of developmental dyslexia. *Cortex, 7,* 127–142.

Liberman, M., & Prince, A. (1977). On stress and linguistic rhythm. *Linguistic Inquiry, 8,* 249–336.

Lindgren, S. D., De Renzi, E., & Richman, L. C. (1985). Cross-national comparisons of developmental dyslexia in Italy and the United States. *Child Development, 56,* 1404–1417.

Lisker, L., & Abramson, A. S. (1964). A cross-language study of voicing in initial stops: Acoustic measurements. *Word, 20,* 384–422.

Lorge, I., & Chall, J. (1963). Estimating the size of vocabularies of children and adults: An analysis of methodological issues. *Journal of Experimental Education, 32,* 147–157.

Lotz, J., Abramson, A. S., Gerstman, L. J., Ingemann, F., & Nemser, W. J. (1960). The perception of English stops by speakers of English, Spanish, Hungarian, and Thai: A tape-cutting experiment. *Language and Speech, 3,* 71–77.

Lukatela, G., & Turvey, M. T. (1980). Some experiments on the Roman and Cyrillic alphabets of Serbo-Croatian. In J. F. Kavanagh & R. L. Venezky (Eds.), *Orthography, reading, and dyslexia* (pp. 227–247). Baltimore: University Park Press.

Lundberg, I., Olofsson, A., & Wall, S. (1980). Reading and spelling skills in the first school years predicted from phonemic awareness skills in kindergarten. *Scandinavian Journal of Psychology, 21,* 159–173.

Malécot, A. (1960). Vowel nasality as a distinctive feature in American English. *Language, 36,* 222–229.

Mangieri, J. N., & Baldwin, R. S. (1979). Meaning as a factor in predicting spelling difficulty. *Journal of Educational Research, 72,* 285–287.

Marcel, T. (1980). Phonological awareness and phonological representation: Investigation of a specific spelling problem. In U. Frith (Ed.), *Cognitive processes in spelling* (pp. 373–403). London: Academic Press.

Mason, J. M. (1980). When do children begin to read: An exploration of four year old children's letter and word reading competencies. *Reading Research Quarterly, 15,* 203–227.

Massaro, D. W., & Hestand, J. (1983). Developmental relations between reading ability and knowledge of orthographic structure. *Contemporary Educational Psychology, 8,* 174–180.

Menyuk, P. (1971). *The acquisition and development of language.* Englewood Cliffs, NJ: Prentice-Hall.

Miller, P., & Limber, J. (1985, October). *The acquisition of consonant clusters: A paradigm problem.* Paper presented at the Boston University Conference on Language Development, Boston, MA.

Montessori, M. (1966). *The secret of childhood.* New York: Ballantine Books.

Morris, D., & Perney, J. (1984). Developmental spelling as a predictor of first-grade reading achievement. *The Elementary School Journal, 84,* 441–457.

Niles, J. A., Grunder, A., & Wimmer, C. (1977). The effects of grade level and school setting on the development of sensitivity to orthographic structure. In P. D. Pearson (Ed.), *Reading: Theory, research and practice* (pp. 183–186). Clemson, SC: National Reading Conference.

Ohde, R. N. (1984). Fundamental frequency as an acoustic correlate of stop consonant voicing. *Journal of the Acoustical Society of America, 75,* 224–230.

O'Neal, V., & Trabasso, T. (1976). Is there a correspondence between sound and spelling? Some implications for black English speakers. In D. S. Harrison & T. Trabasso (Eds.), *Black English: A seminar* (pp. 171–190). Hillsdale, NJ: Erlbaum.

Orton, S. T. (1937). *Reading, writing, and speech problems in children.* New York: W. W. Norton.

Peterson, G. E., & Lehiste, I. (1960). Duration of syllable nuclei in English. *Journal of the Acoustical Society of America, 32,* 693–703.

Phonics workbook, Level A. (1966). Cleveland, OH: Modern Curriculum Press.

Prator, C. H., & Robinett, B. W. (1972). *Manual of American English pronunciation* (3rd edition). New York: Holt, Rinehart & Winston.

Pulgram, E. (1970). *Syllable, word, nexus, cursus.* The Hague: Mouton.

Raphael, L. J., Dorman, M. F., Freeman, F., & Tobin, C. (1975). Vowel and nasal duration as cues to voicing in word-final stop consonants: Spectrographic and perceptual studies. *Journal of Speech and Hearing Research, 18,* 389–400.

Read, C. (1971). Pre-school children's knowledge of English phonology. *Harvard Educational Review, 41,* 1–34.

Read, C. (1973). Children's judgments of phonetic similarities in relation to English spelling. *Language Learning, 23,* 17–38.

Read, C. (1975). *Children's categorization of speech sounds in English.* NCTE Research Report No. 17. Urbana, IL: National Council of Teachers of English.

Read, C. (1980). Creative spelling by young children. In T. Shopen & J. M. Williams (Eds.), *Standards and dialects in English* (pp. 106–136). Cambridge, MA: Winthrop.

Read, C. (1986). *Children's creative spelling.* London: Routledge and Kegan Paul.

Reeds, J. A., & Wang, W. S.-Y. (1961). The perception of stops after s. *Phonetica, 6,* 78–81.

Rosinski, R. R., & Wheeler, K. E. (1972). Children's use of orthographic structure in word discrimination. *Psychonomic Science, 26,* 97–98.

Rubin, H. (1988). Morphological knowledge and early writing ability. *Language and Speech, 31,* 337–355.

Seidenberg, M. S. (1985). The time course of phonological code activation in two writing systems. *Cognition, 19,* 1–30.

Seidenberg, M. S., Bruck, M., Fornarolo, G., & Backman, J. (1986). Word recognition skills of poor and disabled readers: Do they necessarily differ? *Applied Psycholinguistics, 6,* 161–180.

Seidenberg, M. S., & McClelland, J. L. (1989). A distributed, developmental model of word recognition and naming. *Psychological Review, 96,* 523–568.

Selkirk, E. O. (1982). The syllable. In H. Van der Hulst & N. Smith (Eds.), *The structure of phonological representations* (Part II) (pp. 337–383). Dordrecht, the Netherlands: Foris.

Shankweiler, D., & Liberman, I. Y. (1972). Misreading: A search for causes. In J. F. Kavanagh & I. G. Mattingly (Eds.), *Language by ear and by eye: The relationships between speech and reading* (pp. 293–317). Cambridge: MIT Press.

Simplified Spelling Board (1906). *Simplified Spelling* (1st ed.). Washington, DC: U.S. Government Printing Office.

Singh, S., & Woods, D. R. (1971). Perceptual structure of 12 American English vowels. *Journal of the Acoustical Society of America, 49,* 1861–1866.

Singh, S., Woods, D. R., & Becker, G. M. (1972). Perceptual structure of 22 prevocalic English consonants. *Journal of the Acoustical Society of America, 52,* 1698–1713.

Smith, N. V. (1973). *The acquisition of phonology: A case study.* Cambridge, England: Cambridge University Press.

Snow, K. (1963). A detailed analysis of articulation responses of "normal" first grade children. *Journal of Speech and Hearing Research, 6,* 277–290.

Spache, G. (1940). A critical analysis of various methods of classifying spelling errors, I. *Journal of Educational Psychology, 31,* 111–134.

Stage, S. A., & Wagner, R. K. (1992). The development of young children's phonological and orthographic knowledge as revealed by their spellings. *Developmental Psychology, 28,* 287–296.

Stanovich, K. E. (1992). Speculations on the causes and consequences of individual differences in early reading acquisition. In P. B. Gough, L. C. Ehri, & R. Treiman (Eds.), *Reading acquisition* (pp. 307–342). Hillsdale, NJ: Erlbaum.

Stanovich, K. E., & West, R. F. (1989). Exposure to print and orthographic processing. *Reading Research Quarterly, 24,* 402–433.

Stemberger, J. P., & Treiman, R. (1986). The internal structure of word-initial consonant clusters. *Journal of Memory and Language, 25,* 163–180.

Sterling, C. M. (1983). Spelling errors in context. *British Journal of Psychology, 74,* 353–364.

Taraban, R., & McClelland, J. L. (1987). Conspiracy effects in word pronunciation. *Journal of Memory and Language, 26,* 608–631.

Tolchinsky Landsmann, L., & Levin, I. (1985). Writing in preschoolers: An age related analysis. *Applied Psycholinguistics, 6,* 319–339.

Tolchinsky Landsmann, L., & Levin, I. (1987). Writing in four- to six-year-olds: Representation of semantic and phonetic similarities and differences. *Journal of Child Language, 14,* 127–144.

Trager, G., & Smith, H. L. (1951). *An outline of English structure.* Norman, OK: Battenberg Press.

Treiman, R. (1983). The structure of spoken syllables: Evidence from novel word games. *Cognition, 15,* 49–74.

Treiman, R. (1984a). Individual differences among children in spelling and reading styles. *Journal of Experimental Child Psychology, 37,* 463–477.

Treiman, R. (1984b). On the status of final consonant clusters in English syllables. *Journal of Verbal Learning and Verbal Behavior, 23,* 343–356.

Treiman, R. (1985a). Onsets and rimes as units of spoken syllables: Evidence from children. *Journal of Experimental Child Psychology, 39,* 161–181.

Treiman, R. (1985b). Phonemic awareness and spelling: Children's judgments do not always agree with adults'. *Journal of Experimental Child Psychology, 39,* 182–201.

Treiman, R. (1985c). Spelling of stop consonants after /s/ by children and adults. *Applied Psycholinguistics, 6,* 261–282.

Treiman, R. (1989). The internal structure of the syllable. In G. Carlson and M. Tanenhaus (Eds.), *Linguistic structure in language processing* (pp. 27–52). Dordrecht, the Netherlands: Reidel.

Treiman, R. (1991). Children's spelling errors on syllable-initial consonant clusters. *Journal of Educational Psychology, 83,* 346–360.

Treiman, R. (1992). The role of intrasyllabic units in learning to read and spell. In P. B. Gough, L. C. Ehri, & R. Treiman (Eds.), *Reading acquisition* (pp. 65–106). Hillsdale, NJ: Erlbaum.

Treiman, R., & Baron, J. (1981). Segmental analysis ability: Development and relation to reading ability. In G. E. MacKinnon & T. G. Waller (Eds.), *Reading research: Advances in theory and practice* (*Vol. 3*) (pp. 159–197). New York: Academic Press.

Treiman, R., & Danis, C. (1988). Syllabification of intervocalic consonants. *Journal of Memory and Language, 27,* 87–104.

Treiman, R., & Zukowski, A. (1988). Units in reading and spelling. *Journal of Memory and Language, 27,* 466–477.

Treiman, R., & Zukowski, A. (1990). Toward an understanding of English syllabification. *Journal of Memory and Language, 29,* 66–85.

Treiman, R., & Zukowski, A. (1991). Levels of phonological awareness. In S. A. Brady & D. P. Shankweiler (Eds.), *Phonological processes in literacy: A tribute to Isabelle Y. Liberman* (pp. 67–83). Hillsdale, NJ: Erlbaum.

Trubetzkoy, N. (1969). *Principles of phonology* (C. A. M. Baltaxe, Trans.). Berkeley and Los Angeles: University of California Press. (Originally published 1939.)

Tunmer, W. E., Bowey, J. A., & Grieve, R. (1983). The development of young children's awareness of the word as a unit of spoken language. *Journal of Psycholinguistic Research, 12,* 567–594.

Umeda, N. (1977). Consonant duration in American English. *Journal of the Acoustical Society of America, 61,* 846–858.

Van Orden, G. C., Pennington, B. F., & Stone, G. O. (1990). Word identification in reading and the promise of subsymbolic psycholinguistics. *Psychological Review, 97,* 488–522.

Venezky, R. L. (1970). *The structure of English orthography.* The Hague: Mouton.

Venezky, R. L. (1980). From Webster to Rice to Roosevelt: The formative years for spelling instruction and spelling reform in the U.S.A. In U. Frith (Ed.), *Cognitive processes in spelling* (pp. 9–30). London: Academic Press.

Vennemann, T. (1988). The rule dependence of syllable structure. In C. Duncan-Rose & T. Vennemann (Eds.), *On language: Rhetorica, phonologica, syntactica: A festschrift for Robert P. Stockwell from his friends and colleagues* (pp. 257–283). London: Routledge.

Walsh, T., & Parker, F. (1983). The duration of morphemic and non-morphemic /s/ in English. *Journal of Phonetics, 11,* 201–206.

Waters, G. S., Bruck, M., & Malus-Abramovitz, M. (1988). The role of linguistic and visual information in spelling: A developmental study. *Journal of Experimental Child Psychology, 45,* 400–421.

Waters, G. S., Bruck, M., & Seidenberg, M. (1985). Do children use similar processes to read and spell words? *Journal of Experimental Child Psychology, 39,* 511–530.

Why simplified spelling? (Fall, 1987). *Sound Spelling.* (Available from Better Education thru Simplified Spelling, 2340 East Hammond Lake Drive, Bloomfield Hills, MI 48013.)

Zivan, M. T., & Samuels, M. T. (1986). Performance on a word-likeness task by normal readers and reading-disabled children. *Reading Research Quarterly, 21,* 150–160.

Zukowski, A., & Treiman, R. (1989, April). *What happened to the "n" of went? Children's consonant omissions in spellings of final consonant clusters.* Paper presented at the meeting of the Society for Research in Child Development, Kansas City.

Glossary

Affix   a morpheme that is attached to a stem and that modifies its meaning in some way. Prefixes and suffixes are two kinds of affixes.

Affricate   a consonant that consists of a stop portion followed by a fricative portion. The words *chin* and *gin* begin with affricates.

Allophone   a variant of a phoneme. For example, English /t/ has several allophones, including aspirated /t/ as in *till* and flapped /t/ as in *batter.*

Alphabet   a writing system that represents the spoken language at the level of phonemes.

Alveolar place of articulation   an articulation involving the front part of the tongue and the ridge just behind the upper front teeth. The first consonants of *tap, lap,* and *sap* all have an alveolar place of articulation.

Alveolar ridge   the bony projection immediately behind the upper front teeth.

Ambisyllabic   belonging to two syllables at once. According to some linguists, the /m/ of *lemon* is ambisyllabic.

Archiphoneme   a unit that contains the properties shared by two phonemes. For example, some linguists consider the second consonant of *sty* to be an archiphoneme that has all of the properties shared by /t/ and /d/.

Articulation   the positioning of some part of the vocal tract to form a speech sound.

Aspirated stop   a stop consonant that is produced with a following puff of air. The /t/ of *tap* is aspirated in English.

Back vowel   a vowel in which the tongue is close to the upper or back surface of the vocal tract. The vowels of *food* and *good* are back vowels.

Bilabial place of articulation   an articulation involving both lips. The first consonants of *bite* and *might* have a bilabial place of articulation.

Coda   the coda of a syllable consists of the final consonant(s). The /t/ of *bite* is a coda.

Connectionist model of spelling or reading   a theory of the processes involved in spelling or reading single words or nonwords. There are connections between phonological units and orthographic units; the weights on the connections are adjusted to reflect the relation between phonology and orthography in the words to which the model is exposed.

Consonant   a speech sound that is produced with the vocal tract relatively constricted.

Dental place of articulation an articulation involving the front part of the tongue and the upper front teeth. The first consonants of *thin* and *then* have a dental place of articulation.

Derivation the process by which affixes combine with words to form new words. For example, the suffix *-ion* combines with the verb *collect* to yield the noun *collection.*

Destressable word a word that often occurs in unstressed form in connected speech, such as *an, the,* and *of.*

Dialect a form of a language that is peculiar to a locality or a group of people and that differs from other forms of the language in pronunciation, vocabulary, or other features. Dialects of a language are mutually intelligible.

Digraph a sequence of two different letters that represents a single phoneme. The *th* of *thin,* which stands for /θ/, is a digraph.

Diphthong a vowel in which there is an appreciable change in quality during the course of the vowel. The vowel of *boy* is a diphthong.

Distinctive feature a feature that distinguishes phonemes from one another. For example, /p/ and /b/ are distinguished by the feature of voicing.

Doublet a sequence of two identical letters that represents a single phoneme. The *ee* of *see,* which stands for /i/, is a doublet.

Dual-route model of spelling or reading a theory according to which two processes are involved in spelling or reading single words or nonwords. The first process involves rote memorization. The second process involves constructing a spelling for a spoken word from its phonological form or constructing a pronunciation for a printed word from its orthographic form.

Exception word a word that is an exception to a linguistic generalization. For example, *plaid* is an exception to the generalization about sound-spelling correspondence that states that /æ/ is usually spelled with *a. Kept* is an exception to the typical patterns of past tense formation.

Flap in American English, the middle consonants of *latter* and *ladder* are flaps. In the production of these sounds, the tip of the tongue makes one rapid tap against the alveolar ridge and then drops away.

Fricative a consonant that is produced by partially obstructing the stream of air so that a slightly hissing sound results. The first consonants of *ship* and *fall* are fricatives.

Front vowel a vowel in which the highest point of the tongue is in the front of the mouth. The vowels of *bead* and *bid* are front vowels.

Glide a vowel-like sound such as the first sounds of *we* and *yell.*

Glottal place of articulation an articulation involving a constriction at the vocal cords.

Grapheme one or more letters that are used to represent a single phoneme. The *b* of *boy* and the *sh* of *ship* are graphemes.

Graphemic alteration the alteration between different graphemes as a function of their context. In English, for example, *y* usually appears at the ends of words while *i* appears at the beginnings and in the middles of words.

High vowel   a vowel in which the body of the tongue is relatively close to the roof of the mouth.

Homophone   a word that has the same pronunciation as another word but a different spelling and a different meaning. For example, *there* and *their* are homophones.

Homorganic   having the same place of articulation. For example, /m/ and /p/ are homorganic.

Hoosier   an inhabitant of Indiana; the term Hoosier dialect is used to describe the accent of the children in this study.

Illegal spelling error   a spelling that is not a reasonable representation of a word's phonological form. For example, SAIG for *said* is an illegal error.

Inflection   the process by which affixes combine with words to indicate such grammatical categories as tense or plurality. For example, the *-ed* suffix indicates the past tense.

Irregular word   see exception word.

Labio-dental place of articulation   an articulation involving the lower lip and the upper front teeth. The first consonants of *fan* and *van* have a labio-dental place of articulation.

Language-experience approach   an approach to the teaching of reading and writing in which children write and read about their own experiences in order to learn that print is talk written down.

Lateral   a sound in which the air flows over the sides of the tongue. The first sound of *leaf* is a lateral.

Lax vowel   a vowel that may not occur in the final position of a stressed syllable in English. The vowels of *hit* and *hat* are lax vowels.

Legal spelling error   a spelling that is a reasonable representation of a word's phonological form. For example, SED for *said* is a legal error.

Legality principle   the idea that words are syllabified in such a way that syllable-initial consonants are legal in the initial positions of English words and syllable-final consonants are legal in the final positions of English words. Thus, *only* must be syllabified between /n/ and /l/ because the /nl/ cluster cannot occur at the beginnings or ends of English words.

Linguistic awareness   the awareness of the parts of which language is made up, including words, syllables, and phonemes. Linguistic awareness implies the ability to reflect on language in addition to using it.

Liquid   a class of sounds that contains /r/ and /l/.

Logographic reader   a child who reads words in a nonanalytic manner, for example recognizing *dog* by virtue of the "tail" at the end.

Low vowel   a vowel in which the body of the tongue is relatively far from the roof of the mouth.

Manner of articulation   the way in which a sound is formed. In English, the manners of articulation include stop, fricative, nasal, affricate, liquid, and glide.

Maximum onset principle   the idea that words are syllabified in such a way that as many consonants as possible given the phonological constraints of the language are placed at the beginning of each stressed syllable. Thus, the /t/ and /r/ of *patrol* must belong to the word's second syllable since /tr/ is a possible English onset.

Monophthong a vowel in which there is no appreciable change in quality during the course of the vowel. The vowel of *cat* is a monophthong.

Morpheme the smallest meaning-bearing unit of a language. For example, *boy* is a single morpheme whereas *boys* contains two morphemes, *boy* and *s*.

Morphology the internal structure of words and the relationships among words in a language.

Multiple-letter grapheme a grapheme that contains two or more letters. Examples are digraphs and doublets.

Nasal a sound in which the air is obstructed in the oral cavity but escapes through the nose. The first consonants of *my* and *new* are nasals.

Nasalized vowel a vowel is nasalized if part of the air escapes through the nose during the production of the vowel, as in the vowel of *went*.

Nonphonetic spelling error see illegal spelling error.

Nucleus see peak.

Obstruent stops, fricatives, and affricates all fall into the category of obstruent phonemes.

Offglide a rapid movement toward another vowel that occurs in a diphthong. The offglide in the diphthong of *boy* is in the direction of /i/.

Onset the onset of a syllable is the initial consonant(s). The onset of *pie* is /p/ and the onset of *ply* is /pl/.

Orthographic constraint a restriction on the way in which letters may be arranged in the written form of a language. For example, *ck* does not occur at the beginnings of English words.

Orthography the writing system of a language.

Palatal place of articulation an articulation involving the front part of the tongue and the hard palate, or the bony structure at the top of the mouth. The first sound of *you* has a palatal place of articulation.

Palato-alveolar place of articulation an articulation involving the front part of the tongue and the back part of the alveolar ridge. The first consonant of *ship* has a palato-alveolar place of articulation.

Peak the peak of a syllable is the vowel or syllabic consonant. In some views, a sonorant consonant that occurs after the vowel may also belong to the peak.

Phone see allophone.

Phoneme the smallest unit of sound that makes a difference in meaning. For example, *tip* and *sip* differ by a single phoneme. A phoneme is often realized by two or more allophones.

Phonemic awareness the ability to segment spoken words into phonemes. A person who possesses phonemic awareness can compare, count, and manipulate phonemes in addition to using phonemes implicitly in the production and perception of speech.

Phonetic spelling error see legal spelling error.

Phonetic stage of spelling development   a stage in learning to spell, according to some theories, in which children represent all of the segments at the phonetic level of speech. For example, a phonetic speller may spell *trap* as CHRAP.

Phonological constraint   a restriction on the way in which phonemes may be arranged in the spoken form of a language. For example, /tl/ may not occur at the beginnings of English words.

Phonology   the systems and patterns of sounds that occur in a language.

Place of articulation   the part of the vocal tract where there is the greatest degree of constriction in the production of a sound.

Precommunicative stage of spelling development   a stage in learning to spell, according to some theories, in which children string together letters in an apparently random fashion. For example, a precommunicative speller may spell *boy* as SLBF.

Prefix   a morpheme that is added to the beginning of a stem to change its meaning or create a new word. The *re-* of *reread* is a prefix.

Primacy effect   the primacy effect refers to the relatively good performance on the first few items of a memorized sequence.

Recency effect   the recency effect refers to the relatively good performance on the last few items of a memorized sequence.

Regular word   a word that conforms to a linguistic generalization. For example, *bad* is a regularly spelled word, because each phoneme is represented with the grapheme that typically represents that phoneme. *Cleaned* is a regular past tense form.

Regularization error   an error that involves following a linguistic generalization when it does not apply. For example, the spelling of *plaid* as PLAD is a regularization error.

Rime   the vowel and any following consonants in a syllable. For example, the rime of *cat* is /æt/.

Rounded vowel   a vowel in which the lips are rounded, such as /u/.

Semiphonetic stage of spelling development   a stage in learning to spell, according to some theories, in which children represent some of the segments at the phonetic level of speech but omit others. For example, a semiphonetic speller may spell *old* as OD.

Serial position curve   a function plotting recall as a function of the serial position of an item in a presented list.

Sonorant   nasals, liquids, glides, and vowels all fall into the category of sonorant phonemes.

Sonority   the sonority of a sound is related to its loudness or degree of openness.

Sonority scale   a ranking of phonemes in terms of their degree of sonority. Vowels are highest on the sonority scale, followed in turn by glides, liquids, nasals, and obstruents.

Steady-state portion of a diphthong   the more prominent part of a diphthong. The steady-stage portion of the diphthong in *boy* is the first part.

Stem   a morpheme that serves as a base for forming new words via the addition of affixes.

Stop consonant   a consonant that is produced by completely obstructing the flow of air. When the air is released, a small burst of sound occurs. The first consonants of *boy, pan,* and *get* are stops.

Stress   the use of increased respiratory energy during the production of a syllable, which typically leads to increases in vowel length, pitch, and loudness.

Suffix   a morpheme that is added at the end of a stem to change its meaning, give it a grammatical function, or form a new word. The *-ion* of *collection* is a suffix.

Syllabic   refers to a phoneme that occurs as the peak of a syllable. The /r/ of *batter* and the /l/ of *battle* are syllabic liquids.

Syllabification   the division of words into syllables. For example, the spoken form of *only* is syllabified between /n/ and /l/.

Syllable   a linguistic unit that consists of a vowel or syllabic consonant that may be preceded or followed by several consonants. *I, pie,* and *spite* all contain one syllable, while *patter* and *platoon* contain two.

Syllable juncture stage   a stage in learning to spell, according to some theories, in which children learn that double consonants are used to mark "short" vowels, as in *rabbit.*

Tense vowel   a vowel that may occur in the final position of a stressed syllable in English. The final vowels of *he* and *high* are tense vowels.

Transcription   a system of writing used for linguistic purposes that represents the speech sounds of a language.

Transitional stage of spelling development   a stage in learning to spell, according to some theories, in which children move away from complete reliance on sound. They begin to use meaning relationships among words to guide their spelling. For example, a transitional speller may use the same letters at the beginning of *eighty* as in *eight.*

Unaspirated stop   a stop consonant that is not pronounced with a following puff of air, such as the second consonant of *still.*

Unrounded vowel   a vowel in which the lips are not rounded, such as /i/.

Velar place of articulation   an articulation in which the back of the tongue is raised so that it touches the velum at the back of the mouth. The first consonants of *cap* and *gap* have a velar place of articulation.

Velarization   velarization involves raising the back of the tongue into an /u/-like position during an articulation. In English, /l/ is often velarized after a vowel.

Velum   the back part of the roof of the mouth, which is soft and movable because there is no bone under the surface.

Voice onset time (VOT)   the interval between the release of a closure and the beginning of vocal cord vibration.

Voiced   having vibrations of the vocal cords during an articulation, as in /n/.

Voiceless   not having vibrations of the vocal cords during an articulation, as in /t/.

Voicing   the sound made by the vibration of the vocal cords.

Vowel   a speech sound that is produced with the vocal tract relatively open.

Vowel principle   the idea that words are syllabified in such a way that each syllable contains a vowel or a syllabic consonant. Thus, the syllable boundary in *Joey* must fall between /o/ and /i/.

Whole-language approach   an approach to the teaching of reading and writing that emphasizes the use of meaningful texts and tasks and deemphasizes work with isolated words.

Author Index

Italics indicate pages on which bibliographic references are cited

Subject Index

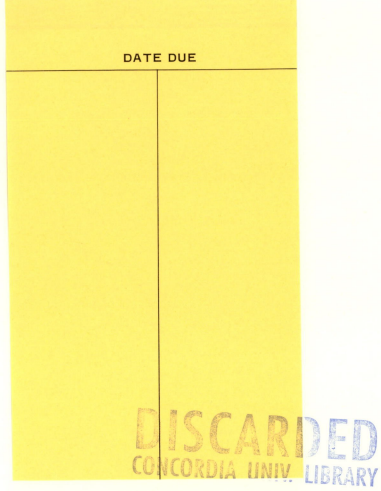

DATE DUE